# Path of Peace and Happiness

Essays in Buddhist Social Philosophy and Ethics

Chulan Sampathge

authorHOUSE®

AuthorHouse™ UK
1663 Liberty Drive
Bloomington, IN 47403  USA
www.authorhouse.co.uk
Phone: UK TFN: 0800 0148641 (Toll Free inside the UK)
       UK Local: (02) 0369 56322 (+44 20 3695 6322 from outside the UK)

Published by AuthorHouse  11/30/2022

ISBN: 978-1-7283-7637-0 (sc)
ISBN: 978-1-7283-7638-7 (hc)
ISBN: 978-1-7283-7636-3 (e)

# SYNOPSIS

Are you happy in this modern world? Or do you need more? Is there something else you are searching for? If you are looking for true happiness, then you just need find the path leading to it. In a world of uncertainty, *The Path of Peace and Happiness* show you directions to safety, stability and building resilience with confidence to help you understand, cope with emotional distress, face life challenges born by man-made disasters and conflicts.

The current state of affairs that we are facing in this 21$^{st}$ century as a global community and no matter where we live in the world, as well as at a personal level, have the potential to trigger mental destress such as anxiety, feeling stressed, worry, and fear of future. It can drain you emotionally making you feel helpless. The book explores and investigate the causes, conditions of uncertainties looming on our doorstep with reference to contemporary and historical events and their impact on our life. What do you currently do to overcome these difficult scenarios about what tomorrow may bring with empathy towards those who are affected too, and improve conditions to reduce unnecessary suffering?

The principal aim of this book is sharing the value of the middle path propounded by the Buddha many centuries ago rejecting extremes. Unlike at the time of the historical Buddha, in this modern world, lots of undue suffering is inflicted on people by bad politics. The pragmatic teachings of Buddhism help to uproot and eliminate the deep underlying causes of suffering.

Narrated through the philosophical background, the book conveys how to relate Buddhist teachings to improve the quality of everyday life and other social institutions including marriage to find true happiness. It discusses the Buddhist ethical values and Western development of thought including how wrong views caused wars, destruction, and misery.

The book shows the practical applications of Buddhist teachings through familiar historical literature not inhibited by traditional interpretations and it is therefore, presented for the consideration of openminded imaginative readers.

Written in a mixture of prose and verse, it presents a code of conduct and provides the basis for a system of moral philosophy. A prime source of both western and eastern philosophies, it constitutes a rational, straightforward simple understanding of the ethics and psychology of Buddhism, advocating peace and nonviolence and respect for life and individual acceptance of social responsibility. Buddhist teachings has been a truly seminal contribution to find peace and happiness.

# PREFACE

This book is intended to be read and studied by those who want to find simple happiness by simple means. It is well-grounded in Buddhist philosophy and the psychology of the Theravada School of Buddhism. Focusing on the theoretical understanding and practical application of ethics, it emphasises its relevance for modern, hectic lifestyles.

The main theme of the discussion is the Buddhist social philosophy as conveyed through a Western perspective. I was inspired by the historical Buddha's teachings and other varied personal studies. My predilections to Buddhist literature drove me in the direction of further research into Buddhism's higher philosophical psychology.

Since 2004 I have been consistently teaching Insight Meditation at the Buddhapadipa Temple in London. Throughout many years I have had the opportunity to study Buddhism in all its branches and almost every tradition. I have had an opportunity to personally meet people from all over the world, each searching for happiness.

I have not let this privilege pass through my hands without coming to an understanding of the diverse nature of personalities and people from all walks of life. The result of these protracted experiences further inspired me to share my own experience with the rest of the world. Buddhism has no policy of converting anyone or forcing them to accept its principles blindly. Buddhism can thus be considered the base religion, irrespective of your beliefs, anyone can benefit from its timeless truths to find happiness.

After many horrific events and the futility of wars and conflicts, the world is poised on a paradigm shift, this is beyond geographical differences, ethnic, religious, or political ideas that have narrowed the human thinking.

In March 2020, the whole world was affected by the Covid-19 pandemic that made life difficult to many by several lockdowns, travel restrictions, social distancing, job losses, and added more misery to our lives, highlighting our limitations and just how helpless we could be. Many Covid-19 patients died in hospitals without having any loved ones at their bedside proving life is uncertain and that death is certain.

The central vision of the Path of Peace and Happiness is to bring ethics and its values to the forefront of our everyday lives whilst in pursuit of happiness.

This book emerged with my inquiry into the philosophical and psychological teachings of the Buddha. Unlike in the historical time of the Buddha, there is much suffering in the modern world because of bad politics and politicians. I was moved by people affected by wars, civil wars and those innocents trapped in conflicts, suffering from no fault of their own.

I attempted to reason out causes and possible simple solutions to alleviate their suffering in a different perspective. Addressing a deep-seated moral crisis is a challenge but worth the pain that more can join the path of peace.

I should like to dedicate this book to my ancestors as a mark of gratitude for their guidance.

In this task I would like to thank Danyal Dunsford and Suraya Dunsford who helped editing, prepare and improve the final manuscript. Danyal's valuable advice helped me immensely to restructure Part II of the book.

I would like to express my special thanks and gratitude to The Buddhapadipa Temple Wimbledon London for kindly giving me copy right permission to use their mural painting images for cover design.

Photography by: Alexandra Kovacs
AK.Foto@outlook.com

*Chulan Sampathge*
*United Kingdom*
*November 2022*

# TABLE OF CONTENTS

# INTRODUCTION

*The Path of Peace and Happiness* is cast as a philosophical teaching of the historical Buddha, a young nobleman, who of his own accord became enlightened about 2560 years ago in northern India.

Buddha succeeded in his quest for enlightenment, thus superseding all other views of his day and firmly establishing his school of thought which expanded rapidly across all six continents. During that time the world was awakening to a new direction of knowledge, to build a utopia based on the ideals of perfection.

Some of these were speculative views of an external power, a superbeing that controls the destination of man-kind, others were unsuccessful theories of self-actualisation and to free themselves from ignorance. The Buddha's teaching is directed towards resolving the problems of mankind peacefully and finding perfect happiness by simple means.

This book is narrated in the context of Western thought of enlightenment and social ideas. It aims to unearth the historical links of many sources in explaining man's struggle for freedom, from the Biblical to Shakespeare. It is helpful to readers in Western societies to understand and appreciate Buddhism in this way, through their familiar stories and ideals. It explores the origin of Western philosophy and its parallels to Buddhism's social ideology. It also discusses political interference to social order, futility of wars and the Buddha's advice on social governance.

Internal conflicts of many countries usually go unnoticed. Mass atrocities are generally understood as genocide, war crimes and crimes against humanity, but many other human rights abuses are committed in conflict-affected contexts. For example, forceful arrests, forceful relocation, illegal detention, political revenge, torture, rape, oppression, insurrection, invasion, and government reaction through counter-insurgency operations to suppress a revolt.

These incidents damage and change people's lives sometimes irreversibly for the worst and might result in death or permanent physical or mental injuries. There are a range of responses to these abuses, particularly by national and international organizations such as Human Rights Watch and United Nations which put pressure on governments, impose trade sanctions, and cut off foreign aid that might result in alienation from the international community forcing social reforms through change of governments' attitudes. Serious human rights abuses occur frequently in severely conflict-affected societies.

These include mass atrocities, but also violations of civil and political rights including freedom of religion, denial of freedom of expression, assembly, and political participation. Violations of rights or infliction of economic harms, including corruption, often precede and occur during conflict. It is essential to understand the root causes of these violations may be both a consequence of conflict, political attitude, race-related hatred, ethnic difference, ideological difference, and drivers of future or further. Conflict in ways that are not sufficiently addressed, could result in complete cultural destruction, harm to innocent internally displaced civilians or the establishment of corrupt political regimes.

Failure to address them may perpetuate underlying causes of conflict, create new grievances and limit opportunities for post-conflict peacebuilding and development without justice to victims and their families.

When you hear about civilians or soldiers dying, it is usually a statistic. Only a person who has been there would know the grim reality. Behind those numbers there are real people, families, and communities completely devastated and grieve for their loved ones. Death of a soldier in combat is generally accepted but those losses are hard even for a fellow soldier.

Mass graves of fallen soldiers who died in battle are a variation of common burial, practiced in dignity in honour of their service. On the other hand, criminal mass graves are a site of horror.

For example, the Crni Vrh mass grave, discovered in 2003, is among the largest mass graves found in Bosnia and Herzegovina after the Bosnian War of the 1990s.

Similarly, in April 1994, throughout the Rwandan genocide, bodies were buried in mass graves, left exposed, or disposed of through rivers. At least 40,000 bodies have been discovered by forensic anthropologists in Lake Victoria which connects to the Akagera River. War crimes were carried out by extremist members of the Hutu government who formed an interim wartime government. They called for an extermination of the Tutsi population, Hutu political opponents and Hutu who resisted the violence. The genocide lasted 100 days and resulted in an estimated 800,000 killings. (BBC News)

The book is addressing a range of historical and contemporary events that led to man-made disasters showing how ignorant political behaviour has added more suffering to innocent people. It is digging deep into fundamental errors in ethics highlighting Buddhist values applying intellect for the purpose of common good. Chapter one discusses recent conflict affected areas focusing the impact of Russian special military operations started in February 2022.

After the collapse of many regimes across the Middle East, Central Asia, and Eastern Europe in the late 80s and early 90s, the newly independent states began the long and difficult journey towards creating strong, democratic systems to make the 21st century free from armed conflicts. One of the questions which quickly arose was how to approach the process of dealing with the trauma of the difficult past and preventing future atrocities.

Buddhism is like a lamp post shedding light to the darkness, showing us the direction to find the path of peace and helping us choose wise resolutions to avoid conflicts.

In this modern world, politics, economics, technological and social changes are closely connected in a manner no single nation could live in isolation. Geopolitics takes a prominent place on the world stage reflecting internal politics of superpower nations affecting small nations.

The role of politicians and lawmakers is to balance the relations with other nations and design an ethical policy framework suitable for their national identity, culture and heritage adapting to modern technological changes identifying economic drivers for social welfare and development with consultation for collective agreement of all players.

Research shows that political participation in many countries among young voters (aged 18-24) has steadily declined over the past two decades.

Alongside this decline, the use of smartphones and computer devices has meteorically risen among the same demographic cohort, resulting in relying on quick online web information is becoming increasingly more integrated within modern society. Perhaps they don't understand the extent to which politics has an impact on them or they are engaged in other pursuits which to them are more interesting and important than what is happening in their government institutions. On the other hand, perhaps they are convinced that they cannot have an impact on the political process in their favour.

The framework of the political society should aim for the understanding and consideration of directing this age group towards meaningful political participation. Improving value goals of them with the traits of confidence and tolerance is important for peaceful coexistence, progress, and personal happiness. They are the demographic cohort to take responsibility in future, in particular, in the post Covid-19 pandemic world more like the "civic-minded" the Greatest Generation, with a strong sense of community both local and global who could contribute to rebuilt better equitable societies.

Nowadays, the themes of political identity are much complicated than we used to think. Over period of time ideological differences have moved from left to right and sometimes leans to extremes. The January 6, 2021 the US capital riots called into question ethical values not only of individual leader's conduct but how to evaluate collective mindset of followers of a political party, their political preferences and behaviour. If majority of peace loving citizens of the world are to accept democracy, protect it against autocracy then leaders must set example showing its true values.

Civilizations evolved over centuries of cumulative work, good governance of generations. Without common values and goals, no community could settle and progress. But after World War II, an entire set of cultural traditions was disrupted. The combined effects of industrialization, the returning of veterans, the economic depression, and the exploding technology pushed young families to a new lifestyle frontier of individualism without the accumulated wisdom gained from traditions, networks, and support systems to guide them. People became increasingly isolated and new culture evolved with urbanisation. Collectiveness was replaced with individualism.

War is defined as a state of armed conflict between different countries or different groups within a country in which the total resources of the belligerents are employed. In modern times, major powers threaten other nations national security provoking war. The most recent armed conflict is Russian invasion termed as special military operation in Ukraine. During the second phase of the war with Ukraine, in April 2022, Russia test-launched a new intercontinental missile that could carry multiple nuclear warheads. The launch was a pointed warning to the U.S. and other nations. Russian President Vladimir Putin perceives that his country is threatened by NATO expansion in Europe and beyond that led to the invasion of Ukraine under the political phrase "Special Operation".

Origin of the word *War* is as old as civilisation. The term, 'first world war' did not yet exist in the Oxford English Dictionary until 1921. It was added to the vocabulary after the major catastrophe in which European nations clashed with each other in an armed conflict. Our modern terminology depends, of course, firmly on hindsight. A first world war, as we now know, was followed by a second. The numerical sequencing offers ominous potential for a third or fourth which, as yet remain unrealised. This indicates a risk pattern, a kind of trend of human behaviour becoming more aggressive with developing more and more advanced weapons.

It calls into question whether war is part of the economy or economy is part of war. Advancement of science and technology is a major driving factor of economic activities and modernization. Knowledge and experience gained from fighting wars have later been used for civil and commercial purposes to make better the economy. For example, internet was a result of developing advanced military command and intercontinental communication lines, later adapted for information communication technology (ICT), and consequently improving employment, income, and standard of living, but it is not clear whether our perceptions, feelings, empathy, consciousness, performance, and concerns of the environment are improving towards a real achievement of peace and happiness.

The Path of Peace and Happiness is a convergence of both Eastern and Western philosophies for a new foundation to enrich human potential to be better and more compassionate towards recognizing others' suffering.

Every citizen of this new emerging Global Village has a dream, ambition, purpose of life and want to live in peace and harmony with nature. Denial of this individual freedom and basic human rights is inhumane. Buddhist teachings certainly encourage irrespective of your religious belief to achieve your peaceful life goal.

Modern ICT has shrunk the world. At the early stage of its development was known as Information Superhighway allowing knowledge to share much easier. The world as a single community of interdependent inhabitants who are interconnected by contemporary ideas and knowledge share can benefit from each other, work collectively, and integrate to make the world a better place for all of us. During the Covid-19 lockdown, work from home became a new norm even living in different time zones.

Buddhist concepts and its deep meaningful philosophy has proven success reaching optimal performance, higher states of consciousness, and human optimization through simple means.

I hope this book inspires readers of many age groups by bringing the teachings into the modern world and exploring how to relate to them in order to improve the quality of life through self-development. One of the themes of the Buddha's timeless teaching is that true happiness is accessible to anyone who wisely seeks it.

This book has two parts. The first part explores the philosophical background of the teaching and how to relate Buddhist teachings to one's life. The second part discusses the Buddhist ethical values and the Western development of thought, including addressing the destruction caused by adhering to wrong views. It narrates the practical applications of Buddhist teachings to social institutions, including marriage, and how Buddhist countries have successfully adapted and applied Buddhist principles for their collective prosperity.

The writer shares his knowledge and experience from over twenty-five years of extensive research on this subject. His personal pursuits led him to explore the Buddha's teachings and includes Buddhism's higher philosophy and psychology, used to help explain complex phenomena to understand inaccurate worldly views and egotistical racist personalities.

The true greatness of a person and his or her potential comes from a deep understanding of the need to drive and manage a change of life according to Dhamma *(Dharma)*. When an individual at a personal level change for the better then, the whole society would change for the better to make it peaceful enjoyable place to live.

The Present is the most powerful moment to create the right conditions for a positive change to happen. Being at present, here and now one can gain the phenomenal insight into the truth of all phenomena how external events influence your mind and condition it to make you believe in false notions and views that are adding unnecessary suffering to people's lives. The book also shows meditation practices in Buddhist traditions as methods to achieve inner peace.

The recent Russian invasion of neighbouring Ukraine in February 2022 will certainly change the existing world order and security architecture of Europe, making NATO countries more united than during the Trump era of presidency in the U.S. The world is awakening to true democracy dispelling the vail of myths and mightiness to economic reality and real issues people are facing on daily basis.

The knock on effect of war in Ukraine on the wider world economy is severe because of rising energy prices that will have a devastating effect on poorer nations and emerging economies making them turn to other oil suppliers and renewable energy sources. People in the world have been watching the terrible events unfold in Ukraine with great concern.

Number of refugees amounted to over three million within less than three weeks since the war began what Russian leader Vladimir Putin phrased as a "Special Operation" to rescue Ukrainians from the US agencies operating in their backyard. Many have made donations to aid humanitarian relief efforts through local and global organizations including UNHCR – the UN Refugee Agency. Those uncertain times might have caused feelings of fear and anxiety as people in the world considered the impact of the crisis. Some were closely monitoring the situation.

All European countries stood together hoping for a swift, peaceful, and compassionate resolution to the crisis. However, Russia directed their fire power mostly at civilian targets reducing cities to pile of rubble. According to Hindu philosophy of the world, there is a creator, protector, and a destroyer. Russia demonstrated to the world that they have all those qualities in them while India stayed neutral on this ancient philosophy. In the Indian religious tradition, Shiva is the Supreme Lord who creates, protects, and transforms the universe. Shiva has many aspects, benevolent as well as fearsome. In his fierce aspects, he is often depicted slaying demons and villains.

President Vladimir Putin is a phenomenal politician and a keen chess player, and as this unprovoked war escalated serious situation of moves developed among other powerplays in Russian circles. Russian President Vladimir Putin lashed out at "traitors" in a speech as his invasion stalls in Ukraine referring to oligarchs living abroad while the US president accused Russia of war crimes. Reuters News reports confirmed an attack on a civilian target, a theatre in Mariupol, by Russian forces where hundreds of people, mostly women, children, and the elderly, had been hiding because of heavy shelling.

"The heart is breaking from what Russia does to our people, our Mariupol, and our Donetsk region," Ukrainian President Volodymyr Zelensky said in a late-night address on Wednesday the 16th March 2022, after referring to the theatre attack. (Reuters 18 March 2022). Russian spokesman denied the incident at the theatre that it was not an attack by their forces but an accident of Ukrainians themselves. Fake news and disinformation are a feature of Russian tactics and in any war situation.

# Part I

War or Peace
Buddhist Approach to
Spiritual Awakening and
Peaceful Co-Existence

# CHAPTER 1

# MORAL AND SOCIAL RESPONSIBILITY OF LEADERS IN GLOBAL ECONOMICS AND POLITICAL SOCIETY

Buddhism has both influenced governments and been identified by governments as a source of their wisdom and guidance for good governance and Rule of Law in the past. Buddhism is founded on a philosophy of nonviolence. The Buddha always advised kings and laypeople to resolve issues through wise dialogues applying ethical values, justice, avoiding hatred and conflicts. He compassionately encouraged people to consider results before their actions. The Buddhist benchmark on good life is Karma *(law of action)*.

Violence and revenge can lead to a spiral of bad Karma producing bad results in many generations to come in the same way good Karma produce good results here and now and in future for the wellbeing of many. The guiding principles are articulated into five precepts which are stem from the Noble Eightfold path propounded by the enlightened Buddha for peaceful coexistence and towards final liberation. Its ultimate goal is true unconditional happiness.

The unique idea of good governance is not a new concept in the modern political arena. 'Good governance' is a combination of the two meaningful words 'good' and 'governance'. In a word, Governance means the way to exercise proper control, good constitution, right management, and also standard administration, financial discipline, prudence with wealth redistribution which are accepted by a government or a king or a state.

The earliest Buddhists texts, the Pali Tipitaka, contain numerous references to and discussions of kings, princes, wars, and policies. Later Buddhist texts, up to the present day, likewise contain advice to rulers about how to govern well, warnings about the dire consequences of poor ruling. In the realm of political practice, there are many ideologies and doctrines causing disharmony, social instability ignoring the needs of the common people.

On the contrary, the Buddha passed the responsibility of social welfare to individual rulers and citizens of a country with added emphasis on spiritual development for lasting peace. His teachings are based on principles of the law of action that every action produce results. The earliest intervention of Buddhism into politics at the time of historical Buddha Gautama is recorded in the classical history of the island of Lanka, today known as Sri Lanka and Ceylon during the British colonial times.

The Book of Chronicles Mahavamsa which is indissolubly linked with that of Sri Lanka (Ceylon) tells that the Buddha had personally visited the island nation to resolve disputes between ruling clans. Circumstance leading to this connection and subsequent resolutions accepted by ancient kings for the benefit of all, which gave rise to revival of civil administration of the island. It laid the foundation for social governance based on nonviolence not confined to Ceylon, and that the time was ripe for the crucial work of sharing values with other neighbouring nations.

There are archaeological sites and monuments corresponding to those records depicting how Buddha advised rival kings on how to live peacefully. The Buddha intervene to change the cause and effect by changing the attitude of rulers', emphasis of the value of patience. Compassionate Buddha could see the suffering of both aggressor and victim and correct both sides.

Primitive laws were laid down based on an assumption about the innate depravity of man - that man, ungoverned, lived according to the law of the jungle - and, therefore, a ruler needed to have the skills, knowledge, and wisdom to understand, conquer, and control differing factions of the society. Under such a system, the ruler had to have the power to impose rules to keep people from harming one another for the sake of social stability and the continuing safety of the government aiming at economic prosperity and social wellbeing of their people.

Buddhism is an important ethical and religious tradition in many Asian countries, even if it is not explicitly incorporated into the political system. This subject of how Buddhism has influenced politics and policies is not fully explored by Western scholarship in the 20th century.

The 21st century has been recognized by many political analysts as the century of peace, avoiding conflicts through diplomatic dialogue. Many powerful nations have now turned to constructive dialogues to resolve issues. The value of Buddhism is yet to discover for peaceful coexistence in multicultural and multi-ethnic societies. Its application is wider both in the global economy and interdependent modern industrialized supply chain activities.

The Cold war era was marked by many disastrous events because of the fight between superpower nations for nuclear weapons supremacy. In the 21st century, new contenders, notably India and China, have entered the game forcing America and European nations, including other NATO (North Atlantic Treaty Organization) alliance, to intervene into the competition to keep the situation under control.

The concept of good governance through democracy is supported by many North American, European, and like-minded nations around the world which recognize multiculturalism, tolerance, and freedom of religious faith. They all share values of morals and ethics that are a foundational corner stone of civilization.

In recent years, Australia, Japan, and India have been active proponents of the Indo-Pacific regional concept known as Quad. By joining the U.S., they have created an informal alliance to collaborate on disaster relief efforts in the Pacific region and that have already made several important contributions to the Indo-Pacific order. They share an outlook regarding the future of regional order, which emphasizes free, open, inclusive, and rules-based principles for governance.

On September 24, 2021, President Biden hosted Prime Minister Scott Morrison of Australia, Prime Minister Narendra Modi of India, and Prime

Minister Yoshihide Suga of Japan at the White House for the first-ever in person Leaders' Summit of the Quad. The leaders have put forth ambitious initiatives that deepen their ties and advance practical cooperation on 21st century challenges: ending the Covid-19 pandemic, including by increasing production and access to safe and effective vaccines; promoting high-standards infrastructure; combatting the climate crisis; partnering on emerging technologies, space, and cybersecurity; and cultivating next-generation talent in all those countries. They would invite and support new member states conditional on meeting their core values of human rights and the rule of law.

The future of the new coalition rests in collaborative and bottom-up diplomacy to build consensus around principles and norms. This should leverage existing institutions and processes to amplify collective voice in an era when the Indo-Pacific and Indian Ocean Region (IOR) are riven by great power conflict. Balance of power is important for the peace and economic prosperity of the regions.

Understanding the differences in superpower nations' specific national interests – particularly in the economic and security spheres is important to small nations in this region, Indo-Pacific rim nations and southeast Asia. For example, Sri Lanka a Buddhist country has come under the spotlight of all contenders in the region for her geographical position which is the hub of the IOR maritime navigation and must decide upon balancing her Foreign Policy and careful internal governance considering the value of Middle Path propounded by the Buddha if Sri Lanka to benefit from next-generation talent and knowledge share from developed countries.

The current dire economic situation in Sri Lanka is reportedly due to debt-driven financing of unsustainable projects and weaknesses in financial management. Over 30 years of civil war, heavy borrowings, waste, and corruption at all levels of successive governments have contributed to the current downgrading of its central bank by international rating agencies.

If the political culture of the ruling party appropriates national wealth for themselves as well as for their friends and families, erodes justice system and ignores the common good, then bankruptcy is inevitable.

The Pandora Papers published by the International Consortium of Investigative Journalists (ICIJ) on 3 October 2021 unmasked the hidden owners of offshore companies, secret bank accounts, private jets, yachts, mansions, and hidden artworks by world-renowned artists. The leak exposed the secret offshore accounts of 35 world leaders, including current and former prime ministers including then British Prime Minister Mr Tony Blair, heads of state as well as more than 100 billionaires among celebrities and business leaders. Not surprisingly, among them there were names of relatives of Sri Lankan ruling politicians who were responsible for managing country's finances at the time. Sri Lanka is a case study of debt financing for government spending.

There is high trade and budget deficit, severe food shortage in the year 2022 which was coined as 'dollar crisis.' Country's US Dollar balance of payment has eroded due to interests and debt repayments and overspending on import goods. People's means of income have been lost and prices of essential goods have increased. Average person's standard of living is falling speedy. Covid-19 has added an additional burden to this hard-hit nation in addition to hyperinflation. Therefore, reversing and correcting corrupt government policies and stopping opportunists making money out of crisis might take longer than expected and that would prolong the suffering of common people who are currently struggling. So, only a critical analysis and intelligent responses can help managing a crisis of this nature. In a democratic society, people have the ultimate power of deciding what is good governance.

Elected representatives must realise the limitations of exploitation of national wealth. Research shows that corrupted regimes use offshore banking to hide their money. The European Union has published a list of international tax havens as part of a crackdown on multinational companies trying to avoid paying tax in the 28-nation bloc that was including UK. The list of 30 territories includes Hong Kong and Brunei in Asia, Monaco, Andorra and Guernsey in Europe, and a series of Caribbean havens including the Cayman Islands and British Virgin Islands. The European Commission's proposals also include reforms to end sweetheart tax deals following a series of investigations into arrangements between EU countries and firms including Amazon, Apple, and Starbucks. 1% tax is one of such low taxes offered by Sri Lanka to induce returning undisclosed money to circulation. In the meantime, the opposition has filed a case in the country's supreme court on 22 July 2021 against the recent legislation that allows 'no questions asked' policy fearing legislation would encourage money laundering and crime.

Super wealthy individuals use Tax Havens and Shell Companies to hide their money. These practices were exposed in the 2016 Panama Papers investigation. The documents show the myriad ways in which the rich can exploit secretive offshore tax regimes. Twelve national leaders are among 143 politicians, their families, and close associates from around the world known to have been using offshore tax-havens. Tax avoidance is not only criminal offence it is also immoral paying as little tax as possible while still staying on the right side of the law.

These tax shelters are often small, low-tax jurisdictions in remote locations, like the Caribbean islands. The EU blacklist, pressures nations to make changes and reforms to their tax codes, and blacklisted countries can face sanctions from the EU. For example, Nauru, a Pacific Island northeast of Australia, was internationally backlisted amid concerned that it had become a centre for money laundering, and it was among the countries backlisted as a tax haven by the EU in 2015.

The increasing global gap between rich and poor and between women and men is generating and sustaining poverty. Consequently, in Europe and beyond, extreme inequality is fomenting divided societies and stoking populist sentiment. Then, the coronavirus pandemic has further exposed and exacerbated these inequalities with the risk of pushing more than half a billion people into poverty. We see this situation in Sri Lanka where many hotel workers are now without any income because drawback in tourist industry which is slowly picking up. But inequality is not inevitable; it is a political choice and can be overcome by sensible and coherent policymaking, not least on EU level.

Our world had gone through many crises, and it has already been proved that it is the quality of leadership and the attitude of governments that matters in the end. In Buddhist Ideals in Government (2011) published by the Buddhist Publication Society, the author, Gunaseela Vitanage, writes:

"It must be remembered that the Buddha was born into a society which, comparatively speaking, was politically advanced and through the ages had developed certain very solid ideas of government. In the Manu Neeti or the Code of Manu, the Hindus already had laws hallowed by time to guide them in their civic duties. These laws discussed not only the rights of the rulers, but also their duties towards their subjects. They also discussed the obligations of the subjects and their rights." (Vitanage 4, 2011)

The seven essential principles (satta aparihaniya dhamma), or the seven rules governing conduct, were taught by the Buddha to the Vajjians of Vesali (in present-day Vaishali in Bihar, India). The Buddha gave these teachings during his stay at the Sarandad shrine in Vesali. These seven essential principles prioritize living in unity, solidarity, and righteousness, reflecting the prime concerns of Indian kings of the time. They contain the principles of governing individuals, families, societies, and the state. It is said that if any nation or society follows these seven essential ideals, they will prosper and suffer no defeats.

Seven essential principles are listed as:

1. Always gathering together through regular meetings and assemblies.
2. Attending the meeting in unison and leaving together at the end of the meeting and performing the proposed work of the meeting together.
3. Refraining from introducing any bad ideas or policies that divide people in any organization or state, not omitting any good trends or policies of the past and abiding by all the traditional laws or policies of the past that have been passed down through the tradition.
4. Honouring and respecting elders and senior citizens and to obeying their orders and advice.
5. Respecting women and not violating their rights, and according to them freedom and autonomy.
6. Preserving, honouring, and worshipping all the religious locations, shrines, and monasteries in the village or town and not abandoning but keeping active the pre-existing religious activities of the sacred places.
7. Religiously protecting the saints and the virtuous religious teachers, arranging the wellbeing of the arrival of new saints, and inquiring whether the saints are living in safety.

These seven essential principles were subsequently followed by the Vajjians of Vesali. The Buddha said that no one could defeat the Vajjians as long as they followed these principles.

These seven principles are also important for nations and communities today. When people meet in assemblies in good faith with open hearts and minds, there is unity and solidarity. When a community agrees to attend meetings in an organized manner and perform their general duties unanimously, the principles of unity and solidarity are reinforced.

When a nation refrains from implementing bad policies and ideas, bad practices, corruption, does not do away with good rules and regulations, and follows those rules, regulations, and judgments that are for the welfare of all, the nation prospers peacefully. When a nation respects the elderly and follows their wisdom, there is unity, solidarity, and good living. When a state does not abuse women or restrict their rights, everyone can reach their full potential. When a nation respects all religions, there is harmony among the different religions. Finally, when a nation respects religious teachers, the community has trust in the government.

There is also a story in the Jataka tales that illustrates the virtue of kingship. A ruler, called King Ummadayanti, once saw a beautiful woman during his rounds of the city and fell in love with her at first sight. But when he learned that she was married, he felt ashamed. As it happened, the woman's husband, who had guessed the secret, out of deference to the ruler, offered his wife to the king as a concubine, but the ruler refused.

The monarch replied, "If I should lack the power of ruling my own self, say, into what condition would I bring the people who long for protection from my side? Thus, considering and regarding the good of my subjects, my own righteousness, and my spotless fame. I do not allow myself to submit to my passion. I am the leader of my subjects, the king." (Vitanage 15, 2011)

Ashoka the Great, an Indian emperor of the Mauryan dynasty, played a critical role in helping make Buddhism a world religion. He sent his enlightened son and daughter as missionaries to spread Buddhism in Sri Lanka and they established Buddhist teaching there. Since then, the Island nation adopted a culture and social system founded on Buddhist ethics and values.

Emperor Ashoka shared not only Buddhism but developed diplomatic, international relations through the exchange of knowledge and skills particularly in the field of agriculture and numerous other industries across Southeast Asia. Over centuries through cultural exchange programs, Buddhist teachings are shared with the neighbouring countries of India, Malaysia, Thailand, Cambodia, Myanmar, South Korea, and Japan. Teachings have spread as far as China and Central Asia along the ancient Silk Road.

Sri Lanka and Thailand share a special relation of cultural exchange and have helped one another to restore Buddhism time to time. Sri Lanka has also extended goodwill to Japan at its most difficult time after World War II in August 1945, to regain international confidence. The Sri Lankan representative (then Ceylon) voiced the sentiments of the people of Asia in their general attitude towards the future of Japan before the assembly of fifty-one nations by requesting them to forgive Japan for War Crimes at the Peace Treaty conference, stating that hatred cannot be overcome by hatred but only through love and kindness.

It is the message of the Buddha, the Great Teacher, the founder of Buddhism which spread a wave of humanism through Southeast Asia across the Indo-Pacific rim states and northwards through the Himalayas into Tibet, China and finally, Japan, which bound these nations together for centuries with a common culture and heritage.

When an unprecedented war broke out between India and China 58 years ago on 20 October 1962 on their Himalayan border dispute, Sri Lankan then Ceylonese Prime Minister, Mrs Sirima Bandaranaike, made a brave effort to defuse the conflict which was threatening to turn the region into a theatre of power rivalry and war.

Through the Non-Aligned Movement, the Commonwealth and United Nations, Mrs Bandaranaike, the world's first woman prime minister was influential in the multilateral arena. Her actions in mediating between India and China led to the reduction in hostilities.

In the period of the Sino-Indian war, the world was locked in a bipolar balance of power led by the U.S. and the former Soviet Union. In a bipolar system, states are rigidly aligned to either pole, but also have great flexibility of strategy within their camp. This was caused by the zero-sum nature of a bipolar system, in which the gain of one side is the loss of the other. As such, the leader of either faction is unwilling to allow client members to fail in policy endeavours.

Finally, in a bipolar system, states that refuse to join either faction drastically increase their security dilemma unless they have the power to challenge the international structure towards a multi-polar balance. Over time, with the development of modern hypersonic nuclear capabilities as well as economic and political changes, the balance of power has shifted and currently in a state of readjusting. For example, in the northern theatre, in January 2022 there was a massive Russian troop build-up at the Ukrainian border and conversation between the U.S. president Joe Biden and the Russian president Vladimir Putin was continued to deescalate the tension through dialogue and diplomacy for a better outcome. An interesting dialogue began between all parties to the showdown.

For weeks Russia has insisted that the U.S. provide written responses before the Kremlin decides on its next course of action and has asserted that it has no plans to invade Ukraine. The U.S. response "sets out a serious diplomatic path forward should Russia choose it," the secretary of state, Antony Blinken, said to news reporters. Formally, the U.S. and NATO stood firmly with diplomatic attempts to resolve the situation with Russia, and the U.S. has deployed extra troops to Eastern Europe to reassure anxious NATO allies over tensions surrounding Ukraine. The U.S. and allies were united with enhanced battle readiness and have offered Russia a path away from crisis and towards greater security.

The role of NATO is to deter, take pre-emptive action, and reassurance of strength of member states against military threats. But resilience is part of Russia's national identity and restoring former Soviet glory is on their agenda. Securing geopolitical position is strategically important to Russia for in the event of deploying modern weapons stationed in their allies' countries in former Eastern Europe whilst it is important for Europe to secure its gas supplies through Ukraine.

During the tension period, the Secretary of State Mr Blinken expressed his wishes to speak in the coming days with his Russian counterpart, Sergey Lavrov, once Russian officials are "ready to discuss next steps" showing the importance of restrain, diplomatic dialogue to resolve a dispute that might lead to a warpath. The document has not been released publicly, but Blinken said it proposed "reciprocal transparency measures regarding force posture in Ukraine, as well as measures to increase confidence regarding military exercises and manoeuvres in Europe" and nuclear arms control in Europe.

The U.S. would not rule out future membership in NATO for Ukraine, he added. Americans have multiple objectives served in one move. The Americans, backed by their Western allies, accused Russia of endangering peace and destabilizing global security by massing more than 100,000 troops on Ukraine's borders. Kremlin diplomats dismissed what they called baseless and hysterical U.S. fearmongering aimed at weakening Russia and provoking armed conflict. (The New York Times 27 January, 01 February 2022).

In this scenario, Chinese state media, have vocally backed Russia in arguing that the current crisis stems from the U.S. "using NATO as a tool to cannibalize and squeeze Russia's strategic space." (Global Times, Dec. 27, 2021). However, not expressed explicitly them supporting Russian leader Putin because it would certainly antagonize the European Union (EU), which is now China's second largest trading partner. In Chinese policymakers' strategic calculation, it is vital to prevent the U.S, from recruiting the EU into its anti-China coalition. It is important China keep good relationship with the U.S. and EU despite previous trade wars because Chines export market depends on the West. Unlike Russia, China is in transition from rigid command economy to more liberal market economy.

After many days of diplomacy about the crisis in Ukraine, the leaders of Europe said their overriding goal was the preservation of peace in Europe, but they warned Russia of dire consequences "politically, economically and surely strategically," according to Olaf Scholz, the German chancellor, if the country launched further incursions into Ukraine.

A potential Russian invasion of Ukraine could have pushed other economies into recession, posing another significant risk for equity markets, it was predicted by one of Wall Street's well-known equity strategists Michael Wilson of the Morgan Stanley investment bank. According to Mr Wilson, a spike in energy prices "would destroy demand, in our view, and perhaps tip several economies into an outright recession," The strategist and his team said, adding that energy stocks are most at risk of a selloff and increase inflation.

Mr Joseph Borrell EU High Representative for Foreign Affairs said that this is the most dangerous moment for the security of Europe after the end of the Cold War. (Bloomberg 14 February 2022). On the other hand, Russia thinks NATO's expansion is a threat to them.

Russian President Vladimir Putin might not be the sole decision-maker when it comes to Moscow's plans for Ukraine. There is a group of Kremlin's elite security advisers known as the 'siloviki', ex KGB officials were stoking tension making a hard-line turn in Russia's foreign policy threatening a major war in Europe in February 2022. Siloviki are members of security services police and armed forces. Also, "siloviki" is an unofficial term for a group of high-ranked politicians in the top state institutions of the Russian Federation who used to be the members of the military or the security services and worked closely with Vladimir Putin in the early years of his career. The term comes from the Russian word "sila" (force), and it means "people with force".

In the early 1990s, right after the collapse of the Soviet Union, many new politicians had heated discussions about the necessity to control the "force structures" ("silovye struktury"): The Defence Ministry, Police, and the KGB (later renamed the FSB – Federal Security Service).

When men of this calibre set their objectives and purpose, they do not see the consequence or concern of the cost of humanitarian suffering, the dire economic situation that would follow their decisions. This was the tensest standoff of superpowers since the World War II, a scenario characterized by President Joe Biden to a journalist as "the world could be very different if both Americans and Russian started shooting at each other and that means beginning of the World War III."

However, diplomacy had its window open, the UK threatening to impose tuff economic sanctions, use less gas if Russia invade which seem imminent on the 14th of February 2022. The U.S. State Department was taking all steps to relocate its embassy and evacuated all staff as artillery moved into the target position. Rationale was to continue diplomatic deliberation to resolve differences when and as there was no de-escalation of Russian aggression. Their concern was the safety of embassy staff and being transparent with partners.

On the morning of the 15th of February 2022, according to Russia's defence ministry there were signs of some Russian tanks returning to their bases after completing drills in districts adjacent to Ukraine, but large-scale drills were continuing. It was not clear how many units were being withdrawn, and by what distance, after a build-up of an estimated 140,000 Russian troops to the north, east and south of Ukraine. Western military analysts said it was too soon to be sure of the extent of any de-escalation.

Civil dialogue is important to avoid war perhaps multilateral talks with Russian, European and the U.S. would have been more constructive than showing military strengths at each other. The Russian leader was demanding with threatening rhetoric equal legitimate security status which he perceived that NATO is expanding and shrinking his dominance in the region. (Reuters – Moscow).

This was a chess game between democracy and authoritarian regime moving military arsenal. Russia has deployed an overwhelming 60 per cent of their combat power to position, poised battle readiness. Both US and Russian Presidents were appeared to give diplomacy "every chance". President Vladimir Putin was expressively seeking a "diplomatic path" to resolving the tense standoff with the West, but he would continue pushing for a rollback of NATO in Eastern Europe and a guarantee that Ukraine would not join the alliance. With these developments of Russian intimidation, NATO members in Europe will up-scale their resources to restrengthen themselves against any strategic threat for effective deterrence. (New York Times 15 Feb 2022)

Ukraine has long played an important, yet sometimes overlooked, role in the global security order. A former Soviet republic, Ukraine has deep cultural, economic, and political bonds with Russia, and it is keen not to let the country become more aligned with Western institutions, chiefly NATO, and the European Union. Ukraine was a cornerstone of the Soviet Union, the arch-rival of the United States during the Cold War. Behind only Russia, it was the second most populous and powerful of the fifteen Soviet republics, home to much of the union's agricultural production, defence industries, and military, including the Black Sea Fleet and some of the nuclear arsenal. Ukraine was so vital to the union that its decision to sever ties in 1991 proved to be a coup de grâce for the ailing superpower.

The early 2022 conflict in Ukraine is viewed by some analysts as part of a renewed geopolitical rivalry between western powers and Russia. The demographic of Ukraine includes large Russians and Jewish population, and Israelis has shown its concerns on the effect any possible armed conflict might have on Jewish lives in Ukraine. Making Ukraine a neutral country, a kind of stifled sovereignty as a diplomatic solution to the military standoff has been considered by the European leaders.

A similar model was used during the Cold War time to protect the independent and unoccupied democracy of Finland. (BBC News February 2022, Council on Foreign Relations December 2, 2021)

It is often said that NATO was founded in response to the threat posed by the Soviet Union. This is only partially true. In fact, the Alliance's creation was part of a broader effort to serve three purposes: deterring Soviet expansionism, forbidding the revival of nationalist militarism in Europe through a strong North American presence on the continent, and encouraging European political integration. The American policy was to prevent the expansion of Communism in the continent. Europe was divided into West and East where all Eastern Europe became communist-backed by Russia. For example, in February 1948, the Communist Party of Czechoslovakia, with covert backing from the Soviet Union, overthrew the democratically elected government. Then, in reaction to the democratic consolidation of West Germany, the Soviets blockaded Allied-controlled West Berlin in a bid to consolidate their hold on the German capital.

The aftermath of World War II saw much of Europe devastated in a way that is now difficult to envision. Approximately 36.5 million Europeans had died in the conflict, 19 million of them civilians. Refugee camps and rationing dominated daily life. In some areas, infant mortality rates were one in four. Millions of orphans wandered the burnt-out shells of former metropolises. In the German city of Hamburg alone, half a million people were homeless.

Learning lessons from World War I and II, today the Western defence analysis is more refined, and the democratic political decisions are taken upon them to avoid mistakes of unnecessary human loss and suffering let alone assessing the damage to the economy.

Although Ukraine is not a member state of NATO, the U.S and European nations were concerned about possible Russian invasion and showcased a force with a critical deterrent. The Biden administration was asserting its relationship with NATO a stark reverse in tone from few years ago when the Trump administration threaten to cut NATO funding under his America first policy. This alliance is critical for the stability of Europe which the Biden administration understood and made speedy changes to rebuild relations. It is a challenge to President Biden when his domestic popularity rating just 41 per cent according to the latest CNN poll in January 2022 and his admiration how they handle Ukraine crisis to rebuild America's image overseas and is a defining characteristic of American politics, in the meantime, managing domestic political front in a time America's digital capital market is changing to join with its industrial capital forming new industrial base of Unicorn companies is another challenge.

In the post-Covid world, we noticed a mega effect of Milton Friedman's New Liberal Economic theory. To meet the economic challenges and market shocks during Covid lockdown period, America and EU countries including the UK applied Quantitative Easing to increase the money circulation adding high inflation rate overriding value of real interest rate, in the U.S, consumer prices have risen by 7.5 per cent while China redirected export production capacity to their internal consumer market, 500 million strong middle-class buying power has now made the Chinese domestic economy stronger. Today, China possessed the world's largest US dollar balance and economic strength, therefore, can make a significant economic influence on Russia and the EU.

Milton Friedman was one of the leading economic voices of the latter half of the 20th century and popularized many economic ideas that are still important today. Friedman's economic theories became what is known as monetarism, which refuted important parts of Keynesian economics. In his book *A Monetary History of the United States*, 1867-1960, Friedman illustrated the role of monetary policy in creating and, arguably, worsening the Great Depression. Friedman argued for free trade, smaller government, and a slow, steady increase of the money supply in a growing economy. His emphasis on monetary policy and the quantity theory of money became known as monetarism.

The influence of Milton Freedman on our lives is significant. His contribution in economic theory and public policy has arguably added tens of trillions of US dollars to world product over time. Friedman lives his life for a purpose, the utilitarian goal of producing the greatest good for the greatest while being happiest oneself. His political goal is the greatest freedom possible. But we witnessed during the Covid lockdown situation limitations of our achievements. The total effect of Friedman's theory would completely change the world politics, culture, social structure, capital markets and notably shift the unipolar power. Mr Putin fears that liberalisation would soon take over Russia's economic model.

## Russian invasion of Ukraine February 2022

On the 18th of February 2022, the Russian president Mr Putin demonstrated his strategic nuclear weapon capabilities to the world with his Belarusian counterpart Alexander Lukashenko. His modern hypersonic air to land missile system is deadly and fiercely accurate sending a strategic message to NATO asking to keep out of his special military operation in Ukraine. Evidently, he has well prepared for the invasion expecting Western economic sanctions to follow for his actions. The Central Bank of Russia (CBR) had over 800 billion US Dollars in reserves and heavily invested in tons of gold. Mr Putin repeatedly mentioned that he had no intention to invade Ukraine but delivered an emotional speech reminding that Ukraine is part of Russia.

According to Mr Putin, it was Russia that helped building modern Ukraine referring to historical events. It is a fact that Ukrainians are not much different to Russians in terms of ethnically, socially, and economically traits, however, Mr Putin ignored the freedom of choice and self-determination of Ukraine accusing American agencies of interfering.

On the ground Russian artillery fire escalated sharply in eastern Ukraine over the weekend, deepening fears of an imminent attack and potentially giving Russia a pretext to invade. Ukrainians reluctantly left their homes, with some evacuating to Russia.

Over the weekend of 19 to 20 February 2022, Russia conducted strategic nuclear weapon exercises, journalists witnessed a very harsh increase in political rhetoric and rising tensions with continued rejections from any overtures from Ukrainians. Russian forces have not crossed the boarders, there was no sign of rollback, but they are still very close to it conducting false flag operations. There is a significant overmatch of weapon power of Russian artillery and tanks that Ukrainians have to defend against. If Putin invades Ukraine, it would be the highest attack in a scale of ground since World War II. Russian capabilities are very sophisticated, and it will change the security architecture of Europe. This is why it is important for the world leaders to discuss the security and strategic stability of Europe as a whole and not in isolation of Ukraine. (NBC, Fox, and Al Jazeera News February 2022)

A false flag operation is an act committed with the intent of disguising the actual source of responsibility and pinning blame on another party. The term "false flag" originated in the 16th century as a purely figurative ex-pression to mean "a deliberate misrepresentation of someone's affiliation or motives". False flag operations carried on throughout the war, but most can be considered in the old sense of the word.

The phrase was coined for the practice of pirate ships flying the colours of other nations to deceive merchant ships into thinking they were dealing with a friendly vessel. While the pirates would usually unfurl their true colours just before attacking, the wrong flag would some-times continue to be flown throughout an attack, hence the term 'attacking under a false flag'. Over time, the term 'false flag' came to be applied to any covert operation that sought to shift the responsibility onto a different party from the one carrying it out, as was the case with the Nazis at Gleiwitz.

One of the most famous incidents considered by many to be a false flag operation is the Reichstag fire, which took place on the night of the 27th of February 1933. A lone communist sympathizer called Marinus van de Lubbe was arrested and charged with setting fire to the German parliament building. This gave Hitler and his propaganda minister, Joseph Goebbels, the excuse they needed to purge Germany of opposition, especially the communists. The sweeping emergency powers Hitler and the Nazi Party grabbed for themselves after the fire are the reason many people think the Reichstag was burned not by a lone communist protesting Germany's treatment of the working classes (as van de Lubbe himself claimed while in custody), but by the Nazis themselves.

20th February 2022 was the last day of the Winter Olympics in Beijing and Mr Putin did not want to tarnish the image of China by showing his aggression. He waited until the end of the games. Geopolitically, Russia and China appear to be in lock step, and the U.S. is trying to build up a global coalition to counter the alliance. Experts say that Putin may be trying to rewrite the security rules and redesign the security architecture of Europe.

Last year, in 2021, President Putin wrote a long piece of thesis in which he described Russians and Ukrainians as "one nation". He also defined the collapse of the Soviet Union in December 1991 as the "disintegration of historical Russia" and considers Ukraine's current leaders as running an "anti-Russian project".

President Putin has also argued that if Ukraine joined NATO, the alliance might try to recapture Crimea. Its other core demands are that NATO does not deploy "strike weapons near Russia's borders", and that it removes forces and military infrastructure from member states that joined the alliance in 1997. That means Central Europe, Eastern Europe, and the Baltics. In reality, Russia wants NATO to return to its pre-1997 borders.

Russia was poised to go much further on the 21st of February 2022, shortly after the Security Council meeting, Russia's President Putin signed a decree to recognise breakaway regions as independent states, recognized two 'breakaway' regions of neighbouring Ukraine and then sent in troops to "secure peace" in a repeat of 2014's annexation of Crimea. Russia's defence doctrine is absolute protection of its people. It includes use of tactical and strategic nuclear weapons if needed to win.

With the backdrop of international condemnation, Russia indiscriminately attacked Ukraine cities, both military and civilian targets from air, sea, and land. Used internationally banned cluster bombs causing maximum destruction to property reducing cities to rubble. There were many civil casualties including children reminding Syrian Civil War. Russia was up to an all-out assault and attempted to destroy a multiple television station and communication tower in the capital city of Kyiv to cut off the country and take over the control so they could change the narrative of this war, but the missile missed the surgical strike. The blast occurred near the Babyn Yar Holocaust Memorial Centre, drawing criticism from Israel. Russian tactics were more violent and destructive striking at residential areas. The situation in many parts of the country was desperate.

Ukrainian President Volodymyr Zelensky, a former actor and comedian who has been serving as the president of Ukraine since 2019 gained international recognition for his bravery and resilience to defend his country by boosting the morale of his people in this unmatched, un-provoked war. Since Ukraine is not a member state of NATO, the U.S. President Mr Biden categorically said that he will not put American or NATO soldiers on the ground knowing the risk of contending a nuclear state. His approach was prudent and diplomatic as he did not wish to provoke Russia to use nuclear weapons. Many Western journalists condemned Russia's actions as a belligerent state and called for a ceasefire while some critics said that the Western media is one-sided, and that President Zelensky is an immature politician who underestimated his Russian brothers and was unable to build a constructive relationship with its powerful neighbour.

Belarus, officially the Republic of Belarus, and historically Byelorussia, is a landlocked country in Eastern Europe. It is bordered by Russia to the east and northeast, Ukraine to the south, Poland to the west, and Lithuania and Latvia to the northwest. Belarus President Alexander Lukashenko, a close ally of Vladimir Putin, appears to be siding with Russia reportedly known top-secret plans of Russian invasion and in support of the rebuilding of the Russian empire. According to Mr Putin's thesis, Russia, Belarus, and Ukraine are all one nation.

The UK has announced its first wave of sanctions against senior military figures in Belarus specifically for their role in joining and facilitating the Russian invasion of Ukraine.

The Belarusian chief of the general staff, Maj Gen Victor Gulevich, and three other deputy defence ministers will all face sanctions, along with two military enterprises.

The EU has accused Belarus of double standards – with which the UK has been working in close cooperation over sanctions – is likely to take similar measures. Belarus has been used as a base for Russian soldiers to pour into Ukraine. Soldiers from the Belarus army have joined the invasion. (The Guardian 01 March 2022)

As the events were unfolding rapidly, Russia showcased a strength of comeback after the collapse of Soviet Union and was determined to rebuild its historical empire. At the time of writing this book large 40 miles long Russian military convoy was advancing towards Kyiv to crush Ukraine Kyiv (sometimes spelt Kiev) is the largest city and the capital of Ukraine, as well as the historical capital of Kievan Rus'.

Kyiv officially celebrates its founding year as 482, but the city may date back at least 2,000 years. Archaeology dates the site of the oldest known settlement in the area to 25,000 years BC. Ukraine officially declared itself an independent country on 24 August 1991, when the communist Supreme Soviet (Parliament) of Ukraine proclaimed that the nation would no longer follow the laws of USSR, only the laws of the Ukrainian SSR, de facto government declaring Ukraine's independence from the Soviet Union. In June 2019, at the request of the United States Department of State, the Embassy of Ukraine to the United States, and Ukrainian organisations in America, the name Kyiv was officially adopted by the United States Board on Geographic Names as the only correct one, which resulted in the federal government of the United States of America.

Co-existence of two different systems is possible but need deep philosophical critical thinking to understand differences and secure your own interest while respecting your adversaries. Military men think in a military way. Especially autocratic leaders have little capacity to compromise. War in mind is the pattern of their thinking to defend or strike the way modern war machine is built for them. They are motivated by aggression to reach the intended target one way or the other.

"I have decided to conduct a special military operation. Russia cannot exist with a constant threat emanating from the territory of Ukraine. You and I have been left with no opportunity to protect our people other than the one we use today."

"Let's imagine Ukraine is a NATO member and starts these military operations. Are we supposed to go to war with the NATO bloc? Has anyone given that any thought? Apparently not." (President Vladimir Putin Sky News 23 February 2022)

"Putin has delivered the most terrifying geopolitically speech of the 21st century," tweeted one US foreign-policy consultant.

Over the last decade, Russia has used cyberattacks as a part of its military activities beyond its borders to undermine and destabilize Ukraine. During the invasion, the use of malware to distort Ukrainian government websites and spreading disinformation to mislead people were common soft attacks yet powerful enough to confuse civilians. President Putin's call to overthrow their elected President and support his long-protracted military campaign was insanity. Putin appeared to be an isolated decision-maker of this Russian autocratic regime without any public consensus.

On the other hand, discussions and negotiation is the democratic way of addressing a crisis. Each year, the Munich Security Council (MSC) offers the unique opportunity for leading institutions to host an official side event within the framework of their flagship conference in February. Many renowned think tanks, government institutions, civil society organizations, and partners from the private sector have made use of this platform, enjoying direct access to an exclusive community of decision-makers and key experts.

From traditional defence and security policy to questions of global order, technological change, sustainability, and human security, the MSC is committed to tackling today's most prominent security challenges. The MSC welcomes side events as enriching elements of the conference program and actively supports their organization and implementation through a dedicated team. This year, 18th February 2022 was a perfect time for them to take up the theme of European Security Architecture at the 58th conference as Russia seems uncontrollable. Western leaders unanimously decided to impose economic sanctions against Russia.

The U.S. and its allies swiftly imposed economic sanctions on Russia for what President Biden denounced as the beginning of an "invasion of Ukraine." Western officials have confirmed that Russian forces have crossed the Ukrainian border into two separatist enclaves in eastern Ukraine. Germany responded by suspending the controversial Nord Stream 2 gas pipeline, the 27 European Union member states discussed targeting all the politicians in Russia's Duma who voted for the recognition last week invasion – plus Russian banks now financing military operations in Ukraine – while the UK added 3 businessmen and 5 banks to its existing financial sanctions list.

The premise of the UK government is to find the corrupt Russian money and freeze them. The sanctions so far include halting the Nord Stream 2 gas pipeline and cutting off global financing to two Russian banks and a handful of the country's elites. The moves fell short of the more sweeping economic warfare that some have demanded, though President Biden warned that more sanctions would follow if Vladimir Putin, did not withdraw his forces from Ukraine. Accordingly, Russia was also cut off from the SWIFT international banking system disabling electronic money transactions.

The Nord Stream 2 pipeline can carry enough natural gas from Russia to fuel 26 million households in Europe. If it were to work at full capacity, it could go a long way to solving gas shortages and high energy prices. However, the U.S. has vowed to "bring an end" to Nord Stream 2 if Russia invades Ukraine. Nord Stream 2 is a 1,200km pipeline under the Baltic Sea, which will take gas from the Russian coast near St Petersburg to Lubmin in Germany. It cost €10bn (£8.4bn) and was completed in September 2021. The Russian state-owned energy giant Gazprom put up half of the cost and western energy firms such as Shell and ENGIE of France are paying the rest. Russia under Putin was engaging in the globalization of the economy taking forward-thinking projects and taking part in popular European football games.

For most of his 22-year rule, Putin has presented him-self as a leader who astutely manages risk to navigate Russia through treacherous shoals. But his attack on Ukraine has revealed him to Russians as an altogether different leader: one dragging the nuclear superpower he helms into a war with no foreseeable conclusion. Putin chose war to resolve his perceived threat. Russians awoke in shock after they learned that Putin, in an address to the nation that aired before 6 a.m. local time, had ordered a full-scale assault against what Russians of all political stripes often refer to as their "brotherly nation," even as the state-run news media characterized the invasion as not a war, but as a "special military operation" limited to eastern Ukraine. Some civilians see this situation as a war between Russia and America as they cannot make any sense of fully-fledged invasion and destruction to their distant brothers. President Putin waged this war with the assumption that Ukrainians would welcome him as a liberator and turn against American backed government which, in his mind, is destroying Russian values; but the truth on the ground would prove otherwise as Russia is now accused of alleged war crimes.

While UK Prime Minister Boris Johnson called Russia's latest action in Ukraine "barbaric" on a visit to NATO ally Poland on the 1st of March 2022, both the US and UK governments rejected Ukrainian pleas to enforce a no-fly zone for fear of provoking nuclear war. UK government goes by the rule book and wise thinking.

Both UK and NATO do not want a further escalation of this war, instead they're open to confrontation and ready to give impunity to Russia if they wish to withdraw troops. There is a major risk of NATO jets could get shot by Russian Airforce triggering Article 5 that could turn into World War III dragging all European countries to the battlefield. Diplomatically, there was a mass walkout of European delegates in protest during the Russian foreign minister's speech in the UN Human Rights Council.

Though not legally binding it has a lot of political weight for brutal violation of human rights by Russia. Many families were displaced because of attacks by missiles and bombs on civilians stemming from Russian aggression. Thousands of people lost homes, and many are now without water and electricity. Reuters reported that the most intensive bombardment has struck Kharkiv, a city of 1.5 million people in the east, whose centre has been turned into a bombed-out wasteland of ruined buildings and debris.

"The Russian 'liberators' have come," one Ukrainian volunteer lamented sarcastically, as he and three others strained to carry the dead body of a man wrapped in a bedsheet out of the ruins on the main square.

On the sixth day of Russia's invasion of Ukraine, the Russian military campaign appeared to have shifted toward targeting civilian areas with increasingly powerful weapons. The U.N. said that at least 136 civilians, including 13 children, had been killed so far. Volodymyr Zelensky, the Ukrainian President, has accused Russia of war crimes. (New York Times 02 March 2022)

Ukrainians said they were fighting on in the first sizeable city Russia claimed to have seized, while Moscow stepped up its lethal bombardment of major population centres that its invasion force has so far failed to tame. Approximately two million people were already displaced internally following Moscow's 2014 invasion of Crimea and support for *separatists* in the Donbas, with 14,000 killed.

"A third world war would be nuclear and destructive," said Moscow's Foreign Minister Sergei Lavrov on the 02nd of March 2022 in comments reported by Russian news agencies RIA and TASS.

With Moscow having failed in its aim of swiftly overthrowing Ukraine's government after nearly a week, Western countries were worried that it is switching to new, far more violent tactics to blast its way into cities it had expected to easily take. On the 2$^{nd}$ of March 2022 and 6$^{th}$ day of war, in Washington, the U.S. President Joe Biden, addressing the Congress, banned all Russian flights from the American airspace.

On the 7$^{th}$ day of the war, while Russian troops outside the city of Enerhodar were shelling the Zaporizhzhia power plant, Ukraine's largest nuclear facility, a fire broke out, according to Ukrainian officials. 20% of Ukraine's electricity is produced by nuclear power and the country is now facing a huge challenge of containing radioactive contamination and power outage.

Ukrainian leaders warn the attacks were creating a "real threat of nuclear danger" at the power station, the largest plant of its kind in Europe. Having a nuclear power plant in a conflict zone is a grave concern not only to Ukraine but to the entire Europe, and Russia appeared to ignore the international Nuclear Safety protocols directing their firepower to the danger zone. Ukrainian firefighters bravely extinguished the roaring fire caused by shelling. Depending on the magnitude of the damage, the plant could be shut down to prevent radiation leaks to the atmosphere.

Russian forces have reportedly taken over the control of the plant transforming Putin's invasion into a global threat. Then the Prime Minister of the UK Mr Boris Johnson at the Munich Security Council on the 04$^{th}$ March 2022 stated that the reckless actions undertaken by President Putin could directly threaten the safety of Europe. The situation on the ground was dire, full of horror and fear of innocent civilians who until 9 days before lived in a country that functioned normally with schools, coffee shops and markets. Steady increase of Russian army shelling with lethal weapons inflicting maximum damage, therefore, sees no end to misery on the ground with increasing death toll. State of the affairs was pretty chilling though Russian leaders deny such actions.

As a matter of fact, President Putin keeps justifying his actions by saying that Russian and Ukrainian are one nation, and that his army is there to liberate Ukraine from Neo Nazis. He went to the extent of criminalizing journalists who report fake news prohibiting telling the truth. (CNN, Sky and DW News 04 March 2022)

"China does not approve of any approach that may exacerbate tensions," China's permanent representative Zhang Jun said to the UN at Monday's emergency special session of the UN General Assembly.

"I hope what is happening in Ukraine will end up to the benefit of nations and the region," said Iran's President Ebrahim Raisi in a phone call with Russia's President Putin last week.

Damage has already been inflicted on civilians both in Russia and Ukraine. As Russian citizens began to feel the devaluation of their currency Rubel, the public sentiment was shifting from confidence to what would happen to their money and future. Some Russian businessmen in London are even more worry about their money than loss of life.

• Oligarchs

Russian oligarchs are business oligarchs of the former Soviet republics who rapidly accumulated wealth during the era of Russian privatisation in the aftermath of the dissolution of the Soviet Union in the 1990s. The failing Soviet State left the ownership of state assets contested, which allowed for informal deals with former USSR officials (mostly in Russia and Ukraine) as a means to acquire state property.

The first modern Russian oligarchs emerged as business-sector entrepreneurs under Mikhail Gorbachev (General Secretary 1985-1991). During his period of market liberalization to prevent economic collapse he encouraged the transition from a Communist socialistic economic model to a more democratic social system. These younger generation entrepreneurs were able to build their initial wealth due to Gorbachev's reforms "when co-existence of regulated and quasi-market prices created huge opportunities for exploitation."

The term "oligarch" derives from the Ancient Greek *ol-igarkhia* meaning "the rule of the few". Since 2018, several Russian oligarchs and their companies have been hit by US sanctions for their support of "the Russian government's malign activity around the globe" (especially in Russia) by a very rich business leader with a great deal of political influence.

The UK has become a safe haven for Oligarchs where Russian money has been channelled through facilitating corporate banks and companies. There is a call from investigative journalists to clean up assets management companies through regulations to stand up for democratic values against corrupt leaders.

During the 1990s, once Boris Yeltsin became President of Russia in

July 1991, the oligarchs emerged as well-connected entrepreneurs who started from nearly nothing and became rich through participation in the market via connections to the corrupt but elected, government of Russia during the state's transition to a liberal economics. Broadly speaking, an oligarchy is a form of government characterized by the rule of a few persons or families.

More specifically, the term was used by Greek philosopher Aristotle in contrast to aristocracy, which was another term to describe rule by a privileged few.

Russia today exhibits a distorted complex economic and political philosophy with money pyramids. Their leadership actions are increasingly become unpredictable without having anyone to question about the nature and purpose of their social contract towards people of Russia. Those sequential events unfolding before our eyes tell the story of human misery created by man himself.

Economics and politics are ideas, doctrines, concepts, and theories formulated by thinkers of the past to improve the standards of living and quality of the life by pure observations of different social systems with broad assumptions. Economic is a dynamic subject. It changes with time. Instead of going forward, Present Russian leadership want to go back in time to an old paradigm.

What we see today in the 21st-century the Russian President and his allies are in a reversal of progress, a come-back to a dark age. Indeed, with their military might and intense bombardment, they're a not only causing a humanitarian disaster but are employing weapons which are banned at home and abroad.

Despite his reputation of good calculator, by leading his country into a high-risk war, the Russian President has caught the attention of the entire world, and his decisions might lead to international isolation and the devaluation of the Rubel, which in turn can cause the political and economic destruction of Russia. Russia has now been cut off from the 21st-century market economy and household technology like Apple, Google and the like the West weaponizing the flow of Finance closing doors to Banking system.

Putin vowed an "uncompromising fight" in Ukraine challenging the Western economy and US central-bank chief Jerome Powell said the Fed

(Federal Reserve) will raise interest rates a quarter-point from zero at March 2022 policy meeting. With surging prices for oil and gas driving US inflation to the highest since 1982 last month at 7.5% per year, "Inflation is too high." Powell told US lawmakers in regular testimony, accepting that Covid Crisis stimulus from both Washington and the Federal Reserve has helped worsen the rise in the cost of living.

"It's going to take some time, but we're going to get [inflation] back under control."

Starting from March 2022, every day the world wakes up to see the latest developments from Ukraine, a tragic situation that is rapidly developing with Russian troops advancing to take the capital city, causing grave concern for all people around the world, especially those in Ukraine, Russia, and their neighbours in Central and Eastern Europe. Feeling safe and secure wherever you call home is a human right, and it is at these moments that unilateral organizations including NATO and the United Nations, and the global community have come together to protect those impacted.

This recent operation as is a lot different from that of Crimea which is smaller in size and had no resistance. As President Zelensky clearly stated that light will dispel the darkness. Mr Putin has to weigh the cost and benefits of his political doctrine which lies behind his decision to invade Ukraine. His "Special Operation" - as he calls it - the extreme military campaign against his brothers in Ukraine will bring the world to judge the merit of communist ideology.

Among all doctrines, Buddhism stands as the pillar of light shining above shedding love and compassion to all nations without any discrimination. There is a reason why revolutionists kept the Buddha statue undamaged in Lenin Grand St Petersburg, Russia. Perhaps Mr Putin has yet to discover what it means and the middle way of resolving critical issues at critical times.

The refugee and internal displacement crisis from and within Ukraine have moved with unprecedented speed and scale. Civilian casualties have been almost entirely a direct result of ongoing combat operations sometimes because of the targeted bombing of residential areas. UN-HCR estimates that roughly 10 million displaced persons, which is nearly one-quarter of the entire population of Ukraine.

Killing or harming human beings is not acceptable to Buddhist teachings. Because of this, some Buddhists would not rise to an attack or to any conflict with violence and in principle would condemn such violent means used to resolve issues. Most Buddhists try to practice nonviolence in their everyday lives and believe that it is wrong to show violence at any time. In times of war, Buddhists must show compassion and help all living beings. They must abandon any fight that crosses their path and view aggression as a weakness rather than a strength. The Buddha has shown us better ways to avoid wars and resolve conflicts wisely without adding unnecessary suffering to people.

The Noble Eightfold Path is at the heart of Buddhist teachings that show the importance of regulating behaviour so that one would not harm another. For example, the Buddha would advise on the importance of right thought, right speech, and right mindfulness and not engage in provocative arguments or actions that would otherwise escalate into war.

According to Buddhism, there is always a way out of a complex situation by applying critical analysis and strategic thinking with wisdom. There are multiple causes of war and noting arise singularly. Buddhist teaching could help us prevent war, crime, and unnecessary loss of lives like the unfortunate situation that unfolds in Ukraine. Most Buddhists are committed to non-violence and willing to help those who suffer through war, spreading love and kindness to those affected.

Compassion is one of the cardinal qualities of the Buddha that all Buddhists want to promote to alleviate the suffering of others. Those who practice his teaching see that ego is a mental delusion and taking a warpath is a blind view. It requires patience; the capacity to accept or tolerate delay, problems, or suffering without becoming annoyed or anxious.

War must be the last resort. Of course politicians have responsibility. There are differing views as to what the term 'last resort' actually means in the context of an ethical war. A state should only go to war if it has tried every sensible, non-violent alternative first. This is because a state should not put lives at risk unless it's tried other remedies first. The decision to use lethal force, and tactical weapons as last resort without considering and evaluating other options available to them reflect the disposition of the leaders and the mindset of their inner circle.

Evidently, in the case of this most recent Ukraine war, western democratic leaders were prudent and have applied alternatives that included diplomacy, economic sanctions, political pressure collectively with other like-minded nations, withdrawal of financial aid, condemnation in the United Nations, and so on. Russia should have tried these alternatives exhaustively and sincerely before violence is used.

Some writers don't think that 'last' in last resort refers to the sequence of time. They argue that last resort means that the use of force is ethical only when it is really necessary and when no reasonable alternative is left to stop the enemy to do much more damage or kill more people than an early war would have done. On the other hand, Moscow has perceived that not acting now may allow their enemy to become so established in another country's territory and far greater force will have to be used to remove the threat than would have been needed earlier.

Mistrust, "to regard with doubt or suspicion; have no trust in" is the cause of the use of heavy-handed aggression for harsh treatment. As described by some Western journalists, Putin is a rational actor living in an echo chamber of political science vernacular, an old school scholar of the Russian Empire. However, during his interview with Financial times (FT) in July 2019, he has demonstrated a deep insight into the Globalization of economy, an appreciation for doing business in good terms with the West and stressed the importance of both the political stability of a country and a free market economy.

So, he believed in the distribution of resources and the benefits of globalization. In replying to a question of the interviewer on new nuclear arms race, President Putin showed his ingenuity of KGB secret service. After a long pose, he replied "I believe there is such a risk, …. the war theatre in Europe is unlikely to be interesting to the US, despite the expansion of NATO and NATO'S contingent at our borders." (Vladimir Putin interviewed by the Financial Times -FT)

Is there a truth in his conspiracy theory that Ukraine is now a fake country run by an American backed anti-Russian drugged addict neo-Nazis, who hold Ukrainian people hostage? Did he twist the modern history to justify his actions framed as a rescue effort operation to de-nazify the country?

So much damage has been done in Putin's choice of war including killing civilians, destabilizing the Western economy, and sending shocks in the world energy market. It is hardly expected both ordinary Russians and Ukrainians to take his side under the circumstances of a dire economic situation born by the war of choice. In spite all the assumptions he predicted, his war turned out to be wrong, a delusion of imaginary history lesson of Cold War.

If this is a fabricated story, then is there another factual classified information the world didn't know about, that pushed Russia into war. Like over 150,000 Russian troops surrounded Ukraine prior to this invasion. So, has NATO encircled Russia? The steady expansion of NATO in the former Eastern bloc has been said to have taken away the Russia's security belt and in return, they have taken this expansion as a serious provocation that reduces the mutual trust.

In this perspective, an act in self-defence claims sounds plausible. Historically, when the peace agreement was signed in September 1990 with former Soviet leader Mikhail Gorbachev and U.S. President Ronald Ragan both Russia and the U.S. agreed that NATO would not expand beyond Germany and no new members would be added to the alliance so to avoid demolishing the Warsaw Pact, but NATO rapidly expanded in the Russia's backyard disregarding past agreements.

Russia rightfully asked for which countries this expansion is intended and what happened to the assurances Western partners made after the dissolution of the Warsaw pact. Many US diplomats and the State Department officials have also publicly made their concerns about this matter many occasions to the successive American administrations overreaching NATO to Russia's proximity.

In 2014, when Russia annexed Crimea and invaded eastern Ukraine, NATO responded by suspending cooperation with Russia and boosting Kyiv's defensive capabilities. It held military training, deployed troops to the region, and funded cyberwarfare protections. The Russia-NATO Council was established in 2002 to handle security issues and joint projects. In response to Russia's false claims, the NATO's Public Diplomacy Division (PDD) – Press & Media Section has published five myths dismissing Russia's claims.

NATO responded by publishing all such claims and explained in detail fact sheet. According to the publication all Russia's allegations proved baseless. Since Russia is a member of UN security council, all activities were carried out with their approval. For example,

- Myth 1: NATO is trying to encircle Russia • Fact: This claim ignores the facts of geography. Russia's land border is just over 20,000 kilometres long. Of that, 1,215 kilometres, or less than one-sixteenth, face current NATO members. Claims that NATO is building bases around Russia are similarly groundless. Outside the territory of NATO nations, NATO only maintains a significant military presence in three places: Kosovo, Afghanistan, and at sea off the Horn of Africa. All three operations are carried out under the United Nations mandate, and thus carry the approval of Russia, along with all other Security Council members.

As already explained by NATO Secretary-General Jens Stoltenberg, geography and physics make it impossible for the NATO system to shoot down Russian intercontinental missiles from NATO sites in Romania or Poland. The interceptors are too few and located too far south or too close to Russia, to be able to do so. They are designed to tackle threats from outside the Euro-Atlantic area. The Russian claim that the framework agreement on Iran's nuclear Programme obviates the need for NATO missile defence is wrong on two counts.

NATO enlargement has contributed to spreading democracy, security, and stability further across Europe. By choosing to adopt the standards and principles of NATO, aspirant countries gave their democracies the strongest possible anchor. And by taking the pledge to defend NATO, they received the pledge that NATO would protect them. NATO membership is not imposed on countries. Each sovereign country has the right to choose for itself whether it joins any treaty or alliance. Invading a sovereign country and committing war crimes are not justifiable acts for any reasons in the 21$^{st}$ century free world.

Ukraine has been under constant attack. Russia has broken the ceasefire and shelling indiscriminately and firing cruise missile attacks were continued. On the 5$^{th}$ of March 2022, the Russian military convoy moved slowly toward the capital like a dark cloud spreading the terror far and wide increasing the number of refugees to 1.5 million separating families making young children orphans. Sadness, pain suffering, and separation were the results of Putin's defence doctrine.

This war was unnecessary and would have been avoided by wise thinking, but tension built up over a period of time without reconciliation of the real concerns and differences. Innocent civilians of the Ukraine are paying a heavy price for the bad politics. President Zelensky is a shining example of bravery and courage facing unmatched combat power of Russian aggression. Putin's end game is to capture and demilitarise Ukraine at any cost.

Resistance forces of the Ukrainian army are credible and the convoy advancing towards their capital city has been ambushed in all directions by heroic soldiers.

On the 12th day, the war was entering into a dangerous stage in the fear that Russia might use chemical weapons. It was difficult to watch graphical images coming from the war zone, with Russian forces relentlessly attacking civilian targets, President Putin has begun to calculate the losses in the close combat in this long-protracted war. Civilians have been armed and have started fighting for freedom.

Thousands of lives have abruptly come to holt by this escalating war. History tells us that confronting a ruthless dictator should be done sooner than later to stop human suffering and longer-term threat to world peace. Slow advancement is not what Russia expected. They expected to decapitate and replace the current government of Ukraine and have a land bridge between Crimea and Mariupol to other close cities. Ukrainian resistance has slowed down the outright capture by using banned conventional thermobaric rocket launches of mass destruction.

Sky Australia reported that isolated Putin is a 'lonely, vulnerable man'. "The emerging trend of personal miscalculation, combined with loneliness of supreme leadership that (Putin) seems to prefer, does not augur well for his future."

Has Putin got everything wrong about NATO? He is not without critiques within his own government. During the last few decades, Russia has preferred to go on a path in contrast with its own values rather than investing in human development and its rich natural resources and participate meaningfully with rest of the world economy.

Putin's inner circle is funded by Oligarchs carrying out businesses in the West, people who control a vast amount of wealth and who are not happy about the strong sanctions imposed against them. He has rarely looked as much isolated as he is now.

Indeed, in his choreographed appearances with his inner circle, he always sits at a resolute distance from his closest advisers. As commander in chief, the ultimate responsibility for the invasion rests with him, but he has always relied on a deeply loyal entourage, many of whom also began their careers in Russia's security services. The question is who has his ear, during this most fateful moment in his presidency? Inside Russia is said to be highly corrupted and those elements have loomed into its once formidable army. If anyone does, it is his long-time confidant Sergei Shoigu, who has parroted the Putin's line of demilitarizing Ukraine and protecting Russia from the West's so-called military threat. This is a man who goes on hunting and fishing trips with the President to Siberia, and in the past, he has been viewed as a potential successor.

Russia was one of the main reasons that contributed to end of World War II and the West should not underestimate the scarifies this country made to secure peace. As a matter of fact, it was Russia that, by encircling Hitlers Germany, ended the war in Europe. Experience and determination which Russia gained by fighting wars, are the pillars of their modern combat power and strategy. The determinant factor of the present war is whether Russia would be successful in taking Kyiv without civilian casualties. At the time writing this book there were 400,000 civilians trapped in the capital city and Russia did not agree to ceasefire.

Besides, it has been reported that there are nuclear power plants and virus testing labs inside Ukraine. Russia was blaming the U.S. for the funding of chemical weapons and the situation has become seriously threatening.

In this critical juncture of the world politics and economy, China has offered unconditional friendship to Russia. This was revealed at the opening games of 4th February 2022 winter Olympics when the two leaders of communist regimes met to sign the friendship accord. Asia showed a strength in silence by not taking sides and Saudi Arabia by refusing to increase oils production but taking the advantage of rising oil price that was then rising to 130 US Dollars per barrel.

Russia has enough reserves, gold and has China which would help them financially to rebuild their economy and even go to war in order to win. Turning against a powerful neighbour, in particular a nuclear state and former partner is lack of political insight of Ukrainian leadership. In this scenario middle path is wiser to balance relations than leaning to strategic alliances. The death, destruction and deprivation of war were mounting in Ukraine, from which an estimated three million people have fled seeking refuge as peace talks failed to bring a diplomatic breakthrough.

In the southern city of Mariupol, Russian commanders appear to be resorting to tactics used in Chechnya and Syria: flattening settlements with overwhelming and indiscriminate firepower is what Russia demonstrating to the world.

Efforts to negotiate a cease-fire to give civilians a chance to escape have failed repeatedly. For the past three days, the prospect that relief could reach the city through a "humanitarian corridor" fell apart in a hail of mortar and artillery fire. (New York Times 10 March 2022)

The transition from the strict communist rule of former Soviet Union to democracy in Ukraine has never been a smooth curve as expected or liked to happen or thought by many Western politicians and strategists.

The Orange Revolution (Ukrainian: Помаранчева революція, Pomarancheva revoliutsiia) was a series of protests and political events that took place in Ukraine from late November 2004 to January 2005, in the immediate aftermath of the run-off vote of the 2004 Ukrainian presidential election, which was claimed to be marred by massive corruption, voter intimidation and electoral fraud.

Kyiv, the Ukrainian capital, was the focal point of the movement's campaign of civil resistance, with thousands of protesters demonstrating daily. Nationwide, the revolution was highlighted by a series of acts of civil disobedience and general strikes organized by the opposition movement.

Reports from several domestic and foreign election monitors suggested that the election was rigged by the authorities in favour of the contestant Viktor Fedorovych Yanukovych, the Russian favourite. The final results showed a clear victory for Yush chenko, the other contestant who received about 52% that ended the Orange Revolution, however, had a negative connotation among pro-government circles in Belarus and Russia. Ten years after, the protests were sparked by the Ukrainian government's decision to suspend the signing of an association agreement with the European Union

(EU). A period of relative calm in the anti-government demonstrations in Kyiv ended abruptly on 18 February 2014, when protesters and police clashed.

The Revolution of Dignity (Ukrainian: Революція гідності, Revoliutsiia hidnosti), also known as the Maiden Revolution, took place in Ukraine, in February 2014 and at the end of the Euromaidan protests, when deadly clashes between protesters and the security forces in the Ukrainian capital Kyiv culminated in the ousting of elected President Viktor Yanukovych and the over-throw of the Ukrainian government. This incident evidently aggravated Russia and they refused to accept Zelensky as the legitimate President of Ukraine.

Nearly six years after the fall of the regime of Ukrainian president Victor Yanukovych, Ukraine's Euromaidan Revolution of 2013-2014 is increasingly becoming a subject of historical analysis, albeit one still fraught with political controversy. This is clear in Mychailo Wynnyckyi's book, Ukraine's Maidan, Russian War: A Cornicle and Analysis of the Revolution of Dignity, published in 2019.

Wynnyckyj, Associate Professor of Sociology at the National University Kyiv-Mohyla Academy, was a participant in the protests held on Kyiv's main square, the Maidan. Here Wynnyckyj stresses that the Maidan was a revolution as understood by Hannah Arendt's *On Revolution* (1963), where a dramatic shift in values and ideas, rather than a shift in social and political structures, took place. Wynnyckyj sees Ukraine's "creative class" – its advertisers, computer programmers, managers (particularly in investment firms, agribusiness, and the IT industry), university professors, and journalists – as the revolution's driving force.

As they entered Ukraine's post-Maidan government and parliament, this group replaced the Yanukoyvch-era oligarch clans that were on the decline. They stood for values such as self-reliance, fairness, and a sense of social responsibility.

Wynnyckyj, whose PhD dissertation from the University of Cambridge focused on small entrepreneurs and large industries controlled by oligarch clans in post-Soviet Ukraine, makes a compelling argument: that the Maidan sped up the decline of oligarch-controlled manufacturing industries in Ukraine's east and south which had dominated Ukrainian political life for decades.

Russian secret service KGB believes all those ideological shifts were works of American CIA contractors. The controversial Special Operation of liberation is a psychological deterrent and strong message to Baltic nations and former Warsaw Pact countries from President Putin that he and his inner circle would not tolerate ideological changes at his doorstep, that they take pride in their century's achievements and developments under Communist banner

The Soviet Union originally formed this alliance as a counterbalance to the North Atlantic Treaty Organization (NATO), a collective security alliance concluded between the United States, Canada, and Western European nations in 1949. The Warsaw Pact supplemented existing agreements. Russian leadership is not yet ready to change, and had the West pushed hard their luck too far.

It is important to evaluate political psychology and profiles of leaders not only in Communist authoritarian regimes but equally important to understand the mentality of West as well to test whether the timing was right to take critical decisions of change regimes and the methods of change management without converting seemingly peaceful time to a crisis crossing the communist autocratic Russian redline. Putin's pushback was no surprise. He responded by taking Crimea a strategically important location.

Russia is now on a mission for rapid regime change in Ukraine by force of might is right. "Welcome to hell", Russia increased intense pressure on many city centres including Capital Kyiv, active terror in the region will be remembered for centuries.

Does the West have a wrong impression of Orthodox Vladimir Putin or a thin assessment of their foreign policy interests? President Putin has warned that Russia could take counter-measures if it felt threatened by NATO expansion.

The current situation was eloquently expressed in the US filmmaker Oliver Stone's 2016 documentary "Ukraine on Fire" directed by Igor Lopatonok. There was a systemic split in relations in order to bring this division between Russia and Ukraine to hate each other over time by using a policy of violence which has elevated to the state policy of both countries.

Resemblance against Russia has been going on for a long time. Anti-Russian policy became more pronounced, revealed the documentary interviews. All sequential events hitherto antagonised Russia including investment decisions made by US corporations implementing democratic leadership without testing the grounds, for timing or deeply analysing trajectory of events. The seed of democracy need to be planted in fertile grounds and nursed to grow and produce its fruits. This transition of autocracy to democracy is now a slow and painful process that need insight and political wisdom.

An apparently bugged phone conversation in which a senior US diplomat disparages the EU over the Ukraine crisis has been posted online. The alleged conversation between Assistant Secretary of State Victoria Nuland and the US Ambassador to Ukraine, Geoffrey Pyatt in 2014, was made public. The US says that it is working with all sides in the crisis to reach a peaceful solution, noting that "ultimately it is up to the Ukrainian people to decide their future". However, this transcript suggests that the US has very clear ideas about what the outcome should be and is striving to achieve these goals.

Russian spokesmen have insisted that the US is meddling in Ukraine's affairs - no more than Moscow, the cynic might say - but Washington clearly has its own game-plan. The clear purpose in leaking this conversation is to embarrass Washington and for audiences susceptible to Moscow's message to portray the US as interfering in Ukraine's domestic affairs.

(BBC News 7 February 2014)

Perestroika as understood by former Soviets is the policy or practice of restructuring or reforming the economic and political system. First proposed by Leonid Brezhnev in 1979 and actively promoted by Mikhail Gorbachev, perestroika originally referred to increased automation and labour efficiency, but came to entail greater awareness of economic markets and the ending of central planning.

The theory of democracy is much wider than its applications on market economy. In his observation, Aristotle stated that "the basis of a democratic state is liberty" and he proposed a connection between the ideas of democracy and liberty that would be strongly emphasized by all later advocates of democracy.

In an ideal free world, sovereign country has the freedom of choice on how and what political ideology they would like to have in order to arrange the state of affairs. However, if it aggravates a powerful neighbour that they perceive such moves as a security threat to them then surely a diplomatic path is the best way to resolve it with an authoritarian leader.

## Geneva Summit 2021

The Geneva 2021 Summit was one of the biggest superpowers diplomatic showdowns of the year where US President Biden and Russian President Putin met in person on the 16 June 2021, in Geneva, Switzerland. The summit was held in the historic Villa la Grange, an 18th-century building overlooking Lake Geneva, chosen as the location for the summit due to its history of political neutrality.

It was expected to set the direction of the relationship between Russia and the Biden administration, however, discussion between two powerful leaders took place behind closed doors. In preparations for these high-profile talks, on the 12 March 2021, the U.S. national security adviser Jake Sullivan told journalists during the press briefing, at the White House that the main objective of the summit was to get the tense relationship more stable and predictable. Sullivan reiterated U.S. backing for Ukraine's sovereignty and territorial integrity.

At the time, there were private diplomatic channels to communicate with the Russians and ongoing security partnership with Ukraine.

"President Biden has indicated in his conversations with President Putin, and publicly, he believes that such a summit would be valuable in establishing better understandings between our two countries and the possibility of getting this relationship on a more stable, predictable path," Sullivan said.

"And the President's also made clear that Ukraine - and this is an obvious point - would be near the top of the list on the agenda for such a meeting." The leaders appeared afterwards for the press briefing.

"The tone of the entire meeting was good, positive," Biden said, adding: "The bottom line is, I told President Putin that we need to have some basic rules of the road that we can all abide by."

Vladimir Putin gave a somewhat similar description. "He is a balanced and professional man, and it is clear that he is very experienced," Putin said.

"It seems to me that we did speak the same language". There were lots of discussions on cyberattacks in the press conference. It was unclear to the world what two men disagreed on Ukraine or anything went wrong or whether the topic was taken seriously. When Putin emerged after the hours-long summit, he acknowledged the meeting with Biden was constructive.

"I think both sides manifested a determination to try and understand each other and try and converge our positions," he said. But he went on to perform the same type of equivocal, denial-filled performance he always does when pressed on issues of cybercrime, human rights, and Ukraine. This was not a surprise to American officials, who did not enter the talks believing Biden would magically be able to change Putin's rhetoric, much less his behaviour. Nor was it out of character for Putin, who has often worked to cultivate relationships with American leaders, even as he blatantly shrugs off their concerns in public.

(The Americas, defensenews.com, Apr 30, 2022, CNN News June 17, 2021)

War in Ukraine highlighted the limitations of approaching democracy vs autocracy game theory to deter autocracy quickly by different means in particular with a geo-political sensitive nuclear power state. The outcome of this recent war is unpredictable but certainly, there are lessons to learn.

Risks and uncertainties are inherited features of economics and politics especially when countries decided to go into war at times of modern hypersonic weapons are testing grounds for superpower nations.

The US-led NATO countries are cautious not to cross the redline but war could prolong by proxy guerrilla type actions or activities performed in an impromptu way, often without authorization. There are already mercenaries fighting for both sides on the ground. Russia was the first superpower to explore geopolitics and was not much successful when economic priories of many countries made them more aligned with open market, rules-based globalisation of economic policies including India and China quickly shifting their policies towards the West to take the best advantage of knowledge transfer. With the collapse of the Soviet Union, Russia lost its influence in Asia, and China quickly filled the gap.

The theory of geopolitics is always working to break the existing dominant power. It requires much more research on political psychology and behavioural science to resolve disputes in a more humane manner than use of violent means as China adapting a business strategy to concur with the world instead. In this current crisis, Chinese ambassador to the US claims that China is an asset for peace talks diplomatic settlement and declined to accept Russia's action as an invasion and indicated that Russia has legitimate security concerns that need to be met. In essence they envisage a new world order where the US hegemonic dominance is declining while Washington is concerned about any possible weapon flows from China to Russia. China seems to be troubled by what they were seeing in Ukraine.

The new development and security assessments of the war have turned opposite. They expected an easy gain and gave the green light as soon as winter Olympic games ended. Fierce ground resistance, the Western countries poring anti-tank weapons and strong economic sanctions made China think twice about their Communist alliance with Russia. Something unexpected happened during this war; Ukrainians were able to create an international legion supporting them in every way to hold advancing Russian troops who were made to believe that the NATO and neighbouring armies were scared of them.

The Washington Post reported that seven Russian generals had been killed in close combat to date. (The Washington Post, 26 March 2022).

The hope is that China would remain moderate and not seek undue gain from this crisis or attempt to support Russia militarily. The elite Ukrainian army would give up their southern cities to Russians, living to fight another day potentially being available for the defensive Kiev at some time in the future. In the second month of the war in Ukraine has failed to give Russia the quick victory it wanted. With the poor performance of the army and the Western sanctions against them, cracks were beginning to appear in the Russian's innermost circle in this climate of selective repressions.

In the absence of political opposition, most of the higher-ranking officers were worried about their careers because of Military halt. Night ambush by Ukrainian volunteers has been an essential element in Ukraine's successful resistance giving grounds for both sides to commence peace talks.

On 29th March 2022, peace talks in Turkey made some significant progress giving President Putin some face savings to hold the fire when

Ukrainian President agreed to neutrality. Russia has reduced and scaled down its military operations near Kiev to build trust, but critiques were sceptical about whether they were using this opportunity to regroup as they had already violated international law by invading the territorial integrity of another state and challenging the world peace order.

A day after, Russia made claims of de-escalation, it increased bomb and artillery attacks in Ukraine and sent conflicting signals about the prospects for peace, suggesting new tensions in the Kremlin hierarchy about the course of the war, New York Times reported on the 31 March 2022. It appeared that there are diametrically opposite views inside Kremlin.

Observers think that Vladimir Putin, the Russian president, had been misinformed about the war's trajectory by subordinates, who feared his reaction to the Russian military's struggles and setbacks suggesting that Putin had miscalculated or overestimated his strength for a quick win. A complex situation had evolved during the Ukrainian war, a sceptical narrative of Pro - Russian Chechen paramilitary mercenaries acting outside the Kremlin authority fighting a war within a war has been identified by the German Council on Foreign Relations.

Within Putin's power structure, there are militia groups loyal to him and their combat experience play a vital role in this war. Yet, in this divided world there are Chechens who are in exile in Europe fighting for Ukraine, they were renewing and extending their fight against Russian system and regime. (DW news 30 March 2022)

Ukraine was a neutral country and by Russian annexation of Crimea and invading Donbas in 2014 they set conditions to change the Ukrainian constitution to be more alliance with NATO. On the other hand, Russia has to accept its strategic failures, that more countries want to join NATO and one day they would take Russia by surprise then it would be Russia's responsibility not to explore diplomatic avenues further, instead planting seeds of hatred for generations to come showing their military might committing war crimes.

There is a significant component of spreading hatred in the younger generation in Europe examining who is the real enemy in deep philosophical investigation of ethics and human nature of greed, and concept of modern state of the art presidency and who runs a country and so on but not creating a peace dividend. Reportedly, in February - March 2022 both US and Germany increased their defence budgets, and many countries are to follow that trend reverting the world back to Cold War mentality.

"We will have to invest more in the security of our country to protect our freedom and democracy," The German Chancellor Olaf Scholz told an extraordinary session of the Bundestag lower house of parliament. Germany also halted its Nord Stream 2 gas pipeline project with Russia and agreed to send weapons to Ukraine after long resisting pressure from Western allies on both issues and facing accusations of being too dovish towards the Kremlin. (Reuters, 27 February 2022).

Russia is devoid of basic liberties. After the 24th of February 2022, it even became more restricted, and the Russian citizens were made to believe that the Ukraine invasion was a special operation to liberate their brothers. Their propaganda machine was so strong that even families were divided on the truth. Other news agencies were barred from operating in Russia so as to cut off them from the rest of the world. This was a difficult scenario for the West to comprehend and Putin has to win to convince his citizens of his theory. What he defines as victory was another, but anyone who disagreed with him was treated as a state enemy even if he or she lives outside Russia.

By attacking another European country, Putin crossed a line that was drawn after World War II and changed the world. But he also changed Russia, from a functioning autocracy to a Stalinesque dictatorship, a country characterized by violent repression, inscrutable arbitrariness, and a massive brain drain.

In 2016 President Putin had a better relationship with the West and was open to dialogue, even ready to cut down nuclear weapons in old Ragan – Gorbachev style. In the contrary, the cynics of war bread grounds for new war products and selling them to others is a huge money-making idea.

When Russia invaded Ukraine in February 2022, under the political phrase 'Special Operation', many observers expected that Russia's military would make a quick win on their mission: to capture the country's capital, Kyiv, depose its democratically elected government and restore Ukraine to Moscow's control. But nearly six months later, in August 2022, after Russian forces failed to take Kyiv, the war has evolved into one of attrition, grinding on with no end to heavy losses on both sides. Since the war started, a staggeringly high rate of casualties was reported in Ukraine almost daily, and sadly, millions of Ukrainians were forced to flee their country.

Since the armed conflict began in the region, fighting has caused nearly three thousand civilian deaths and internally displaced more than seven million people, according to the United Nations. This war, displacement of civilians and loss of lives would have been avoided if Russia had chosen a diplomatic path to resolve the conflict and had mitigated the perceived threat by maintaining peaceful relationships between nations. The invasion only caused unnecessary suffering and increased uncertainty not only in the warzone but extended it to the rest of the world's economy by sending shockwaves because it severely interrupted the global energy markets. Ukraine and Russia are major producers of wheat, corn, and barley and hence the conflict has exacerbated a global food crisis too (The New York Times, August 2022).

The Buddhist doctrine of "nothing arises singularly" suggests that finding a solution to a crisis requires a deeper analysis of causes and their effects, in particular, a conflict situation needs a broader understanding of synthesis and synchrony of dynamic relations. Studies show that the majority of soldiers on the battlefield suffer from Post-Traumatic Stress Disorder: the unending echo of battle etched in the brain affects 15% of soldiers. It can destroy families; it can leave its sufferers unable to work and addicted to substance misuse. It is difficult to understand what they endure. There are also issues of soldier suicide. Statistics from past and present wars tell the sad story of the magnitude of this problem. Unlike in the historical time, much of the suffering in the modern world is a complex phenomenon, aggravated by human-caused disasters.

On 15 October 2022, there was an incident of shooting inside a Russian training camp. At least 11 people were killed and 15 more wounded on a military training ground in the Belgorod region in south-western Russia when two volunteers opened fire on other troops, according to the Ministry of Defence of the Russian Federation. The ministry said in a statement that the two shooters were nationals from a former Soviet republic and had been shot dead after the attack. The ministry called the incident a terrorist attack.

"The two terrorists were eliminated in return fire," the statement, cited by the Russian news agency Tass, said (The Telegraph October 2022).

Saturday 15ᵗʰ October's mass shooting points to growing tensions among Russia's troops, and the issues that have plagued its army since the start of the war.

Tens of thousands of newly drafted Russian men are sent to Ukraine, in what has become a highly unpopular move ordered by the Russian president, Vladimir Putin, in an attempt to halt Ukrainian advances. Inevitably, some draftees have already been killed or captured, stirring ever harsher criticism of the mobilization effort announced last month and considered a shambles from the start. Many Russians have fled the country to avoid conscription. This ground war is the most destructive conflict in scale to be fought in Europe since World War II.

It appeared that the Kremlin has to justify the war to satisfy ultra-nationalist groups, adding legitimacy and supremacy, and showing strength in their action plan. Its adherents have been mounting a sustained critique of the Kremlin's handling of the war in Ukraine. Powerful, well-positioned and ideologically committed, they want a much more aggressive war effort. And judging from Mr Putin's address on Wednesday 21 September 2022 — where he announced the call-up of roughly 300,000 troops, gave his support to referendums in the four occupied regions of Ukraine on joining Russia and repeated the threat of nuclear escalation to take war efforts forward.

"In the face of a threat to the territorial integrity of our country, to protect Russia and our people, we will certainly use all the means at our disposal," Putin warned. "This is not a bluff," he said, with a clear reference to Russia's nuclear capabilities (Washington Post 21 September 2022).

Russia's faltering military performance in Ukraine leaves Moscow relying on its nuclear arsenal to affirm its status as a global power. Brimming with resentment and anger, Putin called the war an effort by Western elites to destroy and dismember Russia, framing it as a confrontation between Moscow and NATO countries.

After winning the referendum, Moscow annexed the occupied regions of eastern and southern Ukraine and called up for men to join the army. Among the new recruits were inexperienced young men to be sent to the frontline and thrown into combat. These young adults are the next generation of "College and career readiness" to take up responsible jobs and citizenship to take Russia forward and both those young men and their parents would agree to this. Sending them to the battlefield is a suicidal mission that the country's leadership should rethink seriously.

There was no imminent threat to Russia as such narrated by political rhetoric, but a false perception was created to build an image of a new Russian empire to rewrite history books with the iconic image of Russia under Putin seeking recognition on the world stage. It would be hard to believe that Russian mothers would agree to send their inexperienced young men to the frontline. In this modern world young generation rejects totalitarianism and brutality. They yearn for the freedom of thought. There are a lot of better ways of getting recognition without harming others and doing good for the world instead.

All war events and incidents have an element of human intent, negligence, or error involving a failure of man-made systems. Correction of those errors needs ethical, pragmatic, and wise interventions through the philosophy of ethics. Uncovering the error of thought and by replacing hatred with loving kindness can reverse the even battle harden mind.

In May 2022, a former Russian diplomat, who resigned from his position after Moscow invaded Ukraine, said the war has led to internal turmoil that could remove Vladimir Putin from power and trigger a civil war in the country. The former counsellor of Russia's permanent mission to the United Nations in Geneva, Boris Bondarev, who resigned in May, wrote a long article published on Foreign Affairs criticising Putin's government. According to Bondarev, the Russian inner circle dangerously supports the warpath and will continue the war but no one in Russia commands his stature, so the country would likely enter a period of political turbulence. "It could even descend into chaos." (Reuters, 17 October 2022). The most important value in international affairs is stability and predictability to which Mr Putin subscribed in June 2021 Geneva summit with the US president. It is a myth to believe that their weapon power could bring stability to Russia.

Russian President Mr Vladimir Putin viewed the collapse of the former Soviet Union as a great tragedy and is now on an aggressive warpath to regain the lost prestige. It was unclear whether the other countries in the former USSR have the same consensus.

We also know from our experience in history the futility and the devastating result of war. As an alternative, we can bring about peace through dialogue, which we must engage in using all available talent. We must also ignite human potential to sustainably grow prosperity around the world, not flames of fire. It is the right thing to do, and it is what we must do to prosper.

We know that we should never stop working towards creating better and more equal, inclusive societies around the world where everyone feels welcome, listened to and seen, and able to unleash their human potential. We will never shift from our purpose, namely that meaningful and sustainable economies be given the power to change the world for the better. We should always take seriously our responsibility and our commitment to reach, assess, train, and provide opportunities for people of all communities to acquire skills and knowledge because we know that work, education, skills, and aspiration are critical parts of community cohesion and prosperity.

These are things that Buddhism can offer to the world at times of difficulty. Buddhism is a light in the darkness. It gives us a choice: we can choose to walk in the darkness and fall into the same pit hole again and again, or we can use a torch and avoid the danger of pit holes. The Northern School of Buddhism says that the Buddha met with eighty-four thousand different people and gave them the advice to resolve their issues concerning life and liberation. There is evidence in the scriptures that the Buddha had intervened in wars and successfully resolved disputes. The Theravada School of Buddhism has a collection of Buddha's teachings and has arranged these into three divisions which are the source of their knowledge. Western thought has yet to discover the contribution of Buddhist social philosophy that has contributed to peaceful co-existence with improved foreign policy.

The foundation of the present Russian communist regime is based on 19th-century German thinker Karl Marx. His most famous book is *Das Capital*. He correctly saw that there was a great gulf between the economic prosperity of the owners of the property and workers in 19th-century Europe. His theory aimed to eliminate the wealth gap between rich and poor proposing a utopian economy in a democratic society where freedom of thought is recognised. The fundamental function of an economy is to resolve the basic economic problem – resources are scarce but wants are unlimited.

Upon Vladimir Lenin's death who led the Russian revolution, Joseph Stalin was officially hailed as his successor as the leader of the ruling Communist Party. Stalin solved the problem by creating a command economy where the state owns the most resources, joining almost all eastern European countries under the common identity of the Soviet Union. However, rigid state control, central planning and bureaucracy of allocating and controlling resources ultimately have not been anywhere near as successful as the free market and mixed economies at delivering economic benefit to their citizens. It was evident not only in the command economy but also in liberal economies that too much government intervention has led to a loss of economic welfare rather than a gain in economic welfare, so government failure exists when there is a net loss of economic welfare.

All planned economies in the 20th and 21st centuries have curbed political freedom to enforce control. Almost all have been totalitarian police states. In contrast, both free markets and mixed economies in the rich industrialised world have been associated with political freedom.

North Korea is one of the last planned economies in the world. But it is slowly moving in a more market-oriented direction. In the 1990s, the breakup of the Soviet Union brought mass famine to North Korea with an estimated 1 million deaths. The Soviet Union had been North Korea's main partner since the end of World War II and had subsidised its economy (Financial Times 2014). The militarisation of civil admiration has dire economic consequences. When a country is under coercive control for a long period of time, the creative ability of the people gradually diminishes. People get normalised in a hard and harsh society.

Throughout history, philosophy arose as a conscious attempt to reshape human life and shift the locus of power. Friedrich Hayek was a 20th-century Austrian economist who moved to the UK in 1931. His most famous book is *The Road to Serfdom* published in 1944. It was enormously influential in the development of the then UK prime minister Mrs Margaret Thatcher's economic thinking in the 1970 and 1980 when the world was gripped in a nuclear arms race known as Cold War. In his book, Hayek argued that ever-greater control of the economy by the state leads to totalitarianism and the loss of individual freedom in the Soviet Union under Joseph Stalin and Germany under Adolf Hitler. He correctly saw that individuals were forced to comply with state wishes through the threat of imprisonment and death. In the 21ˢᵗ century democratic societies widely adopted Hayek's economic ideas. As it evolved, neoliberalism became more strident. Proponents of free markets used Hayek's thoughts to argue that the liberties of the individual are maintained in a free market when state provision and control are removed or minimised with the assumption of increasing allocative and production efficiency. His theory on how changing prices relay information that helps people determine their plans is widely regarded as an important milestone achievement in economics. The market ensures that everyone gets what they deserve. This theory is what led him to the Nobel Prize (Economics, Alain Anderton 6ᵗʰ edition 2015).

On the other hand, critics would argue that neoliberal economics also leads to multinational corporations owned by a few rich classes and rent-seeking capitalists controlling the whole society. Those who own property are able to impose their will on everyone else widening the wealth gap and shifting political power to a new elite class creating inequality. There was a widespread information gap and moral hazard by an economic agent, like a bank or their employees mis-sold mortgages and loans knowing that there are potential adverse risks to buyers. For example, the 2007-8 financial meltdown and banking collapse, Panama papers and recently, Pandora papers revealed how wealthy people avoid tax and hide their money in offshore tax havens. Invariably, deregulation and privatisation of public services shifted economic power to the hands of a few, and budget cuts on education and public health have made those valuable services underfunded.

Neoliberalism sees competition as the defining characteristic of human relations. It redefines citizens as consumers, whose democratic choices are best exercised by buying and selling, a process that rewards merit and punishes inefficiency. Efficiency is measured by profit ignoring environmental pollution caused by production processes. It maintains that "the market" delivers benefits that could never be achieved by planning. This school of thought created a new ideology of market oriented business model to essential services previously provided by state corporations. Where neoliberal policies cannot be imposed domestically, they are imposed internationally, through trade treaties incorporating international laws and monetary fund agreements. It divided society again into rich and poor. The Covid-19 pandemic exacerbated the world economic situation including rich nations. The application of quantitative easing to increase money circulation with a view to increasing aggregate demand has led to high inflation in both the US and UK inevitably increasing interest rates.

It can be argued that these thinkers suggested a solution to solve the economic problem which is dynamic and evolving and those facts were correct for the given time and given economy. However, relentlessly applying a theory without evaluating its cause and effect, linked relations, benefits, and loss would not improve the welfare of many. Those economic theories and models developed later have not taken into consideration the human factor and behaviour of how people would react to different conditions, particularly, how authority is imposed on people. It has shifted the wealth of nations to an unbalanced one-sided argument. Politics is a field to form views, mostly wrong views to justify their ideology and satisfy power bases. In an extreme, it views others as enemies, some uses Hollywood style cinematic art of political rhetoric with a tone to entertain their audience seeking popularity. Russian president is sceptical about liberalisation and believes that it could erode their values. For much of his 22-year reign, Putin has been credited with rejuvenating Russia and returning the country to the forefront of world affairs following the humiliations of the 1990s dismantling the Union. However, having doubts or reservations on a theory is no way can justify use of heavy handed weapon power.

On Wednesday, October 19, 2022, President Vladimir Putin declared martial law in four Russian-occupied regions of Ukraine and in some neighbouring parts of Russia including Crimea. It is a clear sign that his real concerns may lie far closer to home, he also moved to put the economy on a wartime footing and imposed restrictions in more than two dozen areas across Russia. Under martial law, a civil government is substituted by military authorities, granting the government extraordinary privileges that take away legal protections and civil rights. Governments can replace all civil institutions with military operatives, force citizens to take up arms, and appropriate any private property from citizens and any private sector asset which could be used to ramp up military production.

In the annexed territories martial law also means that now President Putin can force Ukrainian citizens to fight for him and against their own army.

As the war entered the 9th month, Russia suffered several setbacks during this time. In retaliation for the attack on the Crimean bridge that happened on October 8, 2022, two days after, on the 10 October 2022, Russia expended as many as 80 missiles including S-300 missile systems at civilian infrastructure targets destroying electricity supplies and bridges. At least one missile ended up hitting a children's playground near Kyiv. Russian president has responded to every setback with more aggression. That involves more indiscriminate attacks on civilians and civil infrastructure. Many able Russians have signed up willingly, following what they believe is their patriotic duty, or for want of better employment amid there is no massive support for the war, according to reliable news media. Independent analysts say that there probably is still a majority in favour, but that it is not monolithic. (The Guardian, 26 October 2022).

Russia is one of the countries that has a stockpile of arsenal. This nuclear state is now threatening centuries of hard-earned economic, political, and social development not only in Ukraine but also rest of the Europe and beyond by destabilising the global economy. Horrors of war mean the outcomes and the after-effects of war. War is a huge fight and a battle between two powers such as two countries. It always leads to destruction including work in dangerous conditions and forcible deportation. It always brings death and sorrow. War affects people mentally, psychologically, physically, and emotionally. The world is praying for the horrors unfolding in Ukraine to end as bitter cold European winter loom.

Apart from the humanitarian crisis in the warzone, the conflict is a major blow to the global economy that will hurt growth and raise prices. Beyond the suffering and humanitarian crisis from Russia's invasion of Ukraine, the global ramifications of the economy will feel the effects of slower growth and faster inflation which is already indicated in the UK economy. The drop in demand from Europe will also hamper global trade. In Asia-Pacific, the impact will be felt almost immediately through higher import prices, particularly in energy prices, with many economies in the region entirely dependent on oil imports such as Japan, China, India, and South Korea. Disruption to the supply chain has seriously impeded the global trade positions of industrial nations. One of the most alarming supply chain issues resulting from the Russia-Ukraine war is food shortages, particularly acute in low-income countries in Africa.

The Buddhist social philosophy and its ethical dimension address a middle way of rejecting extremes not only in the personal spiritual development of an individual but also in how it would be applied to wider socio-economic and political society to improve the social contract between government and its citizens. With the globalisation of the economy, these ethical values can be integrated into specialisation and exchange to maximise the welfare of all.

Russia has a lot more to offer to the world than showing aggression. It was clear and well demonstrated in the great writer Leo Tolstoy's biography. Tolstoy is best known for his two longest works, War and Peace (1865–69) and Anna Karenina (1875–77), which are commonly regarded as among the finest novels ever written. Tolstoy had a vision. Through the characters of his stories, he projected what true human endeavour is. Undoubtedly, Russia has many scientific breakthroughs. For example, the Sputnik Covid vaccination was as effective as any other western invention which they shared speedily with many underdeveloped countries. Russian technology is very much geared toward military application. They have yet to transfer that knowledge to civil and domestic use improving both economic welfare and foreign relations through cultural vehicles should they choose the path of peace and happiness for the welfare of many.

Is there a middle ground for peace or truce to stop fighting or arguing for a certain time? By the end of October 2022, the world leaders face new obstacles to keeping together the bipartisan, multinational coalition supporting the effort to drive out Russian invaders from Ukraine. Russian president Vladimir Putin remains committed to force or even might use lethal force to show strength and on the other hand Ukrainian leaders are unwilling to give ground after their recent battlefield victories achieved through much scarification and efforts. In Europe, allies are divided, with some former Soviet-bloc countries seeking a resounding defeat of Russia, while countries like Germany, France and Italy believe a full-scale Ukrainian victory is an unrealistic prospect.

Taking a critical decision needs much evaluation of all theories, facts, and evidence applicable to conflict resolution. It required wise thinking, judgment made on political wisdom assessing, weighing, and calculating risks and benefits. A peaceful resolution could be found if all parties to the conflict meet at the middle path. In a world of impermance and uncertainty, there is no such thing called absolute power and authority. Whatever may rise must fall. Those who delighting in its attachments to permanence and personality views, it is hard to understand this condition of things, their causal connection, their dependent origination, the cessation of all conditioned things. One may enjoy such position in the short run, however, in the long run all composite creations must dissolved. Only the Middle Path which alone can lead to peace and happiness by avoidance of extremes.

It is clear with evidence that Russian president Vladimir Putin has responded to every setback with more aggression. That involves more indiscriminate attacks on civilians and civil infrastructure, and he will continue doing so to convince that he is in control and win internal support but had transformed international perceptions. It is important that rest of the world know how totalitarian regime and autocratic leaders would react to resolve conflict "whose authority at home depends on projecting strength abroad cannot afford the humiliation of defeat". They would disregard life and suffering of innocent civilians. A conflict that Mr Putin had sort to portray as a "Special Military Operation" to address legitimate Russian security concerns was now widely recognized as a brutal and entirely illegitimate war of imperial conquest.

"Mr Putin intended to harden opinion, appealing to national myths of self-sacrifice for the greater glory of Russia, converting waverers into crusaders." This kind of conditioning is possible when people are isolated from the truth and to develop loyalty and unquestioning obedience to the ruling party. Followers are successfully subjected to indoctrination or ideological remoulding. (The Guardian Editorial 18 November 2022)

On the other hand western leadership believe that full-scale Ukrainian victory is an unrealistic prospect. It is, therefore, wiser to seek all available avenues for conflict resolution. Russian's themselves cannot allow this to go on indefinitely. The war and related war crimes reflects the mindset of "hard-line nationalists who see the conflict as a crusade against the west." Until majority of moderate Russians learn that there are better ways of building constructive relationship with Ukraine and rest of the world than believe in myth of supremacy, until such change happens there is a long road to a better future for Russia.

In the speech, delivered to the annual meeting of the Valdai Discussion Club in Moscow, On the 26$^{th}$ October 2022, President Vladimir Putin portrayed Russia as a champion of rising nations in a new multipolar world, which he demanded that the United States and other Western powers begin to respect as equals. Most of the questioning was on Russia's invasion of Ukraine, Mr Putin's usual grievances and criticisms is pointing finger to the hegemonic "West". He forcefully argued that American dominance is over and defended Russian values blaming the West for "its so-called cancel culture" and for losing touch with its traditional roots but said there can be a peaceful coexistence. (The Washington Post 26 October 2022)

In January 2022, the Executive Director of the Human Rights Watch Mr Kenneth Roth wrote that the conventional wisdom these days is that autocracy is ascendant, and democracy is on the decline. But the superficial appeal of the rise-of-autocracy thesis belies a more complex reality and a bleaker future for autocrats. As people see that unaccountable rulers prioritize their own interests over the public's, the popular demand for rights respecting democracy remains strong.

*Demonstration in Colombo Sri Lanka*

In April 2022, Sri Lanka witnessed one of its worst ever economic crises, as people across the island nation have been protesting against the elected President Gotabaya Rajapaksa, his government, and its handling of the economy. A severe deficit in Balance of Payment, a shortage of foreign currency, in particular, US Dollar balance has left the government unable to pay for essential imports, including fuel. As a result, ordinary Sri Lankans have been dealing with shortages and the crippling impact of soaring inflation.

The residents of southwestern province were protesting at the latest fuel price hike when they clashed with the police. At least one person was killed, and 13 others were injured on Tuesday the 19 April 2022 when police opened fire to disperse anti-government protestors in Sri Lanka's southwestern region. According to the police, protestors had blocked the railway track and started pelting stones at them.

On the 13 Apr 2022, Fitch Ratings – (Hong Kong) has downgraded Sri Lanka's Long-Term Foreign-Currency Issuer Default Rating (IDR) to C from CC; The issue ratings on foreign currency bonds issued on international markets have also been downgraded to C from CC; The Long-Term Local-Currency IDR has been affirmed at CCC; and the Country Ceiling at B. The downgrade of Sri Lanka's Long-Term Foreign-Currency IDR reflects Fitch's view that a sovereign default process has begun. This reflects the announcement by the Ministry of Finance on 12 April 2022 that it has suspended normal debt servicing of several categories of its external debts, including bonds issued in the international capital markets and foreign currency- denominated loan agreements or credit facilities with commercial banks or institutional lenders. People are demanding president's resignation over the worst economic crisis in memory while a team of Sri Lanka's government officials have commenced discussions with the International Monetary Fund (IMF) in Washington for a possible economic bailout.

On 9 July 2022, Reuters reported that Sri Lanka's President Gotabaya Rajapaksa plans to step down, the country's parliamentary speaker said on Saturday, bowing to intense pressure after a violent day of protests in which demonstrators stormed the president's official residence and set fire to the prime minister's home in Colombo. Throughout the day, soldiers and police were unable to hold back a crowd of chanting protesters demanding Rajapaksa's resignation and blaming him for the country's worst economic crisis in seven decades.

Months of largely peaceful anti-government protests over a dire economic crisis, fraud, corruption, and misappropriation of government money by political circles turn into an angry mass rally. On Wednesday the 13th of July 2022, protesters invaded government buildings and seized the Presidential Palace, the Presidential Secretariat and the Prime Minister's Office. President Gotabaya Rajapaksa and his wife fled to the Maldives by an Airforce plane on Wednesday, driven out after an economic collapse unleashed a popular uprising that appeared to end his family's near two-decade dominance of the country. Rajapaksa fled the country on the day he was supposed to handover his resignation. From the Maldives, they flew to Singapore by a private flight, according to the Associated Press. Subsequently, the protesters vacated the government buildings seized by them during the protests.

"We are peacefully withdrawing from the Presidential Palace, the Presidential Secretariat and the Prime Minister's Office with immediate effect, but will continue our struggle," a spokesperson said.

Under the constitution, Sri Lankan premier Ranil Wickremesinghe was appointed as the acting president. He then directed the military to use force to quell the protests. However, the Sri Lankan army had declined the instructions.

As those dramatic events unfolded by foreign media reports, Sri Lankan President Gotabaya Rajapaksa emailed his resignation shortly after reaching Singapore on Thursday 14 July 2022. Sri Lanka's speaker of parliament has received a letter of resignation from President Gotabaya Rajapaksa through the country's embassy in Singapore, his office said. The speaker then made a formal announcement on Friday "after checking the accuracy of the document and fulfilling all legal requirements", the speaker's spokesman said.

Chinese Foreign Ministry Spokesperson Wang Wenbin says Beijing hopes that all parties in the Sri Lanka crisis work together for the sake of the island nation.

"As a friend, neighbour and partner, China sincerely hopes that all sectors in Sri Lanka will bear in mind the fundamental interests of the country and people and work together in solidarity to overcome the current difficulties, strive to restore stability, revitalise the economy, and improve people's livelihood," Wang said (Aljazeera News).

United Nations Secretary-General Antonio Guterres said he was following the continuing political crisis in Sri Lanka.

"It is important that the root causes of the conflict and protestors' grievances are addressed," he tweeted. "I urge all party leaders to embrace the spirit of compromise for a peaceful and democratic transition."

It can be concluded that the power transition was a result of the struggle and strength of the frustrated youth who demanded a system change. Many of them were educated youth with a good political knowledge, among them were university professors joined the protest. They were organised and used carefully measured social engineering tools of popular social media platforms, without bloodshed embracing the spirit of compromise for a peaceful and democratic transition. The economic crisis that evolved into a political crisis is mainly attributed to unsustainable debt financing and more borrowing for debt servicing.

Democracy is at the heart of Sri Lankan politics as it was in the past seven decades since the independence from Imperial Britain and now a commonwealth country. The present Presidential administration has characteristics of both French and Westminster parliamentary systems of elected representatives as such it has 225 elected members in the parliament. However, the majority of current members lack political vision or foundation of any standard, which was instrumental to the current economic crisis voting to support any bill in their favour. Some of them were no different to street entertainers. Realising the mistakes made, in October 2022, the parliament amended the constitution restoring democratic values with an overwhelming majority.

The newly formed government in August 2022 quickly worked with the IMF, World Bank, and other multilateral and bilateral development partners including the Paris Club and has made significant progress in those efforts to stabilize the economy. In order to provide immediate relief, the government with the special assistance of the world bank has initiated many programmes to assist vulnerable groups while identifying malnutrition among underprivileged children. The government has recognised human capital development as the core of the development and growth process. It was expected to resolve the economic and political crisis through negotiations, debt restructuring and compromise with all parties concerned. Having adopted a democratic framework, non-aligned foreign policy, and flexible approach this small island nation appears to be managing the issues without major calamity.

The Paris Club creditors, an informal group of official creditors largely consisting of western nations, have expressed their readiness to negotiate with Sri Lanka for debt relief following the island nation securing a staff-level agreement for a 48-month, US$ 2.9 billion Extended Fund Facility with the International Monetary Fund (IMF).

The Paris Club remains at the disposal of Sri Lankan authorities and non-Paris Club official bilateral creditors to further discuss the next steps of the debt treatment process. However, most of Sri Lanka's debt remains with creditors who are not members of the Paris Club. For example, India and China, who are among the two creditors to Sri Lanka are not full members of the Paris Club. While India has shown keenness to work with the Sri Lankan authorities to provide debt relief in a bid to help the country make its debt sustainable, China's position remained unclear in October 2022.

Following the announcement of the staff-level agreement, the Chinese embassy in Colombo issued a statement that said, "Shortly after the Sri Lankan government announced to suspend international debt payments in April 2022, Chinese financial institutions reached out to the Sri Lankan side and expressed their readiness to find a proper way to handle the matured debts related to China and help Sri Lanka to overcome the current difficulties."

However, the statement stopped short of giving any specific indication of whether China will come on board with a broader debt restructuring exercise, which is likely to be organised by Japan at the request of Sri Lanka. Sri Lanka getting any IMF financing is contingent upon the island nation obtaining assurances from both its official and private creditors for debt relief, most likely by way of haircuts meaning write-off part of bad debt, as IMF has assessed Sri Lanka's debt as unsustainable.

The Bloomberg website reported that Paris Club creditors have reached out to China and India to coordinate Sri Lanka's debt-restructuring talks, according to a person familiar with the matter, in an attempt to bring major global creditors together to rework the obligations of emerging economies, the local news agency reported.

The club, an informal group of mostly rich, western bilateral creditors, is awaiting a response from both countries after it sent an official request in late August 2022 to work together, said an official who declined to be identified because talks are continuing.

The formation of an official creditors committee in which China and India agreed to work together with the Paris Club would help Sri Lanka secure a $2.9 billion bailout from the International Monetary Fund. The Washington-based lender announced a staff-level deal with the government last month and needs assurances from creditors that they're willing to negotiate a restructuring before its board can give final approval and start disbursing the much-needed funding.

Sri Lanka defaulted for the first time in May 2022 and aims to finalize debt-restructuring talks with international creditors by the second quarter of 2023. The government has said it will ensure transparency and equal treatment among creditors. Critics argue that the US-sponsored high-interest junk bonds and credit markets (20 billion USD in debt) created a debt trap and force the pro-creditor Paris Club on Sri Lanka so that Sri Lanka becomes a de facto colony of the West. The Paris Club is notorious for extracting pro-Western geopolitical conditions on developing countries in exchange for debt reduction and restructuring. President Ranil Wickremasinghe has been accused of being the key enabler of this re-colonization plan when he was 'executive' prime minister during the 2015-2019 period by falsely claiming that Sri Lanka was a middle-income country to access high-interest US junk-bond markets. The double-digit usury interest rates on this 20 billion USD US-sponsored junk-bond debt is absolutely strangling the Sri Lankan economy, yet the US wants to blame China for the US debt trap in Sri Lanka, a Colombo news channel reported. The criticism looks like an argument formed to defend China and actual facts cannot be verified without knowing the actual figures borrowed when and why and by whom? Reportedly, Japan has offered low-cost financing in the past, however, Sri Lankan authorities at the time had declined those projects and accepted high-cost borrowing, a matter that needs further investigation.

It was revealed in mid-October 2022 that there had been recent discussions on Sri Lanka's debt restructuring with the Chinese Finance Minister and the government is optimistic that the discussions in this regard would be concluded successfully. In October 2022, a delegation headed by the State Minister of Finance held initial discussions in Washington, with the International Monetary Fund and the three main countries, China, India, and Japan that have given loans to the country, giving priority to immediately solve the problem of the country's bankruptcy and to ensure food security.

Much of the economics assumes that governments will act in a way that maximises the welfare of their citizens. Public choice theory suggests that politicians act in a way that maximises their own utility whether or not this leads to improved welfare for the citizens they are supposed to represent. For example, since 2008, successive Sri Lankan governments had invested in projects with high borrowing costs and in unsustainable projects without a substantial return on investments implementing policies which benefitted their own personal advantage. Or they have adopted policies which would benefit in the run-up to an election showing high economic growth but which in the long run lead to a net loss of economic welfare. Politicians may also engage in rent-seeking behaviour. This is where those in power manipulate the distribution of resources to benefit themselves without creating any extra wealth for society. There was evidence that politicians had received bribes, commissions, and other benefits in kind from investors to make sure they win government contracts.

Economic textbooks define Government failure if governments intervene in markets and that intervention leads to a net loss of welfare to society (Economics, Alain Anderton 6th edition 2015). Evidence suggests that tax cuts, high-interest payments, manipulation of exchange rates and capital repayments have led to the bankruptcy of Sri Lanka. Further, during this time, the Central bank and treasury have not made information transparent allowing a distortion of price signals, information gaps, conflicting objectives and the maximisation by politicians and high-ranking government officials of their own welfare causing unnecessary suffering to the working-class community.

Social unrest is an inevitable consequence of bad economic management and asymmetric information where governments intentionally and knowingly not telling the truth to the public but keeping snippets of information for their own advantage victimising people is a sign of corrupt regimes.

In October 2022, a high-profile financial scandal was revealed by Sri Lankan news media that the Criminal Investigation Department (CID) has arrested a young woman, who operated a company at the World Trade Centre in Colombo, for financial fraud amounting to over Rs.500 million. The woman had cheated money from many individuals including businessmen, artists, politicians, and doctors, and had given the impression that she has intimate connections to powerful politicians. She had acted like a VIP agent representing star hotels in the city of Colombo. The CID said that there were eight complaints against her. Others have not come forward fear of money laundering. The CID said she has registered six shell companies related to gem, jewellery, construction, film production, and land buying and selling. She had obtained investments from various individuals in these companies including clergymen. The incident shows the depth of corruption, moral degradation, and money laundering and how society has been rotten from top to bottom by decades of economic and political mismanagement.

In country after country, Myanmar, Sudan, Russia, Belarus, Nicaragua, Poland, Uganda, even Kazakhstan before protests seemed to have been hijacked by a governmental power struggle large numbers of people have recently taken to the streets, even at the risk of being arrested or shot. There are few rallies for autocratic rule.

In some countries that retain at least a semblance of democratic elections despite the leader's autocratic tendencies, opposition political parties have begun to paper over their policy differences to build alliances in pursuit of their common interest in ousting the ruler. And as established autocrats can no longer rely on subtly manipulated elections to preserve power, a growing number are resorting to electoral charades that guarantee their victory but confer none of the legitimacy of an election. Yet, autocrats are enjoying their moment in the sun in part because of the failings of democratic leaders. (How Democracy Can Defeat Autocracy - https://www.hrw.org/; Kenneth Roth, Former Executive Director, HRW)

Democracy may be the least bad form of governance, as Winston Churchill observed, because the electorate can vote the government out, for example, the importance of these checks and balances was visible in the United States, where they impeded then President Donald Trump's attempt to steal the 2020 election.

But today's democratic leaders are not meeting the challenges before them. Whether it is the climate crisis, the pandemic, poverty and inequality, racial injustice, or the threats posed by major technology companies, these leaders are often too mired in partisan battles and short term preoccupations to address these problems effectively.

If democracies are to prevail, their leaders must do more than spotlight the autocrats' shortcomings. They need to make a stronger, positive case for democratic rule. That means doing a better job of meeting national and global challenges of ensuring that democracy delivers on its promised dividends. Many political analysts predict that during 2022 middle powers will shape geopolitics. Emerging economies such as India and Brazil will rise and mid players, France, Germany, UK, Australia, and Canada will influence world affairs. America's exit from Afghanistan left the country in chaos and made others doubt unipolar superpower.

In January 2021 the U.S., Capital insurrection, a mob of supporters of the then President Donald Trump attacked the United States Capitol in Washington D.C. They sought to overturn his defeat in the 2020 presidential election. This incident of attacking the seat of American democracy which was telecasted live across the world also cast doubt on the credibility of uneven American politics by international observers.

The use of violence to achieve party political goals is creating a toxic public atmosphere that encourages a tiny but growing number to act on disinformation. People who actually commit acts of violence belong to the smallest circle but there are other circles of indirect supporters that might include people who attend meetings, donate money, or read the website of an extremist group. Domestic political extremism might be acceptable to some internal party-political members but internationally such outrageous behaviour paints a different picture of modern American democracy.

One year on from the Capitol riots and Team Trump remains defiant. Mr Trump is as active as ever, as defiant as ever, and seems to have conquered the Republican Party from the bottom up. At the rallies, he has continued to claim - against all facts but to audiences who believe him - that the election was stolen. President Joe Biden has marked one year since the deadly assault on the U.S. Capitol by condemning political violence in an address to the nation, as he also hit out at his predecessor Donald Trump.

The healing of the old wound is far from over. The growing sense of cultural isolation, anger, and frustration among Americans - conservatives, independents, and European partners made rethink of relying on American leadership that led to shaping the contours of what would become the new multipolar world order. The impact of these bigger themes needs serious consideration.

China's Silk Road-Belt and Road economic vision are overshadowing by the so-called String of Pearls hidden agenda as its intentions have become so much visible that small countries keep rejecting China's debt trapped economic support and accepting Western more rules-based order. China wants to recreate its old civilization and culture, the one that developed along the Silk Road. Ancient Chinese wisdom is infused with Buddhist and Taoist spirituality and values thrived for thousands of years until communism took over.

Today, much of this divinely inspired culture has been destroyed or forgotten. For decades, the world witnessed an age-old civilization torn apart by communism and the militarization of civil administration. They made radical changes to their own culture. Ancient China's cultural heritage was founded on courage and inspiration from their practice of spiritual discipline based on the principles of truthfulness, compassion, and tolerance. They shared a message of hope, honesty, and strength for battling darkness with courage, overcoming adversity with wisdom.

The current Chinese Communist Party (CCP) lacks socialist political wisdom on which it was founded by President Mao Zedong. They have distance from socialist values and instead have built a regimental capitalist economic model that is proving to be incapable to accommodate its large population of 1.4 billion people and is creating a huge income gap. China today suffers a trust deficiency among its business partners for quality and reliability. In a modern China grappling with widening social inequality, Mao's philosophy provides justification for the anger many young people feel towards a business class they see as exploitative. They want to follow in his foot-steps and change Chinese society - and some have even talked about violence against the capitalist class, if necessary, all to get closer to a modern socialism with a democratic outlook. Young Chinese people are yearning for the freedom others enjoy in democratic societies.

There appear to be a power vacuum in the world and no force for constructive change. With growing economies and geopolitical stature, mid players will rearrange and establish a multipolar order with alliances to suit their national interests.

The Buddha taught that being a ruler requires clear understanding, studying the past and present, knowing when to be active and passive, temper force with mercy, being kind to one's subordinates, acting to benefit the people, and giving equally. Social inequality, deprivation and poverty are all signs of poor ruling and to favour one privileged class while ignoring the others can cause schism and division. The Buddha emphasises the moral responsibility of both ruler and subjects. Modern liberal societies reject class division demand equal rights, and for people to be treated equally and without favouritism or discrimination which is what the Buddha taught many centuries ago.

Social change through social mobility is possible only in a country of good governance by democratically elected government representatives who listen and implement the will of the people. Violent revolutions and terrorism are things of the past. Even Marxist revolutionists have realized the value of democracy and applications of an open market economy. If a country is going through political instability or coercive control of external powers that wish to destabilise its social harmony by undemocratic means, the history suggests that it's always the people who suffer in the end, for anxiety and worries that sometimes correspond to a complete collapse of the social system.

Lebanon is a good example of social-political self-destruction. Prolonged civil wars have devastating effects in generations to come. Political assassinations, random killing of suspected opponents, mass murder of innocent civilians, suicide bombing are commonplace features of civil revolutions and wars. This violent behaviour is a result of adhering to wrong views, doctrines often mixed up with erroneous religious ideologies coupled with underworld economy of smuggling weapons, hard drugs, money laundering, and human trafficking. Those societies ultimately achieve nothing but misery and more suffering for their people. For example, after many years of violent fighting, Taliban has become a lost cause with international condemnation and isolation where the energies of those young men would have been better used for peaceful development and prosperity of their country. Similarly, Syria and Libya are classic examples of countries that exercise coercive control on their people by both internal and external power struggles for regional dominance.

Those countries have achieved nothing but fast track social degeneration, corruption, economic collapse resulting in poverty although once they have enjoyed oil rich economic prosperity. It is evident that violent means resolve nothing and usually result in misery, to the alteration of ethical values, justice, and to the establishment of lawless states. People who live in such circumstances are constantly suffering from insecurities.

Perhaps after many years of war, the most existential question for them is "what is the meaning of life?"

Their hopelessness can lead to a variety of psychological issues such as sadness or depression, which might prevent them to think clearly. The Covid-19 pandemic and the emerging new variants added more difficulties and slowed down economic recovery, especially for those war-torn countries with no social progress; a situation which forced them back to survival civilizations.

Human nature is bright, and every human being has the potential to live a successful life and make great contributions to the world. However, because of ignorance, sometimes good human qualities could be overshadowed by greed and hatred. When long-standing disputes between countries or divided nations are not addressed correctly, the process of finding a lasting peace could manifest in a different kind of conflict and bring violence.

Some powerful politicians have provided temporary solutions to conflicts but have also left gaps by not taking the whole equation into account. For example, in May 2021 Israel and Palestine conflict was the result of the so-called Abraham Accords. Violent conflicts resurface showing a pattern of political interference.

The 2021 recent power transition in Israel parliament shows instead, a wise political move and a series of sharp choices made by a younger Jewish generation that aspire to a change in the country's political landscape.

## Israel and Palestine Conflict 2021

*Deadly Israel and Gaza Violence in May 2021*

The relationship between Palestinians and Israelis has always been a difficult one. On August 13, 2020, a normalization agreement was made between Israel, the United Arab Emirates, Bahrain, and the United States. Subsequently, the term was used to refer to a collective agreement between these countries known as the Abraham Accords. Notably, Saudi Arabia did not sign this agreement.

This fragile and weak settlement agreement mediated by the past Trump administration has not taken into due consideration of Palestinian course seriously. It has marginalized Palestinian occupation in Gaza Strip, other areas and undermined their leadership by withdrawing Palestinian's veto powers leaving militant group Hamas to take an upper hand to provide defector leadership. This ambiguous situation allowed the forced expulsion of Palestinian families from the occupied East Jerusalem neighbourhood of Sheikh Jarrah, that have been facing multiple court cases filed against them by several pro-settler organizations since 1972.

These organizations claim that the land on which the families live on was originally under Jewish ownership, but Palestinians see this as an extension of an official Israeli policy to displace as many Palestinians as possible from Jerusalem in order to retain a majority Jewish identity in the city. Marginalizing and pushing people to an edge by supremacy ideologies in this way leads to radicalization of young groups, a feature of many societies irrespective of their religious belief in the past and contemporary Palestine is no exception to rise of militia groups.

The United Nations has warned the planned expulsions could amount to "war crimes". Ignoring these warnings of hostility against Palestinian settlers continued. Protests and scuffles between Palestinians, Israeli settlers and the Israeli police have steadily increased since the end of April 2021. The Israeli court in October 2020 ruled that four Palestinian families should vacate their homes and gave May 2, 2021, as the date for their forcible eviction. However, the court date has since been postponed twice. Observers see a systemic racial social injustice suffering by Palestinians in the hands of powerful Israelis not shorter of Apartheid State persecuting defenceless minority.

Apartheid ("apartness" in the language of Afrikaans) was a system of legislation that upheld segregationist policies against non-white citizens of South Africa. After the National Party gained power in South Africa in 1948, its all-white government immediately began enforcing existing policies of racial segregation. According to this description, Palestinians have been denied equal rights after 73 years and pushed out of their occupied land, a history that goes back as far as the crucifixion of Jesus.

Jewish people suffered systemic persecution at the hands of mighty Romans, and they dispersed to Europe. Arabs occupied the land left by Jews the ancient Hebrew people of Israel to Abraham. During the time of Hitler's Germany and World War II, German Jewish people suffered atrocities and genocide. Cyclic nature of suffering continues and reappears in different scales and forms.

This phenomenon cannot be resolved only by existing religious textual knowledge, politics or by applying socioeconomic theory based on circular reasoning. It requires deeper insight and critical thinking into human nature and applying the correct definition of the term "human" and human qualities to find a solution for coexistence irrespective of religious and ethnic differences. This area of studies has been initially introduced by Immanuel Kant's metaethics.

The subject matter has been fully explored in Buddhist Higher Philosophical Psychology many centuries ago in the context of understanding the nature of mind and thinking process. It explains the law of action and principles of cause and effect and other associated laws compatible with modern physics that transformation of energy continues to eternity.

Consciousness is a form of mental energy that transforms from life to life and that can be improved and purified until it finally breaks the vicious cycle of suffering. On the other hand, it can get defiled in many cycles of hatred and become a ferocious weapon that would explode with serious destruction like a volcano eruption.

Hatred and anger are manifestations of a deep-seated frustration in the subconscious mind. For this reason, human activities must be managed and directed towards humanity to defuse tension. Blind faith, arbitrary divisions, hate preaching, provocation, and antagonized attitude towards fellow human beings would result in an upward cycle of violence like adding fuel to fire.

The Israeli - Palestine conflict is an ongoing violent struggle between Israelis and Palestinians since 1948 when the State of Israel was declared soon after World War II. The modern state of Israel was founded in May 1948 in the aftermath of the Holocaust but the conflict that has raged between Israelis and Palestinians since can be traced back much further into the Ottoman Empire in 1799.

The background of those military strategies and British imperial interests is well depicted in the 1962 British epic drama film Lawrence of Arabia based on the true life story of T. E. Lawrence and his 1962 book *Seven Pillars of Wisdom*. Lawrence of Arabia was nominated for ten Oscars at the 35th Academy Awards in 1963 and it won seven of them. After graduating from Oxford, Lawrence pursued his interest in archaeology and travelled to Beirut, northern Syria, and Egypt.

Lawrence was offered a post in the British army for his well-researched knowledge and served as a Colonel. He became renowned for his role in the Arab Revolt (1916–1918) and the Sinai and Palestine Campaign (1915–1918) against the Ottoman Empire during the First World War.

The breadth and variety of his activities and associations, and his ability to describe them vividly in writing, earned him international fame as Lawrence of Arabia, a title used for the 1962 film based on his wartime activities. His daring raids in World War I made him a legend. But in the Middle East today, the desert warrior's legacy is written in sand.

The underlying issues of the decades-old conflict have deep roots in racial differences, injustice and by design, the State of Israel is characterized by a policy of imperialist interests in the past. Those differences surfaced in violent cycles time and time again in our living memories and notably, in the last few weeks of May 2021 it erupted in high tech war never seen before.

During that time, there have been confrontations as Palestinians gathered for iftar meals – the breaking of Ramadan fasts – at the homes of those being evicted. The families have since appealed to Israel's Supreme Court. On a Thursday night, at least 30 people were wounded and 15 arrested. On Friday, tens of thousands of Muslim worshippers gathered at the Al-Aqsa Mosque compound – Islam's third holiest site – to pray on the final Friday the 7 May 2021 of Ramadan, with many staying on to protest against the expulsions.

Heavily deployed police fired rubber-coated bullets and stun grenades at protesters who responded by throwing stones. Some 205 Palestinians and 17 Israeli officers were wounded. After a violent weekend, Israeli security forces on next Monday conducted a flash raid on the Al-Aqsa compound, again firing rubber-coated bullets, tear gas and sound bombs at gathered worshippers, stoking international outrage and wounding more than 300 Palestinians. About 20 Israeli officers were also injured. This incident triggered widespread anger and violence.

Hamas later announced it had given an ultimatum for Israel to remove its security forces from the Al-Aqsa compound and Sheikh Jarrah neighbourhood by 6 pm local time (15:00 GMT).

Twenty-seven days before the first rocket was fired from Gaza in that week, a squad of Israeli police officers entered the Aqsa Mosque in

Jerusalem, brushed the Palestinian attendants aside and strode across its vast lime-stone courtyard. Then they cut the cables to the loudspeakers that broadcast prayers to the faithful from four medieval minarets.

It was the night of April 13, the first day of the Muslim holy month of Ramadan. It was also Memorial Day in Israel, which honours those who died fighting for the country. The Israeli President was delivering a speech at the Western Wall, a sacred Jewish site that lies below the mosque, and Israeli officials were concerned that the prayers would drown it out. The timing was very sensitive. The incident was confirmed by six mosque officials, three of whom witnessed it; the Israeli police declined to comment. In the outside world, it barely registered.

But in hindsight, the police raid on the mosque, one of the holiest sites in Islam, was one of several actions that led, less than a month later, to the sudden resumption of war between Israel and Hamas, the militant group that rules the Gaza Strip, and the outbreak of civil unrest between Arab and Jews across Israel itself.

"This was the turning point," said Sheikh Ekrima Sabri, the grand mufti of Jerusalem. "Their actions would cause the situation to deteriorate."

That deterioration has been far more devastating, far-reaching, and fast-paced than anyone imagined. It has led to the worst violence between Israelis and Palestinians in years - not only in the conflict with Hamas, which has killed at least 145 people in Gaza and 12 in Israel, but violence spread in a wave of mob attacks in mixed Arab-Jewish cities in Israel.

It has spawned unrest in cities across the occupied West Bank, where Israeli forces killed 11 Palestinians on Friday. And it has resulted in the firing of rockets toward Israel from a Palestinian refugee camp in Lebanon, prompted Jordanians to march toward Israel in protest, and led Lebanese protesters to briefly cross their southern border with Israel.

The crisis came as the Israeli government was struggling for its survival; as Hamas - which Israel views as a terrorist group was seeking to expand its role within the Palestinian movement; and as a new generation of Palestinians was asserting its own values and goals.

And it was the outgrowth of years of blockades and restrictions in Gaza, decades of occupation in the West Bank, and decades more of discrimination against Arabs within the state of Israel, said Avraham

Burg, a former speaker of the Israeli Parliament and former chairman of the World Zionist Organization.

The worst fighting between Israelis and Palestinians in seven years intensified on the night of 10th Monday, May 2021, resulting in the deaths of at least 30 Palestinians, including 10 children, and three Israelis. Hundreds more civilians were wounded, according to local officials on both sides. Israeli airstrikes began targeting Hamas's offices in apartment buildings in Gaza City, while militants in Gaza fired back at Tel Aviv, Israel's economic centre.

In Israel's Arab neighbourhoods, Palestinian citizens of Israel expressed fury at the killings and longstanding complaints of discrimination inside Israel itself. The Palestinian militants and Israeli military were unevenly matched - the former armed with crude rockets, the latter with fighter jets and a sophisticated antimissile defence system, the Iron Dome. Israeli airstrikes aim for strategic targets in densely populated Gaza, killing civilians even as Israel insists it takes measures to avoid them, while Hamas's rockets aim for civilian population centres but often miss the mark.

The United Nations Security Council called for an emergency meeting. "If there is a hell on earth, it is the lives of children in Gaza", Mr António Guterres, Secretary-General of the United Nations (UN), said in his opening remarks in the recent virtual summit.

The actions of both sides disregarded the UN Resolution 1265 (1999), Protection of Civilians in armed conflict (PoC), and the number of civil casualties testified to this measurable fact. The Resolution 1265 addresses the "Protection for Humanitarian Assistance to Refugees and Others in Conflict Situations" (S/1998/883), in particular their analysis related to the protection of civilians.

Media attention was very focused on the situation in Israel, West Bank, Gaza, world leaders were deeply concerned about the Hamas indiscriminate rocket attacks targeting civilians and subsequent Israeli airstrikes in retaliation on highly dense population areas were justified as an act of self-defence. Israelis used Iron Dome defence technology to intercept incoming rockets.

The night sky was lit with those images like fireworks. Ironically, Israeli jets bombed the Al Jazeera broadcasting tower and the building that hosted Associated Press (AP) an American non-profit news agency headquarters in

New York City without a credible explanation. International humanitarian law (IHL) provides that civilians shall enjoy general protection from the effects of armed conflicts, protects civilians from being the objects of attack, and prohibits indiscriminate attacks. Israel spokesman claimed that they are targeting Hamas tunnels and given warnings to civilians to evacuate residential buildings. Unfortunately, not all of them were contactable in a warzone of highly dense population.

Thunderstrike air attacks demolished residential buildings in minutes before media cameras that showed the strength of Israeli air force. Those who could not make it were buried under the rubble. Rescue operatives worked tirelessly helping the wounded. Despite their efforts, 66 among the dead were children.

The Geneva Conventions are the essential basis of international humanitarian law applicable in armed conflicts. They evolved from rules of customary international law binding on the entire international community. In the second part of the nineteenth century, when the codification of international law started, most of these rules were included in international treaties, beginning with the 1864 Geneva Convention and the 1899 and 1907 Hague Conventions.

Israeli air raids hit the Qatari Red Crescent Society (QRCS) office in Gaza during the fighting, killing two Palestinians and wounding 10 others. The organization condemned the targeting of its office while asserting the need to "allow relief teams to work in accordance with international humanitarian law". QRCS Secretary-General Ali bin Hassan al-Hammadi slammed the attack as a flagrant violation of the Geneva Convention, of which Israel is a signatory. Palestinians return to their destroyed houses in Beit Hanoun, northern Gaza, following the Israel-Hamas truce [Source: Mohammed Salem/Reuters].

The Gaza reconstruction effort will be an important test. The 11-day war killed more than 250 people, mostly Palestinians, and caused heavy destruction in the impoverished coastal territory. Preliminary estimates have put the damage in the hundreds of millions of dollars. In a boost to those efforts, the energy-rich Gulf country of Qatar pledged $500 million to post-war reconstruction in Gaza. Qatar often serves as a mediator between Israel and Hamas, and it has contributed hundreds of millions of dollars in humanitarian and development aid to support past ceasefires.

"We will continue to support our brothers in Palestine in order to reach a just and lasting solution by establishing their independent state," Qatar's foreign minister, Mohammad bin Abdulrahman Al Thani, wrote on Twitter.

With contemporary wars continuing to produce disastrous effects, the Geneva Conventions signed on August 12, 1949, and two additional protocols adopted on June 8, 1977, are the most important treaties for the protection of victims of war. The treaties adopted include the number of conventions and protocols. The final Goal is to make full compliance by all the parties to an armed conflict with their obligations under international humanitarian law to better protect and assist the civilian population and other victims. Under humanitarian law, the civilian population, in general, is protected from dangers arising from military operations. However, some groups among the population, such as children, women, the elderly, persons with disabilities and displaced people, have specific needs and are entitled to special attention. Civilians can also expect, under humanitarian law, adequate care, and respect. But one of the most acute challenges facing humanitarian organizations at present is access to all the victims of an armed conflict.

The psychological impact of war on civilians is not considered in the equation. There are not enough trained and qualified personnel to treat traumatic psychological syndromes of victims of war. It will take a long time for children and adults alike to recover from such traumas.

Tragically, contemporary armed conflicts are frequently characterized by massive displacement of populations, both within and across international borders. This phenomenon is particularly prevalent in non-international armed conflicts, where displacement is often regarded as a strategy of warfare, and sometimes even constitutes the very objective of the protagonists to the conflict.

*Israel-Hamas ceasefire holds*

A little noticed police action in Jerusalem in the month of April 2021 was one of several incidents that led to the current crisis. The sirens across southern Israel were silent on Friday, and the thunder of bombs bursting in Gaza City was replaced by sounds of celebratory gunfire as a fragile ceasefire between Israel and Hamas went into force, bringing an end to more than 10 days of fighting that claimed more than 243 lives and many wounded. Among them, over 60 children were killed, according to the Gaza health ministry. The Israeli military said that more than 130 of those killed were combatants. Hamas rocket attacks have killed more than a dozen people in Israel, including two children, according to the Israeli authorities.

The truce, mediated by Egypt, began at 2 a.m. in Israel as people on either side of the divide watched nervously to see whether it would hold. 11 days of intense fighting ended on the 20th May 2021 with both Israel and Hamas agreeing to ceasefire. The U.S. President Mr Biden and his administration tirelessly worked hour by hour with their partners, in particular, Egyptians to negotiate a truce while United Nations Security Council met in a virtual summit to discuss a possible solution. Speaking at the White House an hour before an Egyptian-brokered ceasefire was set to go into effect in Israel and Gaza, President Biden expressed gratitude for the deal - which, if successful, would put at least a temporary halt to rocket attacks, airstrikes and other violence that has killed more than 200 Palestinians, as well as at least a dozen Israelis.

Biden's remarks were fittingly brief: just three minutes. The administration shied away from public pressure or public statements throughout the conflict, instead prioritizing what White House officials constantly referenced as "quiet" diplomacy.

Throughout this period of relative silence, the White House emphasized how often Biden and other key figures, including Secretary of State Antony Blinken, were on the phone with officials in Israel, Egypt, Jordan, and other Middle Eastern states. By then, the total number of calls White House officials were touting to reporters had grown to 80, including a half dozen conversations between Biden and then Israeli Prime Minister Benjamin Netanyahu - as well as calls to Palestinian Authority President Mahmoud Abbas, Egyptian President Abdel Fattah el-Sisi and others.

A good portion of Biden's remarks was simply thanking the various officials his administration had worked with to bring about a ceasefire.

"These hostilities have resulted in the tragic deaths of so many civilians, including children," Biden said. "I sent my sincere condolences to all the families, Israeli and Palestinian, who have lost loved ones, and my hope for a full recovery for the wounded." (White House Briefing Room, Washington DC, May 20,2021)

The flare-up was the latest in a cycle of conflict between Israel and Hamas, which have fought similar battles like this three times previously. But this escalated faster than the others. Both sides warned the other that they could resume attacks if the ceasefire was not honoured, and it took some hours to determine whether it was realized.

Challenges are not exhausting but give us an opportunity to reshape our world and make it a better place for everyone. Although Mr Biden hoped to shift America's foreign policy focus away from the Middle East, this deadly conflict between Israel and Palestine forced him to get involved.

Political rhetoric was limited to blame game and add to it, some were pointing fingers at Biden administration claiming that no such wars happened during the previous White House administration referring to American domestic politics. Analysts and media outlets were confused as a spiral of deadly violence continued to be running in spirals. Mr Biden was honoured to lead a strategic region, both for weight and relevance for its geopolitical and global economic stability. Its gravity pulled him to address the issue.

If you put events under the lens of philosophical psychology, it is not difficult to find a longer-term strategy for this region which has become complex by many different approaches in the past. It took four centuries for Romans to understand the simple but powerful message of Jesus until Emperor Constantine made the difference.

"Love thy neighbour as much as you love yourself" was his message, further, Jesus said that his mission was to renew the covenants and replaced them with that of Moses. You need a variety of experience, knowledge, to look through different angles, and insight of political science working with countries in the region with different strengths, capabilities and knowledge and need the confidence to drive political willingness to leverage this richness of experience to achieve favourable results together in partnership to implement a new accord.

Mr Biden had them all. President Biden sent his envoy to the region, the U.S. Secretary of State Mr Antony Blinken to convey his message of equality.

Pushing forward on a diplomatic mission to bolster a ceasefire that ended 11 days of conflict between Israel and the Gaza Strip's Hamas resistance group, U.S. Secretary of State Antony Blinken travelled to Egypt and Jordan Wednesday the 26th of May. Blinken landed in Cairo a day after holding intensive talks with Israeli and Palestinian leaders. In Egypt, he met with President Abdel Fattah el-Sissi and other top officials. Later he travelled to Jordan to meet with King Abdullah II. Blinken has vowed to "rally international support" to rebuild hard-hit Gaza while promising to make sure that none of the aid reaches Hamas. He is instead trying to bolster Hamas' rival, the internationally recognized Palestinian Authority (PA).

In a gesture to the Palestinians, Blinken on Tuesday the 25th of May 2021 announced plans to reopen a diplomatic office in Jerusalem that oversees outreach to the Palestinians. He also pledged nearly $40 million in additional aid to the Palestinians. In all, the Biden administration has pledged some $360 million to the Palestinians, restoring badly needed aid that the Trump administration had cut off.

The truce that ended the Gaza war on Friday (May 21, 2021) has held so far, but it did not address any of the deeper issues plaguing the Israeli-Palestinian conflict. Those challenges include a hawkish Israeli leadership that seems unwilling to make major concessions, Palestinian divisions, years of mistrust and deeply rooted tensions surrounding Jerusalem and its holy sites.

Germany's foreign minister, Heiko Maas, met with Mr Netanyahu on that week and also pressed for peace. Qatari Emir Sheikh Tamim bin Hamad Al Thani, in a telephone call with Palestinian Authority President Mahmoud Abbas, has said Qatar will pursue efforts together with other nations to help stop Israeli attacks against Palestinians and the Al-Aqsa Mosque, the state news agency QNA reported.

An Egyptian-brokered ceasefire between Israel and Hamas, which rules the besieged Gaza Strip, came into effect on Friday morning to end the 11-day fighting. Mr Abbas briefed the emir on developments related to the ceasefire "and the efforts to rebuild the Gaza Strip, expressing his sincere thanks and appreciation to HH the Emir for the role of the State of Qatar and its efforts in support of the Palestinian people to obtain their legitimate national rights", the QNA said on Saturday the May 22, 2021.

Meanwhile, the emir highlighted "the importance of the unity of the Palestinian ranks".

The Qatari ruler reiterated the Gulf nation's ongoing support to the "brotherly Palestinian people and their just cause" and pledged to continue its efforts with Arab and Muslim countries "to stop the Israeli attacks on the Palestinian people and the blessed Al-Aqsa Mosque", the agency reported.

This great accomplishment of reaching a truce to stop killing innocent children, destroying families, damage and disruption to civil infrastructure was attributed to President Biden and his administration. Everyone involved claimed victory. It changed the political narrative from Palestinians to Hamas as the latter expected to gain this attention and their immediate demands are the very reason that triggered violence at the Al-Aqsa Mosque.

Israel legitimately and forcefully claimed impunity as they always do. Their air defence systems, high-quality intelligence with superior kinetics partially destroyed the operational infrastructure of their enemy that has been built over period of time in a highly dense population. The head of Israeli Air Force Air Division admitted some operational losses in the critical role played and in this scenario was regrettably unavoidable.

What needs to be said has been said by all parties at the UN Security Council. Israel is U.S.'s strongest alliance in the Middle East. It provides them with military aid and equipment. There was a 750 million dollars' worth deal in the pipeline.

Powerful Jewish lobbies support both American political parties. In return, Israel provides regional military intelligence useful to U.S. national security. The need for this interdependency was well demonstrated in the September 11, 2001. This incident, which is often referred to as 9/11, consisted of a series of four coordinated terrorist attacks implemented by the Wahhabi Islamist terrorist group Al-Qaeda against the United States on the morning of Tuesday, September 11, 2001.

This partnership is important to both counties and their Western alliance as there are many unpredictable elements and risks to Western territories. Two months ago, few in the Israeli military establishment were expecting anything like this. In private briefings, military officials said the biggest threat to Israel was 1,000 miles away in Iran, or across the northern border in Lebanon. The next challenge is to convert what has been achieved to sustainable peace not only in the region but globally.

"Those who would give up essential Liberty, to purchase a little temporary Safety, deserve neither Liberty nor Safety." Benjamin Franklin. The history of this famous quote goes back to the times of frontier defence during the French and Indian War.

**Operation Opera,** also known as *Operation Babylon,* was a surprise airstrike conducted by the Israeli Air Force on the 7th of June 1981 and which destroyed an unfinished Iraqi nuclear reactor located 17 kilometres (11 miles) southeast of Bagdad Iraq. It was an unprecedented mission success perfectly planned and fiercely executed with engineering precision that sent a chilling message to all their enemies in the world that Israel takes no chances on her national security. Despite international criticism, the operation demonstrated Israeli unmatched air superiority.

Israel called the operation an act of self-defence. It added a new dimension to the Israeli government's defence doctrine and policy on counterproliferation preventive strikes to destroy perceived nuclear threats.

At that time, Iraq was building an Osiris-class nuclear reactor with the help of France. Although Iraq and France claimed it was for peaceful scientific research, the Israelis viewed the reactor with suspicion, believing it was designed to make nuclear weapons that could escalate the ongoing Arab Israeli conflict at the time.

On 7th of June 1981, a flight of Israeli Air Force F-16A fighter jets, with an escort of F-A5As led by squadron leader Ze'ev Raz, bombed the Osirak reactor deep inside Iraq. All eight pilots returned home safely. Jean-Pierre Van Geirt, a French investigative journalist, described in detail the secret nuclear deal between France and Iraq in his book *La France aux cent sects.* (Vauvenargues-1997)

Israeli Air Force planned the mission-critical surgical strike to eliminate only the military target with the help of their secret service Mossad. Iraq purchased a research reactor (called Osirak or Tammuz-1) that used weapons-grade uranium as fuel. Iraq imported hundreds of tons of various forms of uranium from Portugal, Republic of the Niger, and Brazil, sent numerous technicians abroad for training, and in 1979 contracted to purchase a plutonium separation facility from Italy. When

Israeli jets bombed the Osirak reactor, south of Baghdad, demolished the reactor's core and dealt a serious setback to the Iraqi nuclear program.

Faced with a nuclear threat from then Iraqi ruler Saddam Hussein, Israel resolved to eliminate Osirak, a French-built, Baghdad-based reactor producing weapons-grade plutonium. The reactor formed the heart of a huge nuclear plant situated 19 kilometres from Baghdad, 1,600 kilometres from Tel Aviv. By 1981, Osirak was on the verge of becoming "hot," and prime minister Menachem Begin and his closest colleagues in the Israeli cabinet, including Ariel Sharon, knew they would have to confront its deadly potential or face another Holocaust.

Accordingly, Begin turned to Israeli Air Force (IAF) commander David Ivry to secretly plan a daring surgical strike on the reactor. Prime Minister Begin defended the timing of the bombing stating that a later attack after the reactor had become operational, could cause lethal radioactive contamination doses to reach all the way to Baghdad.

After 41 years, in 2022, Israel faces the same dilemma with the new Iranian threat to "wipe out" Israel if their nuclear Programme goes ahead and has already taken countermeasures. At the turn of the $21^{st}$ century, the U.S. Defence Intelligence Agency estimated that Israel had 60 to 80 nuclear weapons.

Forty years after Israel destroyed Iraq's fledgling nuclear program, one of the pilots who took part in Operation Opera warned that an attack against Iran's nuclear reactors "won't be the same."

The strike at the heart of Saddam Hussein's nuclear program at Osirak outside Baghdad in 1981 was, and remains, one of Israel's most daring raids. But any operation to take out the Iranian nuclear program "won't be the same; it can't be the same," Brig.-Gen. (ret.) Relik Shafir told The Jerusalem Post. Unlike in Operation Opera, Iran's nuclear sites are spread across the country, some deep underground or in mountains, and surrounded by sophisticated air-defence systems.

You need a deep political insight, experience, support from West Asia (Middle East), and political will outside narrow party politics to find a settlement for lasting peace and prosperity. Importantly, Mr Netanyahu then Prime Minster of Israel (31 March 2009 – 13 June 2021) in this multiplex equation has not understood wider global politics, range of ideologies, nature of other adversaries, what true democracy is and help his nation evolve to values of co-existence, fair and just giving helping hand to their neighbours through paradigm shift for true liberty.

Jerusalem is a world heritage city. It should be accessible to all Jewish, Christian, Islamist and all like-minded people who appreciate the values of multiculturalism and Kant's cosmopolitanism around the world, to make it a holy city for all pilgrims like Mecca for Islam religion. If you want to recognise the independence of Palestine then you have to reconfigure the region with some political-ideological changes, accelerate modernization, re-education programs and shift people from survival to self-reliance through "peace and cooperation, openness and inclusiveness, mutual learning and mutual benefit" like Dubai and Qatar today.

Israel's strength of defence largely depends on Americans' attitude and their own interest in national security. The public opinion of the international community including within the progressive Democratic Party in the U.S. Congress shifted their perception of freedom of people enclaved in Israel. People become more vocal about Palestinian oppression and the violation of basic human rights such as the right to practice religious worship. Public sentiment on injustice and marginalization of ethnic minorities has dramatically shifted toward empathy on victims in the U.S. and other major cities around the world.

New generations are no longer accepting incarceration, and victimization. Now, they are connected and vocal about injustices suffered by people beyond their shore and stand up in solidarity. It has almost rose to a decentralized political and social movements protesting against incidents of police brutality, unlawful arrests, and all racially motivated violence against young people.

The global political landscape is transforming towards a more inclusiveness and against unjust social-political supremacy. A sequence of events happening since 1948 are now in the public domain, in this information age of transparency and social media platforms.

This social and political trend forced President Biden to recognise that both Palestinians and Israelis equally deserve to live safely and securely, harvest prosperity, and enjoy the fruits of democracy.

It is evident that to establish a longer-term peace and stability both parties must move towards a middle path and away from their current political models to true democracy to reach social justice, resolve issues, and fill gaps in human rights.

It would be very useful to have an independent commission to test the fitness of Palestinian self-governance, how to empower them, design a feasible roadmap to rebuild the war-torn economy, their civil infrastructure, and fill the void in political and diplomatic capacities to address Palestinian course for good.

*Palestinian Political Agreements and Constitution for Self-Governance*

The history of modern-day Palatine goes back to end of World War I in 1918 when the League of Nations issued a mandate for the British administration of the territories of the Palestine and Transjordan both of which had been conceded by the Ottoman Empire. It was formalized by the Constitution of Mandatory Palestine on the 10 August 1922 by the Palestine Oder-In-Council, a type of legislation presents in the Commonwealth realms and directly related to the then British Empire. It was first published on 1st of September 1922 in an Extraordinary Issue of the Palestine Gazette.

Recognition of Palestine as an independent state became a complicated matter after World War II when the State of Israel was established on May 14, 1948, by Mr David Ben-Gurion, the head of the Jewish Agency.

U.S. President Harry S. Truman recognized the new nation straight away. Then, on the same day Israel declared its independence, the fighting intensified with other Arab forces joining the Palestinian Arabs in attacking territory in the former Palestinian mandate.

Israel gained some territory formerly granted to Palestinian Arabs under the United Nations resolution in 1947. Palestine did not receive the attention from any super-powers as all their interest and priorities shifted to Israel. Since then, the struggle has continued with various temporary agreements between the Israeli Government and the Palestine Liberal Organization (PLO), notably, under PLO Chairman late Mr Yasser Arafat.

The Palestinian National Covenant or the Palestinian National Charter is an ideological paper, written in the early days of the PLO. The first version was adopted on 28 May 1964. In 1968 it was replaced by a comprehensively revised version. In April 1996, many articles, which were inconsistent with the Oslo Accords, were wholly or partially nullified.

The Oslo Accords are a pair of agreements between the Government of Israel and PLO: the Oslo I Accord, signed in Washington, D.C., in 1993; and the Oslo II Accord, signed in Taba, Egypt, in 1995. A Constitution was drafted in 2003 and amended in 2005 with totalling up to 121 articles on it widely known as 'Palestine's Constitution of 2003 with Amendments through 2005' to recognize the rights of the Arab Palestinian people and their national entity.

"The birth of the Palestinian National Authority in the national homeland of Palestine, the land of their forefathers, comes within the context of continuous and vigorous struggle, during which the Palestinian people witnessed thousands of their precious children sacrificed as martyrs, injured persons, and prisoners of war, all in order to achieve their people's clear national rights, the foremost of which are the right of return, the right to self-determination and the right to establish an independent Palestinian state, with Jerusalem as a capital, under the leadership of the Palestine Liberation Organization, the sole, legitimate representative of the Arab Palestinian people wherever they exist." However, this constitution has not been recognized on equal footing with other nations.

Palestinian fighters do not have a Minister of Defence equivalent to other developed countries neither they have strong weapons to match the Israel army, something that cannot be comprehended by western journalists. They are often branded as terrorists and they use innocent civilians as human shields, get funding, and support from anti-western groups or secretive organizations. Going forward they need a framework and model of governance suitable for their culture, religion, and beliefs.

After May 2021 conflict, Mr Biden has explicitly stated that his administration would favour two-state solutions, but he has not given a clear roadmap or timeline. The struggle for Independence in Palestine had been fought on the strongly confrontational approach rather than on "constitutionalist" lines that reactive attitude had been developed since 1948 and appears to be continuing in the same line. The Silverline of social justice and recognition for Palestine course is finally in the West Asian sky.

Considering the 73 years of struggling, the sacrifice of so many lives, and the suffering they had been through, it is wiser for Palestinians to accept this solution in a *quid pro quo* for the abolition of Israeli colonial rulings, hostility, and unfair treatment they suffered. Hope for the end of this progressive estrangement of these brothers and sisters has finally come. The dawn of peace is in the twilight.

Regardless of definitions, religious textual narratives and precise lineage, Palestinians, like all human beings, are ultimately descended from the same original mother and father (Genesis 3:20).

Human beings have often forgotten this when constructing cultural, geographic, and political lines. Much of the angst over who should or should not be called a Palestinian, or whether it matters where such a group came from, is based on divisions that forget our common heritage. Jesus has clearly shown how to treat a lost son, a brother who finally returned home.

The International community must not let this golden opportunity go without seizing it and in so doing, end the cycle of violence and recognize the independent Palestine state.

"Every moment wasted looking back, keeps us from moving forward." (Hillary Clinton)

To this end, the international community can appoint a commission to make recommendations for a new Constitution or remodel the existing one so to fit into the existing culture structure, meet the current conditions, and reach consensus. Most importantly, who can take responsibility to run a democratic government, accumulate funds for the modernization of their economy and improve the social fabric and structure or restructure if necessary? This could be a major question.

In this recent conflict, 248 people had died, 66 of them were children, so, only a mother who knows the pain of losing her children in violent air attacks could tell what she needs to protect her children.

Portuguese diplomat and UN Secretary-General of the assembly, Mr Volkan Bozkir stated "If there is a hell on earth, it is the lives of children in Gaza", he said during the UN Security Council meeting in May 2021. This was a measurable fact. Diplomacy is a difficult one but all of them spoke in one voice and both sides appealed to stop violence immediately. The Commissioner must listen to pleas for female suffrage, educate women, and grant suffrage to all women aged 18 in line with the Charter of Human Rights recognized by the United Nations together with their emblements.

Having noted this vacuum of strong leadership, that the society is riven by power struggles between few competing militant groups, spoilers or to avoid such confrontation, Commissioner must devise a system of executive committees that would control all government departments rejecting the principle of communal representation, league, ensuring that no one group could control all levers of power and patronage. Instead, all executive decisions would require a measure of consensus among the different representatives.

Two of the most important reforms that would concern elections and electorates if they are to establish a democratic system of governance. This time, however, to ensure that inclusiveness of minority groups with a fair distribution of representatives to voice their concerns who can think jointly, in joint perspective, work with growing relationships both internally and external world is needed.

Central to this conflict there are other natural laws, unknown to all parties seeking solutions but that are only found in the teachings of the Buddha, once a warrior prince born to be a king, trained in conventional and psychological warfare, who understood the truth, saw the suffering it brings and conquered himself instead.

Is Buddhism a religion?

The question is irrelevant, the Buddha did not intend to establish a religion, but his role was to make known the Truth, a path to end suffering. The understanding truth of suffering is the common denominator that could bring people together.

Religious symbols are used to convey concepts concerned with humanity's relationship to the sacred or holy (e.g., the cross in Christianity) and to social and material world. Ostentatious religious symbols characterized by nationalism that can lead to dogmatic ideologies, provocation, and narrow views in the long run can result in hatred and violence. Over a prolonged period of time those religious ideas surreptitiously and gradually, infiltrate and normalised in politics that becomes doctrines.

The Buddha advocated nonviolence, a path of peace and happiness. Buddhism as narrated in the past has been undersold, made people believe that it is an ascetic practice. Instead, it has true philosophical value, a profound insight, the potential to address critical issues at critical times, and bring light to darkness. Nevertheless, it is yet to be tested this aspect in this 21st century.

Not only Palestine but also West Asia need a progressive culture change from survival to self-reliance through education and training. These societies can greatly benefit from Aristotle's ideas of reform through various associations and knowledge share schemes, implementing economic concept of specialization and exchange.

We can all agree on the importance of sports both indoor and outdoor especially after living in lockdowns for a prolonged period of time. Communities and nations need to come together.

There are many countries that share a national passion for sports, which are an integral part of their culture. National sport event is an opportunity to bring communities together through participation, based on the principles of team building, inclusion, unity, fitness, and health and discipline. It can also improve mental health and physical wellbeing.

## Israel Politics after the War June 2021

The war between Israel and Hamas killed 260 Palestinians and 13 Israelis, totalling 273 lives. Still, these numbers impressed neither observer nor Israel citizens themselves. Then, Prime Minister Benjamin Netanyahu made the biggest political gamble in his career by ordering heavy bombardment and expecting support from his opposition in the Israel parliament Knesset to secure his coalition government. Yet, the complete opposite happened.

Israel's perspective "change government" is a coalition of unlikely partners contended with only one goal in mind – changing the country's prime minister. But will Benjamin Netanyahu's ousting from power lead to positive change in Israel, or for that matter Palestine?

The long journey that led to the formation of this motley coalition, including four national elections and tough protracted negotiations, has demonstrated that in a confident and prosperous Israel, personal ambition trumps politics, and politicking outweighs ideology.

In fact, it was Netanyahu who first revealed unrestrained willingness to pursue all paths to further his personal ambitions and interests. It was he who after demonizing any cooperation attempt with Palestinian Arab parties as un-Zionist, pursued a coalition agreement with the United Arab List to preserve his premiership. And it was he who helped organize and legitimize the most openly racist elements in the Israeli society, ensuring they pass the threshold and enter the Knesset.

But Netanyahu "the magician" seems to have lost his touch. He has gone too far, lied too much, and stepped over too many associates to stay on top. Indeed, nothing explains the formation of this new coalition of political extremes better than animosity – the animosity of political leaders exacting revenge against the man who once and again deceived or outright burned them. Israeli Prime Minister Benjamin Netanyahu's 12-year hold on power is ended when the parliament votes on a new government, ushering in an administration that has pledged to heal a nation bitterly divided over the departure of the country's longest-serving leader.

Netanyahu, 71, the most dominant Israeli politician of his generation, failed to form a government after Israel's March 23 election, its fourth in two years. Israel like any other democratic country has a wide generation gap. The younger generation is too much influenced and benefitted from developed Western technology and Israel is one of the largest contributors for IT and software development. This means that their views are too much different to what the world known as historic Israel.

The new cabinet, which will be sworn in after a Knesset confidence vote was expected to win, was cobbled together by centrist opposition leader Yair Lapid and ultra-nationalist Naftali Bennett. When the votes were counted on the June 13, 2021, evening, Netanyahu was ousted by the new coalition with a thin margin and not by an absolute majority. This extraordinary power transition unseated the Prime Minister after 12 years, it was a much anticipated change in Israeli that bitterly divided politics.

Bennett, a hawkish hi-tech millionaire, will serve as Prime Minister for two years before Lapid, a former popular TV host, takes over in an interesting dynamic of rotating premiership. Veteran leader Benjamin Netanyahu handed over power in Israel to new Prime Minister Naftali Bennett but remained defiant as the patchwork government faced tensions with Palestinians over a planned Jewish nationalist march. Just after 13 hours of taking the office, this ultra-nationalist leader approved the traditional march after consulting the chief of police, carefully avoiding the previous flashpoint East Jerusalem temple. Thousands of Israeli far-right nationalists marched in a flag-waving procession through East Jerusalem on Tuesday, an event that reignited tensions with Palestinians and posed an early challenge to Israel's new government.

In a democratic country, people's freedom of expression of national interest could not be cancelled even at a time both sides are trying to heal the deep cut wounds. It is important for Naftali Bennett to show his leadership, prove what he stands for and maintain the morale of his fractious coalition.

Balancing power within the Knesset is ultra-sensitive than the leftist ideology he represents. He has been in politics long enough to understand the internal dynamics notably undertaking several responsibilities of important cabinet ministries in Netanyahu's previous governments.

He entered politics in 2006, serving as Chief of Staff for Benjamin Netanyahu until 2008. He has given up his passion for high tech to serve his country. He clearly understood his adversaries and helped bring into his country the American liberal culture and a cooperate approach to business with which he wishes to modernize Israel.

Contemporary Israel state is a combination of ideas that exhibits the full spectrum ideologies from far left to far right indicating complex evolution from biblical times to modern high tec society via World War II holocaust. The newly formed government has many domestic challenges. Political polarization is almost a permeant feature and an ongoing rift in the nation that was well illustrated during the power transition inside the Knesset.

Divergence of political attitudes to ideological extremes was demonstrated by the opposition party members by shouting and interrupting speeches of the members of the government. Almost all discussions of polarization in political science consider polarization in the context of political parties and democratic systems of government.

"This rift that tore the threads that hold us together, threw us into one election after another, into a whirlpool of hatred and brotherly quarrel. These fights between the people who were supposed to run the country led us to its paralysis as can be seen at these very moments. And so, the state of Israel caused to be unmanaged, Lack of governance of the state and loss of 12 years progress."

Israel also faces numerous security challenges with its new government composition. Its defence doctrine is a very traditional religious doctrine of redemption, action of saving or being saved from sin, error, or evil based on patience, truth, wisdom, knowledge and understanding of religious teachings. Safety of Israel is in the hands of the government and the strength of the defenders which is their armed forces and assets.

The new Prime Minster Bennett clearly understood his primary responsibility in the first hour of his job. He has served in the special commando forces unit of the Israeli defence forces. The biggest threat to Israel as perceived by all parties is the growing nuclear capabilities of Iran.

Minutes after meeting Bennett, Netanyahu repeated a pledge to topple the new government approved on Sunday by a 60-59 vote in parliament.

"It will happen sooner than you think," Netanyahu, 71, who spent a record 12 straight years in office, said in public remarks to legislators of his right-wing Likud party. This charismatic leader personifies the complexity of Israel politics, its history, and its determination to survive in a country surrounded by adversaries playing politics and with the blessing of their strongest allies the US. His entire attitude and ideology reflect survival strategy. Jewish people believe that there is evil in the world, and that they should fight against it. Netanyahu perceived that he was surrounded by enemies outside and within. He was a man determined to succeed but was unable to balance the global power factors.

Formation of the alliance of right-wing, centrist, left-wing and Arab parties, with little in common other than a desire to unseat Netanyahu, capped coalition-building efforts after a March 21 election, Israel's fourth poll in two years.

Instead of the traditional toasts marking Bennett's entry into the prime minister's office, Netanyahu held a low-key meeting there with the former defence chief, who heads the nationalist Yamina party, to brief him on government business. Ceasefire was violated on June 16, 2021, by Hamas that sent some toxic balloons into Israel territories.

Washington Post and Reuters reported that Israeli air-strikes struck Gaza in the early hours of Wednesday in retaliation for incendiary balloons that crossed into the country from Hamas-controlled territory - an exchange that highlights the fragility of a cease-fire in the region and poses a first test for Israel's new government.

Israeli jets struck military compounds allegedly belonging to Hamas, the militant group that controls Gaza, according to an Israel Defence Forces (IDF) statement. Hamas "is responsible for all events transpiring in the Gaza Strip, and will bear the consequences for its actions," the IDF said. It said Israel was "prepared for any scenario, including a resumption of hostilities."

There were no immediate reports of casualties from the airstrike. Israeli authorities reported that the incendiary balloons had sparked 20 fires near the Gaza border, according to Reuters. Strategic analysts and observers of the Israel new government believe that security policy continues while others in the government set the agenda from different positions recognizing the inward government and potential flashpoints to review policies. Israel is currently facing endless scenarios; observers fear miscalculation and misjudgement of their decisions. Strategic coherence of Israel's foreign policy predominantly on American interest. Government planning mechanisms, intelligence capabilities, and organizational provisions cannot expect to be dramatically changed.

If there are not any other better proposals, then the new government will continue with the defence policy. Government must hit the ground running prioritizing security establishment components and challenges of adversaries when domestic issues take precedence. The situation can become complicated unless the government conducts a serious reform to stop the declining of other domestic services. What is needed is a fresh thinking pattern outside the previous mindset of governance under Netanyahu.

Behavioural scientist Professor Shaul Kimhi in his book, Profiling Political Leaders: Cross-Cultural Studies of Personality and Behaviour explains the psychological profile of this extraordinary charismatic career politician.

Professor Kimhi describes a number of Netanyahu's behavioural patterns that most key dimension of his personality is egocentricity. Personal success is more important to him than ideology and he constantly strives for it. Example of this pattern of behaviour was demonstrated by his acceptance of help from US contributors who held extreme views, very different from his own (Kim, 1996a).

He doesn't hesitate to exploit other people, including colleagues to succeed. Journalist Yoel Markus describes Netanyahu: "he is charismatic, driven, from an extremely ambitious family, egocentric, a lone wolf, the kind of person you might say has no God" (Markus, 1996). He over values his own perceptions than others. Thus, he undermines those who disagree with him that they don't understand historical/political processes correctly and maintained an attitude of I know best.

According to the testimony of a journalist who interviewed him, Netanyahu is convinced that he discerns the historical processes that others do not and believes that it is his heroic task to rescue his homeland. (Shavit, 1996). Some behaviour betrays self-involvement to the point that others receive no consideration. This trait is also manifested in Netanyahu's manipulation of colleagues (Kim, 1997a).

Netanyahu has difficulty distinguishing between personal and public/ political dimensions of his life and justifies his actions by pointing to the loyalty and support from all areas of the nation. He made to believe himself that success of the Jewish people, the success and security of the State of Israel, depends on him (Verter, 1997).

Netanyahu is chronically tardy for meetings even with heads of state, interpreted by foreign leaders, politicians, and others as offensive, insulting, and even degrading (Benziman, 1997e). One can safely assume that the Prime Minister is aware of these reactions (some of them have been published in the press), but these reports have not influenced his behaviour.

Ambition and determination are perhaps Netanyahu's most prominent character traits. Ambition is expressed in his desire to be the very best, to be first, to triumph over others, to reach the top (Horowitz, 1992: 6). He sets high goals and is not satisfied with partial successes. Netanyahu rarely despairs and never gives up.

Among other traits, Professor Kimhi lists several distinct, recurring behavioural patterns that have been identified since Netanyahu's emergence into politics.

- Aggression and Manipulation, Netanyahu sees the game of politics as governed by the "laws of the jungle," where the strong survive and the weak fall by the wayside. To him, the achievement of the goal justifies any political means (Sheory, 1985).
- Suspicion, this suspicion that "the entire world is against him" is accompanied by feelings of victimization and mobilize his inner

resources enabling him to fight and win in an effort to "show them" (Kim, 1997b). Individuals who are not members of his close staff are often and automatically suspected of disloyalty and conspiring against him. The threat, as he sees it, is primarily personal.

It can be ascertained from those personality traits, that circumstances have been conditioned this career politician and made him to believe that there is no successor equal to him who could rule Israel better until his retirement. In October 2022, Netanyahu was campaigning with a hope of returning to power even as he stands trial on corruption charges. The good thing about democracy is that the ultimate power is vested in citizens of Israel who could decide on their future and what is suitable to them.

## Brief history and summary of the Israel-Palestinian conflict

The Israeli - Palestine conflict is an ongoing violent struggle between Israelis and Palestinians since 1948 when the State of Israel was declared soon after World War II. The modern state of Israel was founded in May 1948 in the aftermath of the Holocaust but the conflict that has raged between Israelis and Palestinians can be traced back much further into the Ottoman Empire.

In 1799, the British revived the failed attempt of French commander Napoleon Bonaparte to establish a European stronghold in the Middle East in favour of Jewish people. Their aim was to conquer and populate the land area central to Jerusalem with Jewish immigrants as a means of countering the considerable influence of Egyptians.

French philanthropists encouraged and sponsored other Jewish people from Europe to join them and established settlements, the most notable being Rishon Le Zion, founded in 1882. Austrian writer Nathan Birnbaum coined the term "Zionism" in 1885 as Jews, particularly from eastern Europe, continued to arrive in Palestine.

By 1907, Britain was considering the need for a "buffer state" in the Middle East to bolster its dominance, to safeguard and strengthen its grasp on the Suez Canal. For this end, British proposed annexation of Palestine land, supported, and established a "national home for the Jewish people" in Palestine under the Balfour Declaration on 09 November 1917 overpowering the resistance and revolt that followed this announcement. The outbreak of World War I made Europeans and British shift priorities to their home countries while developing an allied presence in Palestine.

Following the Allied victories in Europe and the Pacific in 1945, world powers turned their attention towards the ending of violence in Palestine. The State of Israel was founded on the 14 May 1948 while ignoring the civil war between Israelis and Palatines with ending of the British Mandate, winning immediate recognition from the US and Soviet Union but prompting the outbreak of the bloody Arab-Israeli War, which saw 3,000 resistance fighters rise up against the new nation and forced 700,000 Palestinian people to flee the fighting, seeking refuge in Jordan, Lebanon, Syria, the West Bank and Gaza, often without citizenship being granted.

The displacement of the Palestinian people on that date is still marked every year on "Nakba Day", named for an Arabic word for "catastrophe" and on which Palestinians give speeches, hold rallies, and brandish the keys to the homes they were forced to leave behind and still hope to return to.

Since then, various attempts have been made to resolve the conflict as part of Israel - Palestinian peace process but without a satisfactory solution for the real issues and concerns of Palestinians. In the past, all settlements were in the favour of Israel. The most recent violence started in April 2021, in the middle of the global coronavirus pandemic, and ended in a ceasefire agreement on 20 May 2021 killing about 248 including children, injuring 2,000 others, and destroying buildings and critical infrastructure.

At least 12 people in Israel, including two children, were killed by rockets fired from the Strip by Palestinian armed groups. New Biden administration was proactively involved in securing immediate peace and was fundamental to reaching the ceasefire agreement. Circular reasoning concerning religious texts would provide very little help for a lasting resolution for this long conflict.

The intellectual community needs to look beyond historical records with a new understanding and in a new light of co-existence to see things as they are without forming opinions and judgements.

Racial inequality, injustice and discrimination which are widespread in big cities in the world need also to be addressed through constructive dialogues. The sentiment of the people in those cities have recognized the

Palestinians course in one voice to change this injustice, state-sponsored racism, and treat everyone in dignity.

*'No justice no peace'* has become a popular theme in big cities around the world promoting inclusiveness to end racial injustice. Innocent civilians have been caught up in superpower games and their internal politics while the region is being destabilized by new nuclear power interest by ambitious Iran in the middle of global pandemic.

Currently, NPT (Non-Proliferation Treaty of nuclear weapons) talks are continuing in Vienna for a diplomatic resolution. The U.S. Secretary of State Mr Antony Blinken visiting the region on 24 May 2021, stated shared recognition of both sides and opened the door for constructive dialogue with a financial aid package to rebuild the damage caused by the recent bombing (Reuters and Al Jazeera).

Blinken repeatedly alluded to the underlying issues of the decades-old conflict and expressed empathy for both sides, but he showed little interest in launching another U.S. push for lasting peace, perhaps because previous efforts by past administrations have all failed. Instead, he expressed hope for creating a "better environment" that might one day yield peace talk.

Despite these modest aims, Blinken made clear that President Joe Biden will pursue a more even-handed approach to the region than former President Donald Trump, who sided overwhelmingly with Israel in virtually every area of disagreement with the Palestinians.

Israeli new Prime Minister reiterated their claim of self-defence against Hamas's aggression and stated that improving the life and conditions of Palestinian people is his responsibility along with building economic growth in the West Bank with the cooperation of the international community. He also expressed his concerns about Iran's Nuclear Programme. To end violence and human suffering requires a middle path of peace with a vision, compassion, and insight wisdom of the nature of life to devise an action plan with a substance and commitment to restore civilization and achieve a purpose.

*Path of Liberation*

Worldly peace is a temporary concept. It does not guarantee lasting stability, peace, and happiness though there are many eloquent economic and political science theories. As long as human nature is defiled with greed, hatred, ego, and delusion, man will continue to be subject to suffering, will make others suffer and will add other anxieties that will haunt him because of his insecurities. The long essay of conflicts describes the nature of suffering, uncertainty, and despair it can bring in this modern world unless wise intervention to settle differences. Most of scientific development has directed to develop weapons that can destroy hard earned progress by aggression. Evidently, autocratic leadership has less tolerance to negotiate than democratic governments towards seeking resolutions and quick to use firepower intimidating peace loving nations.

Personality is the product of society, political regime, or political game. It has limited time for dominance. Like any other phenomenon, ego centric personality is subjected to impermanence, rise, and fall. Such regimes had added unnecessary suffering to people and clearly, they would reject them. New generation of Israelis has shown to the world that they are ready move from traditional thinking toward more progressive politics.

Contemporary and historical politically motivated events described in this chapter are testimonies that worldly knowledge needs reshaping with ancient wisdom and ethical values to evaluate political behaviours that add unnecessary suffering.

Central to the Buddha's teaching is the Four Noble Truths that allows us to find the cause of suffering by diligent investigation and by applying principles of cause and effect. The fourth noble truth is the path to end suffering. Buddhism has provided us with a path to discover inner capacities for wakefulness, joy, dignity, and compassion – your Buddha-nature. By following this Noble Eightfold path, you could explore unused energy and your true potential by mindful meditations and teachings on love, purifying consciousness, healing, and developing the nature of mind toward full liberation to end suffering. Having or showing fine personal qualities or high moral principles is the best one can achieve and it is possible in this very life.

Buddhism has successfully mitigated worldly issues with personal attributes. Starting from having a balanced view of politics and economic theories one must choose between right and wrong. Ethical values, justice, and moral compass are given as Right in every factor of the path that is interconnected and intertwined.

The Buddha taught both "Dhamma and Vinaya" which are moral disciplines towards final liberation. For a lay practitioner, there are five moral principles given as five precepts to maintain and ensuring ethical conduct. If the society one lives in is just and equitable then achieving inner peace could be much easier, but one must put an effort to make it happen.

The path is further grouped into three dimensions that are morality, meditation, and wisdom. In most of the Western approaches to Buddhism, they are starting with mindfulness meditation practice. When you are beginning to see the effect of tranquillity you can advance in the path toward acquiring wisdom to 'see clearly' things as they are removing the blind faith, wrong views of delusion. In Buddhism the quality of the thought matters. The right view that sees suffering of others generate right thought of compassion and loving kindness gradually softening heart and mind.

The Buddhist higher philosophical psychology provides a detail analysis of the consciousness, how we are trapped in a net of wrong social-political views, ideas, concepts, ego, and it also provide a practical method to liberate ourselves and to find true happiness beyond illusions.

Buddhism implicates a quality of will theory, on which agents can be morally responsible and their underlying motivation determines whether they are praiseworthy or blameworthy rejecting the free will that is dangerously coupled with moral retribution that is every action has a corresponding result. Good actions produce good results and bad actions produce bad results whether they are politically motivated, collective actions, or individual personal choices.

Buddhist writers describe a way to live with the practical consequences of the absence of free will and avoid narrow pollical motives.

Noble Eightfold path is progressive, and one can reap benefits here and now in this very life finding peace of mind and happiness. A lot of suffering in this contemporary world is because of bad politics and as a result, many innocent people have been victimized.

It is easy to start wars, but consequences are always severe. This is why, wise people choose the personal liberation, inner peace instead.

Buddhist psychological and spiritual skills can guide you to address the root causes behind painful patterns, scars whether politically inflicted, torture, subjugated to mental pressure or caused by personal injuries, and show how to address them with comprehensive practices to be resilient. Teachings inspired by the Buddhist tradition in particular, the practice of generosity, kindness, and joy of being a part of a spiritually rich community allow you to cultivate the mindfulness and compassion that are the heart of Insight Meditation.

Buddhist meditation practices are to connect you to the real world through mindfulness, awareness, and concentration. There are only six objects of insight meditation: seeing, hearing, smelling, tasting, touching, and thinking. By paying attention to these momentary experiences, you can gain a better understanding of life experiences letting go emotional traumas. When the mind is not busy then it sees experience more subtly.

A concentrated mind does not wander off all over the place but stays settled and gives the opportunity to observe some aspects of the mind in a more subtle way.

It's like looking through a clear glass.

In addition, you would be able to detach from feelings, emotions, wondering thoughts and be able not to react to them. And in doing so you come to see how things come to be in life.

For example, stress is a common syndrome of busy urban life built throughout daily challenges. Our minds are usually defiled by hindrances such as stress which make us unable to correct our judgment. Meditation would allow you to withdraw from a mechanistic routine, find work-life balance and understand how stress comes to be, how to manage the factors contributing to it, and how to live a healthy happy life.

Mindfulness and awareness can be brought into any circumstance in life even when you are angry and allow you to step out immediately and look objectively leaving the subjectivity aside. Though it is useful to spend some quality time withdrawn away from the bustle of society to enjoy the quiet nature when body and mind are settled, it is not always possible to go away on holiday or sit and meditate at the beach at sunset.

If mastered, these techniques, can help you create your own space by mindfulness in your own living room. When we are aware in the present moment, we are aligned with nature then we see clearly and are able to accept the reality of life, that all life experiences are impermanent, subject to suffering, and without enduring self.

The dynamic nature of all phenomena is common, and the Buddha formulate his doctrinal teaching of change from the pure observation of body and mind continuum. The idea of permanent-self coupled with ego is a destroyer of goodwill and view your fellow human beings as enemies. Insight meditation as the word implies gives an insight into operating laws of nature, that human nature is part of the larger cosmic universe. Once understood these laws, we will be able to change our attitudes, behaviour in the world, and we'll become more kind, loving disciplined responsible individuals, and therefore, happier.

One of the most beautiful qualities of human nature is our ability to love and be kind to others. It is a method of connecting to the outer world and could be expanded further to limitless other beings who share this world with us. Its Pali name is *Metta* better described by practising than defining in words. Its liberating quality is most effective in every given circumstance whether at work, with family, or any other relation.

When *Metta* is present hatred cannot be. It frees the heart from jealousy, judgment, fear, greed, hatred, and all negative emotions. These qualities of mind are mutually exclusive with Metta because its mental quality overrides negative states of mind and heart, making consciousness purer.

It is a mindfulness way of healing the pain and an effective method of reconnecting with broken relations.

The present moment is the moment you can make a change and extend to make the world a better place for everyone. One who practices *Metta* can enjoy many positive aspects from feeling free, to sleeping well, wakeup energetically, living healthily, and develop caring attitudes that lead to benefits for oneself and others. You can release accumulated physical tensions and habitual thought patterns so you can begin the day with a kind and empathic heart.

Buddhist writers describe Metta as boundless and immeasurable as it is explained well in the discourse given by the Buddha himself – the *Metta Sutta*. When Metta is strong, it is inclusive and wide, welcoming all forms of life, which is a very pleasant experience free from hatred. Metta is a wisdom factor equated to dwelling places of gods. It includes Compassion, Joy in others' success, and Equanimity. They are all alternative states of mind that could be cultivated through meditation practices. One who live accordingly to them enters the Noble Eightfold Path of peace and enjoys its fruits in this very life.

Buddhist teaching direct an individual to take responsibility of control at a personal level, over life and wellbeing. Mindful living can improve conditions by taking positive steps to reduce unnecessary suffering and empathy towards others as well. One of the powerful insight of impermanence would help letting go attachments to cyclic phenomena and free yourself from repetitive cycles of suffering and become resilient, face life challenges with courage.

Resilience is the ability to cope with the loss, change, and trauma that have been affecting our lives whether a global emergency, dramatic changes to how we conduct our daily lives, economic uncertainty, or political turmoil, aggression as well as personal traumas such as separation, violent crime, or tragic accidents. Most of the news we read in daily basis is disturbing, it brings anxiety and worry adding more uncertainty. Building resilience can help you better adapt to life-changing events, cope with turbulent times, and bounce back from hardship and tragedy.

Generally, Buddhist teaching views life and death as a continuum, believing that consciousness (the mind) continues after death and may be reborn. As long as mind is defiled by three main roots of greed hatred and delusion that mind continue to be reborn in a realm corresponding to strength of its defilements. For example, person with angry disposition mind reborn in woeful realm and on the other hand generous mind might be reborn in heavenly realm. This process is colloquially known as Karma as such bad Karma like killing has long consequence of present and future suffering, it follows a chain of cause and effect as a revenge in many cycles to come. War, war crimes and arm conflicts are grounds for accumulate bad Karma hence must be avoided and encouraged to resolve by wise dialogue. The principles of Karma and rebirth provide an emotional and intellectual account of suffering and evils in both Buddhism and Hindu religions. They see Karma as responsible for suffering and reincarnation or rebirth, and the final goal is to achieve liberation. All the suffering is associated with evil deeds that occurred earlier in life. Because of Karma, there is no bad act that will go unpunished. Buddhists consider the intention behind an action is the factor responsible for formation of Karma. All intentional verbal, physical and mental actions are producing Karma. Death can be an opportunity for liberation from the cycle of life, death, and rebirth when mind is free from defilements and pure.

> *"Though one may conquer a thousand times a thousand men in battlefield, yet he indeed is the noblest victor who conquers himself".*
> *Dhammapada - 103*

CHAPTER 2

# INTRODUCTION TO BUDDHISM

I F WE LOOK BACK IN history, there are some major events that have come to change the lives of mankind. Some of these are now established as religious events and have a significant place in our calendar. Every year people celebrate these events to keep alive the principles they have established. For example, Christmas, Good Friday, and Easter Sunday are very important days in Christendom.

The Buddha's enlightenment is similarly significant as it is a historical event that happened in May around 563 BC. After his enlightenment, the Buddha decided to teach what is today known as Buddhism. These teachings have influenced the life of many. In fact, Buddhism has been adopted in many Asian countries and is embedded in their local cultures and beliefs. Thailand is one of those countries in Far East Asia, where Buddhism is socially inseparable from their culture.

It has become the way of life for the majority of people in Asia. They share their knowledge and experience of Buddhism both with neighbouring countries and Western countries. There are many Westerners who have come to learn about Buddhism in Thailand, and some have made a significant contribution by establishing the practice across the UK, Europe, Australia, America, and many other Western countries.

## What is Buddhism?

Buddhism is a gentle, peaceful, non-aggressive, and ethical philosophical system of teaching as expounded by the Buddha when in an enlightened state. After his enlightenment he did not expect anyone to believe his experience and so instead he invited people to come and see. There is no place for blind faith or dogmatic creeds in Buddhism, it instead encourages questioning and an investigation to be tested with reason.

Buddha rejected the animal sacrifices and killings that prevailed during his time hence he excluded superstitious rites and rituals as serving no real purpose. Buddhism recognises the right livelihood and prohibits unscrupulous trading practices, advising individuals to choose a right career path. Disciples of the Buddha are guided by the golden rule of pure living and pure thinking in order to reach the supreme vision. This reveals the unique path of purification to reach deliverance from all suffering. The path comprises of "Dhamma and Vinaya," these Pali words that I will further explain shortly. They are interlinked to form a doctrine founded on reality (Dhamma) and practice of discipline (Vinaya).

To describe Buddhism as non-aggressive is to say that it is non-violent. The Buddha is sometimes known as the Prince of Peace, he not only resolved problems peacefully but taught how to find inner peace or peace of mind.

In other words, Buddhism is a way to find happiness, although Buddhism redefines happiness as a state of mind, for where there is peace there can be happiness.

Being a moral and philosophical system of teaching, Buddhism offers an explanation of the nature of the mind and how happiness can be achieved by living according to Buddhist teachings.

Siddhartha Gautama was born into a royal family of a small kingdom in the 6th century BC in India. By invitation of his father, King Suddhodana, learned astrologers investigated and predicted that the new-born prince would one day be a great king or a great religious leader. The young prince was brought up in a protected environment of luxury to prevent him from developing an interest in religion and was trained in military warfare in preparation for kingship.

As a young prince, Siddhartha Gautama contemplated the meaning of life and the nature of true happiness, he was deeply moved by human suffering and was disgusted by temporary sense of enjoyment.

To his father's disappointment, one day he left the palace in search of a higher calling, embarking on a journey to find a permanent solution to the suffering of mankind. He struggled for six years living the life of an ascetic and going from one school to another, but Siddhartha Gautama found himself going nowhere.

When contemplating his failures, he reflected the two extremes, self-indulgence which retards spiritual progress, and self-mortification which weakens the intellect. In their place he discovered and followed the middle path, deciding to go his own way.

Having practised this path on a full moon day in the month of May, ascetic Siddhartha Gautama was enlightened and became the Buddha, a title given to a self-enlightened one. The Buddha is not a God, nor a saviour who can save others.

After his enlightenment, he explained that deliverance from suffering can only be gained by self-exertion and advised his disciples to be self-reliant.

"Striving should be done by you; the Buddha only teaches."

After his enlightenment, the Buddha taught for 45 years, becoming the longest-serving teacher on this earth. During his long ministry, the Buddha expounded 84,000 discourses. Even in his last minutes, Buddha taught to his disciples, saying "Listen up monks, the master is about to pass away. If you have any questions, please ask now; do not regret after I go".

After the Buddha passed away his enlightened disciples arranged his vast array of teachings into an order useful to new students. It is taught in a form of discourses known as *suttas*. The teachings are philosophical in the way they explain the nature of the mind and its relation to human conduct, but it is pragmatic in its application.

The whole set of teachings is known as the *Pali Canon*, Pali is the language or dialect spoken by Buddha. His teachings were first documented in Pali and Sanskrit, for this reason, Buddhists still use many Pali and Sanskrit words which have meanings that stem from root words, similar to the way Latin and Greek are used in English.

The Pali Canon constitutes the sacred scriptures of Theravada Buddhism which is one of the schools of thought founded on the historical Buddha's teachings. It is the collection of discourses most widely esteemed by Western religious scholars. The discourses are recorded transcripts of the original words spoken by Buddha in response to particular events.

Some are simple dialogues between an inquirer, who is asking the questions, and the Buddha, who in return explains the principles of nature and how to resolve the problem. On other occasions, the Buddha gave direct instructions and expositions to his disciples. The teaching provides a form of counselling, advice, and intellectual inspiration to the seeker of truth, reflecting the pure wisdom of the Buddha and his realistic understanding of life. The teachings were passed down from one generation to another with unbroken continuity. They are still relevant today because they are based on indisputable facts of life. They provide a valuable purpose and vision through the darkness of the confused and obscured views of our time. The Pali Canon is arranged in a methodical manner unfolding the doctrines that extricate the roots of suffering.

The original Pali term for Buddhism is *Dhamma*. Dhamma is a multi-faceted term. It signifies 'that which upholds or sustains him who acts in conformity with its principles, protecting him from falling into woeful states'. The Dhamma is the Doctrine of reality; it distinguishes what is real from illusion. It is the method of deliverance in accordance with the universal moral law that governs our lives, similar to medicine, which is prepared according to the nature of life so that it cures an illness. The Buddha is like a doctor who understood the illness of life and prescribed the appropriate medicine.

Whether a Buddha appears in this world or not, the laws of nature exist. These are the eternal governing laws of our existence throughout the galactic system of this universe. Dhamma is a non-personal, universal moral law that applies equally to everyone who seeks to find deliverance from suffering and attain liberation.

The Buddha discovered this law, which was hidden from the ignorant, untrained mind of men and out of compassion he revealed it to the world to enable us to find a balanced and happy life. The Dhamma is not something that is completely outside of us, our very being depends purely on our actions and their consequences. An individual has to gain insight into how actions dependently arise and the intricate web of relations that make up one's life. According to the enlightened perspective, everything originates in the mind and therefore the solution is not outside of us. For this reason, we are encouraged to look inwardly.

The sublime Dhamma is the profound truth without any speculation, it can thus be tested and verified by personal experience. The Buddha did not expound on any revolutionary philosophical theories to change the social order, nor did he attempt to create a superior order. He explained in plain terms both what is relevant and irrelevant for emancipation from the ills of life, in doing so he revealed the unique Path of Deliverance.

Practising and understanding the teachings requires certain disciplines, *Vinaya*, without which learning and progression in the path are not possible. They are important for one's personal growth in wisdom and as norms for harmony within a community.

In his first sermon to his former colleagues, the Buddha consolidated his discovery and formulated his teaching into Four Noble Truths: that all life experiences are subjected to suffering; that there is a cause to suffering; that there is a cessation to suffering; that there is a path leading to the cessation of suffering.

They are to be seen and understood by our individual experiences of life as these constitute the fundamental components of reality. Similar to a scientist discovering, elementary components of matter by his diligent application of thought and experiment, a disciple has to unravel the truths of suffering by his own diligent practice. Although Buddhism has a scientific mode of application, it is not itself a science but is the truth of our nature.

The fourth Noble Truth gives two sets of practical training schemes. The first is the practice of generosity, morality, and meditation. When a disciple has reasonably improved, his practice can go to the next level, that is to say, the practice of morality, concentration, and wisdom. The ultimate goal of happiness comes from gaining wisdom of life and its experiences as they really are. The final liberated state of mind is known as 'Nibbana'.

Our minds are conditioned by views, opinions, judgments, and analysis. There are three ways we ask questions: what, how and why. In most situations, we know tackle what and how, but we do not often ask why. Little children always ask this question, and adults often ignore it. Wisdom comes from asking the question 'why?' For example, asking: Why am I angry? or in fear? or impatient? and so on. The right answer to 'what' and 'how' comes from the right answer to 'why'. If our answer to 'why' is wrong, then we wrongly understand what the question is and how to resolve it.

Buddha discovered the principle of cause and effect and restated it as the nature of *kamma* the Sanskrit term is *Karma* (the law of action) which explains the compounded nature of phenomena and their interdependency.

The discovery of the principles of the law of action made Buddhism unique compared to all other teachings. This law explains how beings are trapped in the cycle of suffering and how liberation from it is achieved. Liberation comes from seeing the true nature of phenomena. That is to say, the cyclic, transient nature of things brings dissatisfaction, and these are beyond the control of any permanent self.

Buddhist training schemes are to help us identify our own inner hindrances preventing our happiness and overcoming them. When wisdom increases, our ability to resolve our day-to-day problems also increases and then we can find peaceful solutions to problems which increases our overall happiness. For example, when we are angry and frustrated about a situation, our reactive solution can be aggressive and damaging. When resolving a problem with wisdom we can change an apparently difficult situation into a peaceful one.

There are many stories where Buddha resolved problems peacefully. The Buddha once intervened in a war between two clans. In another situation, Buddha subdued a serial killer peacefully. He was able to engage his princely qualities and diplomacy to bring order.

Buddha and his disciples walked across India from village to village to teach, refusing to take vehicles drawn by animals such as chariots, carts or to go by horseback. They had no disputes crossing borders of countries and all rulers of the northern Indian subcontinent allowed them to enter their countries in order to teach. Buddha gave strict instructions to his disciples not to perform miracles for worldly gains and not to upset local people and their local cultures. His mission was simple and pure – to enable peace and happiness to be attained by all.

The teachings have three primary aims. These concern the welfare of the individual and family life. Buddhism recognizes life after death according to the law of action and claims the ability to achieve a favourable rebirth. Good actions produce good consequences, whereas bad actions produce bad consequences. For those who do good, a good destination is expected and for those who do bad, a bad destination is expected. In the end, the attainment of the unconditional reality of ultimate happiness (Nibbana) is for those who are prepared for the journey to cross the cycle of rebirths and death. The final journey is also known as the *Path of Purification* leading to the *Path of Liberation*.

Because of impurities in the mind, human relations can be infected by bitterness, conflict, and revenge. Buddhism provides practical guidelines based on basic ethical values which propose injunctions against improper behaviour that leads to bad destinations.

The Path of Purification given in the Fourth Noble Truth is to develop the sterling qualities of human beings by acquiring virtues. The Buddha said that the scent of virtue is sweeter than the scent of all flowers and perfumes. The highest wisdom factors manifest themselves as sublime qualities of the mind. They shine and radiate from the personality, namely compassion, loving-kindness, sympathetic joy, and equanimity. When the mind is free from greed, hatred, and delusion of every kind we can see the suffering of ourselves and others developing empathy.

Compassion is seeing the other's suffering and actively wanting to help those beings to alleviate their suffering. Loving-kindness comes from the mind that is free from hatred and anger.

Sympathetic joy comes from the mind that is free from jealousy and envy, whereby one can appreciate the success of others. Finally, equanimity comes from the mind that is free from delusion and judgment. These qualities have immense practical value and are closely interwoven with the entire fabric of Buddhist societies.

## Family values for those who value family

Buddha taught monks, family men, and other lay investigators about how to resolve their problems.

In Buddhism, family is regarded as the fundamental unit of society. Family unity, its values, wellbeing, and happiness resemble the characteristics of a good society.

The matrix of family values is explained in the discourse named

'Singala', where Buddha advised the young man, Singala, about the duty of each member of the family and relations.

Marriage is one of the main events in a person's life, forming the foundation of family life. A family unit consists of husband, wife, and children. The stability of the family depends on a stable relationship between the husband and wife. They should not pursue conflicting interests that destabilize the family unity. The family should have common goals such as economic prosperity, family wellbeing, and self-development.

The ideal householder possesses four kinds of happiness. These are: the happiness of possessing wealth; the happiness of spending wealth; the happiness of freedom from debt; and the happiness of blameless conduct. The Buddha did not set a limit for wealth, as long as one does not use wrong means to acquire it and doesn't become attached to it.

Children have a duty towards their parents as much as parents have a duty towards their children. Having been raised, educated, and guided towards adulthood, children in return have to respect, love, and support their parents, especially when they are old or unwell. Family relations are then extended to teachers, religious leaders, relatives, friends, employers, and employees.

Good relationships stem from the philosophical tenets of compassion, loving-kindness, generosity, responsibility, truthfulness, and mindfulness.

These are wisdom factors. They are important for the unity and harmony of the family as a foundation for lasting happiness. Therefore, the family needs to set aside time to grow in wisdom. Most religious institutions provide a framework to help their members to gain spiritual wisdom as well as conventional wisdom. In Buddhism, growth in wisdom is a gradual progression which encourages people to be reflective, contemplative, to understand, to reason and to know good from evil. The Four Noble Truths explain the benefit of good conduct in thought, speech, and deed, this avoids harming others.

There are eight Right Factors leading to enlightenment. Buddhist contemplative thought is applied to what is useful and separates us from what is useless, to see things as they really are. Our senses can otherwise deceive us. We must, therefore, use our wisdom to investigate causes and conditions, solve problems wisely, and carry out tasks effectively. When wisdom increases, the unlimited qualitative factors of wisdom can be extended not only to the family but to the wider world.

The discourse of loving-kindness is the charter for world peace, and if correctly understood, peace on earth and heaven can be achieved by living accordingly.

## Philosophical and ethical values

The first part of this book examines philosophical values and how they relate to teachings on how to lead our lives. The second part examines the ethical criteria and their practical values. Ethical values based on the law of action are important, not only for the intellectual investigation of human behaviour but also for how it reveals new psychological aspects of behaviour to reduce suffering and improve wellbeing.

The Buddhist doctrine of action means volitional action that manifests physically, verbally, or mentally, all of which are born by intention. The origin of this intention remains deep in our unconscious mind as desires, cravings, wants or revenge to harm others.

When mental contact is made with the world through our senses or mind, such contact acts as a sense-avenue.

It is by this process of contact those feelings, thoughts, perceptions, and emotions arise. Reacting to these mental states triggers a chain of further mental activity. The nature of these results is dependent on the intention. Intention rooted in greed, hatred and delusion produces results of more suffering to one who commit such action and others as well. On the other hand, intentions rooted in generosity, compassion and wisdom produce favourable results of happiness that help us to rise upward in life.

Some of these results occur immediately, while others can remain in the unconscious mind and produce results at a future point in time, in the same way that a dormant seed will sprout when the right seasonal conditions are met.

To adhere to ethical values has great benefits. Their importance for self-development and self-reliance has been identified by both Eastern and Western philosophers in earlier centuries. The Buddha discovered the moral law that governs the behaviour that consequently leads to rebirth in higher or lower realms. This is popularly known in the East as *kamma*. Richer life experiences such as happiness and joy are products of good actions.

To violate the law of action and to deny that there is retribution is to take a nihilistic view.

The truth, according to Buddhism, is that bad behaviour leads to moral deterioration and suffering.

Hatred, violence, and social disorder are the result of an unethical upbringing. When children are neglected at a young age and not shown the principles of morality in their broader social context, they become selfish and antisocial.

Ethical injunctions are there to prevent evil, to bring social order and to create harmony in society. To cultivate what is good and to purify the mind are the way to progress in life and towards true happiness.

The following words of wisdom from the Buddhist texts brings conclusion to this introduction.

"All conditioned things are impermanent and unsatisfactory. When one sees this with wisdom, one turns away from suffering. This is the path to purification". Dhammapada.

<blockquote>
May all beings be free from enmity, ill will and
suffering. May all beings be well and happy.
</blockquote>

CHAPTER 3

# BUDDHIST SOCIAL PHILOSOPHY

"Is Buddhism a philosophy?"

The main purpose of this chapter is to discuss if we accept that Buddhism can be considered as a philosophy, and then to explore what is known as Buddhist Social Philosophy and how we can find a way to relate the teachings to our lives.

It is seen as a philosophy by some western writers, some scholarly Buddhist monks in the East also write about Buddhist philosophy. Importantly, the answer is not relevant if we know how to relate the teachings to our lives.

The word philosophy is derived from the Greek language word 'philosophia' meaning love of wisdom. According to the Oxford Advanced Learners Dictionary "philosophy" is defined as "The study of nature and meaning of the universe and human life. It can be a particular set or system of beliefs which results from the search for knowledge about life and the universe. For example, we may study *moral philosophy* or *the philosophy of science*".

Philosophy today is an academic discipline with a history spanning many centuries. Its origin goes back to the time of Greek civilization. During the time of the Roman civilization, philosophical ideas were widely applied in order to expand and stabilize the Empire. For example, Plato and Aristotle's ideas were widely adopted, further developed, and have now become the foundation of modern western philosophy.

With the explosive growth of the subject, it has now grown into five branches of individual study. These are metaphysics, ethics, aesthetics, epistemology, and logic. Metaphysics has two subdivisions namely ontology and cosmology.

On the other hand, the history of Eastern thought goes back about seven thousand years. Evidence of the search for knowledge can be found in the Indian scriptures of Vedic science known as 'Vedanta' literally meaning knowledge. Vedic scriptures were written in a contemporary Indian language of Sanskrit. The 'Pali' word 'dithi' stands for philosophy. Pali was the language or dialect said to be spoken by the Buddha.

During the time of the Buddha, there were many views pertaining to the purpose of life. In his quest for enlightenment Buddha rejected extreme views and found the middle path to liberation. Views are classed as wrong views if they are a hindrance to enlightenment and as the right view if they are conducive to liberation. Yet, most Buddhist scholars agree that the middle path established by Buddha is the only path for liberation.

In Brahmajala sutta, an exposition, the Buddha analysed sixty-two different philosophical views. They were summarized in three views: Materialism, Eternalism, and Nihilism.

Materialism says the purpose of life is to entertain the senses as much as we can by consuming materials. Materialists saw no basis for any paradox since they counted as real only the observable material world. Eternalism says that a permanent soul is transmigrating from life to life for eternity in many different planes, both pleasurable and painful. The idea of cosmology was formed according to such an eternal theory. Nihilism claims that the soul annihilates after death and the material body disintegrates, making an end to all existence.

Some of the modern social, economic, scientific theories and ideologies proliferate such nihilistic and materialistic ideas. For example, for the last three decades, people in the world were divided in opinion as to what is the best political and economic ideology, viewing each other as political enemies. World resources, including all human capabilities, were used to meet the enemy threat, world economic models were changed, and we consumed all our resources at such a rate without having to replace them by natural order which creates an economic erosion and depletion.

There are many people in the world who are caught up in such views of life and make their followers suffer too. Buddha rejected such views which serve no real purpose to life. Some of them were speculative philosophies coupled with metaphysical theories of origin and the destination of man. There is no scriptural evidence that Buddha taught any metaphysics, instead, he categorically rejected metaphysics and remained silent when such questions were posed to him.

## Ethics

Buddhism can be seen as a set of ethical teachings. Buddha addressed the moral consequences of our actions. Kamma is the law of volitional action; it conditions our life and binds us to cycles of unhappy destinations. Out of compassion, he taught how to reduce levels of bad kamma. Buddhism is the name given to his teachings which comprise two branches.

One is called 'Dhamma' *(Dharma)* meaning moral laws of our existence; the other is called 'Vinaya' meaning moral discipline.

The entire teaching of the Buddha is embedded in ethical grounds. Mental, verbal, and physical actions are further divided into wholesome and unwholesome. Ethics are guidelines to regulate all kinds of actions.

## Aesthetics

Aesthetics is a branch of the study of beauty and its appreciation.

Undoubtedly, Buddhapadipa Temple in London is a beautiful place, located in a conservation area surrounded by a grove and a lake. It represents Thai Buddhist architecture, culture and art, its mural paintings are masterpieces of Thai artists. Statues placed in the alter represent majestic images of Buddha often to the amazement of visitors, the entire Temple is an immaculate piece of artwork by master's in art and craft.

Casting a Buddha image is considered a wholesome action and marking Buddha's eyes are a special ceremony performed by both monks and the artist. The artist has to undergo special preparation before and during the casting process. In Buddhism, art and sculpture are used as teaching devices and as methods of propagating the teaching.

It is also the vehicle that artists and sculptors use to pay tribute to their traditions and cultures.

In the cultural triangle, North of Thailand, in the cities of Chiang Rai and Chang Mai, there are amazingly beautiful ancient and new Buddhist temples surrounded by mesmerising misty mountains adding panoramic scenery that testify to the Thai architectural marvel and art of presentation. They define aesthetics and beauty.

In Buddhism, temples and monuments serve the purpose of performing religious ceremonies rather than simply places of worship. But the use of art, sculpture, architecture, and design to build religious places are not unique to Buddhism.

During 500 BC there was a gigantic awakening of religious and philosophical thought in many civilizations across the world including India, Central America, Middle East, and China. There is a marked evolution of art, sculptures, architecture, and their application to religious thought can be found in all these civilizations. Knowledge and skills gained from building religious places were later applied to the development of structural engineering and architectural masonry.

Art and culture are inseparable manifestations of an underlining religious philosophy. Appreciation of the beauty of nature, making beautiful ornaments, monuments, and pieces of art are a way of achieving material perfection as a projection of religious beliefs for many religions.

For example, ancient Egyptians, Greeks, and American Indians *(Mayan Civilisation)* produced miracles of material perfection in honour and glory of their religions, this was a method of worship.

Aesthetics now deals with such issues as, what it is for an object or a performance to be a work of art. It is concerned with whether there are objective standards for judging it, what meaning, and function can be ascribed to art and the concept used within it.

In this context Buddha images and alters are considered as worthy objects for contemplation, to consolidate one's thoughts and deeds by reminding the person that there is much more to life outside of their ordinary patterns of thought. Art is also used for inspiration, where religious and historical works can be used as subjects.

The use of art and sculpture was magnified by Renaissance architecture in the 16th Century when the style spread throughout Italy, especially to Venice and much of Western Europe.

For example, *Leonardo Da Vinci* used religious objects and stories for his artwork. Similar applications of art can be found in Southeast Asia and the Far East, where Buddha images and Temples are the centres for magnificent architecture, art, and sculptures.

Historically, the kings of Asia supported the Buddha, and since Emperor Asoka of India, Buddhism has become the state religion in many countries including the Kingdom of Thailand. As such, across the cultural triangle of northern Thailand, there are many applications of artistic skills amassed into Buddhist temples. It is common in many Buddhist countries like Sri Lanka, Myanmar, Cambodia, Japan, and Korea where Buddhist temples are the places of inspiration for devout Buddhists.

In Parinibbana Sutta *(discourse given at the last moment)* the Buddha gave very specific instructions to his disciples, informing them on how to cremate his body and what to do with his remains. It was according to such instructions that great pagodas were built to deposit Buddha's relics. "When people see those pagodas, they will come to learn my teachings".

Buddha's relics are shared between many nations and deposited with much veneration, including in Buddhist temples of Great Britain.

## Epistemology

Epistemology is the branch of philosophy that studies the theories of knowledge. According to the Buddha's own words, the knowledge he discovered in this universe was infinite. The Buddha achieved omniscience of knowledge, yet he only taught a handful of that knowledge.

Buddha possessed knowledge of five branches, which covered how a being comes into existence, including the formation and deformation of the physical universe. In this regard, Buddhism can be classed as a philosophy. However, the Buddha limited his teachings to the understanding of suffering and the way out of suffering. He formulated his teaching in Four Noble truths which set the framework for all his teaching.

During his long ministry of teaching the Buddha unfolded the theory that leads to wisdom. He advocated that knowledge itself can be a hindrance, therefore only a pragmatic application of knowledge will lead to wisdom.

"Wisdom that sees the truth" can bring suffering to an end. Buddha's assertion of truth was not through knowledge or the application of logical reasoning. The discovery of truth and enlightenment occurred to him during deep meditation. The ultimate truth is comprised of insight and wisdom into the transcendental dependency of mental and material phenomena.

Buddha discovered the operating laws of the mind, how it is bounded and how to liberate it from bondage.

Our usual method of assertion is through logical reasoning; however, we cannot discover or discern the nature of things as they are by pure speculative reasoning. It is only when reasoning is closely tied up with experience that there is a discovery and understanding of facts in the objective world.

Rational thinking and statements of facts can assist in finding the fundamentals of truth.

The meaning of the words we use and the context of such use, by cultural background and origins, also contribute to the true meaning. This branch of study is called Etymology. Still, Buddha rejected the strong application of these methods without questioning their validity. There is a discourse that supports freedom of questioning called 'Kalama sutta'.

Kalama was the name of the city in which people were perplexed by many contradictory teachings each claiming to be true. The Buddha advised thus, "Kalama's be cautious, do not believe it because of tradition or because it is written in a sacred book, or because of the reputation of the teacher, or because it is logical. Believe only if you can comprehend the truth".

Buddha's method of assertion of the truth was empirical. The Buddha succeeded in discerning the truth from sense perceptions by penetrating sense-data presented at the moment of observation.

The method is called "insight meditation".

Modern psychologists turn to the Buddhist way of thinking because classical and neo-classical concepts cannot address the real problems of the mind and get nowhere close to understanding the nature of the mind. The discernment is not some kind of mystical revelation for it also involves rational and logical thinking. For example, Buddha found the Middle Way by seeing a musician tuning his musical instrument; the fine tuning is in the middle, where strings are neither slack nor too tight. This thought of balancing mental and physical effort prompted him to reject the extremes.

Buddha taught "monks pay wise attention and contemplation and reflection on the four foundations of mindfulness". The understanding that comes from seeing things as they really are, is the right understanding. Mindfulness is associated with the present moment where only true facts could be observable. That is to say knowing true characteristics of all phenomena that constitute life forms and material world. Direct knowledge gain from observations is compatible with scientific knowledge that physical and organic matter are made of compounded materials. Over period of time all compounded and composite matter disintegrate decay and die. So does the mental formation, they arise, persist for a while, and pass away.

When one sees the impermanence, unsatisfactoriness, and non-substantiality of all bodily and mental phenomena one turns away from attachment to them.

Detachment from worldly things is the renunciation that gives the space for freedom of thought. Such renunciation has to be practised on many different levels in order to eradicate the defilements that are clouding the clarity of thought.

Different writers use different terms to explain the process of discernment. I would like to use the word "wisdom" as it is widely used in our tradition.

The Pali equivalent of "wisdom" is 'panna' literally meaning 'to cut off'. The term thus emphasises the cutting off of attachment to worldly things. The Buddha compared the gradual awakening of wisdom to the ocean:

"Just as the ocean has a gradual shelf, a gradual slope, a gradual inclination, with a sudden drop-off after a long stretch, in the same way, this Doctrine and Discipline has a gradual training and a gradual performance, a gradual progression, with a penetration to gnosis only expected after a long stretch". In this context, "gnosis" means the ultimate depth or ocean floor.

When propounding his irrefutable thought and discoveries as perceived by the enlightened mind, Buddha exhibited the knowledge of truth by logical presentation. All his teachings are presented in a natural, logical order without any speculation. The truth of life and existence is an experience beyond conceptual thought. However, for the purpose of communication and teaching we interpret our experiences with the aid of language. Words in languages were introduced, developed, and taken into usage according to semantics, thus words are not mere arbitrarily chosen sounds, they are used according to conformity with their etymological meaning.

Pali language very well expresses the meaning of what Buddha wanted to teach. Buddha's teaching cannot be excluded without its ethical dimension; Buddhism is a philosophy that leads to the perfection of man's moral conduct. Buddhist social philosophy addresses a wider spectrum of activities in all walks of life.

Buddhism provides a practical application of its doctrines to everyday life. Evolution of the Buddhist schools of thought and culture directly applies Buddhist doctrine and teachings to their societies by using many different methods. In Buddhist countries, this can be considered as the Buddhist social philosophy. These schools have provided meaning and purpose to people's everyday life activities.

## Buddhist Theory of Knowledge

Prior to the emergence of the Buddha's enlightenment and the subsequent establishment of the Four Noble Truths, there were many schools of Nihilistic, Eternalist and Materialist thought in contemporary India. They projected various views according to their epistemological doctrines. At that time, religious texts and mystical experiences surrounded by various kinds of rituals and practices were the authority of knowledge. Some of them were superstitious knowledge, a notion maintained despite evidence to the contrary. For example, occult practices and witchcraft.

The Eternalists believed life forms have a soul that transmigrates, reincarnating from life to life in different realms, whereby heavenly birth was possible through following their doctrines. The Materialists rejected the argument of authority; interpretation of perception and verifiable inference were the means of knowledge recognised. The kind of reasoning employed by the Materialist was based on empirical evidence and experiments devised to test hypothesis. They rejected metaphysical concepts that lacked rationale and critiqued the claim of intuitive knowledge held by the Mystics. The Nihilist school denied the validity of all means of knowledge, the conflict of theories was the main motive for the birth of this scepticism. By rational and logical arguments, they could defeat one another's philosophical position.

The Buddha avoided confrontation with other schools. He was familiar with certain rules of reasoning, he used the existing intellectual culture and their beliefs as a vehicle to convey his teaching. He used appropriate means according to the level of knowledge and background of his audience. For example, he explained and illustrated his doctrinal teachings by similes, parables, and metaphors to a range of people. He taught farmers how to plough their fields, traders how to treat their employees, householders how to live a happy life and disciples how to liberate their minds. In epistemology, the Buddha sought a middle way between dogmas and scepticism and rejected Eternalism, Materialism, and Nihilism as they provide no means for final liberation.

When posed with provocative arguments by agents of those schools of thought the Buddha had adopted an approach of epistemic rationality. To take one example in the Pali Cannon, the Buddha showed the futility of debating to an eloquent teacher, Punna Mantaniputta, who was filled with pride by his wealthy background, as he was with his own philosophy of life. The Buddha showed him that instead of engaging in debate, people should seek liberation through dialogue.

Epistemic rationality is roughly defined as the kind of rationality that one displays when one believes propositions that are strongly supported by evidence and refrains from believing propositions that are improbable given one's evidence. Traditionally, epistemic rationality has been distinguished from practical rationality.

In philosophy, practical reason is the use of reason to decide how to act, it is basically goal-directed reasoning selected from some action as a means of carrying out the steps to achieving that goal. It contrasts with theoretical reason, often called speculative reason, which is the use of reason to decide what to follow.

In the view of many thinkers, to be epistemically rational, one's beliefs should approximate a number of ideals: coherence with the canons of logic, axioms of probability, and rules of evidential support; only then are beliefs deserving of our trust. On the other hand, instrumental rationality is a form of practical reasoning that allows a person to decide how to do things or how to take a course of action towards an end goal. In philosophy, instrumental rationality refers to the pursuit of a particular goal by any means necessary. Instrumental rationality is all about making decisions that maximize efficiency. It's about using the approach that is the most economical, even if it compromises other things.

For example, a paramedic attending an emergency medical service (EMS), such as a call for a cardiac arrest, a critical incident or an accident involving patients with illnesses and injuries which the patients or bystanders believe constitute a medical emergency. The paramedics need to have certain epistemological knowledge in medical procedures and dynamic high skilled training in using electronic and biomedical instruments. Paramedics providing out-of-hospital acute care go through various steps assessing patient's neurological, cardiological, and functional abilities including those with an altered level of consciousness.

They should be able to take a rational decision between life and death. As such, well-trained emergency medical technicians (EMT) check patients' pulse, breathing, chest movements, blood loss and examine other life-threatening injuries, performing a primary assessment and deciding upon the best course of action to follow in the shortest possible time. Paramedics are advanced emergency medical care providers trained to take a sequence of actions that can optimize care and the outcome for their patients. They provide advanced life support to patients and have knowledge of cardiovascular procedures, staying on the scene to perform high quality care and medical interventions to save lives. For example, EMS personnel are often the first response medical providers to initiate care of critical patients outside of the hospital. As the first contact with patients, they often encounter difficult medical and ethical situations, none more so than when critical patients are in the peri arrest and cardiac arrest state.

Medical assessments of these situations are needed to clearly determine the patient's condition including issues of whether to initiate cardiopulmonary resuscitation, rapid defibrillation versus the determination of death already being present or when to terminate an active yet futile resuscitation. Traditional approaches to patients who are not breathing or do not have a pulse is to transport patients to the nearest hospital as quickly as possible with medical care performed in a moving ambulance, a rational decision to be taken by EMS crew members.

The Buddha has shown that life is short and that similar to what would happen in an emergency when we must deal with it and work diligently at the present moment like EMS persons with attentive awareness, men need to sort out their entanglement with worldly affairs, use skilful means and find liberation.

He asked to his audience "what would you do if your house is on fire? would you keep arguing about who set fire to your house or save your life first?" His teaching demonstrates the ability to significantly increase one's capabilities in the present moment. In order to convey his teaching, the Buddha appears to have applied both epistemic and instrumental rationality without spilling emotions into the latter.

Moral discipline is maintained by a strict code of practice, adopting a simple lifestyle compatible with the existing culture and principles of law of action is conducive to progress. Progress in the sense of feeling less stressed and ability deal with issues more efficiently, wisely disentangling with unwholesome activities and development towards an improved or more sublime qualities.

In the end goal is specific with clear learning objectives transforming lives towards supreme happiness. A Buddhist order of monks is established according to a broad understanding of practical reasoning.

It is an inferential process through which new intentions are formed or old ones modified into compliance with other standards of consistency and coherence aligned with normative beliefs. This is to safeguard the best interest of the order. Buddhist monks are to live in the peaceful pursuit of their end goal of happiness with excellent conduct. The Buddha set these rules to build a good relationship within the monastic order and with the lay community. His pragmatic attitude towards teaching emphasised personal experience, he encouraged his disciples to critically reflect on the conventional worldly knowledge and focus on wisdom.

The Pali term 'panna' is often translated as *insight wisdom*, it goes way beyond mere knowledge and has a connotation of *intelligence* or *understanding*. Buddhism is concerned with Truth rather than knowledge. It is described in Buddhist commentaries as understanding the true nature of phenomena. There are three levels of insight wisdom that have been described. The first level of wisdom can be gained from reading and listening. The second level of wisdom comes from reflection and mental investigation or critical thinking, engaging with the analysis of concepts and the intricacies of different mental formulations.

Buddhism describes the third level of wisdom as wisdom gained from introspective meditation. It involves a direct realisation of Truth by practice, a kind of intuitive knowledge that sees things as they really are meaning an accurate and deep understanding to uncover what is hidden or intricately connected like a cobweb. The philosophy of relations – the book of Patthana explained in Abhidhamma shows twenty four types relations how body and mind are interconnected and dependent nature of mind, consciousness mental factors and body to one another. In simple terms, wisdom is to let go of mental burdens rather than carrying the heaviness of all past and future concerns.

The Pali term *"panna"* has an etymological meaning of "sharp blade" literally to cut off, metaphorically to let go of attachments that cling to worldly desires. All you need is the courage to let go of an attachment, the freedom you may gain from letting go allows you to live a more productive life towards the end goal of full liberation.

The key to this level of understanding is Mindfulness and living in the present. The Buddha proposes a three-fold understanding of action: mental, verbal, and bodily. He advised his disciples to be mindful and look inwards on all three aspects of actions. Meditation retreats designed by masters, organised, and attended by well-meaning people are to gain this experience of inner peace through inward observation of physical and mental movements allowing them to settle.

All phenomena experienced through six senses have similar characteristics in that they are impermanence, subject to suffering and without an enduring substance or permanent self. Sense, pleasure, and worldly happiness are very temporary, as there is a supreme happiness to be found beyond sense indulgence.

This profound knowledge is encapsulated in the theory of the four Noble Truths, first delivered by the Buddha to his former five colleagues.

In metaphysics, the Buddha argues that there are no self-caused entities, that everything dependently arises from or upon something else.

This allows the Buddha to provide a criticism of souls and permanent self-identity; this criticism forms the foundation of his views about the reality of rebirth and an ultimate liberated state called "Nirvana."

He limited his teaching to the end of suffering.

Nirvana *(pali - nibbana)* is not primarily an absolute reality beyond or behind the universe but rather a special state of mind in which all the causes and conditions responsible for rebirth and suffering have been eliminated.

As long as cause and effect continue, beings will continue to remain trapped by ignorance in the cycles of birth and death. The Buddha succeeded in breaking this cycle and identified that ignorance is the principal factor or central force of craving that propels the cycle. One who sees this clearly has a perfect vision and moves away from mundane worldly happiness to the supramundane path of liberation which is the Noble Eight-Fold path.

# CHAPTER 4

# HOW TO RELATE DHAMMA TO YOUR LIFE?

THE MIND AND HUMAN BEHAVIOUR are largely the subject matter of Buddhism.

According to its philosophical analysis, a man is a being with a higher mind. His quality of life can be improved by education and training. However, by improper functions it gets defiled and so continues to produce unwholesome actions, becoming trapped in a cycle of births and deaths known as 'Samsara'.

The Buddha saw that the suffering of the world was due to man's inability to see how his own unwholesome actions contributed to his suffering. Thus, out of compassion, Buddha taught how to escape this vicious cycle.

The three main roots that produce unwholesome actions are greed, hatred, and delusion. In Brahmajala sutta, the Buddha vividly explained the all-encompassing net of delusion in which man is trapped. Greed and hatred can coexist with delusion; delusion is the most difficult to identify among the unwholesome thoughts and actions.

"As rust arises out of iron, eating itself away, even so, his own deeds lead the transgressor to the states of woe."

Having recognized the truth and the cause of suffering and the possibility of escaping it, the Fourth Noble Truth provides the path leading to the cessation of suffering for anyone willing to meaningfully practise Buddha's teachings.

"Knowing this O' good man that evil things are uncontrollable. Let not greed and wickedness drag you to suffering for a long time."

There are various scholarly studies that have been done under various topics to apply Buddhist teachings to social philosophy. In many Buddhist countries, Buddhist doctrines are interwoven into the social fabric, even at higher levels such as being written into government constitutions. Other areas, such as the ethical criteria of human behaviour, social ideals, individual responsibility, interpersonal relations, and qualities of leadership also apply Buddhist concepts.

For example, the head of the state of Thailand is a King, whose role as the state leader is institutionalized by Buddha's advice on the king's duties, known as Raja Dharma (qualities and responsibilities of a great king).

An account of such duties can be found in the "Nandiya Migaraja Jataka" story, which is a source of non-canonical Buddhist literature. The ruling class of Thailand descends from the Rama dynasty when the development of Buddhism was characterized by a strengthening of its relations with the order of Sangha (Buddhist monks). The late King of Thailand, His Majesty the Late King Bhumibol Adulyadej, was a personal supporter of Buddhism and the patron of the order of Sangha. His elder sister, Late Her Royal Highness Princess Galayani Vadhana, had magnanimously dedicated her time to bringing Thai Buddhism to the West.

The role of Sangha (Community of Buddhist monks) provides a strong impact on society through its teachings, such Buddhist institutions provide the socio-cultural framework.

Significant concepts such as non-self, kamma, rebirth and the Four Noble Truths are the main applications to the framework. For example, Venerable P. A. Payutto from Thailand contributed a lot through his many scholarly works and in 1994 he won the UNESCO prize for Peace Education.

In his historical speech "Peace through Freedom and Happiness" he mentioned that when education is out of balance, it only promotes our abilities to acquire material possessions and gratify the senses, failing to develop our ability to be happy.

If we view our fellow human beings as enemies or rivals, then we are in a constant struggle of fear and insecurity. We have no opportunity to promote goodwill and the sublime qualities of love, kindness, and compassion, neither can we then be happy at others' success.

Conversely, Buddhist doctrines help us to look inward to find true happiness and inner peace by depending less on material wealth and less exploitation of the environment.

Venerable Payutto continued to say that "people who are happy within themselves tend to make others happy. Because their material gains are no longer the sole source of their happiness, they are able to share their gains with others. What was initially contentious, happiness becomes a sharing and a harmonious kind of happiness".

One of the main and most basic teachings of Buddhism is to practice generosity. The generous person does not become possessive and liberates his mind. For the first time in the world, a constitution for living was compiled by Venerable Payutto, whose book is based on the Sigalovada sutta (discourse given to Sigala).

It relates to the application of Buddhist principles to daily life, showing a layperson how to improve his social interactions in all aspects of social relations. The Buddhist constitution of relations recognizes the values of a society and each being who lives in that society. It is not about what to eat, what to drink or how to dress. The Buddhist constitution for living is a set of character-building guidelines to live in moderation.

Buddhist teachings offer guidelines for behaviour based on timeless truths, harnessing the positive wealth created by compassionate and wise relationships within society. For example, good relations can build a good neighbourhood and care for the elderly, children, and the sick. It is to live an honourable, righteous life, aimed at the ultimate goal of spiritual freedom, living in the world, and yet rising above the average consciousness of sensuality whilst avoiding becoming entangled with unwise worldly affairs that are born of ignorance.

First, a man must learn how to relate to his own life by having moral discipline as a foundation for life, aiming to realize his full potential, and become a valid contributor to his family and the society he lives in. Having enjoyed the worldly life, he then can become a social benefactor by developing sublime qualities of love, kindness, and compassion, to develop equanimity towards the everchanging worldly conditions.

This is achieved by way of contributing his wisdom to social harmony. In a society, people are related to each other in many different ways such as husband and wife, employer/employee, and teacher/student.

The Constitution of Living covers all aspects of these relations and how to strengthen them by accepting the deriving responsibilities. For example, Buddha went to the extent of recommending that a husband should honour his wife in that status and give her occasional gifts.

Besides, in Buddhist families, grandparents have a higher status as mentors and advisers to the family; as people reach maturity in knowledge, wisdom, and experience, they can become an adviser or mentor to others.

Buddhist doctrines are frequently misconceived by some as an ascetic religion, only practised by monks living in a solitary state. Others view Buddhism as a metaphysical and spiritual teaching with no relation to society. Buddhist social ethics stem from the Middle Path, as discovered by the enlightened one. The basic principles are the Five Precepts and higher principles which are derived from dependent co-arising.

"Dependent on ignorance arises formation and dependent on formation arises becoming," therefore one who sees dependent origination sees dhamma.

The comprehensive conditioned genesis of origination is explained in eleven detailed stages.

The Buddha transcended the aggregates of physical forms, feelings, perceptions, thoughts, mental formations, and consciousness. He then saw these in truth, as irreducible processes, functions, and forces that are final to their ultimate realities called dhamma.

He reformulated a dynamic philosophy of change and presented them in a way for us to easily understand by our general perceptions. He explained the transitoriness of objects, their ceaseless mutation and transformation into different forms; how things appear and disappear in the world and how they conceal the truth.

The doctrine shows how our own craving brings a never-ending cycle of suffering. The higher doctrines are articulated into an integrated philosophy based on psychology and ethics which provide a path for the full liberation of the mind.

The American Buddhist monk Bhikkhu Bodhi says the higher teaching of Buddhism can therefore be described as a philosophy because it proposes an ontology, a perspective on the nature of reality and discovery of truth.

The ethical dimension of the path protects the mind from defilements, thus supporting and sustaining the process of purification of the mind towards perfection, this leads to the direct knowledge of truth. For laypeople, the Buddha showed how to live a complete life by not getting deeply entangled in worldly affairs. Nevertheless, Buddha's investigation into life and subsequent assertion of its truth is for a specific purpose.

The study and practice of Buddhism are therefore not for the sake of knowledge and intellectual interest but for ferrying across the floods of Samsara to a final supreme, permanent peace and the happiness of Nibbana (the ultimate peace of blissfulness).

For laypeople, individual success can be achieved by integrating with the common goals of society and the world at large. Buddha didn't prohibit laypeople from acquiring wealth, thereby he did not set limits on their success, so long as they do not break the precepts. Laypeople are allowed to enjoy the wealth they rightfully earn, of which four kinds of worldly happiness are mentioned.

A family man may possess wealth acquired by energetic striving. Amassed by the strength of his arms, earned by the sweat of his brow, righteous wealth, righteously gained.

When he thinks, 'I possess wealth' acquired by energetic striving, righteously gained, he experiences happiness and joy.

When he does meritorious deeds, he experiences happiness and joy.

When he is not in indebtedness to anyone, he has a greater potential to be happy.

When he is endowed with blameless conduct, deed, and word and thought he experiences happiness.

Happiness is deeply connected to our own conduct of how the material wealth is acquired and how we perceive it. One of Buddha's foremost supporters was a rich banker. He was originally named Sudatta, yet because of his unparalleled generosity, he was later known by his new name, Anathapindica, meaning feeder of the helpless. Anathapindica gave generously to Buddha and the Sangha (order of monks), donating his estates, building monasteries and large-scale offerings of food to many.

In Buddhism, there are two communities, the monastic community, and the lay community. For laypeople, Buddha taught differently than he would to the monastics or those who had left the householder's life. For laypeople, the value of society and social norms are very well demonstrated in the Buddha's advice to a young householder Sigala.

The discourse named *Sigalovada Sutta* stands in fact, as the charter of social norms and as a model for the householder's life.

One day, while Buddha was walking down the road early in the morning, he met a young man, Sigala, performing a ritual at a crossroad junction. When asked to explain why he was worshipping the several quarters of the earth and sky Sigala replied that he was simply carrying out his father's last words to him. But Buddha disapproved of such superstitions and old practices and for this reason, he gave them new meanings by interpreting the meaning of the matrix of six quarters as six classes of social relations that a householder interacts with on a daily basis.

Among other things, the Buddha advised Sigala that the six quarters should be understood by acknowledging parents as the East, teachers as the South, wife, and children as West, friends and companions as the North, servants and employees as the nadir, the recluse and religious community as the zenith. These six quarters set the model framework of a society and how a person can relate himself to the society and the world he lives in.

Buddhists are supposed to lead good lives and contribute to the growth and stability of society in accordance with the laypeople's discipline. Buddhist social ethics are derived from a broad social philosophy that people are related to one another in many ways. It is impossible to live in complete isolation or separation from society. In this context Buddha recognized an individual has to develop many character attributes, the most important one's being love, kindness, compassion, truthfulness, social responsibility, a caring attitude, giving due attention and thought, being cautious to avoid dangers or loss to oneself and others, giving protection to the family, and to be generous.

These attributes need to be cultivated throughout our life until perfection is reached. The Five Precepts stem from the above social philosophy and the doctrines of karmic retribution for immoral actions. While maintaining one's relations towards the six quarters, these precepts are important so that one may not harm others or oneself. To construct a good social relationship and harmony we have certain duties towards each of the six quarters. For example, irrespective of their religious belief, everyone undoubtedly has a responsibility towards their parents.

Buddha's advice on this matter was "Having been raised by them one looks after them in return when they are old".

The discourse provides a detailed web of relationships and how to relate our lives to society.

While performing duties, one relates oneself to the society in which one lives. So, life is a dynamic process, and it is only through acts of goodwill that we can develop good relationships.

CHAPTER 5

# STEERING LIFE TO ITS OBJECTIVES

ONE SHOULD HAVE AN OBJECTIVE in life. Buddhism does not encourage living in idleness, in fact, the Buddha advised people to be industrious. Buddha taught to people of all walks of life; he taught farmers how to plough their fields, businessmen how to run their businesses and kings how to rule their countries.

There is evidence in the teachings that Buddha was deeply moved by inhumanities and addressed the unjust social, economic, and political backgrounds which prevailed during his time. Indeed, Buddhism has a wider social application where individual and social responsibilities are the underpinning principles of Buddhist ideology. Moreover, Buddhism recognizes the family as the fundamental unit of society.

"Whosoever is energetic, mindful, pure in conduct, self-restrained, right living, vigilant; his fame steadily increases."

Right livelihood is the fifth factor of the noble eightfold path. It is evident that the Buddha recognized the fact that choosing a right career is important. There are three levels of objectives specified, the temporal, spiritual, and the highest objectives one can set for one's life. Setting a career objective is important to be economically self-reliant.

Employment or self-employment is one of the main ways we relate to modern society and the family. Having a happy family and establishing the good reputation of one's family depends on one's temporal objectives.

Therefore, these objectives must be chosen carefully so that there is no conflict of interest in one's wellbeing and the welfare of the family. For example, Buddha emphasized that the head of the family is responsible for sustaining the family's prosperity by knowing how to make a living.

It follows that, unemployment could have a bad effect on the welfare of the family. The parent's duties are wide in many ways, these include helping children according to the Buddhist principles of conduct, helping them to understand such principles while protecting them from evil, providing an education and to live in harmony with society. One should be energetic, mindful, and productive in one's livelihood, investing and reinvesting in skill development to secure one's career.

Especially in the present economic climate one should be flexible, to adapt, to change, and acquire new skills as demanded by modern industry.

Philosophical teachings are the guidelines to setting objectives in life and how to relate them to the society whilst staying on the middle path.

A person without wisdom is like a ship without a rudder or compass. Buddhist guidelines provide assistance on how to navigate one's life through troubled waters and avoid unnecessary obstacles, to steer towards one's objectives without sinking into the bottom of Samsara.

For example, Buddha's advice to Sigala vividly explains the gravity of the undisciplined mind and how it could ruin his life.

"And which are the six doors of dissipating wealth? They are drink, frequenting streets at unseemly hours, hunting fairs, gambling, associating with evil friends, idleness. Therefore, the young householder, these dangers of drink, the actual loss of wealth, increase of quarrels, susceptibility to disease, an evil reputation, indecent exposure, ruining one's intelligence."

There are three levels of wisdom. Firstly, wisdom that comes from hearing and learning the teaching. Secondly, wisdom that comes from the practice of Dhamma. Finally, wisdom that comes from applying the wisdom so gained from both learning and practice to resolve the problem and cut off the entanglement.

"Who strive not when he should strive, who though young and strong, is given to idleness, who is loose in his purpose and thoughts, and who is lazy – that idler never finds the way to wisdom."

Once established in a career, being endowed with warmth, deep appreciation, and happiness, having an ideal to adhere to, one may set an objective to develop one's spiritual side of life. There is always time, if managed carefully, to do meritorious deeds with virtue.

As mentioned before, there are moral consequences to our actions. Wholesome or meritorious actions produce wholesome results, whereas unwholesome actions produce unwholesome results. There are immense benefits in having spiritual objectives to life and practicing meritorious actions, such as giving offerings to monks, needy people, helping and giving a hand to support community work.

The virtues of Buddha and his great disciples are very well illustrated in the recommended daily chanting. Buddha had five close disciples who also became Buddhas by following his teaching. The meaning of the blessing is simple and pure:

"These Buddha's are indeed worthy of blessings, and they are well established here. We pay them homage and respect them with offerings. By their virtue may wellbeing and blessings be always with us. We are now paying homage to the Triple Gem, by the highest virtue of this merit; we may achieve great happiness and peace of mind. By virtue of the Buddha may we be free of dangers and obstacles."

In the Maha Mangala Sutta, Buddha explained the blessings of life. These are not any divine powers but the simple and wise application of thought to daily life. Such as not to associate with fools who drag your life into ruins but to associate with the wise and those worthy of honour, make an effort to set your life on the right course by doing meritorious deeds, spend time learning new skills and choose a good career.

To support one's parents, family, and children and to engage in peaceful and purposeful occupations are the characteristics of a good person. To have a steady mind and self-control are blessings for life. In this discourse the Buddha describes 'blessings' that are wholesome personal pursuits or attainments, identified in a progressive manner from the mundane to the ultimate spiritual goal. Suttas (discourses), deal with the way of life that is conducive to progress and happiness.

On the other hand, the Parabhava Sutta pointed out the causes of downfall. For example, one who loves dhamma progresses while one who is indifferent to it declines, such as those keeping bad company.

In Vyagghapajja Sutta, Buddha explained to Dhigajanu, a well-off householder, the conditions which lead to progress and happiness. These are persistent effort, watchfulness of earnings, association with people of higher moral standards and living a balanced life. Buddha and his teaching shed a new light on Asia. Literally speaking, Buddhism civilized Asia.

The British explorer Edwin Arnold was the first westerner to write about Buddhism. He named his book "Light of Asia". Later, he was given a knighthood by the Queen Victoria of England for his work.

We should have higher objectives in life as there is no guaranteed happiness in worldly affairs.

According to higher Buddhist doctrines' there is nothing permanent, the impermanence of both material and mental phenomena is the subject of suffering in life. For this reason, Buddha advised people to learn and practice Dhamma. In Buddhism we often use the word Dhamma as a term with many meanings and contexts.

At the level of the higher doctrines, dhamma means principles that govern our lives.

For example, The English scientist Sir Isaac Newton woke up to the reality of why an apple fell on his head, by investigation he discovered the law of gravity. Similarly, Prince Siddhartha woke up to the reality of life by seeing early four aspects of truth namely old age, sickness, death, and the quest for religious life, he then renounced the royal comfort and investigated for six years until discovering the laws of life by self-enlightenment.

Whether we like it or not there are principles or natural laws, and we are subjected to them. They apply to each and every one of us irrespective of our social and ethnic differences. For this reason, Buddhist teachings are universal. The monks' role is to make these teachings available and accessible to us. In return the laypeople look after them. The order of reciprocal inter-dependency was founded by Buddha as the order of monks (Sangha), which is based on moral discipline and conduct. Both parties are benefited by acts of generosity.

The relationship between monks and lay people was emphasized by the master himself. "Monks, Brahmins (ruling religious class in contemporary India) and house-holders are most helpful to you, since they support you with robe and bowl, with lodging and seat, medicines, and necessaries for sickness, Ye also monks are most helpful to them since ye teach them the dhamma that is lovely. Thus, monks this holy life is lived in mutual dependence, for ferrying across the floods for utter cessation of suffering."

The common goal of the Buddhist community is to finally overcome suffering. Different individuals are at different levels of their maturity of understanding to be able to end suffering. Monks teach people how to tread the path, not only as an act of returning favours, but out of their own virtue of compassion for the cessation of other's suffering. Such compassion was stressed by the Buddha when he sent out his first group of disciples to teach dhamma. "Go monks on your journey, for the profit of the many, for the happiness of the many, out of compassion for the world, for the welfare, the profit, the happiness of gods and men."

The principle of generosity is fundamental to Buddhism. The path of purification begins with this mere act of giving. The summary of Buddha's teachings is "Not to do evil, but to do good and purify the mind."

To understand and realize higher teachings one has to study and practice the central teachings, the four noble truths. To set a higher objective to your life would be to tread the path of your life according to the noble eightfold path, which is the fourth noble truth. Mindfulness, calmness, and stability are given an importance in order to understand Dhamma within you.

Buddha not only had supporters he also had enemies, rivals and people who insulted him out of jealousy. There was a time when some people under the influence of a rich woman abused the Buddha, she was offensive to him for his advice on how to overcome pleasure and passion. On this occasion, his disciple suggested they left the city, but Buddha advised him, "as an elephant in the battlefield withstands the arrows shot from bow even so will I endure abuse. Verily most people are undisciplined. The best among men is the disciplined who endure abuse" thus exhibiting his royal, princely qualities. The Buddha is considered as a spiritual monarch.

The mind trained by introspective meditation and moral discipline can overcome all kind of greed, hatred and delusion and withstand the abuse or repulsion of others.

Trained minds can see things as they are, born of a conditionality to form a variety of phenomena dependently arising in the world outside and world inside us. According to His highness the Dali Lama, ultimate happiness depends on elimination of our negative behaviour and mental states, like anger, hatred, and greed.

These kinds of emotions seem to be a natural part of our psychological makeup, many people think it is natural and that aggression is necessary to compete with others. A 17th century philosopher Thomas Hobbes saw "human race as being violent, competitive, in continual conflict, and concerned only with self-interest".

Before the second world war, in the earlier part of the 20th century, a Spanish born philosopher George Santayana wrote that generous caring impulses, while they may exist, are generally weak fleeting and unstable in human nature. To dig a little beneath the surface is to find a ferocious, persistent profoundly selfish man.

According to Sigmund Freud "the inclination to aggression is an original self-subsisting instinctual disposition." Early writers of psychology identified the mental disposition of an average untrained person. Their observations were pretty accurate, but they failed to see that there are natural laws operating in nature and within us. They confronted the normal and abnormal behaviours of the mind and began to analyse behaviour into psycho-physical processes.

Modern consumer-driven marketing and the advertising industry vigorously apply these psychological concepts and promote indulgence of our desires as the only life worth living. The most obvious way to worldly happiness appears to lie in the gratification of the senses, however the truth is that our senses cannot be satisfied because there is a law of diminishing satisfaction that operates behind our consciousness. Our senses are like a bucket with a hole in it, because of this continuous leak the bucket will never get filled.

People become slaves to their passions until their minds become unclear and confused.

In Buddhism this is called ignorance, with skilful means we can dispel ignorance. Buddhist higher philosophy and psychology recognises that human nature can be changed. People behave according to a certain pattern because of certain conditions. The Pali equivalent for the word 'human' is 'Manussa' meaning being with a higher mind; thus, the mind can be further developed through education and training.

The Dali Lama emphasises that a flexible mind can be trained to objectively examine our problems from a variety of perspectives and develop a flexible mode of thinking. According to him, "ethical behaviour is another feature of the kind of inner discipline that leads to a happier life."

The great spiritual teacher, Buddha, taught us to perform wholesome actions and avoid indulging in unwholesome actions. The importance of ethical conduct was shown by the Buddha himself while admonishing his own son Rahula who had broken the codes of discipline.

The discourse, an exposition given to Rahula, stands as the charter of child discipline and developing their character at an early learning stage of child development.

According to the higher philosophy and psychology of Buddhism, the unwholesome mental factors of our mind are the cause of suffering, these cause the continued acquiring of more unwholesome factors by acting as conditioning factors which are themselves conditioned by their own conditioning force. It is mere impossibility to separate them and interrupt the self-perpetuating nature of suffering without higher mindfulness. Buddhist higher philosophy and psychology gives detailed classifications of consciousness, mental factors and how they associate with each other.

In Cula sutta MN (Majjhima Nikaya - The Middle-Length Discourses) 40.107 Buddha instructed his disciples on how to investigate the mind and identify unwholesome factors:

"How monk, does a monk practice the way proper to the recluse? When any bhikkhu who was covetous has abandoned covetousness, who had a mind of ill will has abandoned ill will, who was angry has abandoned anger, who was resentful has abandoned resentment, who was contemptuous has abandoned contempt, who was insolent has abandoned insolence, who was envious has abandoned envy, who was avaricious has abandoned avarice, who was fraudulent has abandoned fraud, who was deceitful has abandoned deceit, who had evil wishes has abandoned evil wishes, who had wrong view has abandoned wrong view, then he practices the way proper to the recluse. I say, because of his abandoning of these stains for the recluse, these faults for the recluse and these dregs for the recluse which are grounds for rebirth in a state of deprivation and whose results are to be experienced in an unhappy destination. He sees himself purified of all those evil, unwholesome states, he sees himself liberated from them. When he sees this gladness is born in him, when the glad rapture is born in him. In one who is rapturous, the body becomes tranquil. One whose body is tranquil feels spiritual pleasure, in one who feels spiritual pleasure the mind becomes concentrated. He abides pervading on quarter with mind imbued with loving kindness, like wise with compassion, like wise with altruistic joy, like wise with equanimity."

In this discourse the adverse psychological aspects are clearly identified and given a proper method to correct them. By mindfulness and clear comprehension of those mental states one can abandon them by adopting a nonreactive mental attitude.

The middle path is not to get overwhelmed about any reactive emotions but to learn to let them go.

In this way, one can cultivate an equipoised mind. The freedom that comes from this abandoning is called 'deliverance by wisdom', it is the true liberation of the mind that paves the way to true happiness. There are three ways to develop one's life.

Understanding its philosophy intellectually and forming an idea about Buddhism will not help anyone to shape up their character. Buddha provided a three-stage training scheme to practice his teachings. These are the practice of generosity, morality and mental development or meditation; by these one may come to gain a higher awareness, to identify one's own mind and improve their character attributes, in so doing becoming a worthy contributor to your own life, family and the society you live.

There is a fine tradition in Thai culture that allows young men to admit temporary ordination as a monk. Monkhood gives a space to renounce the world. During the time of their stay as a novice monk they are given an opportunity to directly experience monastic order and cultivate the basic character attributes needed to build good social relations, namely, love, kindness, sharing, and caring. The novice monk gets further training in accepting responsibility for his own action. They are also taught to practice mindfulness meditation, paying attention to their thoughts, feelings and emotions which helps the practitioner to identify his own mental disposition.

There are mainly two meditational practices in Buddhism. They are Tranquillity and Insight.

The Pali terms are "Samatha and Vipassana." They go hand in hand. Vipassana meditation is based on the four foundations of Mindfulness, extracted from a discourse named "The Four Foundations of Mindfulness" which has become popular in the west. This method helps to develop mindfulness, momentary awareness of one's actions, inner emotions and thought patterns.

Self-awareness helps greatly in being able to take corrective actions and letting go of attachments or resentments, aversions to clear the mind from the confusions of discursive thinking. It could be supplemented by tranquillity and breathing meditation to find calm, peace, and happiness.

You can try this as little as fifteen minutes a day and see remarkable changes happening to your both physical and mental wellbeing. The combination of Tranquillity and Insight is proven as a successful method of putting the burning emotions of anger, restlessness, anxiety, and worry permanently out the window and welcome a breath of fresh air to your life.

CHAPTER 6

# THAI TRADITIONS AND FAMILY VALUES

IN APRIL AROUND THE 11ᵀᴴ to 14ᵗʰ Thai people celebrate New Year. The festival is called '*Songkrant*' – it derived from the Sanskrit word meaning 'moving'. Ancient Indian astrologers have observed that the Sun travels around twelve constellations and completes its journey from Pieces to Aries. This time of the year is the harvesting time and there are not much other economic activities.

People use this time to enjoy themselves and for family reunion. In Thailand Songkrant is the day for family, the time of the year when everyone comes home to celebrate the day with their family.

Making merit is a strong part of Thai culture, an idea based on Buddhist doctrine of kamma. Thai people believe good action brings good results in this life and also in future lives. The day starts with the family visiting a village temple and make offerings to venerable monks.

Apart from making merit on New Year's Day, the most important activity is that of children paying their respect to parents and asking for forgiveness for any wrong doings, misunderstandings, and anything undone during the year. It is a very moving event, tying the family together and bringing balance to the family's emotional welfare. Both parents and children get an opportunity to forgive and forget their mistakes and look forward to a new year. At the Buddhapadipa Temple they teach these fundamental Thai traditional values to both parents and children.

Buddhism regards the family unit as the basis of both community and society. Family behaviours are the building blocks that eventually determine how society behaves by holding the moral and ethical values. A family's emotional wellness is important for each member to grow strong and face the challenges of life.

In the Anguttara Nikaya (AN), Buddha reveals that "Whatever families endure long, all of them do so because of four reasons, or because of several of them. What four? They recover what is lost, repair what is decayed, eat and drink in moderation, and they put in authority a man or woman of virtue." Buddhist families are organized in accordance with Buddha's advice. Family is usually arranged in line with some generational hierarchy so that such families can balance intergenerational continuity and maintain ties among all levels of generations. Family unity improves the communication between member's ideas.

A healthy family unit depends on communicating, transference of facts, or feelings that clarifies, informs, notifies, and counsels. These are deemed essential so that conflicts and controversial situations are avoided.

Concerning right speech In Anguttara Nikaya II/ 172 Buddha advised "For my part, Brahmin, I do not say that everything one has seen, heard, or sensed should be spoken of and I do not say it should not speak. If one speaks and profitable states grow, one should speak of what one has seen, heard, sensed, and understood." To maintain the balance of a family's emotional and intellectual support to each member, it is important to share and express feelings accurately and directly so that no misunderstanding arises.

Traditional values help families to function properly by understanding their individual role and responsibilities. A happy family usually faces minimal conflicts and are able to resolve family matters that often arise from generational gaps, social changes, and personal views.

Understanding the natural laws governing our lives and the law of kamma would enable a family to cope with momentous events such as divorce, separation, ageing, long term or terminal illness and loss of loved ones. When understanding of dhamma grows, the family members will accept responsibilities rather than avoiding them, becoming accountable rather than denying and blaming each other. Matters can be negotiated and mediated through senior members.

In Sigalovada Sutta, the Buddha explained the importance of family unity as well as individual duties and responsibilities to manage the family economics. Adherence to this advice would result in wealth gained from energetic striving which is related to security and emotional welfare of the family.

Can these Buddhist values apply to western society?

Is western thinking totally different to that of Eastern thinking?

Let me begin by looking at a range of Buddhist beliefs and then match them with similar ideas from a wide range of western schools of thought and individuals who have contributed to western philosophy.

Buddha taught that mind is the forerunner of all our action and much of the suffering is caused by unwholesome states of mind.

The Greek philosopher Epictetus had a similar view of suffering. His investigation suggested that men are disturbed not by things that happen but by their opinions of the things that happen. His school saw suffering as inherent in the human condition. It proposed that men should accept this reality and balance themselves against it by developing a cheerful disposition and a strong character.

For Buddhists, strong character is valued in both family matters and in a wider social context, where individual contribution and charismatic leadership is needed. Buddhist doctrines aim at the cultivation of an individual's character. Hence, it could be argued that Buddhism is a moral philosophy directly addressing human behaviour.

In the pre-Christian era, the Romans too saw the vital need to develop character. They adopted non-Roman beliefs that deviated from power, namely culture and individualism. For example, they used a series of tests designed to build character by stages, adherence to them would strengthen the personality to overcome varied life challenges other than the military and political challenges. Followers saw themselves as being on an upward path of personal development.

What is taught to children on Songkrant day are these fundamental, character-building steps that are needed to move on in life and keep the family unity. To forgive and forget the mistakes done in the past and move into a New Year requires tremendous courage and real character. The family unity and their emotional welfare is important for both parents and children to grow, therefore being able to face the real challenges by responding to day-to-day problems and demands throw at them.

In Buddhism we give much importance to self-control, awareness, and mindfulness. We perceive insight wisdom as vital for a true understanding of life and to resolve the problems it brings.

Fifth century philosopher Socrates taught the central dictum "know thyself". Descartes introduced his famous philosophy "I think there for I am".

Our thinking and the consequent decisions we make are much influenced by the way we perceive the world around us. Our conventional identity and understanding of the limitations of our abilities are important to make the correct decision at critical time. Most people do not have a realistic understanding of themselves, instead daydreaming on imaging. There is a marked difference between who we think we are and who we really are. Most of the confusion in the world is due to a misconception and an unrealistic identity of the self. The acceptance of self as 'myself' or to state 'I am' as a concrete reality can be dangerous because it can lead to a self-centred, egoistic view of life. Buddhists recognise the conventional identity of self but at the higher doctrinal levels Buddha denied the existence of a permanent self. To understand the doctrine of non self and address the challenges of self-identity one needs to go deeper into the practice of insight meditation, Buddhism is not involved in the continual affirmation and maintenance of the personal self.

Before understanding the doctrine of non self, one has to master the doctrine of impermanence unsustainability and non-substantiality of all phenomena both as the inside and outside worlds.

To find out the truth of life and our own mental disposition one has to make an inward journey.

This journey is known as insight meditation.

Appreciation of meditation by 19th century German writer Elizabeth Kubler Ross is overwhelming in regard to the development of personal qualities. Elizabeth wrote "By silent meditation and withdrawing from the day-to-day hectic life, we take our self on board.

As we discover our self, life starts to make sense and we see the sense of life and what the world is about. We begin to answer the question 'Who am I?', 'Where have I come from?', 'Where shall I go?' and 'What are my tasks here?' We find our centres and can then build our hub and wheel of life. We strive for self-improvement, turning ourselves from rough stones into well-hewn blocks that can fit squarely into the building of life. We mature and, as our spirit and wisdom grow, we are able to engage positively with the world and with our fellows. Only can you work on yourself but practicing awareness and serious supportive discussions with those on the same path can help you."

Very much similar to Buddha, Aristotle also studied human behaviour and the ethics that lead to the good life. Aristotle declared that strong character development of a person begins with properly managing his mind. Further, he stated consistently and persistently that by behaving well and guiding one's action one can shape up their character and becomes a good person.

Socrates had taught Aristotle the merits of self-knowledge gained via contemplation and meditation. The word meditation and contemplation imply the Buddhist mental training method of the four foundations of mindfulness.

Aristotle shared the views of Socrates that the understanding gained from examining a life, itself comes to permeate that life and direct its course. Aristotle argues strongly that men usually fail to see what makes them truly happy, but the greatest happiness comes from helping others.

He encouraged men to see reality as it is by removing mental distortions and metaphysical speculations. 4th century philosopher Plato expressed the allegory of the cave - demonstrating Socrates' idea that sense experience cuts us off from the real truth of things, since our five senses present us only with shadows of reality similar to the prisoners in the cave, separated from others by a screen. Socrates was accused, sentenced to death in 399 BC for corrupting the youth with his philosophizing, Plato therefore was cautious in introducing his theories. Freedom of thought is an essential part of a society if it is to ascertain the truth.

Aristotle's teaching resonates with what Buddha had taught many centuries prior. Buddha directed his search precisely to the problem of suffering, he penetrated the conventional reality and succeeded in discovering the absolute truth, his claim to the truth was empirical.

When the Buddha was an unenlightened Bodhisattva living in royal comfort, he was moved by the four early signs of the truth of suffering. On this, he decided to renounce the world in order to find a solution to the sufferings he saw. It could be argued that by living in the realms of sense comforts one cannot find a reality outside of it.

There is an interesting and pragmatic theory of truth introduced by 19th century American psychologist and philosopher William James. James held that a statement is true insofar as it works towards the desired goal or as it pays in monetary terms. Truth is created not discovered. It is created through the successful organization and manipulation of what is given in experience. The theory is derived from the practice of successful inquiry, especially that of empirical science.

For example, what we see, hear, and experience can be manipulated by mass media and drugs, this can brain-wash a person into believing that what he experiences is the truth. James' findings suggest that freedom of thought can be exploited by one's circumstances and the conditions a person is subjected to. James' thinking certainly extends its relevance to today's worldly conditions which can drive a society to extremes of self-indulgence followed by irrecoverable suffering.

In Ariya pariyeshan Sutta (discourse on noble experiments) the Buddha explained various meditation methods he practiced, yet he finally rejected them all because there is no truth to be found in extremes because at extremes it is difficult to distinguish between what real and illusion.

Jayathilleka, a Sri Lankan born philosopher, conclusively established that the Buddha held as true a version of correspondence theory, this was presented by evidence in the form of passages from the Majjima Nikaya (MN) Apannaka Sutta.

Correspondence theory states that a statement can be factually right but only if you are in affirmation with it would that statement be considered true. For example, factually there is another world, therefore one who holds the view that there is another world has right view.

On the other hand, if a belief occurs to him that there is no next world that would be a false belief.

From there onwards many false conceptions and statements would be made and that person falls into the wrong path. Buddha also considered that coherence and consistency are essential factors for judging the validity of an assertion. It has been shown in the MN Culasaccaka Sutta when especially engage in discussions and arguments one should maintain coherence and consistency throughout in order to maintain the validity and reliability of his assertion.

Buddha advised to Saccaka, a wanderer asking illogical and inconsistent questions, "Pay attention Saccaka, pay attention to how you reply. What you said before does not agree with what you said afterwards, nor does what you said afterwards agree with what you said before."

Verifiability is also anther characteristic of the doctrine. Logical positivists hold the view that if the meaning of a statement is devoid of verification, therefore its cognitive meaning of truth or falsity is meaningless.

The truths expounded by Buddha and his enlightened disciples are verifiable by perceptions and extrasensory perceptions. Buddhism accepts both sense and extrasensory perceptions as valid means for the assertion of truth. It is stated in AN that the doctrine and discipline shine when laid bare but not when covered. It is free from metaphysical, theological, or divine secrets of any kind. Unlike other Indian doctrines Buddhism was not taught to a selected few but meant for all and is open to all; for the good it is uncovered like the light. Buddha taught both conventional and ultimate truth.

Buddha didn't encourage men to waste time on metaphysical questions. For example, whether the world is finite or infinite? Whether the soul and body are identical or different? Whether the enlightened one exists after death or does not exist after death?

When one of his disciples made a demand for an answer by saying that he would leave the order if the Buddha could not answer such a question, he was given the following parable:

Suppose a man is wounded by a poisoned arrow. His friends want to take him to the physician, but he refuses until he knew the clan of the man who shot him, his name and caste, whether he is tall or short? What kind of an arrow and poison he used etc.? What would happen to that man? Surely, he would die. This is the case of the man who refuses to enter the path of liberation.

Buddha explained our minds are not capable of finding such answers therefore it would be a waste of time searching metaphysical questions that have no bearing on the quest of enlightenment. Buddha was pragmatic and clearly showed the limitations of life and also the rare opportunity of birth in human form. If a question or line of inquiry is not leading to Nibbana then Buddha wouldn't want to engage in such discussion, instead he taught the middle way.

In this way, the Western philosopher of science A K Warder said, "Buddhism has scientific attitude", going on to state that "the doctrine is not speculative but empirical". The Buddha emphatically rejected all speculative opinions and propounded no such opinion himself, only an empirical account of conditioned origination and the way to end unhappiness. There is however an exception, the Buddha answered with a different type of explanation to a wandering ascetic by the name of Vacca. He gave the following simile to the question of whether the enlightened one is born after death:

Suppose a fire which had been burning before you were going out. If someone were to ask you in which direction the fire had gone, north, south, east, or west, what would you reply? Vacca wisely answered "The question would not fit the case." We can say that a car travelled in the direction of north or that a fire was burning in my garden this evening; such assertions are possible when the object is no longer visible there. This predicate however cannot be applied to an extinguished fire. Applying the same principle would commit a categorical mistake, as such, rebirth does not apply to the enlightened one.

If we ask the wrong question or if the question is incorrectly formulated, then we get a wrong answer. This was the case in scientific research, whereby hypotheses made on limited observations can be proved by testing its validity. Yet though we may satisfy ourselves with the outcome and take our assertion to be the truth, if we apply that same principle under a different set of conditions it could give a completely different set of outcomes. We have come to tinker much with nature by this fallacy and made ourselves fools by assuming we have found the truth.

Buddha limited his teachings to the field of experience that are present here and now, and thus the laws and principles which can be readily explored. By paying wise attention to experiences through the six senses, by mindfulness and clear comprehension one can discover the truth.

"Truth should be realized by the wise, each for him-self."

"Only the meaning and purpose should be heeded well by the wise."
The Buddha

CHAPTER 7

# MINDFULNESS

I<small>F THE ENTIRE TEACHINGS</small> OF the Buddha could be reduced to one word it would be 'Mindfulness'.

Practice of mindfulness is regarded as the highest in the training methods because the culmination of wisdom is not possible without it. Wisdom is synonyms and co-exist with Insight, the capacity to gain an accurate and deep understanding of life experiences focused on mental experiences and based on corresponding external reality.

"Though one may live a hundred years with no true insight and self-control yet better indeed is a life of one day for a man who meditates in wisdom."

"All conditioned things are impermanent; when one sees this in wisdom then one becomes dispassionate towards the suffering. This is the path to purity." (Buddha's words of wisdom)

To experience, understand and realize the deep philosophical doctrines of Buddhism one has to practice mindfulness meditation. Meditation, otherwise known as mental training, is a pragmatic application of the teaching. Mindfulness is not a religion or philosophy, it is a technique to stay at present. It is a unique function of the mind. Past issues could only be resolved at the present and future resolution could only be made at present to make them effective. The Truth of life is discovered by the empirical evidence presented to the mind through mindfulness. Mindfulness is capable of observing the vacillation and understanding the other mental functions within the mind. An exposition of mindfulness and the method of practice is given in the discourse of the Four Foundations of Mindfulness.

Mindfulness is a mental culture, presence of mind, training the mind to be at the present moment, because the truth of life is not elsewhere. It has to be found here and now within the body and mind. With a penetrating insight into reality one can discover its true nature, conditions, conditional states, and conditioning forces that operate to give various feelings, thoughts, and emotions.

The cognition process makes us conscious of the world within and outside of us. By consistent and persistent practice one can awaken to the truth beyond conceptual thought. To be mindful you need an object, natural movement such as breathing or rising falling of the abdomen is often recommended. Unique to Thai culture is walking meditation where one can pay attention to foot movements and become aware of how the foot moves. There are six levels of awareness paying detail attention to dynamic movements as one walks to discover that intention is the driving factor of all movements.

The structure of an Insight meditation practice includes time for sitting or standing meditation, walking or movement meditation, rest and reflection on daily routine activities, mindful observation of both physical and mental activities are the objects of meditation. When mindfulness is well established then contemplate and observe mental movements present in the form of thought patterns, emotions, and mental objects such as attachment to sense pleasure, anger, and ill will, restless and worry, sloth and toper and sceptical doubt. By regular practice, meditator can overcome those hindrances preventing progress and clear the mind from confused thought patterns.

In his book "Understanding Our Mind: 50 Versus on Buddhist Psychology" (Parallax Press, 2006), Thich Nhat Hanh wrote, "Consciousness always includes subject and object, Self and other, inside, and outside, are all creation of the conceptual mind.

Buddhism teaches that we have created a conceptual veil or misty layer on top of reality, and we mistake that conceptual veil for reality. It's a rare thing to perceive reality directly, without distortion. The Buddha taught that our dissatisfaction and problems arise because we don't perceive the true nature of reality. Because of this reason ignorance beings acquires Karma.

Karma is formed in three different ways of mental, verbal, and physical actions through mind and sense avenues when there is strong intention to act upon the object in contact. Both attachment and aversion attract or reject objects respectively. Desire arises for pleasant and pleasurable objects and on the other hand mind is repulsive to unpleasant painful experiences.

Being mindful of the mind and five senses, notably sight sound smell taste and touch one can become aware of the formation, appearance, and disappearance of all phenomena that they are impermeant, unsatisfactory and without an enduring substance. Not knowing this reality, some, impose their views on others. Sometimes forcefully on their followers. This concept is extended to psychology and psycho analysis to understand personalities.

Excessively conceited or absorbed in oneself; self-centred, selfish desire to dominate make a person egotistical, and arrogant. Political psychology attempts to relate leadership traits of a person to his or her actions in a given situation.

It is an interdisciplinary academic field, dedicated to understanding politics, politicians and political behaviour from a psychological perspective and a psychological process using socio-political perspectives. Political psychologists use cognitive and social explanations to study the behaviour of politicians, the foundations for their beliefs, political dynamics between parties, and the outcomes of political behaviour.

If this foundation is not built on ethics and moral values, then the results of their decisions could be dangerous. According to Buddhism, personality is a product of the society, created through complex psychological factors.

Instructions and practical guidance of methods of insight meditation are designed to stay aware of the present for self-discovery of who you really are than whom you think you are. This helps us to deepen our connection to our direct moment to moment experience, cultivate continuity of mindfulness, and awaken the heart and mind for greater ease, balance, and clarity in daily life.

The mind has a function of cognition and create live 3D picture, largely an illusory formation.

When a sense come into contact with an object, there arise consciousness and variety of associated mental factors of feelings and emotions depend on the nature of that object and according to circumstances.

Reactive attitude to these formations multiplies emotions and thoughts and could go spiral out of control causing breaking social relations. Benefits of the practice can be seen here and now, how it expands our hearts and minds connecting us to the real world with love and compassion, overcomes our fears and self-doubt, and we thereby gain faith and trust in Buddha's teaching and turning to peaceful path of progress. When you start to see things as they are then it is easy to let go things that are not worth holding.

We have a freedom of choice to decide our path between that which is wholesome or unwholesome. The happiness or unhappiness we seek in the sense sphere is dependent on the sense object and our opinions which are coupled with judgments. A mind trained by introspective meditation is secure, peaceful, and stable. It is unshaken, even when affected by the ways of the world and when confronted with vicissitudes, namely the four favourable conditions and their opposites: profit and loss, praise and blame, prosperity and recession, happiness, and suffering. The awareness you may gain from the practice of mindfulness would clarify the causes and conditions of all mental and material phenomena, as such, wisdom will creep into your rescue.

The Buddha identified craving as the centre of all entanglement and suffering; on seeing this truth, it is wiser to turn away from causes and conditions of suffering.

"Lead by craving they run this way and then like an ensnared hare, so do men chase pleasure. Therefore monks, who wish his detachment, discard craving."

"There is no fire like lust. There is no grip like hate. There is no net like delusion. There is no river like craving." The Buddha (source: Dhammapada)

Being mindful by earnest practicing one can identify the craving and its supporting conditions. For example, we may get irritated if someone we dislike steps into our space, the unmindful reaction to such a situation could end up with an irrecoverable criminal conviction.

Buddha succeeded in attaining true permanent happiness outside of the sense sphere, reaching far from the mundane world to the supramundane world of happiness. He lived a life as an example to all. During his long ministry he propounded his doctrinal teaching in different ways to different people according to their level of understanding. Buddhism is not a philosophy as philosophy for its own sake. Buddhism is a way of life, applying doctrinal teachings to regulate man's conduct.

Buddha's last advice to his closest disciple venerable Ananda emphasizes the purpose of the master's endeavour during his forty-five years of ministry.

"Ananda the greatest honour one can give to me is to live according to my teaching".

Buddha is also known as *Thathagatha*. When he refers to himself, he used this term. It gives a broader meaning to the title of Buddha. Thathagatha has two root words "tatha agato and tatha gato", literally meaning, one has thus come, and one has thus gone. This is to emphasise one who has come to the real characteristic of dhamma.

One of his disciples was once staring at him, on this occasion Buddha advised him "when you see me you see dhamma and when you see dhamma you see me".

Buddha had awoken to the dhamma therefore he surpassed the world and became supreme. He thus perfected the ten Buddha training factors in three degrees of the same lineage as all past Buddha's with the same aspiration for the welfare of many by practicing generosity with an unbroken conduct of morality, requiring the renunciation of pleasures, and giving time to develop wisdom. He used his energy and efforts to continue the practice with patience life after life.

Always being truthful and determined, to practice loving kindness and equanimity for the welfare of others. He thus had superseded all other teachings of the world, by defeating his rivals, and shattering the ignorance of the world.

In contemporary India among the truth seekers of the day there were a variety of traditions and teachers, everyone claiming their teachings were the truth. There was thus a confusion of philosophical thoughts and ideas as different schools taught doctrines diametrically opposite to each other. For example, one school taught, "whatever a person experiences pleasant, painful or neither pleasant nor painful, that is all caused by what was done in the past".

Another school argued that these experiences were caused by a super being's act of creation, yet another school taught they were all without causes and conditions. They were skilled in debate and logical argument, like hair splitting marksmen shooting down the philosophical views of others to pieces with their verbatim. Their ideas were followed by a variety of social and religious practices and rituals. When asked to explain, or when cross examined and questioned by the Buddha they could not answer as to what established their own theories.

Thathagatha taught the middle way. He had deeper insight into the arising and passing away of dhamma according to their dependency on changing conditions, he also firmly established the path leading to the cessation of suffering. Buddhist schools of thought and culture evolved after the Buddha passed away. They adopted the doctrines of his teachings to suite their local culture and enriched them by opening avenues to relate its principles to people's day to day life, providing an opportunity to actively apply them.

Buddhist temples are the centres of Buddhist culture, and the order of 'Sangha' was founded based on the principle of exchange of goodwill by both monks and laypeople. For two thousand five hundred and sixty years this has continued without breaking its traditional values. Underlining this are three objectives, for the benefit of both the individual and society, helping others to achieve success, guiding, and encouraging them to develop their lives. This is the fundamental constitution of Buddhist societies, in this way all benefit from the cultivation of virtues. People with different skills give their services, time, and knowledge, such as artists, craftsmen, teachers, lawyers, businessmen, all donate their skills for the benefit of the community.

Material perfection through these conventional skills is achieved by not claiming their ownership or possession, the main principle of dhamma is to help overcome attachment thus reducing suffering. The purpose of propagating the dhamma is for the benefit of many in the world.

Over twenty-five years through his long association with the Buddhapadipa Temple, the writer has witnessed the fine aspects of Thai culture whereby they support each other to develop moral virtues, and to understand and practice dhamma on all three levels.

Mindfulness meditation practice is given priority that helps the meditator see things clearly as they are that is to say identify causes and conditionality of suffering and letting go the attachments and aversion. Insight mediational wisdom is to understand four noble truths and escape suffering. Cooling effect of being living in seclusion and withdrawal from tensed worldly activities one can immediately feel the difference of stress reduction, feel energised and resilient.

Four foundation of mindfulness is practiced by way of standing, walking, sitting, and lying down. During intense retreats, meditators are trained to be mindful from moment to moment on daily routine activities from morning to evening including eating breakfast and lunch.

These exercises are designed by masters of meditation to make meditators help develop self-awareness and stay connected to the present moment. Mindfulness makes activities slow down and one can pay close attention to details to become aware of mind body relation. Mindfulness of bodily movements, feelings, thoughts and emotions and consciousness are the four foundations upon which concentration and wisdom can be developed to a level to break the cycles of craving.

It can be combined with loving kindness and compassion in our daily interaction with others with shared connection, open our minds to understand suffering of others. Non-judgemental empathetic view of life forms including your own could be reached to overcome self-criticism and negative thoughts to arrive at a balanced, happy, peaceful state of mind within short period of time.

Mindfulness is now a common theme; it could mean different things to different people. Mindfulness Based Stress Reduction is a clinically proven application of meditation to emotionally vulnerable people by mental health professionals. Participants of retreats are able to manage stress, fear, anger, anxiety, and depression without addiction to medications. They can benefit from having less hospital visits and other professional healthcare providers.

When your mind settles you would be able to look deep into your own life and understand the obstacle and limitations that preventing your progress.

Insight meditation is an inward journey to discover one's potential, and the full development of one's abilities and appreciation for life. By further exploring transcendental knowledge, insight wisdom gained through mindful living, Buddhist philosophy all intersect to understanding purpose of life and you would be able to design your goals, moderate life-style, and plans, take practical steps to optimize for fulfilment and quality of life rather than giving it for chances.

There are many thousands of school children who visit the Buddhapadipa temple in London year after year, they are given an opportunity to freely question what they see, this maintains the historical Buddha's tradition of 'come and see' and 'free inquiry'.

Thathagatha had showed us the way to ferry from life to life safely without acquiring bad kamma *(karma)* or to undergo undue suffering. This is to acquire good kamma, literally meaning good actions conducive to understanding the true nature of life, impermanence, suffering and non-self. This is the path leading to the complete cessation of suffering and to true happiness.

Through experience as a meditation teacher, I have identified that the basic premise for the purpose of life is to seek happiness. Many people do not know how to find it. It was a misconstrued idea to think that true happiness is outside of us and depends on something else. Many people have lived in the sensory world believing that subjective pleasant experiences are happiness until they are dragged into an unsustainable, imaginary, fantasy world. When their world collapses, the happiness they had enjoyed vanishes without consolation.

Over time these habits become basic traits of their character, it is difficult for a person experiencing such a trauma to understand the way out of that situation. Buddhism is a complete change of paradigm. Buddhism is compared to a raft that facilitates the transition across a river from one bank to another.

# Part II

Fundamentals of Buddhist Ethics and Development of Western thought

# CHAPTER 8

# BRING LIGHT TO THE DARKNESS

Buddhist social philosophy and ethics are coherent systems that facilitate individuals in their search for inner peace and true happiness. It presupposes that life is suffering.

Suffering is not a supposition but real, it may not always be overtly apparent as when concealed by temporary enjoyment. From the time of birth to death we go through various types and stages of suffering, both physical and mental, the obvious one's being sickness, diseases, and injuries. But the suffering from gambling, drinking, and associating with evil friends are not immediately apparent.

Departure of a loved one is suffering, associating with unkindness is suffering. By objective observation we can identify a mass of suffering inherent in life.

People come to learn these things with the effect of hindsight.

This understanding of reality gives a real strength so that we may confront with the truth of suffering objectively and removing subjective opinions from it. By practicing insight meditation one can get a deeper insight into the truth of life. The truth of life could be stubborn, difficult to handle, only a one who grew up with wisdom might be able to face the real facts of truth concerning life that is suffering.

> *"We can easily forgive a child who is afraid of the dark; the real tragedy of life is when men are afraid of the light."* – Plato

Systems of interrelated dependence on each other, the harmony between the individual and society is essential to progress in life and to alleviate suffering as one cannot live alone. Buddhism recognizes family as the unit of society, family emotional welfare is important for both temporal and spiritual growth.

Ultimate human development leads to the full realization of truth with a complete understanding of interdependency within the physical world and all the other beings around us. When we understand reality there is a freedom within.

The characteristics of impermanence, conditionality and suffering in all phenomena are not apparent unless we objectively search for them. Misunderstanding reality creates conflict, stress, tension, and undue suffering to everyone in the ecosystem.

The interpretation of reality by different schools of thought has created a vast net of views which carries from the past to the modern world. These views that prevailed at the time of Buddha still exist, although the form of it may differ. Buddha's teachings remain valid to the modern world because there is nothing new to the world; man has not changed since then, and the cycle of suffering continues for sake of the wrong views we adhere to.

The worldwide financial crisis we are currently experiencing is due to the unsustainable economic model of debt driven consumption that ravages the world's resources, while building a stockpile of nuclear arsenal and maintaining them has eroded the wealth of all nations. A government meeting for the G20 summit was looking for a transition towards a sustainable economy, this involves nothing but the Buddha's advice to millionaire banker Anathapindika on how to invest in environmentally friendly projects that improves the welfare of the people.

In February 2022, Russian President Vladimir Putin's war of choice has added many uncertainties to the world economy that has been recovering from the prolonged worldwide Covid-19 pandemic.

Democratic leaders are now contemplating expelling Russia from the G20 community for their aggression displaying smart hypotonic weapons. Running up to Easter holidays in Europe, in April 2022, western countries added more sanctions on the Russian oil supply but there were no signs of slowing down the Russian offensive. On the other hand Russia has lot to contribute to the world economy.

Instead of spending on modern weapon development, there is much scope to engage constructively and investing in renewable energy new agricultural processers, new equipment to increase food production. Scientific knowledge can be used for economically efficient innovative surgical and healthcare industry to benefit the world. There are hardly any Russian brand names in global market.

Majority of Russian citizens outside main cities still live in World War II conscripted mentality to accept authority without question. They were not given an opportunity to move on, see the world and improve personal growth. While Philosophers, theologists, and psychologists are continuously trying to figure out the way to live up to our greatest potential, Russian leadership trying to go back in time to medieval ages.

Russia's GDP is largely made up of three broad sectors: a small agricultural sector that contributes about 5.6% to GDP, followed industry and service, which contribute 26.6% and 67.8%, respectively.

The initial transition period for Russia after the fall of the Soviet Union in 1991 was tough, as it inherited a devastated industry and agricultural sector along with a formerly centrally planned economy. The regime introduced multiple reforms that made the economy more open, but a high concentration of wealth still continued.

Russia's economic growth rate remained negative during most of the 1990s, before the start of the subsequent golden decade. From 1999 to 2008, Russia's GDP grew by at least 4.7% each year. This expansion made Russia one the fastest-growing economies. This growth, however, was mostly driven by the boom in commodity prices, notably oil. The Russian economy then grew at a decent pace for 2011 and 2012, but structural issues started to emerge that caused a slowdown during 2013. Evidently, Russia benefited by joining global economy.

In the year 2020, Covid-19 lockdown also reduced global demand for oil but gradually increased with successful global projects of vaccinations then driving oil price upwards. In February 2022, Russia once again invaded Ukraine. On Feb. 22, 2022, U.S. President Joe Biden announced sanctions against Russia in response to its military aggression against Ukraine, including the advancement of Russian troops into two separatist regions of eastern Ukraine. The administration noted this is the "first tranche of sanctions that go far beyond [the previous invasion of Ukraine in] 2014, in coordination with allies and partners in the European Union, United Kingdom, Canada, Japan, and Australia." (Investopedia August 2022). It is Russian authorities to decide to reduce hostility against Ukraine if they want to be a contributor and global leader and remain in G20.

After meeting with Vladimir Putin on 11 April 2022, Karl Nehammer, the Austrian chancellor, said he feared that the Russian president intended to drastically intensify the brutality of the war. In fact he did fire indiscriminately at civilian targets.

"The battle being threatened cannot be underestimated in its violence," Nehammer said. (New York Times April 2022)

War, in general, is very complex and all incidents cannot easily verify by independent journalists. Situations on the ground and at sea could be very different to the scripts issued by both the Ukrainian and Russian military.

The actual numbers of reported attacks, targets and casualties had been increased from both sides since the war started in February 2022. Russia expected to step up its operations escalating assaults in every possible way with its military and naval might despite obstacles they face in this faltering war when the flagship of its Black Sea fleet the Moskva sank after a catastrophic explosion and fire in mid-April 2022.

The primary aim of this Russian intervention in Ukraine is to eliminate the perceived threat of NATO, drive out American interference and restore Russian authority in the territories of Eastern Europe.

Our intelligence makes us very smart, but at the same time precisely because of that fact we also have more doubts, suspicions, and fears. By fear and mistrust, coupled with the ego, is the beginning to viewing others as a barrier to our freedom. In addition, many conflicts within the human family and within one's own family were born out of greed, hatred, and delusion.

The basis for all conflict is the clash of different ideas and views that our intelligence brings. In this way, intelligence shadowed by mistrust can create an unhappy state of mind.

Buddhist social philosophy is a branch of study providing us with a method to improve our actions, to live a happy life by applying its doctrines, principles and ethics as related to our own life, our family and world at large. If you have the determination, there is a real possibility of transforming the human heart to become a better person.

Theravada Buddhist teachings are directed towards the individual, we believe an individual is the key to all the rest. Many are affected by other people's views, opinions and other things happening around them, whereas authenticity and who you really are is everything and all that matters. For change to happen in any community, the initiative must come from that person.

You could be that exceptional person who could inspire others to bring light to the darkness.

Mindfulness meditation helps a person to overcome the inner struggle born of wrong views.

Clarity of thought helps to identify one's strengths and weaknesses to improve knowledge, skills and become a more productive person. If an individual can become calm, peaceful, and self-reliant, He or she can bring positive atmosphere to the family, to the community, and extend that goodwill to the rest of the world and help build a kind and braver world.

Although Buddhism has most of the aspects of philosophy, the question as to whether Buddhism is a philosophy becomes irrelevant if you know how to relate the teaching to your everyday life.

Understanding the four noble truths and living according to the noble eightfold path is the pragmatic application of its philosophical teaching, that is the way of life for many people in Thailand and other Buddhist countries.

The practical value of his teachings was sealed by the Buddha's last advice "the highest honour you can give me is to live according to my teaching."

Buddhist doctrines are profound and hard to glean, it requires determination and dedication.

For anyone who is seeking it, Buddhism also provides the path leading to the full realization of ultimate truth, beyond the conventional world to the highest and most sublime supramundane reality, 'Nibbana'.

I wish you all the greatest happiness.

*"Nibbanam paranam sukham".*

*Nibbaba is the greatest happiness.*

# CHAPTER 9

⸙

# WHY MORAL PHILOSOPHY?

T HE PURPOSE OF THIS DISCUSSION is to look at the origin and meaning of 'ethics' and 'morals' as they are understood in Western philosophy and Buddhism. In the West, the search for moral excellence can be traced back to ancient schools of philosophy at the time of the Greek civilization.

In Western thought Socrates was the first to question the subject of ethics, he also founded a school of thought which focused on speculative reasoning. However, in 399BC, Socrates was eventually executed on suspicion of misleading and subverting the youth.

Plato, his student, then took up this study, putting forward Socrates' work from a different angle. Aristotle who was a student of Plato developed this further, amalgamating a comprehensive system of Western philosophy. Their ideas are the foundation for modern Western ethics.

Ethics and morality are also a firm foundation of the Buddhist path to liberation. Buddha stated that the meaning and purpose of his teachings were more important than the teaching itself.

To understand the correct meaning, a comparative study of both Eastern and Western schools of thought can be useful. They serve as a collection of experience and evaluations concerning human behaviour.

The Buddhist view of behaviour is regulated by precepts which serve as guidelines, directing one's behaviour so that no harm is made to others. Observation of these precepts protect the practitioner and society alike.

In the Noble Eight-Fold Path the middle three training factors are regarding morality; the manner of mental, verbal, and physical actions so as not to produce adverse effects on the path of progress as one head towards the cessation of suffering.

Both Western and Eastern thought apply ethics to a wider field of social economic institutions, to achieve social harmony, economic development and reduce unnecessary suffering.

The Development of Ethics is a selective historical and critical study of moral philosophy, an enquiry into social justice. Over many centuries these ideas have been developed by prominent philosophers and scholars to includes topics of moral philosophy as they have developed historically, including the human good, human nature, justice, friendship, and morality.

The methods of moral inquiry have changed to include virtues and their connections to ethics and morality.

Freedom of will and free inquiry was valued over aristocratic power; political freedom, responsibility and reasoning was widely accepted by the Western Enlightenment movement. In parallel to Christian values, ethics were integrated within social institutions.

During the period of economic decline in Europe these valuable ideas were suppressed by extremists who took over political power. This resulted in World War II and large-scale atrocities that reappeared at the end of the Cold War era. These historical events are lessons from which to learn.

It is important to disentangle moral philosophy from politics, allowing us to clear our minds from confusion, giving more space for self-examination of our thoughts and emotions and to have a better understanding of human nature. Development of science and technology helps economic growth, but it has limitations as to what extent we could or should exploit nature.

The 5th Generation computer technology has a direct impact on our personal lives, affecting our social life, making us isolated or excluded in some ways, which in turn has direct consequence on mental health issues born by self-isolation.

Social Media and news platforms have contributed immensely to stay virtually connected, informed as well as transmitting disinformation causing schism, racism, and social division. Recently in the US, the disinformation campaigns waged against political oppositions has caused severe damage to the social fabric and has undermined trust in American democratic institutions, voting system to the extend threatened the personal safety of police officers on duty. It is always wiser to check the provenance of information you read, assess the passive or active danger involved in it and find facts from fiction to avoid making mistake.

Fake news can destroy trust, damage learning culture and sap curiosity. Dissemination of disinformation subvert the integrity of those platforms and regular exposure to them erode the moral foundation and weaken the user. We must choose what is really beneficial to mankind and redirect ourselves by inference to past experience. The manifold aspects of senses play an important part in the critical theory of knowledge, but it is left in an obscure and perplexed position by political narratives. We need a new vehicle to express thoughts whilst respecting our great moral problems.

Psychological phenomena cannot be understood by reasoning alone, it requires a human mind to open different perspectives and to explore the truth concerning human nature. The aim of writing this book is to provide insights into a multi-faceted understanding of ethics whilst highlighting its practical value by addressing the complex issues surrounding moral dilemmas within the context of real-life situations.

The latter part of the book examines various historical and contemporary events which have had a significant impact on our lives and threatened the value of democracy. These incidents are analysed to seek patterns and causes of human behaviour through various conflicts in the context of anthropology, social science, economics, and political sciences. These analyses of behaviour are discussed with the advantage of hindsight of major wars, conflicts and incidents that have shaped our world. Examples of these events illustrate key concepts of literature in social science disciplines.

By these we can attain an in-depth understanding of the psychology of human behaviour as an integrated whole, not only as societies in different geographical regions but also the global impact of the modern world. In so doing, the writer refers to different epistemological approaches of the West and East, particularly focusing on the Buddhist theory of knowledge and personality.

Illustrative political narratives have a long continued historical connection leading up to present day dilemmas. A pattern seemingly emerges in conformity with repeating cycles of history at different intervals of time.

This book aims to provide an insight into ongoing, unresolved conflicts to find a permanent solution to men's common factor of suffering, thus lend itself towards illustrating broader lessons to be learnt.

Having thought deeply about how to improve behaviour and enrich cultural values, these conceptually defined ethical values, philosophical views, and related examples, describe in detail what is right and wrong as is still relevant to today's divided world.

Many mistakes and errors in judgment have led to manmade disasters and obstructed the development of the Age of Enlightenment's thinking. Through these narratives that cross the philosophies of the West and East, the book explores professional attitudes to and experiences of new policy initiatives in economics, politics, social governance, and service development.

More generally, it investigates contemporary phenomena in view of benefiting mankind and releasing them from ideological dogmas going forward. The book draws on particular well recognised published literature from the field of ethics to that of epics, to investigate and decouple politics from ethics.

The part II of the book is mainly structured around the following questions: What is right and wrong? Does the end justify the means? What is the true path to peace and happiness? What are the psychological barriers to true happiness? What are the potential pitfalls and how can these be avoided?

# CHAPTER 10

# NEED FOR AN ETHICAL INQUIRY

T HE KEY THEMES OF WESTERN ethics typically look at recent development theories concerning social justice, human rights, and basic economic needs. Since these three are closely interrelated to the field of human behaviour, the enquiry into its ethical dimension mostly reflects man's struggle to meet his ends and the justification of the means he employs to satisfy his basic economic needs.

The main focus is thus on the "ethics of the means", how behaviour manifests and what methods are applied.

First, this enquiry implies the asking of many questions to establish what ethically desirable development is, including its effects and consequences to man himself. In one of its articles, The Routledge Encyclopaedia of Philosophy summarises Development Ethics as an ethical reflection on the ends and means of socioeconomic change. Further, it says; "Development ethicists agree that the moral dimension of development theory and practice is just as important as the scientific and policy components. What is often called 'development' - economic growth, for instance - may be bad for people, communities, and the environment. Hence, the process of development should be reconceived as a beneficial change, usually specified as alleviating human misery and environmental degradation especially in poor countries.

Still, development ethicists do not yet agree on whether their ethical reflection should extend to destitution in *rich* countries or aspects of North-South relations apart from development aid. Other unresolved controversies concern the status and content of substantive development norms. Finally, agreement does not yet exist as to how the benefits of and responsibilities for development should be distributed within and between countries."

For example, we can decide to cutdown rainforests and build a factory that employs many locals, producing plastic bottles, and exporting them to rich nations.

The questions then raise an investigation into the level of pollution it causes during the process of production, distribution, and the final product itself. Is this ethical? What would be the long-term effect to the environment we live? It questions not only the goal but also the ethical limits in their pursuit. Negative externality is a recognised economic concept. A negative externality exists when the production or consumption of a product results in a cost to a third party those who are outside the economic transaction. Air and noise pollution are commonly cited examples of negative externalities. By this line of enquiry, the concept of "sustainable economy" was developed.

Such large developments are undertaken or granted by government legislation and treaties which now require those in authority to consider the ethical dimension of development projects.

Government contracts are passed on to private agents through a mechanism of legal tender.

Denis Goulet one of the founding fathers of this discipline of principal agent relation, argued in his *The Cruel Choice (1971)* that "Development ethics is useless unless it can be translated into public action. By public action is meant, action taken by public authority, as well as actions taken by private agents by having important consequences for the life of the public community. The central question is: How can moral guidelines influence decisions of those who hold power?" In his book, Denis calls into question the moral values of the decision maker and his ability to make an ethical judgment.

New light was shed onto the dilemma of Development Ethics by Terence Irwin, a Professor of Ancient Philosophy at the University of Oxford England.

In his recent book titled 'Ethics Through History', Terence asks a range of questions, which takes the topic a few steps further from mere economic development: What is the human good? What are the primary virtues that make a good person? What makes an action right? Must we try to maximize good consequences? How can we know what is right and good? Can morality be rationally justified?

Terence Irwin addresses such fundamental questions as central debates to the 21st century.

Terence brings back Aristotle's values to the political platform, reiterating that a leader's virtue and ethical values impact the masses.

Relating this to meta-ethics, which was first introduced by Immanuel Kant, Terence provides a link between eighteenth-century rationalism, sentimentalism, and twentieth-century debates concerning the metaphysics and epistemology of morality. These debates are explored in Moore and Ross' meta-ethical discussion on utilitarian theory. They argue that man is motivated to undertake a task by the satisfaction he derives from pleasure or pain, rejecting anything that brings pain.

Pleasure as a utilitarian theory can be traced to the time of Cyrenaic, around the turn of 3rd century BC in the Greek school of moral philosophy. This school of thought was founded by a follower of Socrates, it held that the pleasure of the moment is the criterion of goodness, and that the good life consists in rationally manipulating situations with a view to their hedonistic (or pleasure-producing) utility. They believe that we can have certain knowledge of our immediate states of perceptual awareness, e.g. that I am seeing a flower, and derive pleasure from the object at the present moment.

However, they concluded that we cannot go beyond these experiences to gain any knowledge about the objects themselves or the external world in general.

Cyrenaicism deduces a single, universal aim for all people, pleasure, not only sensuality but pleasure can also be from associations, friendships, and justice.

These are only useful insofar as the pleasure they provide, thus they believed in the hedonistic value of social obligation and altruistic behaviour. Yet, in explaining his behaviour, none of these theories attempt to investigate the psychological aspects related to man's thinking and their subsequent manifestations. Some of the arguments prefigure the positions of their school of thought, such as distinctions between the incorrigibility of immediate perceptual states versus the uncertainty of belief about the external world.

These became key distinctions to the epistemological problems confronting philosophers of the 'modern' period. Descartes equated thinking and perception to the person who experiences it and was unable to go beyond the experience.

In ethics, they advocate pleasure as the highest good. Furthermore, bodily pleasures are preferable to mental pleasures, pursuing whatever will bring us pleasure in the moment rather than deferring present pleasures for the sake of achieving better long-term consequences.

This appears not be practicing moral values but instead proliferating a materialistic view of life.

Open criticism and reasoning, as encouraged by the late Western Enlightenment, changed political leadership into a new and more extremist face. This adopted fascist views that attempt to create an economic power by a new world order, using military means to achieve their political ambitions.

Fascism is a form of far-right, authoritarian, and ultra-nationalist movement. It is characterized by dictatorial power, strong regimentation of society and the economy and forcible suppression of any opposition. It came to prominence in early 20th century Europe, where the violent destruction, atrocities, and harm they did was far more damaging than any economic utility produced.

This proved the futility of war, violating human rights, social injustice, and defeating the objective of Development of Ethics through economic development.

# CHAPTER 11

# HISTORICAL BACKGROUND OF ETHICS

## Socrates 469 BC – 399 BC

SOCRATES IS CREDITED AS ONE of the founders of Western philosophy. One of the best-known sayings of Socrates is "I only know that I know nothing." Among the elite class of people in Athens this paradox made him wiser since he was the only person admitting it, and who was aware of his own ignorance.

Socrates believed the best way for people to live was to focus on self-development rather than the pursuit of material wealth. He encouraged community spirit and friendship as the best way for people to grow. Socrates' ideal stated that "virtue was the most valuable of possessions"; therefore, the best way to live is to be in search of 'the Good'.

Socrates broke down problems into a series of questions, these were then applied to examine key moral principles such as Good and Justice.

This method of inquiry was his most enduring contribution to the development of modern Western philosophy. Socrates had the opportunity to escape his death sentence, but he voluntarily accepted it without fear, and by agreeing to the laws of Athens he implicitly proved his own philosophy and principles.

## Plato 428 BC – 348 BC

Plato was the most devoted student of Socrates. Indeed, he put forward Socrates' ideas and focused his contribution on the field of ethics. All Plato's work reflected the loyalty he had to his teacher, and he always maintained that Socrates' execution was unjust.

Plato's famous allegory of the cave exemplifies the Socratic idea that reality is unavailable to those who only use their senses. It is by ignorance that we accept only the shadows as real, rather than investigating observable phenomena to access a higher insight into reality.

According to Socrates, physical objects and physical events obscure the true vision of reality, they are shadows of their ideal or perfect forms. Shadows are temporary and inconsequential epiphenomena produced by physical objects; in the same way, physical objects are themselves fleeting phenomena born of more substantial causes.

Socrates' teaching, as magnified by his student Plato, resonates with the Buddha's enlightened view of the transcendental dependency of phenomena. However, Socrates and Plato inadvertently applied their theories to social justice and politics. Socrates admitted that few climb out of the cave, as most people are said to be living pitifully in a den of evil and ignorance.

Socrates formulated his political ideology based on reasoning. He further stated that a philosopher has reason, will, and desires that, unite in a virtuous harmony, only such virtuous men are fit to rule. The concept of the "philosopher-king" was used to justify these personal and political beliefs.

## Buddha 566 BC – 486 BC

In Northern India, Prince Siddhartha Gautama became enlightened and introduced his doctrinal teaching for one's liberation from all suffering. For six years he struggled to find the truth, but he eventually discovered the "middle path" thus rejecting the extremes.

Of his own efforts, the Buddha achieved omniscience, dispelling ignorance through his esoteric knowledge. He founded a school of thought based on the Four Noble Truths by which he formulated his teaching.

'Buddha' is an honoured title meaning "the awakened one" which is given to a self-enlightened sage.

In the discourse of The Great Forty (Mahacettarisaka Sutta), the Buddha stated that worldly knowledge is clouded by defilements. By practising the Noble Eight-fold Path one can dispel ignorance and obtain a complete understanding of things as they really are without any admixture of any personal view on it. Knowledge gained through sensory perceptions is not perfect. One may see but not necessarily understand their experience as the result of craving, conceit, and wrong views. These conceptual proliferations are the shadows of reality.

Buddha explained how this sensory knowledge is acquired, how one sees the world through one's experiences and how these are based on the situation of one's mind.

The Samyutta Nikaya (SN) gives the analogy of a magic show:

"What essence, monks, could there be in a magic show? Even so, monks, whatever consciousness be it past, future, or present, in oneself or external, gross, or subtle, inferior, or superior, far, or near, a monk sees it, ponders over it and reflects on it radically. He would find it empty, hollow, void of essence. What essence, monks, could there be in consciousness? Form is like a mass of foam and feeling but an airy bubble. Perception is like a mirage and formations are like a plantain tree. Consciousness is a magic show, a juggler's trick."

Buddha discovered the principles behind behaviour and clearly set the path of progress to its improvement, guiding it towards mental development.

These behavioural guidelines or disciplines are known as "vinaya".

## Aristotle 384 BC – 322 BC

Aristotle was Plato's student. Along with Plato and Socrates, Aristotle contributed most towards forming a firm foundation to Western philosophy, encompassing morality and social governance.

Aristotle studied almost every subject available at that time and made significant contributions to most of them, including politics. He became the head of the royal academy of Macedon in Greece. He was also the teacher of Alexander the Great and taught two other future kings Ptolemy and Cassandra, restating the Socratic idea of the "philosopher-king".

Aristotle claimed that "only one thing could justify a monarchy, and that was if the virtues of the king and his family were greater than the virtues of the rest of the citizens put together".

Aristotle considered ethics to be a practical matter rather than knowledge for its own sake. He taught that the purpose and function of life in the human form is to direct all actions towards 'happiness' and 'wellbeing', for both the individual and society. Such attainment necessarily requires good character, virtue, and moral excellence.

Through education and training, the human character can be improved to a level where one chooses to follow higher pursuits, Buddhism shares the same sentiment of practical wisdom. When people come to live life in this way their intellect can develop towards the highest possible human virtue.

The Buddhist order of 'Sangha' (order of Buddhist monks) represents the Buddha's practical wisdom of moral excellence; monks are to search for happiness through virtuous conduct.

There are two hundred and twenty seven precepts that they adhere to in order to regulate their behaviour.

## Immanuel Kant 1724 AD – 1804 AD

Immanuel Kant was a German philosopher born in Prussia, now Germany. Like Aristotle, Kant studied many disciplines including ethics, religion, law, aesthetics, astronomy, and history. He was brought up in a strict religious family background and was a keen student from an early age. Kant studied at the University of Konigsberg and showed an interest in the philosophical investigation of mathematical physics, from this he moved on to rationalism and idealism. His most important work on ethics was *Metaphysics of Morals* published in 1797. In this book, he introduced a new line of thinking which aimed to resolve the problem of moral philosophy.

He stated, "it always remains a scandal of philosophy and universal human reason that the existence of things outside us… should have to be assumed merely on faith, and that if it occurs to anyone to doubt it, we should be unable to answer him with a satisfactory proof."

Empiricists argue that knowledge comes through sensory experience, while the rationalist's approach maintains that reasoning and innate ideas are required to gain knowledge. Kant's argument was that reasoning must be tested and balanced with experience without any subjective judgment held against it. Anyhow, he failed to explain the connection between the senses and our intellectual faculties. Experience is associated with a sequence of feelings, images, and sensory perceptions. Kant argued that reason can remove the scepticism of ideas that are born by perceptions.

His ideas influenced many thinkers in Germany and later spread to the rest of Europe. In England, his previous work, '*Groundwork of the Metaphysics of Morals*' was more highly accredited. In this earlier work, Kant searched for a supreme, unconditional law of reasoning. This could have been prompted by his interest in transcendental, idealist philosophy; that time and space are not materially real but merely the ideal, a prior condition of our internal intuition. This idea presupposes existence of an absolute reality.

Kant studied the English scientist Isaac Newton's great contribution to the field of mathematics and physics published in 1687. Thus, knowledge of mathematics and physics definitely contributed to his inferential knowledge of absolute reality because time and space are abstracts for the scientific mind. His idea of Meta-Ethics is closely connected with an idealist philosophy which suggests that there is an absolute value to ethics. As a matter of fact, the German scientist Albert Einstein developed a theory of relativity and the absolute, however, he explored it in a very scientific way, applying that knowledge purely to the material world of nuclear science.

## Jean Jacques Rousseau 1712 AD - 1778 AD

Another development of ethics is the natural rights movement which developed alongside the Western Enlightenment. In 1762, Jean-Jacques Rousseau a Swiss philosopher published his most important work on political theory, *The Social Contract.*

His opening line is still striking today: "Man is born free, and everywhere he is in chains." Rousseau agreed with his contemporary

English philosopher John Locke on the theory which states that the individual should never be forced to give up his or her natural rights to a king.

Locke argued that personal identity (the self) "depends on consciousness, not on substance" nor on the soul. We are the same person to the extent that we are conscious of past and future thoughts and actions, in the same way as we are conscious of present thoughts and actions.

This gives us ownership of our contribution to society, our dignity and belongingness.

Natural rights theory holds the view that individuals have certain rights, such as the right to life, liberty, and property. This is determined by virtue of their human nature rather than on account of prevailing laws or conventions.

Rousseau's political philosophy influenced some aspects of the French revolution. The idea of natural rights reaches far back in the history of philosophy and in legal thought. Arguably, it was already recognised by ancient Greek thinkers such as Aristotle, who argued that citizens are equal by nature and thus have the same natural right to political office.

This idea of political freedom concerning individual property rights was gradually developed through heated debates stretching from medieval times to the modern-day. Personal right of freedom of expression and human rights are developed from this early contribution of learned thinkers.

## Hugo Grotius 1583 AD – 1645 AD

Hugo Grotius, a 17th -century Dutch legal scholar and philosopher, was the father of modern international law and a staunch opponent of war. He was a proponent and defender of natural law having been influenced by Rousseau. Grotius maintained the position that natural law is the basis of natural rights: "Civilians call that faculty a 'Right', which every man has to his own…This right comprehends the power, that we have over ourselves, which is called liberty…It likewise comprehends property…Now anything is unjust, which is repugnant to the nature of society, established among rational creatures. Thus, for instance, to deprive another of what belongs to him, merely for one's own advantage, is repugnant to the law of nature."

This statement echoes the teachings of many religions which say that it is not right to steal or take what is not given.

In the process of working out these ideas Grotius saw the value of human life, he saw war as the destruction of this 'Right' to another human being.

Historically, war was a perfectly legitimate government policy. Rulers pursued wars to spread their religion, to gain territory, seize assets, or in other ways expand their power, this clearly contradicted their religious teachings.

Hugo Grotius declared that war was wretched and that it harmed all participants. If war can't always be avoided, Grotius pleaded, then at least the killing and destruction must be limited. He believed "it is folly, and worse than folly, to want only to hurt another...War is a matter of gravest importance, because so many calamities usually follow in its train, even upon the head of the innocent. So, where counsels conflict we ought to incline toward peace...It is often a duty, which we owe to our country and ourselves, to forbear having recourse to arms...[the] conquered should be treated with clemency, in order that the interests of each may become the interests of both."

Grotius originated international law as we know it, refining principles to help improve the prospects for peace. He declared: "On whatever terms peace is made, it must be absolutely kept from the sacredness of the faith pledged in the engagement, and everything must be cautiously avoided, not only the savouring of treachery, but that which may tend to awaken and inflame animosity."

Grotius' thinking greatly influenced later changes in political power and the reconfiguration of government structure and policies. He was one of the first to define expressly the idea of one society of states, governed not by force or warfare but by actual laws and mutual agreement, to enforce those laws recognising individual rights.

## Thomas Hobbes 1588 AD – 1679 AD

The English philosopher Thomas Hobbes (1588-1679) is best known for his political thought, and deservedly so. His vision of the world is strikingly original and still relevant to contemporary politics. His main concern was the problem of social and political order: how human beings can live together in peace and avoid the danger and fear of civil conflict. He poses stark alternatives: we should give our obedience to an unaccountable sovereign, a person or group empowered to decide every social and political issue. Otherwise, what awaits us is a state of nature that closely resembles civil war – a situation of universal insecurity, where all have reason to fear violent death and where rewarding human cooperation is all but impossible.

Hobbes' was concerned by the unfair competition for economic resources. At that time, there was no fair market to distribute economic resources or goods to benefit many. As laid down by Romans, people were compelled to accept authority without questioning its validity. Society was divided into a class structure of ruling class and working class; by adopting a capitalist mode of production, one provided the capital and the other provided the labour.

A few years after Hobbes, John Locke developed his own work from the terms of debate that Hobbes had laid down: how can human beings live together when religious or traditional justifications of authority are no longer effective or persuasive?

How is political authority justified and how far does it extend? Are our political rulers unlimited in their powers as Hobbes had suggested? And if they are not, what system of politics will ensure that they do not overstep the mark by trespassing on the rights of their subjects?

## René Descartes 1596 AD – 1650 AD

René Descartes was a French-born philosopher, mathematician, and scientist who spent a large part of his working life in the Dutch Republic, initially serving the Dutch States Army of Maurice of Nassau. He is credited as the father of analytical geometry, the bridge between algebra and geometry. His mathematical projections helped to understand the physical universe and outer space through a different perspective.

One of his unique contributions to mathematics was infinitesimal calculus, an analysis that influenced Isaac Newton. It helped Newton to develop a unique foundation of Calculus and Newtonian Approximation that largely improved Engineering Mathematics today.

Application of these advanced mathematics increased the understanding of properties of the material. It vastly contributed to modernization and continuous engineering improvements. The curiosity of the mind is complex, and mathematics helps to resolve complex problems. Space travel, jet engines, rocket science, modern weapons, and missile technology are developed by applying this complex engineering mathematics.

Descartes was also one of the key figures in the Scientific Revolution. More importantly, he offered a new vision of the natural world that continues to shape our thought today: a world of matter which possesses a few fundamental properties and interacts according to a few universal laws. This natural world includes an immaterial mind that, in human beings, was directly related to the brain; in this way, Descartes formulated the modern version of the mind-body problem.

In metaphysics, he provided arguments for the existence of God, to show that the essence of the matter is extension, and that the essence of mind is thought.

Descartes claimed early on to possess a special method, which was variously exhibited in mathematics, natural philosophy, and metaphysics, which in the latter part of his life included, or was supplemented by, a method of doubt. His philosophical arguments influenced Baruch Spinoza to critically investigate religious texts in-depth, challenging contemporary beliefs, and in so doing, developing a new foundation for ethics.

Few of Descartes famous quotes are "It is not enough to have a good mind; the main thing is to use it well. The greatest minds are capable of the greatest vices as well as of the greatest virtues. If you would be a real seeker after truth, it is necessary that at least once in your life you doubt, as far as possible, all things." (The Stanford Encyclopaedia of Philosophy).

https://plato.stanford.edu/entries/descartes/

## Karl Heinrich Marx 1818 AD – 1883 AD

An alternative socio-economic theory based on socialist communism and revolutionary ideas were introduced by Karl Heinrich Marx.

Marx's thinking clearly has distance from the lineage of early philosophers, he postulated an economic system and society that emerges from technological advancement. Marx's critical theories about economics, politics, and philosophy were introduced in his volume of books *The Capital* (1867 - 1883). This work came to greatly influence subsequent intellectuals in economic and political history, it divided the world into two completely different views.

Due to his controversial political publication, he became stateless and was in exile with his wife and children in London. His thinking was much influenced by class systems which were seen as unfair treatment of the working class man's struggle to meet his ends. He thus envisioned a classless society in place of ethical enquiry.

An economy based on technological production became the priority. This resulted in the industrial revolution that accelerated production output in the hope of alleviating poverty in the world.

Yet, in the 21st-century we still doubt whether man's welfare depends solely on economic models and political ideology alone, or whether development ethics brings balance that has a greater benefit for happiness. Looking back, it seems obvious the world was on a collision course with different political views, some were 275 resolved with dialogues and some with military means. It is worth revisiting Hobbes' question of whether human beings are purely selfish, self-centred, self-interested, and egoistic. No matter what side they play in the economic tug of war, this aspect of human behaviour should be investigated in relation to the inquiry of ethics.

It may be argued that Karl Marx overlooked this factor, contributing to a conflict of interest that "the self" is, or should be, the motivation and the goal of one's own action.

Egoism has two variants, descriptive and normative.

The descriptive (or positive) variant conceives egoism as a factual description of human affairs; to say that people are motivated by their own interests and desires and cannot be described otherwise. The normative variant on the other hand, proposes that people 'should' be so motivated, regardless of what presently motivates their behaviour.

Altruism is the opposite of egoism. The term "egoism" derives from "ego," the Latin term for "I" in English. Egoism should be distinguished from egotism, which means a psychological overvaluation of one's own importance, or of one's own activities.

Behavioural economics is a new subject increasingly becoming useful in studying how people make decision other than being rational. It combines elements of economics and psychology to understand how and why people behave the way they do in the real world. It differs from classical and neoclassical economics, which assumes that most people have well-defined preferences and make well-informed, self-interested decisions based on those preferences. Behavioural economics examines the differences between what people "should" do and what they actually do and the consequences of those actions. The study can explain people choices not only in economic decisions, but also social behaviour related to preferred political ideology.

# CHAPTER 12

## DEVELOPMENT OF WESTERN THOUGHT

IMMANUEL KANT'S ESSAYS GREATLY INFLUENCED the 18th century Western movement of Enlightenment.

According to Kant, the Enlightenment was "Mankind's final coming of age, the emancipation of the human consciousness from an immature state of ignorance and error." During this period, freedom of thought was valued more than the authority of traditional institutions, customs, and morals.

Kant argued that without human freedom, moral appraisal and moral responsibility would be impossible. Kant believes that if a person could not act otherwise, then his or her actions can have no moral worth. His arguments set a new direction on the political philosophy and discussions on the social contract.

He was the author of '*Critique of Pure Reason*'.

It can be argued that the application of reasoning originated in the time of Britain's remarkable scientific and economic development.

In the mid-18th century, the public overwhelmingly supported this reasoning, and it became the primary source of legitimacy and authority. This period is thus also known as the Age of Reason.

During this time people were beginning to critically question the authority of institutions and the political power of the aristocracy.

This resulted in two major revolutions on both sides of the Atlantic, the American Revolution in 1776 and the French Revolution in 1789. After these landmark events, many political systems in the world recognised Human Rights, thus changing their constitutions to reflect this.

Freedom of thought changed the social and cultural out-look. Many public decisions were made by applying rational and critical thinking. This included having genuinely open discussions, whereby public opinion was also sought to avoid confrontation.

Scientific inventions and innovations made a major contribution to economic development at this time. The invention of the printing press allowed the communication of ideas to spread rapidly, giving the opportunity for public debate and also a public space for sociability. The public was thus empowered to critically examine the state and religious authority. People discussed these matters openly in coffee shops and salons.

Western political ideology moved into a new phase with the German philosopher Karl Marx's critical evaluation of Capitalist economic systems. His ideas were mainly trialled in the former Soviet Union. The application of science and technology along with a mechanistic worldview, achieved higher levels of production and distribution of wealth through the Industrial Revolution to eliminate poverty.

The economic concept of self-sufficiency brought the countries that adopted this model to isolate themselves from the rest of the world, therefore, freedom of thought suffered. It soon progressed towards the dictatorial self-interest of the leaders, contradicting the value of 'common concern'. For example, during Stalin's regime (1924-1953) the main emphasis was on power and controlling the freedom of his own people. Karl Marx critically examined economics and social sciences but did not sufficiently consider human behaviour under different economic conditions and its relation to political power. He assumed a democratic society might evolved from redistribution of wealth and predicted a violent transition of power to working class people which actually happened in Russia.

His theory was strong enough to shift the political power from the elite class to the working class and to create a 'classless' society but failed to give a method for sustainable social order. That is to say, the psychological factors of human behaviour were overlooked.

In autocratic societies, state power was used to crush democratic opposition, as was any protest against the violation of human rights or civil liberties when asking for more freedom. It thus evaded the opportunity to resolve conflicts through intelligent dialogue and peaceful means.

Covert surveillance and instruments such as Public Order Ordinance were used to keep any public demonstrations under control. These harsh measures retard authentic thinking, gentleness, and creativity of the mind, therefore making it dull, depressed and allowing cruelty to surface instead making far left revolutionary views not support progressive reforms, especially those seeking greater social and economic equality defeating their principle objectives. At that time reasons for any irrational behaviour were unknown to the world whether in a clinical setting, at workplace or in public domain.

Sigmund Freud was the first person to investigate a clinical method for treating neurotic patients in the Western world. He was an Austrian neurologist who studied human behaviour and is the founder of Western Psychology to become the Goethe Prize winner in 1930.

His initial study of psychoanalysis was further developed by his successors into what is now known as *psychotherapy*, a new way of understanding the human mind and behaviour.

## World War II 1 Sept 1939 – 02 Sept 1945

Many valuable ideas from the Age of Enlightenment were doomed during the period of economic decline in Germany 1933-1945. It turned into fascism and the development of racist, nationalistic ideas, pinnacle with extreme Nazism when Adolf Hitler took power in 1933.

The Jewish community, as well as various other minority groups in Germany, were persecuted and subjugated to large scale atrocities. Hitler's Nazi regime eliminated any opposition, even within his own race. They arrested religious priests who disagreed with Nazi ideology. For example, Protestant pastor Karl Friedrich Stellbrink and Catholic priests Hermann Lange, Eduard Muller, and Johannes Prassek were arrested and murdered in Hamburg prison in Nov 1943.

Hitler was the main cause of World War II, the man who led Germany to war with the rest of the world.

Hitler's military decisions brought a catastrophic effect to Germany and to the rest of the world. At the same time in Italy, there was radical, nationalistic political changes were developing under the leadership of Mussolini who sided with Hitler to gain his share of the war. Mussolini wanted to invade France but did not have enough fire-power. He was waiting for his opportunity, building his army, tanks, and artillery batteries. He waited for Hitler to advance first and then struck when France became weak.

It was a race to gain nuclear supremacy after German Jewish physicist Albert Einstein developed his general theory of relativity. He was awarded the Nobel Prize for Physics in 1921 for his services to theoretical physics. But Einstein left Germany when Hitler came to power in 1933 to become an American citizen and advisor to American President Roosevelt, he was worried that Germany might develop a nuclear weapon.

During 1922-1932 there were ground-breaking discoveries in Nuclear Physics after Danish physicist Niels Bohr's theories of atomic structure and quantum mechanics were introduced.

Bohr received the Nobel Prize for Physics in 1922. His assistant, German physicist Werner Heisenberg improved 'quantum physics'. Werner introduced the 'uncertainty principle' that largely contributed to the development of nuclear energy. He was awarded the Nobel Prize for Physics in 1932.

There was a considerable amount of work carried out in atomic research in many Western countries including England and America. It was Bohr who suggested that atomic secrets should be shared by the international scientific community in order to speed up the results, to which many top-ranking politicians in the West disagreed. Hitler had many secret scientific programmes, the primary interest of which was in gaining nuclear weapons. His army forced scientists to carry out various experiments including gynaecology experiments to create a superhuman race.

Sigmund Freud branded Hitler as 'crazy and mad'.

The Nazi atrocities are well documented in Australian novelist and playwright Thomas Keneally's *Schindler's Ark*, the story of Oskar Schindler, a compassionate entrepreneur's rescue of Jews during the Holocaust with which the author won the Booker Prize in 1982 for non-fiction Biographical novel.

In 1993, an American historical drama film was produced based on Thomas's exceptional story.

Titled 'Schindler's List', it reproduced the emotional experiences of Jewish civilians' struggling to survive under the Nazi regime. The horror and brutality of war were again recreated in the 1977 epic war film 'A Bridge Too Far'. Based on the 1974 book written by historian and journalist Cornelius Ryan, it describes the hard and harsh conditions of war, the lessons to be learnt from failed military strategy and the value of unity of American, British, and European nations against the common enemy of humanity. The story also depicts the failed military strategy of code name 'Operation Market Garden'. The consequences of ignoring the aerial reconnaissance and the fate of 35,000 including British servicemen in the battle operation was very well demonstrated by the film director Richard Attenborough.

The Nazi symbol of the 'swastika' is a diagram of nuclear physics known to the Aryan race which lived in ancient India, it represents the time travel of electron particles. Aryans were a very intelligent superhuman race that Hitler was dreaming to recreate. They possessed advanced scientific and mathematical knowledge that they used to live in harmony with nature without exploiting it.

The theory of nuclear physics is embodied in their ancient religious scriptures. The theory of ultimate power was metaphorically presented by way of various divine gods. Their ancient Indian dancing contains the language of mathematics and the way they understood the behaviour of subatomic particles. This knowledge is not accessible by reasoning alone. Aryans applied their knowledge to find peace and understand the divine nature of beings.

It is presented in 'Vedanta' as a sacred religious teaching. Hitler misunderstood the Indian philosophy that teaches the equal and opposite forces of all phenomena.

On the other hand, in 1940, Japan made a pact with Germany and Italy to cooperate with their own political, economic military adventures to create a new European and Asian world order excluding the Soviet Union which was seems unapproachable. This was known as the Iron Pact.

Soon, other Eastern European countries joined them. Among them were Romania, Hungary, and Bulgaria which had already been allied in World War I.

Japan had a completely different tradition of a military ideology centred on the loyalty for their Emperor that promulgated feudalism. They had a vision of creating a Greater East Asian Empire by military means. Japan went on ruthless missions attacking American and British military interests in Asia Pacific to fulfil their ambitions.

The nuclear theory was tested by dropping the first atomic bomb on Hiroshima and the second one on Nagasaki within three days. This bombing had a devastating effect on Japan that ended the War in Asia. In Europe, Mussolini was captured and summarily executed by the Italian Resistance Movement. War in Europe ended when Nazi Germany signed its instrument of surrender after Hitler committed suicide.

## Cold War 1947 AD -1991 AD

After the War, the world united to rebuild what had been damaged in terms of the economy and cooperation between nations. However, the nuclear know-how soon divided political ideology and led to the Cold War due to the advancement of science and technology. The North Atlantic Treaty Organization was created in 1949 by the United States, Canada, UK, and several Western European nations to provide collective security against the Soviet Union.

America and its allies led by NATO (North Atlantic Treaty Organization) as well as the Soviet Union (USSR, Union of Soviet Socialist Republics) went on an unprecedented arms race which came close to nuclear conflict. America took the lead with the capability of a nuclear first strike and advanced virtual military command base technology.

In 1987 the former president of the USSR, Mikhail Gorbachev, understood the danger and damage to his economy, he, therefore, came to a settlement by attempting to bring democratic reform to his country.

While the superpower conflict continued, it also triggered conflicts in small nations. They appeared to be separatist movements or political unrest, but the underlining strategies were very complex.

Both superpowers wanted to control the small countries for their own geopolitical interest. For example, beginning in 1983 in Sri Lanka, the Tamil Tigers fought for a separate independent state. They were initially supported by invisible Russian powers through their partners to destabilize the country and prevent American military interest in that region. Militants were trained in camps in Libya. Lately, the Tigers have carried on the civil war under their own momentum. Tamil diaspora is still strong and influential in many western countries.

Sri Lanka is a tropical island in the Indian Ocean which is the hub of Asian maritime and the gateway to Far East Asia, one of the prime targets for the geopolitical interest of superpowers. Neighbouring India and Pakistan also had superpower interests and gained nuclear weapons.

The Cold War was not just a race for sophisticated nuclear weapons, Russians had a strategy to control world oil and energy resources through their partners in the Middle East. Iraq secretly built their weapon capabilities during the long battle with Iran, while the Russians provided them with superior weapons in return for monopolising the oil industry.

Iran, also known as Persia, is one of the oldest civilizations in the world with a long history of revolutions, it became the Islamic Republic in the 1979 revolution, regaining its ancient identity by overthrowing the pro-Western authoritarian monarchy and the Shah's regime. It was a relatively nonviolent revolution based on the concept of Guardianship of Islamic Jurists, a theory based on Shia Islam, it surprisingly produced profound changes at great speed with relative prosperity resulting in the exile of many Iranians. Iran survived without any internal or external revolt, gained nuclear know-how and in the centre-stage of world politics was seen as the winner out of all odds of revolutionary catastrophic failures and Middle Eastern turmoil. Political analysts have speculative views on Iran's nuclear capabilities as a threat to Israel and their intelligence service has already responded by assassinating the country's top nuclear scientist in broad daylight. This increases the tension in the region and weakens relations, pointing fingers at the US for providing Israel with modern military technology and capabilities.

Iran has economic sanctions from the west whilst struggling with the Covid-19 pandemic in March 2020, they were without basic medical protective equipment and medications. Coronavirus cannot be eliminated by nuclear power. It requires good relations with the world's best pharmaceutical companies and best medical scientists in the field. This is a good example of what is more important to our survival than carrying weapons and investing in military capabilities or building bridges with other nations for economic prosperity and social reforms. (Source: Al Jazeera Media Network February 2021)

The American-led allied invasion of Iraq was known as the Gulf War I & II and started in 1991. During 1970 -1989 Kurdish people fought for autonomy in northern Iraq. They were the main victims of the Iran-Iraq War (1980 -1988) who suffered systematic attacks and genocide at the hands of the Iraqi Army. There were other minority groups also affected in that region such as Assyrians, Shabaks and Jews. The Iraqi regime was accused of possessing weapons of mass destruction and was invaded for the second time in March 2003 to finish the job and secure its oil supply.

Public opinion in the UK was divided on these invasions. Since then, the political leadership in many Middle Eastern countries have continued to change. For example, Egypt's President was forced to resign in February 2011. In Libya, the regime was changed by a military conflict in Oct 2011. The unrest in that part of the world is not yet fully settled.

At present, there is an uprising in Syria causing tension with neighbouring Turkey. This may soon further change the political outlook in the Middle East.

## Israelis' resettlement after World War II

The Israelis' resettlement and returning to their home-land after World War II was a carefully controlled and remarkably successful process. Since the State of Israel was declared they have been resilient to all threats from unwelcome attitudes of all neighbouring Arab counties.

The Middle Eastern region is known for many stubborn conflicts. For more than three decades, the Palestinians have sought an independent state in East Jerusalem, the West Bank, and the Gaza Strip; territories seized by Israel in the 1967 war with Arab states.

Israel withdrew from Gaza in 2005 but imposed a blockade after the militant group, Hamas, seized power two years later. Recently, in 2020, the normalization of relations between Israel and two Arab states, the United

Arab Emirates and Bahrain, is, on the face of it, of good and beneficial development.

This has risen from decades without any substantive progress, combined with growing frustrations in many Arab capitals over the corrupt and demanding Palestinian leadership. This has steadily pushed the Palestinians to the background. The Palestinians have lost their veto power over Arab-Israeli relations in recent developments in the region. This isolation and the natural economic and geographic difficulties of resettlement in Israeli occupied land will make Palestinians agree to a peace process or it will be a continuous conflict.

"Middle East peace" has long referred to the peace between Palestinians and Israelis only.

Balancing power in the region is sensitive to this constructive relation, with both claiming equal rights to the same piece of land in the West Bank which Israel want to annex. The threat of annexation had the potential of inflaming Arab citizens and will not reach peace. Ulterior motives and national interests are inherent elements in politics and international relations, as long as men have hidden political agendas, it is hard to expect lasting peace in any agreement irrespective of who is brokering it. (Source New York Times 06 September 2020)

During May 2021 Covid-19 period, again war irrupted between Israel and Palestine but this time it was settled quickly because of wise American intervention under Biden administration.

The history of the Cold War goes back as far as 1947.

American President Harry Truman advocated the foreign policy to support free nations who were resisting attempted subjugation by armed minorities or by outside pressures. His doctrine was based on the reasoning of safeguarding the security of the United States from 'totalitarian regimes' coercing 'free people'.

The Doctrine was informally extended to be the basis of the American Cold War, as a policy to counteract the direct threat from Soviet Russia.

Americans had a backlash when applying this theory in Vietnam (1965-1973). It was implemented as a wider strategy to contain communism from being spread in the region of Indochina. The Vietnam War was part of the Cold War era. Military conflict ended in April 1975 with the 'Fall of Saigon' to the hands of the communists.

The War cost heavy casualties in all parties involved including Laos and Cambodia.

The strategy of the Cold War changed with the advancements in electronic engineering. The switch from analogue to digital completely changed communication technology and weapon capabilities, as such the invention of new missile technology.

Today, the superpowers are capable of striking at each other with precision over great distances at the press of a button. The Americans came up with a new idea of shielding themselves from any possible missile attack. This was known as the Strategic Defence Initiative (SDI). It was a futuristic idea based on George Lucas's Star Wars film. American senators argued to increase their defence budget but some of them described it as insanity.

In 1951, a British science fiction writer Arthur C. Clark wrote *The Exploration of Space* (1951) and *The Promise of Space* (1968). In these books, he predicted the use of satellites for communication. Arthur was a Royal Air Force pilot (flight lieutenant) and radar specialist in World War II. He was involved in the early warning radar defence system and contributed to the success of the RAF's Battle of Britain. During his flights, he tested radar reflections and thought about a way to improve space navigation.

The idea of satellite communication was born in search of space relay stations.

Arthur's knowledge of mathematics and physics largely contributed to his imaginings in science fiction. His ideas were further developed in both fictitious and military applications. SDI is an elaborate application of Arthur's imaginings.

The later collapse of the USSR resulted in the breaking away of Balkan states.

The former Yugoslavia was part of the Eastern Bloc in the Balkan region which disintegrated with a violent eruption of racial hatred and genocide of Bosnians. This was a campaign of ethnic cleansing carried out by Bosnian Serb forces in 1995, they specifically targeted Bosnian Muslims and Bosnian Croats.

The conflict started in 1992 with the Referendum for the independence of Bosnia and Herzegovina which was a multi-ethnic country. The Referendum was rejected by the political representatives of Bosnian Serbs causing the ethnic division. These atrocities were similar to the incidents which happened during World War II but on the grounds of securing the sovereignty of the borders of Serbia.

Use of nuclear energy to produce electricity is also much debated. In 1986, there was a catastrophic nuclear accident in Chernobyl nuclear plant in Ukraine (USSR). An explosion in one of the reactors released large quantities of radioactive contamination into the atmosphere affecting a large area of the Western USSR and Europe.

A similar disaster occurred in Japan's Fukushima Daiichi nuclear facility which belongs to Tokyo Electric Power Company following the March 2011 earthquake and tsunami. It was a nuclear meltdown due to a series of equipment failures causing the cooling system to go out of control.

These accidents suggest that nature is more powerful than our knowledge, that we cannot guarantee a complete control over it, and that our reasoning has limitations. These lessons dictate that we adopt more concern before the use of nuclear power either in commerce or military application. There are no ethical criteria to measure the use of technology. Some of the technology developed during war times is now used in commercial applications. For example, the use of mobile phones and the internet has spread like wildfire in civil communication and social networking.

It was initially developed for Cold War military network communication and now further developed with Fifth Generation computer technology (5G). This social trend is struggling to make a positive impact on social and economic relations. If wisely used, it can be a good tool to build social harmony with improved social inter-action, similar to the impact on the communication of ideas that newspapers and printing had when they were invented.

The Socialist ideas that emerged through reasoning and questioning turned into fascism and totalitarianism when worker's parties and political powers were led by self-centred military personnel. This change caused the world to experience many man-made disasters. Self-interest is a delusion that can blind otherwise all-embracing humanity. Irrespective of political narratives, reasons given, war is a situation of mass destruction and cause for human suffering. In the modern world it is theatre to showcase power and strength displaying waste of human resources otherwise would have been utilized to improve human condition.

The war in Ukraine started in Feb 2022 has led to outrage in the West, it may last for weeks or even years. An account of this development was discussed in the Chapter 1. As the horror of war unfold, the United Nations General Assembly voted to suspend Russia from the Human Rights Council for abrupt violation of human rights. Both U.S and E.U. tightened trade sanctions against Russia. The moves came as evidence grew of atrocities committed by Russian forces, including intercepted radio transmissions in which members of the Russian forces discussed carrying out indiscriminate killings north of Kyiv, the capital, according to two officials briefed on an intelligence report. Russia has denied any responsibility for atrocities.

This unfortunate situation and unnecessary human losses that resurfaced Cold War issues would have been avoided if Russian leaders were prepared for constructive dialogue to resolve their differences with the West. (New York Times 08 April 2022)

Marxist economics had gone from a blind alley to tyranny; the fundamental difference between the capitalist and socialist economic models is that socialists rejected the property rights of an individual. This principle contradicted the freedom people were yearning for since the feudalist medieval time.

Their attempt to improve their standard of living came to induce more suffering to all. On the other hand, capitalism is driven by greed for wealth, exploiting natural resources, and labour to satisfy the theory of man's unlimited needs. Allocation of resources is still much debated. There are many market failures and government failures in all economies. For example 2007-8 banking collapse highlighted limitations of economic theories.

The Americans promoted monetary economics and increased the speed of money circulation.

Credit purchases were encouraged, unsecured loans and subprime asset mortgages were sold in unregulated financial markets which increased consumer spending and capital investments to an unsustainable level of economic growth. People re-mortgaged their houses and spent on unnecessary luxury items. This artificial economy and lifestyles were maintained for a considerable length of time, exploiting world wealth.

During the last few decades, the West adopted a boom and bust economy. Those civil, economic, and military concepts during the Cold War era were based on unrealistic imaginings and people were driven towards a mirage of reality.

At the end of the Cold War, the world economy plummeted into a recession causing crisis in the Banking and financial sector. Many regimes were guilty of hypocrisy and countless atrocities, causing people to repudiate them. They sought a system that includes the consideration and fairness to all people.

# CHAPTER 13

## VLADIMIR LENIN'S NEW ECONOMIC POLICY 1921

THERE ARE ETHICAL PRINCIPLES THAT when consistently and systematically applied can determine what is right and wrong. It is often possible that people become so immersed in their political activities or revolutionary cause that they do not recognise whether the way they are directing people is consistent with established ethical, moral, and economic principles.

People can blindly follow ideologies that are taught in a given philosophical thought or doctrine inspired by a leader. Economic policies that are derived from these doctrines are not necessarily practicable when applied to real-life situations. These policies change from time to time, adapting to newly adopted political ideologies.

New Economic Policy (NEP) is the term given to a re-vised economic strategy developed and introduced by Vladimir Lenin in the early 1921 after the Bolshevik Revolution in 1917.

It was masterfully designed to bring capital into the state, which it did, and to help economic prosperity. The NEP ended the policy of grain requisitioning and introduced elements of capitalism and free trade into the Soviet economy. This was done, in Lenin's words, to provide "breathing space" for the Russian people. Under the NEP, Russian farmers were once again permitted to buy and sell their surplus goods at markets.

This led to the emergence of merchants, retailers, and profit-makers - the characteristics of which are found in a free-market economy introduced by Adam Smith, a Scottish moral philosopher in his famous "The Wealth of Nations" – 1776 the book to describe the industrialised capitalist mercantile trade system.

During the civil war, these activities would have been punishable by harsh death sentences. The NEP was welcomed by many Russians who had endured years of requisitioning, shortages, hoarding and restrictions on free trade. Not all revolutionists agreed to this business and economic model, so it created ideological tension and divisions amongst the ranks of the Communist Party. Many Bolsheviks interpreted it as a surrender or retreat towards capitalism.

The new Economic Policy reintroduced a measure of stability to the economy and allowed the Soviet people to recover from years of war, civil war, and governmental mismanagement. The small businessmen and managers who flourished in this period praised the changes made by the NEP.

The Russian revolution changed all that could be changed, including all religious interference with communist political social governance. The most profound of the changes was the nationalisation of capital. They seized farmland, factories, mills, railroads, banks, and other properties with no compensation to owners. Peasant's harvests were forcibly requisitioned by the state, with the idea that it would be evenly distributed.

Lenin found himself in a difficult position when the unemployment rate skyrocketed. Lenin underestimated the problems within the country, not only economically but socially as well.

Karl Marx had not addressed clearly human behaviour under different economic conditions but assumed that people would accept social changes without questioning the hard and harsh consequences of this sudden impact from capitalism to socialism.

Lenin made the mistake of taking it for granted that the current government and its people were economically equipped for such a conversion straight from Imperialism to dive into full-blown Communism. This economic deprivation increased the risk of rebellion or a counterrevolution by the far-right Bolshevik regime and revolutionary Marxist groups.

When looking for an alternative economic theory, Lenin seems to agree with other prominent economists in Europe.

Friedrich Hayek is a famous economist born in Vienna, Austria, in

1899. Hayek is considered a major social theorist and political philosopher of the 20th century. His theory on how changing prices relay information that helps people determine their plans is widely regarded as an important milestone achievement in economics.

This theory is what led him to the Nobel Prize. He is well-known for his numerous contributions to the field of economics and political philosophy. Hayek's approach mostly stems from the Austrian school of economics and emphasizes the limited nature of knowledge. He is particularly famous for his defence of free-market capitalism and is remembered as one of the greatest critics of the socialist consensus.

The New Economic Policy was cleverly created in order to cure a time of dire economic failure, famine, and unemployment. The mistake was made in transitioning straight from Imperialism to Communism, which, according to the basic economic and social laws, cannot happen. As a result, a new approach was made which incorporated the collective effort, capitalism, and service to the State all in one. Yet again it proves the utilitarian theory, that people reject painful conditions, hardship, and accept appropriate economy that would increase comfort and pleasure.

Naturally, the NEP was not intended to be a permanent fixture in Soviet economy or politics, but rather something of a steppingstone, as well as a way to improve the economic state by the utilization of capitalism, but with a Communist twist. Despite the free markets and the chance for free trade and sales, the economy would still be subservient to the State and the main goal of the capital brought in by the NEP would be to strengthen the State, in this regard Lenin has taken a moderate view of economics.

This was the right thing to do at a difficult junction of decisions, doing what he perceived as best for his people and its party in order to prepare them for the real benefits of Communism.

History suggests that expansion of ideologies, doctrines, and empires are common to all those who hold such views no matter what principles they uphold characterised by slogans, banners, flags, and iconic symbols.

Communism without exception under Lenin and Joseph Stalin had a massive expansion programme. For this end, foreign trade and foreign capital investment were permitted through carefully measured leasing of certain enterprises. Before such ambitious and optimistic endeavour began, they had to address the burning domestic issues of dire economic failure that had affected the workforce of industry and farming sectors.

As an emergency short-term policy, capitalist market mechanisms were accepted to bridge the old Czarist economy and the envisaged Communist economy. This hybrid policy of capitalist economy and communist policy was strategically tailored with a strong political-philosophical thread, stitched onto the social fabric to ensure that capitalism would not lead to imperialism. The success of introducing a capitalist taste to the Soviet economy allowed them to agree with neighbouring states to accept a communist ideology for the expansion and consequently build the USSR.

When introducing the NEP, Lenin showed the ingenuity of Communist doctrines. He replaces capitalist self-interest with "The Principle of Personal Incentive and Responsibility", to benefit many by rounding people to accountability. It includes paying taxes to the government but promises it to be a small amount, taking into consideration the hardship of the war-torn economy. So, he puts a great amount of trust and faith into his people on behalf of the state, showing the importance of a leader's integrity no matter what doctrine, you follow.

Once again, using the wise words of the genius behind this intelligent plan, "We must see to it that everyone who works devotes himself to strengthening the workers' and peasants' state" (Lenin, 72). He was able to gain more of an understanding of the devotion, passion, discipline, and almost obsession with the State, its well-being, and, most importantly, the Soviet People.

By wise responses, he avoided counter-revolutions but built unity among his people. Vladimir Lenin believed that after having experienced the consequences of instant Communism, a stable, successful economy would be harvested with time, the length of which was unknown and had no limit. He did not live long enough to make it happen.

The Soviet nationality policy for Central Asia in the early twentieth century was the acceleration of a modernisation programme of the Russian Empire. It began with the Tsar: Emperor Nicholas II (Nikolay Nikolayevich) in the late 19thcentury, who expected all his subjects to obey him, but he did not expect non-Russians to become Russians.

He detested the Poles *(Polish)* because they had been disloyal subjects and revolted against him, this exemplifies the pride and dignity of

Russian nationalism. However, building socialism in a region of multi-ethnic, multilingual and multireligious communities was difficult, where intellectual knowledge was only based on limited orthodox religious texts.

New Communist regime's challenge was to introduce modern concepts of trade practices, industries, and farming technology to these tribal societies, this required stable long-term multi-ethnic policy instruments.

In the beginning, the Communist Party did not have a predetermined nationality policy. Over seventy years with many alterations they struggled to form a consensus and keep everyone faithful to the central Russian control. The national delimitation of the Central Asian republics was a complex task, setting the autonomy of self-governance through federal states and implementing a practical policy under common Soviet and Socialist identity was a tremendous effort.

There were many indigenous people in the territory of Russia. These arbitrary borders set by the union authority did not correspond to cultural or linguistic boundaries. In some cases, these even divided a single nationality, resulting in the displacement of people outside of their own territory, in some ways, these ethnic groups were marginalised avoiding sedition.

From the central hub of Moscow, it was more of a divide and rule strategy rather than the Marxist ideology of nationalism. It ignored the psychological impact on people's lives, their cultural meaning, including social norms and values. This was mitigated by promoting "titular national cultures", giving some consideration to the anthropology perspectives of these societies. There are valuable ethical principles to be learned from anthropology such as Do No Harm. Be Open and Honest Regarding Your Work. Obtain Informed Consent and Necessary Permissions. Lenin was wise to integrate those values to build nations. Within these institutionalised nationalities, individuals had to perceive themselves as belonging to the nationality of the titular nation they found themselves in, regardless of whether it actually corresponded to their own.

Moscow's indigenisation policy provided state-controlled benefits such as education, housing, and employment to these people keeping them in their side. The policy agreed upon by Lenin and Stalin to form the union was formulated on the theory that once nationalism was institutionalised, the class division would emerge with knowledge workers.

Additionally, nationalism was a natural stage for society to experience before becoming modernized; for example, Japan and Singapore are industrialised social systems that have systematically developed over a period of time based on improved professional work ethics. These modern societies are motivated by capitalist business models and are driven by rule-based social ethics containing elements of feudalistic loyalty to the State.

Emphasizing nationalistic views would ultimately drain it from the minds of people, causing it to fade away and be replaced with a unified state. The last premise for this policy was in response to Russian chauvinism, exaggerated or aggressive patriotism, similar to Western white supremacists, which was seen as a greater danger than local nationalism. They did not want their policies to be seen as Russian imperialism and so inevitably the status of Russians in the USSR would have to be curtailed to further cohesion of the state.

During World War II and the Cold War era, these Republics considerably invested in their military and equipped themselves with modern weapons in response to the superpower's arms race, however, this was to the detriment of the social and economic welfare of their people. For example, the Balkan Federation was formed with an emancipation that unified the region, this was later disintegrated with violent eruptions of racial hatred.

Lessons were learnt from previous mistakes of the Marxist view that nationalism was a powerful mobilising ideology. The collapse of the Ottoman Empire and the dangers of their own previous identity of Russian Empire greatly helped Mikhail Gorbachev to take early steps to devolve the USSR. Through foresight, Gorbachev persuaded the Union to agree to democracy and successfully disintegrate the former USSR. Instead of democracy, Russia has now adopted an autocratic leadership style.

The Republic of Uzbekistan is one of the breakaway Central Asian nations of the former USSR. It is known to have been in the region's cradle of civilization for more than 2000 years.

Uzbekistan is the home to spellbinding magnificent landmarks of Islamic architecture and preserved character of ancient cities set in the midst of snowy mountains. It is linked to the Silk Road, the ancient trade route between China and the Mediterranean. Since its liberalisation, the Uzbek economy has been in a gradual transition to the open market, with foreign trade policy being based on import substitution. In September 2017, the country's currency became fully convertible at market rates.

Uzbekistan is a major producer and exporter of cotton. They inherited the gigantic power generation facilities of the Soviet era and with abundant resources of natural gas, Uzbekistan has become the largest electricity producer in Central Asia. It has come to gain the World Bank's higher rating for economic growth.

The neighbouring Kazakhstan is another emerging economy in the region, with a large-scale modernisation programme for economic transition. Kazakhstan has a land area equal to that of Western Europe but one of the lowest population densities globally. Strategically, it links the large and fast-growing markets of China and South Asia to those of Russia and Western Europe by road, rail, and a port on the Caspian Sea.

Since gaining independence from the former Soviet Union, the country has transitioned from a lower-middle-income to an upper-middle-income status in less than two decades, moving to the latter group in 2006. Since 2002, GDP per capita has risen sixfold and poverty incidence has fallen sharply, thus significantly improving the country's performance on the World Bank's indicator of shared prosperity. Kazakhstan's economy has been in the upper reaches of the moderately free category for the past four years. GDP growth has also tracked steadily higher during this time. Its largest export commodities are oil and gas which contribute 75% to the national income.

The fallout of the Covid-19 pandemic has hit the economy more than the crises in 2008 and 2015.

The pandemic halted global activity in the second quarter of 2020 which depressed global demand and consequently price of oil, which is Kazakhstan's main commodity for export.

The pandemic also significantly depressed their domestic economic activities in 2020. GDP contracted by 2.8 per cent over January-September 2020, compared to a 4.1 per cent increase in the same period of 2019. The Kazakh government acted early to contain the spread of Covid-19. A global economic slowdown in 2020 has much affected economic growth. Kazakhstan has a strategic direction and potential for diversification of the economy toward downstream processing industries by diverse and mixed export markets.

These include agribusiness, mechanical engineering, and petrochemicals, which could promote technology and skills transfer along with job creation and fund in-flows with existing trade agreements. (World Bank reports September 2020)

These land block countries are much safer and easier to control by coordinating the efforts to fight the pandemic, impose quarantine control, and provide support to those people whose lives and livelihoods were affected by coronavirus or the consequent emergency restrictions.

The country has risen to international competition with many talented performers like multitalented classical and contemporary singer Dimash Kudaibergan, who is known for his exceptionally wide vocal range in twelve different languages. Kazakhstan is the first county in the world to locally produce Russia's Sputnik V Covid-19 vaccine after pharmaceutical company Karaganda Pharmaceutical Complex (KPC) received government approval to make the jab. (The Moscow Times 16 February 2021)

These examples show that countries can prosper and gain economic freedom when they become independent of extremism, ideological dogmas, and superpower interventions for their military interests. On the other hand, small nations cannot invest in infrastructure development on their own, they need aid from the World Bank and International Monetary Fund which are funded by rich super-powers. We need a middle ground for economic success rather than the extreme ideologies that ruined us.

The world is awakening to the Truth and Middle path propounded by the Buddha, that there is no solution in extremes. Covid-19 has brought new challenges that encourage us to look closer at humanity and with compassion, it has shown just how fragile economies can be when immobilised by a virus threat.

It has already been confirmed by the pandemic that unity and cooperation among nations are more important in facing a common global threat to mankind than investing in weapons that only bring destruction and suffering. Many developing countries apply the NEP with additional elements of monetary economics.

New Economic Policy in the modern world refers to economic liberalisation, relaxation in the import tariffs, deregulation of markets, opening the markets for private and foreign players, and reduction of taxes to expand the economic wings of the country. However, over the past few decades the gap between the rich and poor has widened, and over-exploitation of nature has largely contributed to environmental pollutions, greenhouse effect, rising sea levels, melting glaciers, flooding, plastics in the seabed, and many natural disasters. There are calls for a sustainable economy from intellectual and scientific communities, but none has materialised yet.

Political rhetoric speeches are convincing but often they over promise and under deliver. State provision and providing public goods is needed to avoid market failures and missing markets. On the other hand well intentioned legislations and government interventions often acts against the interests of those it is intended to serve. Government failure occurs when an intervention lead to a deeper market failure or worse a new failure may arise. In other words intervention creates further inefficiencies, a misallocation of resources and loss of economic and social welfare. There are many examples of total government failures in underdeveloped countries because of polices might have ineffective in meeting their aims or there were hidden agendas of corrupted politicians circumvent their own policies. None of these ideologies have addressed the dividing line between inequalities and insecurities facing the world today, whilst adhering to wrong views is the cause for political chaos.

The world's resources are limited, economic and business cycles have a limited lifespan, in principle, we have to learn to share and care for each other nationally and globally. The faster we consume, the sooner we will face economic depletion of finite resources.

Through these narratives of political-economic doctrine, with the corresponding evidence in the real world, we see clearly that none of these ideas formed by reasoning alone are sustainable or long-lasting, sooner or later they must come to an end because there is nothing that can escape the truth of impermanence.

Man's true happiness, welfare, peace, and prosperity need a more profound dimension of ethical principles and moral values integrated into social governance to achieve a real deal of peace and economic prosperity.

Indigenous societies have survived for many centuries under harsher economic conditions and oppression because their superior and richer ethical values and customs have helped them to live through their difficulties with attuned to nature, this is incomprehensible to western thought let alone to communist regimes. For example, consumption of cheap alcohol, heavy drinking and smoking is recognised as demerit goods that produce negative externalities destroying lives in economics but a common feature in Russian society.

It is not too late to understand and appreciate such authentic indigenous values and integrate them into the modern world and benefit from them.

Buddhism and its rich culture are based on nonviolence, it is such a valued social philosophy based on its timeless truth, on being all-embracing and adaptable to enrich any society regardless of religious beliefs.

Western moral thought is much entangled with economics and politics. Economics and leadership address the issues surrounding morality at a particular interval of time. The struggle for survival is a prominent feature of this, adopting whatever means necessary to meet the end goal, preserving the right to live while obeying political authority. During the past decades there were many conflicts repudiating political authority, this was extended to the international political stage including superpower's interventions of civil wars.

It can be very useful to separate ethics from politics to ascertain the true understanding of moral philosophy and human nature with a view to achieving one's true human potential. People are motivated by many reasons, the questions we might ask ourselves are: for whose interest and for what benefit does our motivation stem? Can we act without motivation? Can a human being only be motivated by his or her interest or could there be a common ground with regards to other people's interests?

Such an in-depth inquiry into man's entire substratum of mind and human nature could be found enumerated in the ancient text of Pali Cannon propounded by the enlightened Buddha Gautama.

These texts have now been translated into English and many other European languages for further research.

# CHAPTER 14

# MODERN DEVELOPMENTS

As PHILOSOPHERS APPLIED THE CONCEPT of natural rights to the secular world, the focus shifted from rules concerning individual behaviour towards the claims of rights that individuals could make against the state.

The Bill of Rights (1689) is a landmark Act in the constitutional law of England that set out certain basic civil rights and clarifies the role of a constitutional monarch. It set out the rights of Parliament, certain rights of individuals including freedom of speech in Parliament. These ideas reflected those of the political philosopher John Locke, and they soon became popular in England.

By issuing the Declaration of Independence, adopted by the Continental Congress on July 4, 1776, the 13 American colonies severed their political connections to Great Britain. The American Revolution was an ideological and political revolution that changed the world's political landscape setting a milestone achievement of political independence from imperial Britain, paving the way to the United States (U.S.).

Bill of Rights comprises the first ten amendments to the U.S. Constitution added further specific guarantees of personal freedoms and rights. Since then, constitutional reforms concerning freedom is an ongoing process to adjust to the contemporary needs not only in the U.S. but in many counties that choose to adopt this democratic system of parliament.

## US Moral Crisis

Abraham Lincoln was credited as the greatest American president for taking the country through its biggest moral, cultural, and constitutional crisis in its history. Its sudden and unexpected dissolution happened soon after his inauguration as the 16th president of the United States (1861) when seven of the then 31 states already voted to secede from the Union.

The Union's military victory in the Civil War was not inevitable but became overshadowed by disagreements of other Confederate presidents and Lincoln's displeasure of slavery largely contributed to the division. While he welcomed differences of opinion, he did not shirk his responsibility. In a mid-19th century world dominated by aristocracies and monarchies, only in the United States was it possible for a man of such a humble background to rise to be head of state. In his view, the insurrection of slaveholders jeopardized the survival of their experiment in democracy and social mobility.

Lincoln was a statesman of principle, integrity, and vision, he was a confident and experienced politician as affirmed by his convictions and ideals. He built a good relationship with people, especially the military commanders. Lincoln overruled generals who strayed into politics.

He attended daily briefings with them, thus addressing critical issues in a timely manner. Lincoln understood his command was essential and a had central part of achieving success in conventional warfare. Having developed a carefully crafted ordinariness over his 30 years as a career politician, his White House was open to all visitors and petitioners.

Confederates attempted throughout the conflict to negotiate a peaceful coexistence between the independent slaveholders' republic and the United States in the post-Civil War. His strategy was to win the war first and then to establish the Union. He gave responsible strategical positions to his rival contestants. In withstanding this effort and persevering against a determined military enemy, Lincoln left three noteworthy lessons about leadership: When fighting a lethal foe on home soil, he expertly managed his top politicians; he related well with people, and he dealt clearly with the military as commander-in-chief.

His master wisdom of politics was conveyed by his great speeches, he used familiar words and phrases from Shakespeare and the Bible to present fighting the war both as a sacred mission to achieve God's aims and as a universal, ideological imperative: to save republican self-government for the world.

Ultimately, Lincoln successfully enlisted political rivals, generals, and the people to support the Union's cause and won the Civil War. In order to accomplish this great task, the president had to simultaneously inspire, delegate, and establish clear lines of authority for those around him.

Lincoln hoped "that this nation, under God, shall have a new birth of freedom – and that government of the people, by the people, for the people, shall not perish from the earth." Unfortunately, Lincoln was assassinated in 1865 by John Wilkes Booth, a famous actor and Confederate sympathizer.

The United States of America is the first country to claim self-governing democratic freedom.

By doing so they have taken most of the philosophical ideas of the Age of Enlightenment. Since its formation, the country has gone through many social changes. At its core, the democracy and the social system were strengthened on fundamental values such as a dedication to truth, justice, humility, service, compassion, forgiveness, and love.

By this definition, all these fundamental elements are religious values to which the majority of Americans have their faith. Indeed, most Americans are churchgoers, and among other things religious freedom is valued most by these people. The recognition of intellectual property, patent rights, and the freedom of expression in literature, music, and performance art were widely accepted among well-meaning citizens because of these developments.

The United States of America (USA) was the first country to claim such freedom, as recognised by the Senate and being well articulated in their constitution.

This was achieved most notably during the time of President Abraham Lincoln, who led the American nation through the country's greatest moral, constitutional, and political crisis. This reform is symbolised by the Statue of Liberty as an icon of freedom, which was gifted from the people of France to the people of the United States to commemorate the national abolition of slavery.

These changes made a significant difference to the way people think, the development in science, technology, and exponential growth in the music and entertainment industry. Economies and social arrangements became increasingly complex.

This was the pursuit of mundane happiness, allowing people to do as they pleased. The freedom people were seeking extended to the freedom of worship, liberalising the Christian Church, and giving birth to different interpretations and research of religious texts. However, this freedom did not resolve the moral dilemma and individual freedom caused people to distance from religion, beliefs, moral values, and their faith.

At the beginning of the 21st century, there appears to be a shift, alterations, and new definitions that have been added to these traditional values along with a new form of fundamentalism.

Division has emerged as the leading diagnosis of the ills for the American political community, but this division is only a symptom of more fundamental problems. Former president Mr Jimmy Carter (39th president 1977 - 1981) recalls his childhood in which many of his church congregation clung to these values.

In his book titled "Our Endangered Values: America's Moral Crisis" (Simon & Schuster, 2005), Carter states "Extensive and profound are the transformations that are now taking place in our basic moral values, public discourse, and political philosophy."

From Carter's perspective, contemporary politics has taken a dangerous turn from traditional political and religious values. According to Carter, this turn is a result of a fundamentalist intrusion into American politics and religion, as well as the melding of the two.

Carter explains that the contemporary fundamentalists, to which he attributes recent political divisions, are identified by their rigidity, domination, and exclusion. These fundamentalists believe that they alone are aligned with their authentic religious beliefs and thus their beliefs should prevail over others.

The new principles of fundamentalism seem very different to Carter's childhood memories of his church. Contemporary fundamentalists, says Carter, believe others are wrong and inferior and thus essentially sub-human (which allows one to engage in atrocities against these "others").

Ironically, this fundamentalist attitude is in direct conflict with the basic (or fundamental) elements of faith identified by Carter such as compassion, justice, and the like. According to Carter, this process is taking place in some sects of many major religions but not identified in Buddhism and the Shinto religion.

This new wave of religious fundamentalism appears to be widespread; it is thought to be a minority movement but tends to have a disproportional influence on society because controversial issues are spread quickly in news and media platforms, attracting political and social debate despite lacking any sound theological grounds. Carter says that it is human nature to be both selective and subjective in deriving the most convenient meaning by careful choices from religious texts to support their arguments.

The moral repertoire they provide is inadequate. Some of these ideas have themselves become corrupted. According to Carter, such divisive issues have been "successfully injected" into the contemporary American political landscape by the fundamentalists, he is most concerned about in his book.

As a result of this calculated and highly organized campaign to inject divisive social issues into politics, American politics has become more fractured and partisan over time.

One of the most challenging tasks for Carter during his administration was the Iranian hostage crisis. On November 4, 1979, Iranian militants stormed the United States Embassy in Tehran and took approximately seventy Americans captive. This terrorist act triggered the most profound crisis of the Carter presidency and began a personal ordeal for Jimmy Carter and the American people that lasted 444 days. President Carter committed himself to the safe return of the hostages while protecting America's interests and prestige. He pursued a policy of restraint that put a higher value on the lives of the hostages than on American retaliatory power or protecting his own political future.

The toll of patient diplomacy was great, but President Carter's actions brought freedom for the hostages with America's honour preserved. These momentous incidents outside the USA led them to change their policies concerning national security.

During the last phase of the Cold War era, American public policy changed dramatically.

One of the most significant recent changes to public policy which Carter identifies is aggressive and unilateral intervention in foreign affairs.

This includes the rejection of major international treaties that eventually led to the war in Iraq.

In relation to the Iraq War, Carter specifically challenges the policy of "pre-emptive war," which he believes is a catalyst to a cycle of escalating violence in the Middle East making peace and happiness a distance mirage, an illusion in the desert land.

Pre-emptive war is thought to be both illegal under international law and a blatant rejection of war as the last resort. While Carter is against the Iraq war, he also rejects what he calls "blind pacifism."

According to his view, war is sometimes necessary; to be justified, though, it must meet certain criteria such as being a "last resort after other options have been exhausted", and that "the peace to be established is a clear improvement over what currently exists".

Though, the Gulf War did not meet any of those criteria. Carter was concerned that a fundamentalist ideology was systematically changing political policy and theological philosophy in destructive ways.

The book's eponymous reflection says it best: "Carefully altered fundamentalism is present in all religions and is embodied in the U.S. politics whose ridged, dominating, and exclusive policies are threatening the fundamental political and religious values of the United States".

## Obama Presidency

The US political party division widened during the Obama presidency. Barack Obama campaigned for the U.S. presidency on a platform of change.

As he prepared to leave office in January 2017, the country he led for eight years was undeniably different.

Profound social, demographic, and technological changes swept across the United States during Obama's tenure, as have important shifts in government policy and public opinion. Indeed, Obama's election quickly elevated America's image abroad, as intended especially in Europe, where George W. Bush was deeply unpopular following the U.S. invasion of Iraq.

This strategic change of leadership was designed to rebuild a good diplomatic relationship, especially with Middle Eastern counties. In 2009, shortly after Obama took office, residents in many countries expressed a sharp increase in confidence in the ability of the U.S. President to do the right thing in international affairs.

Americans declared that they are no longer the international policemen, there seemed to be a change in foreign policy. While Obama remained largely popular internationally throughout his tenure, there were exceptions, including in Russia and key Muslim nations.

The election of the nation's first black President raised hopes that race relations in the U.S. would improve, especially among black voters. But by 2016, following a spate of high-profile deaths of black Americans during encounters with police there were protests by the Black Lives Matter movement and other groups, many Americans - especially blacks - described race relations as generally bad.

Apple released its first iPhone during Obama's 2007 campaign, the use of Twitter and other media platforms quickly got the foothold in American politics as the key method of reaching out to supporters. Today, the use of smartphones and social media has become the norm in U.S. society, not the exception. The technology provided fingertip access to information, whilst so did the use of disinformation and toxic views that spread faster than wildfire.

Mr Obama took the office at the most difficult time of the economic climate when both sides of the Atlantic banking sector collapsed.

This led to the Great Recession which cost millions of Americans their homes and jobs and led Obama to push through an approximately $800 billion stimulus package as one of his first orders of business. There was a significant increase in unemployment in late 2009. But by some measures, the country faces serious economic challenges: A steady hollowing of the middle class continued during Obama's presidency and income inequality reached its highest point since 1928.

Views on some high-profile social issues shifted rapidly. Such as the legalisation of certain drugs for recreational purposes, the Supreme Court's rulings on momentous legal battles during Obama's tenure, and in 2015 it overturned long-standing bans on same-sex marriage, effectively legalizing such unions nationwide which challenged traditional values. Additionally, poorly managed immigration and notable changes in the demographic has contributed to political division. The tide of demographic changes in the U.S. has affected both major political parties in different ways.

Democratic voters are becoming less white, less religious, and better-educated at a faster rate than that of the country, while Republicans are ageing more quickly than the country as a whole. Education, in particular, has emerged as an important dividing line in recent years, with college graduates becoming more likely to identify as Democrats and those without a college degree becoming more likely to identify as Republicans. This shift of identity led conservatives become even mode distance from others. In most democracies, political conservatism seeks to uphold traditional family structures and social values. Religious conservatives typically oppose abortion, LGBT behaviour (or, in certain cases, identity), drug use, and traditional moral values. They uphold conventional institutions, a social order based on strict norms. Traditional institutions have a role in a society. They set standards and values for ethical behaviour without which civil society might not function smoothly. On the other hand conservatives are reluctant to address sensitive issues publicly that might damage their public image thereby leaving an issues unaddressed causing unfair treatment to some minority sects in a political society.

As the Obama era drew to a close the nation has almost divided, not only politically but also racially.

As part of a state visit in May 2011, the then US President, Barack Obama gave a keynote address to both houses of the British Parliament, gathered at London's Westminster Hall. Mr Obama arrived in his smart appearance and started his speech with humour.

*"I have known few greater honours than the opportunity to address the mother of Parliaments at Westminster Hall. I am told the last three speakers here have been the Pope, Her Majesty the Late Queen, and Nelson Mandela, which is either a very high bar or the beginning of a very funny joke. I've come here today to reaffirm one of the oldest, one of the strongest alliances the world has ever known. It has long been said that the United States and the United Kingdom share a special relationship."*

The smooth rhetoric of the US President's address to Parliament won him a standing ovation. But the speech also made two important and substantial key points in relation to foreign policy.

In a spirit of unyielding optimism, neatly combined with a message of hard-headed pragmatism, Barack Obama insisted that the time for American and European leadership "is now", in spite of the continual rise of new global superpowers. He was the first United States president to address MPs and peers in Westminster Hall and received a standing ovation before he began his speech. He covered issues such as shared values of foreign policy, economic development, and international security.

It was an eloquently delivered and partly platitudinous speech that displayed his knowledge and background, a textbook example of the value of democracy and the strength of long-standing alliances.

The theatrics of a state visit from Mr Obama is unavoidably mesmerising. Even the long wait in Westminster Hall for his arrival had a compelling quality; former prime ministers of Great Britain Tony Blair spoke animatedly with Gordon Brown, David Cameron exchanged what seemed like a joke or two with Nick Clegg and opposite them sat the film star Tom Hanks giving the event a touch of Hollywood glamour. The delay in the presidential arrival led to an even greater sense of anticipation. Abroad at least, Mr Obama still casts spells as he did before the hard grind of power took hold.

Mr Obama's visit to the UK reassured traditional relations and inspired his audience. His speech defending democracy and shaping US-NATO strategy with European partners was viewed by many observers as a concept of diplomacy conveyed to attract the attention of other peace-loving nations. It was a sign that the US is committed to strengthening a rule-based order to maintain global peace going forward.

Obama's administration tried to build bridges not only in Europe but also with Arab nations and Indo Pacific regions. Nevertheless, there were stark differences in approaches to the financial crisis, as individual countries were taking different paths in tackling the economy and their own deficit. Rich Arab countries did not want to bail out the West, instead they invested in their own countries. For example, the emergence of ultra-modern cities in Dubai and Qatar shows ambitious projects of Arab nations integrating into the Western economic model.

Global economic issues are far from over, US policies are short term and aim to be implemented for the four-year term of each administration.

Ten years later from Mr Obama's speech, his successor, Mr Donald Trump had a cosy isolation from global policies reversing American leadership. There was a lack of rational constructive dialogue to actively participate in global issues for lasting peace. Mr Trump's political rhetoric and his actions eroded trade relations with China, during his entire period in office. He was largely engaged in pleasing his domestic political base by pushing his "America First" policy.

Evidently, he mishandled the Covid-19 pandemic. The U.S. death count from Covid-19 continues to soar upward with horrifying speed. On Tuesday, 5th January 2021, the last full day of Donald Trump's presidency, the death toll reached 400,000, a grim milestone - a once unthinkable number. Instead of building bridges to unite, Mr Trump invested in building walls to separate. Further, US-China relations deteriorated to their worst point in decades allowing China to work on unilateral policies particularly in the Asia Pacific region and South China sea. However, notably, during Mr Trumps tenure there were no wars in the world.

In 2021, the new Biden administration immediately started communicating with China to rebuild trade relations which still appears to be discontent, following the footsteps of Mr Trump they continue to point fingers at each other on human rights and other issues such as those concerning the independence of Hong Kong and Taiwan. Beijing pushed claiming legitimacy that Taiwan is not an independent country but part of mainland China.

President Biden's top foreign policy officials were in the middle of meetings in Anchorage with their Chinese counterparts, the first high-level talks between the two global powers since the start of the Biden administration.

Relations between the countries were as complicated as they were consequential. Conflicts have arisen recently over the Trump administration's trade war, China's increasingly authoritarian policies in Hong Kong, its campaign of internment and mass sterilization against Uyghur Muslims and its suspected role in cyberattacks against the United States.

The run-up to this meeting in Alaska has only brought those tensions into clearer focus. Antony Blinken, the secretary of state, travelled a week ago to visit the two closest American allies in Asia, Japan and South Korea, with the defence secretary but pointedly did not meet with Chinese officials.

In Seoul, South Korea, Antony Blinken and Pentagon chief Lloyd Austin were holding talks with their Japanese counterparts in Tokyo to reaffirm the trans-Pacific partnerships in the face of an increasingly assertive China and hostile North Korea.

China responded with diplomatic composure, castigating them for not welcoming any Chinese delegates to the Alaska summit while imposing sanctions on the Communist Party leaders; matters that could mutually benefit both superpowers were on the table to mitigate.

The real issue is China is close to outmanoeuvring the US and the rest of the world both economically and militarily to become a formidable superpower.

From the outset, China has grown at extraordinary speed, fast acquiring a manufacturing capacity much greater than the U.S. They have obtained sufficient technical and production capabilities to be competitive in the supply chains of industrial and domestic goods, hence a partnership and collaborative ethics are vitally important in any diplomacy for both countries.

Compared to the U.S., China has long term plans perhaps looking100 years ahead from now, therefore their vision of the future is obscure to the western perspective of limits.

The only possibility to engage in trade and military competition between these democratic and authoritarian regimes is to have strong diplomacy, impose necessary countermeasures, constructive dialogue, and robust international policies to avoid any kind of clashes and to achieve progress.

In relation to foreign policy and diplomacy, this is not an occasion for provocative assertion, but for binding messages. The U.S. delegates share the view that people across the world yearn for democracy but understand an important qualification: that democracy cannot be imposed from the outside, particularly on a regime that lacks an appetite to give such freedom to its people, perhaps not so soon.

China is in transition from a rigid communist economy towards social mobility and to a free and open market economy, willing to engage in trade, however, on their terms.

While the Alaska summit trade talks continue, in mid-March 2021, Britain and the EU have taken joint action with the US and Canada to impose parallel sanctions on senior Chinese officials who are involved in the mass internment of Uighur Muslims in the Xinjiang province, this is the first of such western action against Beijing since Joe Biden took office. The move also marked the first time in three decades that the UK or the EU had taken a multilateral unified front to punish China for human rights abuses, and both will now be working hard to contain the potential political and economic fallout.

China hit back immediately, blacklisting MEPs, European diplomats and think tanks.

The US and Canada also imposed sanctions on several senior Chinese officials as part of the coordinated pressure campaign.

The UK then foreign secretary, Dominic Raab, said China's treatment of the Uighur minority was "the largest mass detention of an ethnic and religious group since the second world war". Evidence of repression in Xinjiang "is clear as it is sobering", he said. Mr Raab argued that Britain and the rest of Europe have a moral obligation to take such actions in principle against oppressive regimes whilst defending against criticism from the parliamentary opposition for not taking leadership earlier. Mr Raab has a clearer precedent for this proposition. First applying diplomatic pressure in concert with other NATO partners.

The sanctions will be imposed immediately and include travel bans and asset freezes on four officials, Raab told MPs. China is facing mounting criticism from around the world over its treatment of the mostly Muslim Uighur population in the north-western region of Xinjiang.

"Amid growing international condemnation, [China] continues to commit genocide and crimes against humanity in Xinjiang," said the US secretary of state, Antony Blinken.

"We will continue to stand with our allies around the world in calling for an immediate end to the PRC's crimes and for justice for the many victims."

Chinese ambassador to the EU, Zhang Ming, had given advance warning that there would be countermeasures including against those organisations spreading "lies" about the situation in Xinjiang. China said it was also sanctioning 10 EU individuals and four entities.

Economically and strategically Asia, in particular Pacific Asia, remains an important area to Britain and the South China Sea is the choke point connecting Britain with the region.

Recently, China has shown an increased interest in international water in this region hence proving that keeping a good relationship with China and regional partners is more important for UK's national interest than joining the U.S. naval competition.

As a country of islands, the UK's economy depends much on its foreign trade, in particular seaborne trade. Sea lanes of communication (SLOCs) in the South China Sea play an important role. According to a report by a UK think-tank, 12% of UK seaborne trade, £97 billion in imports and exports passes through the South China Sea each year. This amount will surely increase as the East Asian economy continues its robust growth and assumes a greater share of the global economy.

Meanwhile, the South China Sea is an entry point for British trading relationships with Southeast and East Asian countries. China is the fastest growing market for UK exports and the UK's second-largest non-EU trading partner.

In 2018 bilateral trade totalled more than $80 billion and UK exports to China increased by 6.9%. Chinese investment in the UK tops $20 billion. Southeast Asia is the UK's third-largest non-EU export market while the UK is the second-biggest EU investor in the area. Moreover, Southeast Asia is the UK's third-biggest market for defence exports.

For all these reasons, the safety and security of sea lanes of communication South China Sea have significance for the UK's economy. Historically, the UK has had a strong link with Asia, possessing many colonies in both South and Southeast Asia. This connection continues today even after it abandoned Singapore and withdrew from its commitments "East of Suez" in the 1970s.

Current disagreement with superpowers has roots in U.S. domestic issues and is well reflected in the attitudes of past Trump administration which repeatedly accused China of unfair trade practices.

China was the first country to recover from Covid-19 pandemic in 2021 while its regional contender, India, was still struggling to cope with the rising number of infections and related deaths.

China's ambition programs are now apparent to the world, and they are closing to annex Taiwan to its territory, its naval dominance in the

South China Sea appears resilient to collation challenges as the Chinese fighter jets are increasingly visible in the skies of the Western Pacific Ocean where U.S. navy also has a presence.

The magnitude of Chinees investments in economic programs in Australia and New Zealand combined with its growing influence in the region on one hand and its close military partnership with Russia on the other hand, have made the nation more resilient to international pressure. Neither the U.S. nor its alliance can afford to go into confrontation with China now.

Conflict is profoundly against the interest of both U.S. and China or even to head that direction. The complicities behind these nations' relationship are made complicated by the tensions with other adversaries, competitiveness, and by additional challenges related to the demoralized internal state department which needs to work on alliances to restore international order. China is accused of stealing trade secrets, intellectual property, and unfair competition.

America is prepared to rise to these challenges in many ways, by identifying human capital as the most important element for the wealth of nation, the Secretary of State Mr Antony Blinken stated in an interview with journalist Keith Sharman.

The recent G7 summit hosted by Britain in May 2021 is going through reshaping, redefining, and rebranding the purpose of G7 to meet the economic challenges and building relation with other member states.

The new Biden administration is in a testing period of forming its foreign policy, one of its principal challenges at this point of time, particularly with competing superpowers. Mr Biden held an interview with ABC news channel which aired on 17 March 2021.

The meandering comments he made concerning the Russian leader in relation to alleged interferences in the 2020 elections caused concern in the diplomatic community.

Moscow has responded by sending a strong signal, recalling its ambassador to the US for consultation. This was an indication that relations between the two countries are under strain. But even as relations between the countries lurched into crisis, Moscow stressed it wanted to prevent an "irreversible deterioration" in relations.

"The main thing for us is to determine the ways in which the difficult

Russian-American relations that Washington has led into a dead end in recent years could be rectified," the Russian foreign ministry said in a statement.

In his interview, Biden also expressed a hope that the US could cooperate with Russia on issues such as arms control, saying that the US and Russia can "walk and chew gum" at the same time. "There's places where it's in our mutual interest to work together such as renewing the Start nuclear agreement," he said.

These new developments indicate that the new administration needs time to position itself and get a good grip before establishing a firm foothold in international politics again. The US National Intelligence's reports on this matter underscored allegations that Trump's allies played into Moscow's hands by amplifying claims against Biden, using other parties linked to Russia with a hidden agenda to boost Trump's re-election an activity attempts to undermine democracy. These unhealthy domestic divisions are now reappearing within the games of the superpowers. Russia denied all allegations and challenged to produce evidence of any interference.

Recent diplomatic moves (March-May 2021) between US and Russia show some correlation to the previous Trump administration and their party politics.

America as a world-leading nation needs proper intellectual understanding to comprehend the scale of the challenges that they are facing both internally and externally. The new administration needs to rebalance relationships with other nations and renew its grand geopolitical strategy. In this, they need to identify China as the principal challenge.

To respond to these potential challenges posed by both Russia and China, individually or collectively, the US has to consider or construe a new strategy with an emulation more or less corresponding to their power.

The US and Russia should resume strategic stability talks that would hopefully cover a wide range of topics to benefit other small nations economically and help bring world peace with an aim to end unnecessary suffering.

Issues on the domestic front are more challenging than international affairs. During President Biden's first news conference on the 25 March 2021, answering a journalist's question on the voting system, Mr Biden said it was being "abused in a gigantic way" and signalled that he would be open to more aggressive steps to limit or abolish it, starting with a proposal that would require senators to keep talking in order to block legislation.

Answering later questions, Mr Biden said he expected to run for re-election in 2024, with Vice President Kamala Harris as his running mate, and reiterated that it would be hard to pull all U.S. troops out of Afghanistan by May 1, as his predecessor, Donald J. Trump, had agreed to do.

His approach to problem-solving and deep-dive policy decisions are very pragmatic. He made a point of striking a contrast with his combative predecessor, who labelled the press as the "enemy of the people."

Mr Biden also hinted that America is preparing for international competition with Chinese counterparts, in this fourth-generation industrial revolution they would need to invest in infrastructure development, research in science, and technology.

The president was characteristically long-winded, self-deprecating, and intent on projecting the image of a convivial and candid leader - as he has throughout his career. He apologized to reporters for over talking or for assuming they did not have background information on issues, and he went out of his way to praise them for their reporting on the immigration crisis at the country's border.

Competition is the act of striving against others. It is a cycle that repeats in history as some nations strive to regain their place in the world. History is not kind to those who play power games, it is made of many cycles of rising and falling empires, great civilisations, and natural disasters.

In the aftermath of the Trump era, it is not a misconception to assume what disinformation could do to destroy a great nation both morally and politically.

What is freedom? Freedom is understood as either having the ability to act or change without constraint or to possess the power and resources to fulfil one's purposes unhindered.

However, individual freedom was still much restricted by the prevailing laws of jurisdiction.

Without an enforced law, there could be anarchy, misuse of freedom and no protection against coercive control, fraud, theft, enforcement of contracts and so on. On occasion people do not accept responsibility, even if the most ethical act is widely accepted, this behaviour is therefore controlled by instruments of law.

For example, the liberal use of firearms led to many mass shooting incidents. Also, during March 2020 with a worldwide pandemic people were asked to use facemasks, social distance and self-isolate; these preventive measures were introduced by medical and health advisors to prevent replicating a contagious virus.

It is the most ethical thing to do in such a situation but the Government, seeking prevention control, had to legislate it and introduce a fine to make it compulsory to comply with social distancing rules as a moral obligation and to reduce the economic consequences of a national lockdown. Fines were introduced, proving the utilitarian theory that man is motivated by pleasure and pain, not by ethics. The March 2020 pandemic highlighted many issues of ethical conduct and moral values. Coronavirus changed life as we know it, it was the biggest health crisis in our living memory.

Not everyone in society was affected in the same way. In October 2020, England and Manchester United football player 22 years old Marcus Rashford has become an MBE (Member of the Order of British Empire) in the Queen's Birthday Honours list.

Marcus campaigned for the government to allow about 1.3 million children to claim free school meal vouchers in England's summer holidays during the coronavirus pandemic, without which those children might have starved with their parents losing income due to the national lockdown. Marcus said that he himself has benefitted from this scheme when he was a schoolboy.

The development of ethics has a clear relation to the economy and man's welfare at any given time.

## Synthetic World View

The Synthetic worldview is a multi-disciplinary approach that can be found in anthropology, biology, engineering sociology, psychology, informatics, and economics amongst others. It enables an open-minded thinker to understand the underpinning philosophy and theory of systems, science and systems thinking.

It enables one to draw upon concepts from one discipline to provide insight into others. Connecting thinking across disciplines avoids the artificial separation and conflict of interest that discipline-oriented thinking can lead to.

It is this multi-disciplinary approach that enables one to gain insight and achieve resolution of the most complex issues faced by society today, and which describes the philosophical underpinnings of the systemic paradigms and the synthetic worldview, comparing and contrasting with both reductionist and analytical approaches.

When we understand the holistic view of a system, we also see the cause and effect of one to another.

This connected approach allows us to critically assess various methodologies and approaches from the perspective of understanding and knowledge, relating them to philosophical concepts such as ontology and epistemology.

In this way, we are able to comprehend the interrelationships between thinking approaches and justify them from a foundational perspective. The challenge of developing a synthetic worldview still remains to address much widely to benefit from its application.

Freedom of thought has limitations when it breaches the freedom of others.

Western philosophy lacks insight and intellectual integrity because ideas were simultaneously developed in very divergent cultures without a coherent value system.

All these views still contain an element of prejudice and ignorance as they do not take into account the true values of humanity.

## Historical and other Developments

During the time of Confucius in China, along with Greek and Judeo-Christian civilizations, human qualities were evaluated which brought about a common set of values. These values are the basis of virtue, mainly 'love of people' and 'to love your neighbour' thus focusing on kindness and generosity. These are the main human values as recognized by evolved human beings.

Plato and Aristotle considered 'courage, justice, temperance, truthfulness, and friendliness' as equally important for social harmony and individual progress.

Immanuel Kant's original thought of Enlightenment had not yet crystallized. In the Western world, sublime thoughts were limited to a few noblemen, noblewomen, and scholars who were immune from worldly conditions. Valuable thought arises only in independent thinkers whose mind is free from defilements. When translated and mapped into social ethics these human values were manipulated and wrongly interpreted by the blind views of political leaders.

Other than Christianity, a convergence of a sustainable world view and value system is yet to arise in Western thought. For example, in 1860 English nurse Florence Nightingale was compassionate with wounded soldiers of the Crimean War and looked after them by herself. Nightingale had a noble idea and laid the foundation for professional nursing.

Similarly, Mother Teresa of Calcutta was a catholic nun who dedicated her life to care for sick and poor children in India. In 1979, she won the Nobel Peace Prize and numerous other awards including Pope John XXII Peace Prize for her charitable services.

These examples are relatively few, people who have seen the suffering of others and proactively done something to help those who couldn't help themselves. Severe winters and adverse weather conditions add difficulty in the Western hemisphere for sublime thoughts to arise in the mind, instead, they are supportive conditions for instinctual survival.

Human behaviour has a direct relation to external conditions. Experiences of war harden the hearts and minds of people, where defence against any threat becomes the priority. As long as mistrust, greed, and hatred prevail in the mind it cannot see the true human nature.

In Buddhism, these experiences are classed as suffering. In times of uncertainty awakening to the truth is more important than choosing the right ideology. The Buddhist teachings of generosity, virtue, loving-kindness, and wisdom are not theories or philosophies. They are great human qualities to be cultivated through mindful living. Instead of becoming entangled in an embattled bitterness or cynicism that exists externally, we need to begin to heal those qualities within ourselves. Suffering is universal message for spiritual awakening and transform rivalry into compassion.

Buddha addressed deeper psychological aspects of the mind and provided a solution for it. Buddha advocated "right thought" which comes from "right view" and gives rise to "right wisdom", seeing things as they are.

According to the enlightened perspective, all phenomena are impermanent and subject to suffering.

The solution to suffering can be sought by the guiding light of wisdom. Therefore, before accepting a theory, concept, or doctrine, it must be evaluated by insight wisdom. Reasoning alone does not make man wise; it must be balanced with experience and its consequences to all beings sharing this planet, including nature itself; exclusion of any of these parts will result in nature retaliating in its own way.

This is known as 'karma' in Sanskrit and 'kamma' in Pali among Buddhist people. Literally means actions or deeds. It refers to the conditioning aspects of the mind by volitional activities and nature. Kamma produce results. This is compatible with physics that every action has a reaction. Kamma not necessarily a reaction but reactive actions are results produced by bad kamma meaning unwholesome actions. For example, climate change is caused by excessive addition of carbon dioxide toxic gas to environment and people face the consequences. Abhidhamma enumerate four types of kamma according to its function, analyse deeper than environmental issues but how it effects an individual or collectively to a society. They are productive, supportive, obstructive, and destructive kamma. The law of kamma is self-subsistent in its operation, ensuring that willed deeds produce their effects in accordance with their ethical quality.

In the 20th century, we experienced various violent conflicts; in war, no one wins, it only adds more suffering to all beings. Buddha saw the dangers of extremes and therefore rejected them. In the middle path, there is hope and solution rather than using aggression or violence to resolve problems; hatred cannot be overcome by hatred.

On the day (11 May 2006) marking Buddha's birth, enlightenment and passing, the United Nations Secretary-General Kofi Annan accepted Buddhism as a world religion, reminding us of the importance of world peace.

"As we mark this year's Day of Vesak, let us recognize, as Buddhism does, our essential interdependence."

He called for a collective resolve to work towards the common good, for the harmonious and peaceful coexistence of all the world's people to meet the challenges of the 21st century.

The 20th -century American philosopher Wilfrid Sellars (1962) was inspired by Immanuel Kant's transcendental idealism. Wilfrid had worked in military intelligence and must have clearly seen the need for a unified world system. He was one of the pioneers of Synoptic Philosophy and explicitly popularized the term. The word synoptic comes from the Greek word συνοπτικός *sunoptikos* (seeing everything together) and has the meaning of bringing ideas together. As a philosophy, it refers to the love of wisdom that emerges from a coherent understanding of every-thing together. It is a synthetic worldview, embracing all other views and their opposites.

It encompasses both the visible and invisible things. For example, every action has a reaction and consequences. Western thought could enrich greatly by Buddhist principles. Isaac Newton studied the action and reaction of physical forces but did not extend it beyond classical physics.

Theoretical physics studies the forces of atomic and subatomic particles and has observed peculiar behaviour that cannot be explained by any conventional means; we cannot have experience if the object is not receptive to our senses.

As claimed by Buddhism, the mind is a sense that can recognise infinite objects including that of extra sensory perception. The mind can be trained to experience different worlds, but Buddha limited his teaching to understanding the true nature of life and a way out of suffering. Buddha transcended abstract knowledge and gained insight into the reality of life; ethical values were paramount in his teachings.

Buddhism is founded on empirical evidence and the real facts of life. The fundamentals of Buddhist principles can be used as a measure of other ethical values.

Albert Einstein also recognised the value of ethics, appealed to the world to recognise its humanity, and showed an inclination towards Buddhism. According to him, Buddhism should be the base religion of the world, "If there is any religion that could cope with modern scientific needs it would be Buddhism".

Buddhist ethics are concerned with how our volitional actions affect ourselves and others, thus directing them towards social harmony.

The mind trained in higher ethical values has access to concentration which can be used as a valuable tool to purify views and gain direct knowledge.

There are various stages of insight knowledge that come to finally liberate the mind from all kinds of views and defilements. Buddhism addresses the common denominator of man-kind that is suffering and way out of suffering.

The liberating power of mindfulness can transcend all boundaries of religious and ethnic differences thus Buddhist social philosophy and its practical applications are universal. Insight wisdom coexists with insight meditation, a technique being living at present beyond reasoning and can be practised with anyone irrespective of their religious beliefs.

In this modern world, the demand for things to do that fill one's life can be endless, challenging, and exhausting. Fortunately, meditation and mindfulness practices have served as a welcome refuge from the tension of the endless work in constantly changing environment and stressful irritating thought patterns that are unproductive.

By taking refuge in mindfulness practices, one can acknowledge thoughts, be detached from them, and not become caught in them, finally gaining wisdom through awareness. When the mind is clear and clean you can see things as they are and accept the reality of life.

There are multiple wisdom factors that nourish and revitalize the mind. Through the practices of loving-kindness and compassion, you can respond to the demands of life with more kindness beginning with your close family and then extending to unlimited wider circles changing attitudes even with enemies.

Learning to pause and anchor attention in the movements of the body, you begin to trust in the goodness, honesty, and truthfulness of being humane.

The more you practice more benefits you gain, and you will find the joy in life.

After consistent practice your perceptions, ideas, and views of the world would beginning to change. This is a great freedom accessible to anyone who willing to choose the path of peace and happiness.

CHAPTER 15

# ETHICS DEFINITIONS

I WANT TO BEGIN WITH THE word "ethics" itself, derived from the Latin word "ethos". It means the disposition, character, or fundamental values peculiar to a specific person, people, culture, or movement. *Ethos* is also an English word based on a Greek word which denotes the guiding beliefs or ideals that characterize a community, a nation, or an ideology. The word was popularized by Aristotle.

The traditional term was used by Plato for ethical inquiry and politics. And this is also the term Aristotle himself first used to describe questions such as "What is justice? What is virtue? What is a good human being and so on?"

Still, Aristotle soon made a distinction which is found nowhere in Plato, between two classes of human excellence or virtue, the first called intellectual (that is, excellences of speculative reason) and a second class called ethical (roughly speaking, excellences of behaviour).

Aristotle coined the term *ethics* to mark this distinction. He drew this from the root word, ethos, which then referred to what is "typical or customary", as in the dwelling places of animals or people, or as in the manners or customs of people.

This word has the same force as the Latin word, "mores", from which we get our own word, "moral". But while Aristotle was calling attention to what was customary or traditional in human societies, and in that sense *moral*, he was more concerned with examining what is customary or characteristic in the life of an individual, specifically the distinctive habits of individuals, the dispositions, or states of the soul, which lead us to act in certain ways. To inquire into this characteristic is what he meant by ethical inquiry. (Dr. Thomas Slakey)

According to the Oxford dictionary, *ethics* means "moral principle". The word *ethics* derives from an application of principles as a code of acceptable behaviour. Ethics became a branch of social governance i.e. politics; in this context it is important to understand the meaning of the word *moral*.

"Moral" is concerned with right and wrong conduct based on a sense of distinction, where right and wrong are mainly value judgments which seek to establish principles of socially acceptable behaviour.

## Development of ethics in the Western philosophy

Ethics in Western thought is concerned with the meaning of certain words like 'good, bad, ought, right, duty, praise, and blame'. Correct meaning and definition with reference to words are sought after lengthy investigations that lead to traditional theories about them. For the purpose of ethics, the meaning of these words is limited to human relations. This is why, the true meanings of these words, even in the context of human relations, are still much debated.

Pleasure Utilitarianism Theory argues that everything called "good" is good because it increases pleasure or diminishes pain, and pain is thus considered "bad". This theory has many criticisms, Bishop Butler was the first British philosopher to emphasize this.

Butler believed that "all particular appetites and passions are towards external things themselves, distinct from the pleasure arising from them; there could not be this pleasure were it not for the prior suitableness between the object and the passion. Pleasure comes when I get what I want. The pleasure could not occur unless I want the object. A man who gets what he does not want gets no pleasure". For example, in window shopping, a shopper does not get pleasure from what they see in the window until he or she wants to buy it but derive some satisfaction pleasing the sight. Pleasure is always a by-product of the achievement of some goal other than pleasure.

G. E. Moore argued against this utilitarianism and introduced instead Ideal Utilitarianism. It maintains aesthetic enjoyment and personal enjoyment are good in themselves, but an act can be judged right or wrong without any reference to motives or intentions.

Motives and intentions are relevant to make a second judgment whether an act is a praise or blameworthy. For example, "the politicians did the wrong thing, but you couldn't blame them as they couldn't have known the Iraqi did not have weapons of mass destruction".

Ethics become complicated when mixed with politics and taking the advantage of ethics for political gain.

Ideal utilitarianism was criticized by W D Ross and H A. Prichard. Their point of argument centred around the basis of moral rules and how such rules can be justified. For a rule to be valid, the use of them needs a sufficient degree of maturity. What is self-evident to one may not be so to another. If rules are to be applied, special rules are needed for exceptional circumstances to the general rule.

"Different factual beliefs held by different people in question may act differently in similar situations. For example, the duty of a Briton to help the police to arrest a murderer and the duty of a Sicilian to kill a member of the murderer's family are basically the same duty of requiting murder or deterring murderers applied to a different set of circumstances those with and without an effective central legal authority."

Moore and Ross have different views of what is right and wrong. They both thought that in any given circumstance there is one act which is the right act for a man to do, this act is his duty and what he ought to do. They further argue that what makes it right are the existing circumstances, the man's own beliefs and motives have nothing to do with it. According to Moore's view, an act is right which, of all courses open to the agent, will produce the best result. For example, suppose a surgeon diagnoses a disease for which he believes an operation is essential, but unknown to him, and unknowable to him, the patient has a blood condition which will make the operation fatal. The surgeon's duty here is not to operate. According to Moore and Ross, duty also is objective.

To know whether a man has done his duty or done what he ought to, one need only know the facts surrounding the situation and actual consequences of his action, his beliefs and motives are irrelevant.

J. D. Mabbott (1966), on the other hand, whose book is the main source for these theories argued that the theory of duty has limitations. He suggests that beliefs about the situation, beliefs about the consequences of action, and moral beliefs are equally important to decide on right and wrong. The man's motives and what he has set himself to do, whether he is successful or not at achieving it, always proves that, on his part, he has done his duty. Criteria for 'duty' and 'right' were tested further with reference to standards of knowledge.

The term 'well meaning' is used to evaluate an action in order to establish blame when a conscience action leads to bad results. For example, can we blame an eighteenth-century surgeon who operated with chloroform or a nineteenth-century physician who failed to prescribe penicillin? We cannot blame them because they could not have known any better. We condemn the well-meaning man in cases when he could have found out the relevant facts or thought more effectively about them.

In such cases, we are blaming him not for a present dereliction of duty but for a past one. i.e. Why did you do it?

"Well-meaning" is the duty to think diligently. A crucial argument put forward by Prichard says that 'before action, I must consider as fully as I can whether my action will be appropriate'.

There may indeed be exceptional situations in which a man is unable to see any distinctions between right and wrong. It may be that exhaustion, starvation, the use of certain drugs, brainwashing, brain damage, may make recognition of all or any moral distinction impossible.

Under these circumstances, a man cannot have the motive of duty or duties. It makes no sense to blame him. So, the exception confirms the rule. If the motive is not present, neither is duty.

To convict a person of a crime there must be proof of the mental intention as enjoined to the act itself. How are we to determine this?

These arguments on moral theory reflect the morals of twentieth-century middleclass intellectual Britons. They can be very different to moral terms in other parts of the world. For example, to this day, human rights in UK and China seem very different. Views on morality differ and it is to be expected that theories built on them will consequently differ too.

In the last fifty years, science and technology have greatly changed. Only the observable, verifiable facts are acceptable as evidence to determine truth. To support criminal investigations there are crime labs to search for scientific evidence and in principle, behaviour is completely predictable.

In this new field of scientific determinism, subjective judgment, and free will are not acceptable terms. That is to say, a man's choice is already fixed to A, where his freedom to choose B is not there.

The writer has discussed only a very limited section of the moral theory, this discussion in full is beyond the scope of this essay. The field of ethics has also developed in line with the development of science and economic activities. Change of economic model also change the way people think about moral values. Political freedom has shifted the boundaries of traditional conservative value towards more liberal ideas about social behaviours strong enough to address variety of discrimination including sexual orientations challenging traditional institutions.

Arguments for the subjectivity of ethics has been removed as much as possible by making ethics objective this aims to remove personal preferences such as attitudes of liking or disliking an act.

Ethical values and meanings of words are very well defined and integrated into the law and legal systems.

Undefined terms and new circumstances are open to debate, as dealt with in the democratic political system. For example, new laws are passed through the Parliament system which is a legislative body of government. In the UK it is through the House of Commons and House of Lords, which finally requires the Royal Assent.

A new approach to ethics was introduced by Kant. Immanuel Kant was a German philosopher whose thinking greatly influenced moral philosophy. He thought of moral values as unique and believed in a universally identifiable property with an absolute value.

Kant's thinking put distance from traditional theory of ethics. He argued that the traditional theory is relative, and that judgment is made with reference to a condition. As an influential result, the intrinsic value of something has to be identified as 'good'.

Kant identified 'goodwill' as being the only intrinsic good. Intrinsic value is an ethical and philosophical property, it is the ethical or philosophical value that an object has 'in itself' or for its own sake. It is an end. For example: 'happiness' and 'family value'. It can be argued that Kant's approach comes close to a Buddhist way of thinking.

Kant states that there is nothing "which can be regarded as good without qualification, except a *goodwill*". Goodwill is the moral compass that always seeks good: if an agent fails, it is not the fault of the goodwill but of the agent's ability to carry it out.

In the opening section of his book, Kant explains what is commonly meant by moral obligation and duty. He writes that an act done out of inclination for the self is not considered moral by common sense. A shopkeeper with honest prices does so foremost to be respected by his customers, not for the sake of honesty. He thus "deserves praise and encouragement, but not esteem."

It is common knowledge that people, for whose good actions there is no reward, are those who act most morally. Kant revises this in his declaration to say that they are the *only* people acting morally. We esteem a man who gives up his life for others because he gains nothing in doing so.

"Duty is the necessity to act out of reverence for the [moral] law." Therefore, to follow moral law an intrinsic sense of right and wrong is our greatest obligation.

Similarly, in the Buddhist path, the final liberation is sought by giving away all possessions without expecting anything in return. A purified mind is radiant; it has an intrinsic nature without any stains of defilement. For example, an aspirant of future Buddhahood will practice ten different types of perfections of morality combined with wisdom, these are divine qualities of one's intrinsic nature in accordance with the moral law.

It establishes a higher degree of certainty and results in the practitioner and the natural law becoming one.

# BUDDHIST THEORY
# OF KNOWLEDGE

THE BUDDHA REJECTED *A-PRIORI* REASONING and abstract speculation as a means of knowledge. According to him, the reasoning was only concerned with validity, not truth; though a piece of reasoning may be logically valid, it may not be factually true.

The Buddha maintained that one must neither accept nor reject an idea because of a liking or disliking without proper investigation. Until the idea is verified, one must safeguard it temporarily because what one may reject could turn out after all to be the truth. The Buddha says that many unnecessary philosophical problems can arise due to the confusing nature of our concepts and language, he, therefore, advocated clarity in thought and language. Buddha also analysed questions and says that not every question can be categorically answered.

The basic idea of the Buddhist system of thought is very different to that of Western thought; the intellectual landscape differs. An aspect of this is exemplified by the way that the phrases in which Buddhism clothes its thought could scarcely be accurately translated to another language. For example, the word 'dhamma' in Pali needs much interpretation in the English language.

Buddhist writers certainly aim for precision of meaning and to a large extent achieves this. To live a moral life is to live according to 'dhamma'. Its meaning in the context of ethics is as a universal moral order that governs both the physical universe and organic life. However, the Buddha limited his teachings to suffering and the end of suffering. The meaning and application of his words are thus interpreted in the context of the path as leading to cessation of suffering.

Buddha refused to engage in a conversation if the meaning and purpose of the discussion was not leading to 'nibbana' (state of suffering's end). Buddhists also seek happiness, but altruistic happiness is ultimately attained through a full understanding of suffering. The purpose of the Buddhist's path to enlightenment is aimed at eradicating mental defilements. Therefore, Buddhist ethics and moral values are set to recognize mental factors that hinder progress and improve mental factors that encourage progress. Mental factors are real, though they cannot be knowable by mere concepts or by logic.

Buddha discovered a method to direct knowledge, that is to say, there is no conceptual knowing of the intrinsic nature of phenomena. The ability of the mind to acquire direct knowledge is clouded by perceptions that are inevitably associated with defilements. Ethical guidelines serve as protection against further pollution of mental factors, they reduce craving and allow for one's focus on mental development.

Any act that reduces suffering can be classed as 'right', while actions that increase suffering can be classed as 'wrong'. Seeing the suffering of others and willingness to help them is considered compassion. The philosophical background of Buddhist virtue leads one to refrain from cruelty, show kindness to all sentient beings who are struggling upwards to overcome suffering, accept responsibility for one's action, recognize the property rights of others, be truthful, honest, and not harm oneself.

Generosity (dana) is a practice to reduce its opposite attachment of greed. Cultivating a mind of loving-kindness and compassion while understanding their purpose is to develop wisdom. For example, giving food is to support and sustain life which naturally includes the beauty, health, and strength of the receiver. Offering requisites to Buddhist monks is central to Thai society, a vibrant culture has evolved from this principle of giving. Many Thai festivals are arranged and organised in a scale to include all classes of the society without an exception to practice generosity beginning from Royals. It is customary for the King of Thailand to be first to make offering and show support to the order of Sangha after the end of every rainy season so that all subjects follow the tradition no matter where they live in the world. It not only strengthens the Buddhist institutions but also give opportunity to everyone to make merits that brings good fortune in time to come.

'Mindfulness' is given a higher place. Mindfulness and awareness are the key to understanding and regulating one's actions. The moral efficacy of volitional action is the basis of deciding its ethical value.

## Buddhist perspective of ethics

The end of October is also the end of British summer time. The clocks turn one hour backwards effectively giving us an extra hour in the day. What did all of you do with this extra hour? Perhaps you stayed in bed for an extra hour. How many of you chose this extra hour to meditate?

This is an example to show that we have choices. When we wake up in the morning, we have a choice of which direction to go. I will come back to this point but let me first explain to you some traditional Buddhist activities pertaining to this period of time. Similar to the end of October being the end of summer in the UK, the end of October is the end of the rainy season in Southeast Asia, the monsoon.

During the time of Buddha, lay supporters offered robes to the Buddha and his disciples at the end of the monsoon season, offering robes has since become the custom. Ethics and moral values are encapsulated in these Buddhist customs, traditions, and activities. They are virtues of character which develop towards higher wisdom.

By practising insight meditation, the Buddha became enlightened and realized that morality and wisdom were the two main paths to attaining ultimate happiness. Buddha is the embodiment of moral excellence; the personification of moral perfection is Buddhahood. His enlightened mind perceived suffering as being closely related to our actions, he, therefore, taught people how to improve their behaviours in order to alleviate suffering.

Ethics is the study of moral principles. The behaviour of a person or group is a manifestation of their level of understanding moral principles.

The course of action one chooses depends on his or her understanding of life in general.

A few years ago, our Temple was burgled. One or two men broke the window panel, entered the shrine room, and stole all the money from the donation boxes. Whoever did this, did not understand Buddhist teachings. Taking what belonged to the community of monks, who have dedicated their lives to teaching, is fundamentally wrong. The donations were for the upkeep of the Temple, it has no other income.

Buddhism investigates this sort of harm by its fundamental ethical level. According to the natural law, those who have taken what is not given have to pay back equally or greater at some stage in their life cycle. Understanding what we do or what we refrain from doing is to understand our choices. Wisdom helps us in making our choices. Buddhism teaches us that what we are at this present moment is the result of our past actions and we inherit its consequences whether good or bad. The consequences of our actions follow us like a shadow.

Why ethics? The easiest way to answer this question is to look at what would happen if there are no ethics to regulate the behaviour of individuals and society at large. The legal model of trial and punishment is best suited to the enforcement of society's laws. These laws are necessary for the preservation of the state's authority and the well-being of society. The legal model is used to evaluate personal moral conduct and behaviour, laws prohibit certain actions and classify them as criminal. If we allow uncontrolled criminal activities to continue, then society will break down in three ways.

1. Direct consequence to the economy
2. Individuals will take the law into their own hands
3. Anarchy

Not every action or behaviour can be monitored by law and policing. Transgressors can slip under the net of the law and law enforcement agencies, although a person can be brought to justice retributively if they eventually get caught.

Buddhist ethics is a means of education. These ethical values are taught to children from a very young age to regulate moral conduct. When children are educated in an ethical background, they are likely to be more productive and law-abiding citizens in the future. Buddhist ethics are not intended to replace the law of society, neither are other ethical systems evolved on religious and philosophical foundations.

Criminal law and its consequent punishment are designed to seek effective control of human behaviour, prevent damage to property and loss of life. Law does not take into account feelings, thoughts or the emotional trauma of victims and transgressors alike. Criminal law will seek the intention of the action to establish the intensity of criminal nature.

Can we forgive a criminal? The theory of crime and punishment is very much debatable. Dostoyevsky's controversial book, *Crime and Punishment,* opens a discussion on this subject. The theory of punishment works in three different ways. They are preventive, deterrent, and reformatory. Punishment should not have the purpose of inflicting pain on the criminal. Rashdall describes retributive punishment as adding evil to evil. It was argued that the standard punishment of the legal system is not the infliction of suffering but deprivations i.e. Capital punishment, imprisonment, and fines are to deprive of life, liberty and of property (The Theory of Good and Evil 1907 Oxford Reference).

Hastings Rashdall FBA was an English philosopher, theologian, historian, and Anglican priest (1858 – 1924), he expounded a theory known as ideal utilitarianism and was a major historian in the Middle Ages. Legal authority is clearly stated in Sir Alexander Paterson's statement:

"The first duty of a prison as an institution of the State is to perform the function assigned to it by the law; and its administration must ensure that sentence of imprisonment is a form of punishment. Men are sent to prison as a punishment and not *for* punishment."

Moral rules vary in the degree to which they are constitutive or merely regulative. Rules are employed to maintain law and order, some of which no civilized society could survive without. The rules against killing, theft and promise-breaking are a few examples of this kind.

Buddha's position on this matter was different to our conventional mode of thinking. According to the Buddha, hatred cannot be overcome by hatred; hatred can only be overcome by loving-kindness. There is evidence in the scriptures that Buddha once subdued a serial killer, this man eventually became a saint.

Regarding the theft, at the Temple, one of the meditators commented that Buddhism encourages giving and we must give more by not punishing the thief.

One day a man came to my meditation class. Before coming to the class, I saw him very respectfully venerating a portrait of Late Venerable Ajahn Chah, so I asked him how he knows that monk. He confessed to me that he was a convicted criminal for armed robbery. In prison, he had met one of Ajahn Chah's students, Ajahn Kema Dhammo, who visited to teach Buddhism. I asked a few questions and he said he knows the law of impermanence. I explained to him that suffering is closely related to impermanence, what he had robbed from others was their happiness, he broke down and began to cry.

It reminds me of Dostoyevsky's words in Crime and Punishment; *'Can this be the punishment already beginning? Indeed, indeed, it is!'* The man had reformed by hearing Buddha's teaching.

"There are two kinds of suffering: the suffering that leads to more suffering and suffering that leads to the end of suffering. If you are not willing to face the second type of suffering, you will surely continue to experience the first." (Ajhan Chah)

Knowing our own behaviour, its consequences and directing our action towards our own happiness and that of others is wisdom in Buddhism. The principles behind our actions that lead to happiness are presented as a code of ethics or more precisely the Buddhist precepts.

## Buddhist view of personality

According to higher Buddhist philosophy, there is no acceptance of personhood, as an absolute point of view, there is no permanent self or person to be identified. Of course, it is a problem for moral discourse if there is no "person" there.

A story in non-canonical Buddhist literature, Melinda Panna, supports the argument of non-self.

Written in Platonic dialogue, this abridgement provides a concise presentation of this masterpiece of Buddhist literature. The introduction outlines the historical background against which the dialogues took place, indicating the meeting of two great cultures, that of ancient Greece and the Buddhism of the Indus valley, which was a legacy of the great Emperor Asoka.

Melinda was a Greek King during the time of Alexander the Great, who ruled the northern part of India corresponding to present-day Afghanistan and Pakistan. That was the area where young Prince Siddhartha studied in a school named Taxila. The King was a philosopher who associated with Buddhist monks.

One day, the King visited a distinguished Buddhist monk Elder Nagasena. After exchanging common respects, the King asked what the Elder's name was. The Elder said his name is Nagasena, his parents gave him that name and his colleagues call him by that name, but there is no real person to be found by that name.

The King further questioned the Elder but was not satisfied with the answers and accused the Elder of lying. He further asked, if there is no real person then who guards morality and who meditates and attains happiness? The elder contested with the learned king that similar to a chariot which the king says he travelled on is made of a collection of conventionally defined parts and no real chariot implied no discovery or could be found in absolute sense.

In this dialogue between the King and the Elder, they established that what we refer to as person is actually the five aggregates, namely form, feelings, perceptions, mental formations, and consciousness. Buddha broke down a person into these five aggregates and formed a basis for further philosophical analysis of their ultimate constituent parts. (Melinda Panha 100 BCE - 200 CE, Indo-Greek King Menander)

Though Buddhism does not accept the idea of a person as an enduring entity, it accepts the existence of a person as a composite physical and mental entity. There are two criteria used in determining the identity of a person. A person is made up of two types of components, physical and mental; mental activities are further analysed into four aggregates as above. What we do physically and mentally make up our personality. All these components or events are ever changing, preceding events disappear and change giving birth to succeeding events. Thus, the succeeding events inherit the characteristics of preceding events. These causal and consequential events are the activities of our life.

In Buddhism, it is through this unbroken continuity or coherence of the series of events that personal identity is traced. The psychological principle or law of causation, Kamma (Karma), says that it is the conditioning force of preceding events that condition the succeeding events. This gives rise to a continued chain of activities that follows the principle of cause and effect. For example, bad thoughts now will generate further bad thoughts until they form a karmic mental complex. This mental complex can be the cause of various types of mental illnesses like anxiety or guilt, which would gradually lead to further complications such as physical illnesses.

In another discourse, the Buddha explained the basis of inference from oneself to another. Inference works in two ways. The first way is thinking of oneself in terms of others, that is to say, what is our social relationship with one another? According to Buddha, the sense of one's value or personality is derived from others, we can thus conclude that personality itself is a value concept. If one is to gain personhood, it has to necessarily be done in a social context, for this reason, one should always be considerate of the value of others.

In today's terms we have personality profiles such as celebrities, TV personalities, fashion icons and sports personalities, add to the list are high profile politicians, etc. These status personalities are created by mass media and consequent social acceptance that propagates new value concepts.

They also have added commercial value, adherence to such value concepts gives leadership and recognition of social status. There are many personalities evolved from the past and in the present moment. Followers can gain their own satisfaction by imitating leaders as role models.

Man's personality is largely a product of the society around him. One becomes good or gains any value to one's personality through society only, that is why one has to consider and respect others. One does not become oneself without the help of others. Shaving the head, taking the saffron robe, and going forth is the first step of overcoming the personality view. Holding on to their personality view may bind a person to further wrong views.

Buddha stated his inference principle, "Therein, you monks, the self ought to be measured against self as shown by a monk. That person who is of evil desire and who is in the thrall of evil desires, that person is displeasing and disagreeable to me and similarly if I were of evil desires and in the thrall of evil desires, I would be displeasing and disagreeable to others." These principles are the basis of Buddhist Ethics.

Buddhist ethics and therein training schemes to improve behaviour, this is to cultivate a mind of friendliness that is far-reaching, widespread, and immeasurable, without enmity, without malevolence. One with such mental qualities dwells having suffused the first quarter of the mind with compassion, likewise sympathetic joy, loving-kindness, and equanimity. In Karaneya metta discourse (of loving kindness) we are taught to give loving-kindness to all beings without exception. These are the four cardinal virtues of Buddhism.

## Social Injustice

During the time of Buddha, society was dominated by a religious clan called Brahmins. People were divided into a class system according to the Brahmin's religious theory. The lowest classes of people were denied basic human rights; they were denied education, political freedom, not even admitted to their religious places.

Buddha was outspoken about this social injustice which prevailed during his time, and he proclaimed no one would become upper or lower class by birth, but only through his own action to become distinguished. By his own conduct one chooses his social position. Buddha was the first religious thinker in history to emphasise the equality of humanity by addressing inequalities and social injustices.

Buddhist ethics and moral values are presented as a code of practice aiming to improve individual behaviour. They stem from principles of social philosophy, that one cannot live alone but only as a part of a larger community. The code is the basic five precepts which are laid down to be accepted voluntarily, for one's own protection and the benefit of society at large. Ethics in Buddhism is traditionally based on the enlightened perspective of the Buddha.

Moral instructions are included in Buddhist scriptures or handed down through tradition. According to traditional Buddhism, the foundation of Buddhist ethics for laypeople is the five precepts (*pancha sila*). These are: no killing, no stealing, no lying, no sexual misconduct and not taking intoxicants. These precepts are not formulated as imperatives, but as training rules that the follower undertakes voluntarily to facilitate practice towards higher wisdom. In Buddhist thought, the cultivation of generosity and ethical conduct will themselves refine consciousness from the three evils of greed, hatred, and delusion towards ethical conduct.

Social relations are very well defined in Buddhism. The matrix of social relations is the way one relates to society, this can be by way of parents, children, teachers, students, relatives, friends, employer, employee etc. They are mainly duty to one another. Buddha also advised kings, as to their duties to the country and people. Concerning wealth, Buddha did not set a limit as long as it is righteously earned. One who does not attach to their wealth with greed will succeed in life.

In Buddhism, ethical values are converted to good moral conduct because the Buddhist principles that govern behaviour were sought from a natural law of cause and effect. For Buddhism, morality is the basis for searching for happiness. The doctrine of transcendental dependent origination explains how beings are trapped in cycles of suffering due to ignorance, it teaches us how to break from these cycles through higher virtues.

"Dependent on ignorance arise formation and dependent on formation arise becoming". The cycle continues in many stages but only a purified mind can clearly see the causes and conditions of suffering. The reverse application of the doctrine is the cessation of suffering, "By cessation of ignorance ceases suffering".

Ethics is a branch of Western philosophy, though every religion in the world addresses this subject. There are a variety of religious practices which have evolved from this branch of study. I will discuss the Buddhist point of view of ethics and how its meaning relates to wider Buddhist teachings. The study of ethics as a philosophy or as an academic subject is only of little use for life, therefore I will discuss the practical application of ethics within a Buddhist framework and other religious and cultural backgrounds.

Most of the conflicts in the world are due to different views of life. Man's struggle to survive has resulted in the formulation of varying economic theories over time. These theories necessarily focus on the control of scarce resources and are shaped by political views. For instance, classical economics evolved from the idea of profit maximisation and the self-interest of individuals (Thomas Hobbes 17th Century British philosopher), although these economic theories are less focused on human behaviour. To avoid confrontation deeper insight into human behaviour must be addressed.

The present economic crisis, compounded by the Covid19 lockdown in 2020, suggests the need for a shift from the old economic paradigm. This could concentrate on building constructive human relations to improve the considerateness of individuals and rearranging resources to obtain optimal results and fair distribution. Sharing mutual values can strengthen the trade ties between nations avoiding trade wars.

A trade war occurs when a nation imposes tariffs or quotas on imports, and foreign countries retaliate with similar forms of trade protectionism. As it escalates, a trade war reduces international trade. A trade war starts when a nation attempts to protect its domestic industry and create jobs or protect high wage jobs and high-value-added manufacturing industry. One of the most important factors trigger rift are intellectual property theft and forced technology transfer.

The organisation of resources can be done in such a way that it takes into consideration methods of improving interrelations and increasing goodwill. Game theory is an example of an unconstructive approach, it divides people into winners and losers. Economic decisions affect human behaviour and should be examined in terms of how they improve the efforts of individuals to collaborate with one another in order to improve living standards for all. If you view others as enemy then it builds up fear and mistrust. Following that thought would lead to extreme blind view of eliminating enemy threat by using all available means. In a world of nuclear states possessing devastating nuclear weapons, if such power would unleash, there would be no winners.

The gap between rich and poor has widened during the recent past, many families are struggling to make ends meet while a few are enjoying a mega-rich lifestyle, which, could be argued, contradicts the common values of humanity.

CHAPTER 17

# ECONOMIC DEVELOPMENT

THERE ARE MANY DEFINITIONS OF economic development, and this has always been an integral subject to political debate. Economic activities have become increasingly complex due to the transition from an agriculturally based economy to one of industrialisation. The tertiary sector is the sector of the economy that concerns services such as banking. It is distinct from the secondary sector (manufacturing) and the primary sector (which concerns extraction such as mining, agriculture, and fishing), therefore mathematics and scientific ideas were introduced to measure these activities and their effect. The measure of economic performances and indicators are not simple. Economics is thus now a scientific subject.

Because of increased scientific development and modern banking systems, the understanding of economics is no longer simple but requires specialised knowledge. Governments control their economies by fiscal policy and other legislation. These policies reflect the nation's political ideology.

In a democratic society, people decide what suits them best according to their level of understanding, beliefs, and value systems. We can argue that the standard of living of a society depends on the level of understanding of economics; how the economic resources are arranged and used for production and distribution irrespective of the political ideology. This subject has two dimensions: the wider study of economics is known as macroeconomics, and the small-scale study of markets or activities of a firm within an industry sector is called microeconomics. Usually, governments take care of the macroeconomics and determine how the nation's wealth is managed.

It is reflected in the government fiscal policy.

Microeconomics is the study of how business enterprises arrange their individual resources. The more wisely these limited resources are used the better it is for the welfare of the nation. Main economic indicators are GDP, inflation, interest rate, and employment rate. The balance of payments (BOP) is one of the important economic indicators that records all international financial transactions made by the residents of a country. The balance of payments is a summary of all the international transactions, imports and exports of that country and its citizens engaged in foreign earnings during a specified period of time. This period is usually one year, though many countries have now started preparing the quarterly accounts for the purposes of forecasting.

The word 'residents' has a wider meaning to include business firms, governments, and international agencies located in a particular country. The residents are not necessarily always citizens of the country. According to the International Monetary Fund (IMF), "The Balance of Payments is a statistical statement for a given period as described below.

There are three main categories of the BOP: the current account, the capital account, and the financial account. The current account is used to mark the inflow and out-flow of goods and services into a country. When the value of imported goods and services is higher than the value of a country's exports, there is a trade deficit which is an indicator of poor export performances, high consumption of foreign goods such as expensive cars, oil and poor global trade relations that might have resulted from poor foreign relations. The high deficit in BOP could be a result of debt financing for capital goods on higher loan interest rates.

Therefore, it is important for countries to have good foreign policy components with developed nations for greater economic benefits taking primacy of comparative advantage and fair trade.

Deardorff's Glossary of International Economics defines "economic development" as "the sustained increase in the economic standard of living of a country's population, normally accomplished by increasing its stock of physical and human capital and improving its technology. A stock or stock variable is an economic magnitude that describes a quantity that exists at a given economy at a given time. It could include a country's international reserves in terms of foreign currency, gold, and bonds. A consumer's wealth and country's labour force are also counted as stock".

Traditionally, total economic activities were measured by Gross Domestic Product (GDP) and Gross National Product (GNP), these are the country's total economic activity and exports respectively. Economic growth is the increase in the amount of goods and services produced by an economy over time and is used interchangeably with economic development. The term 'sustained economic growth' has been added recently due to many economic failures in the past.

Economists are beginning to realise the damage caused by an over-application of monetary theory, this is unsustainable in the long term. By this approach, resources are consumed too quickly, and pollution increasingly becomes a problem in the environment in which we live. A sustainable economy suggests the moderation of consumption, such as the middle path of Buddhism.

Buddhism is the only religion that specifically recognizes 'right livelihood'; one must choose a career that is not damaging to society and the environment alike. Buddha prohibited his disciples from even breaking a branch off a tree without due consideration. There are a few trades that are banned for laypeople, such as selling poison, weapons, and animals for slaughter, because the damage of such trades contribute to the economy is much greater and its moral retribution is cyclical.

The danger of selling poison and weapons to society without a proper license is self-explanatory, there are many stories of senseless killing sprees in modern societies, particularly in the USA. For example, on 15th December 2012 just before Christmas in the USA, a gunman killed 20 children and six adults in the State of Connecticut at Sandy Hook Elementary School in Newtown. The gunman is thought to have had several weapons, including two handguns, a Glock, and Sig Sauer and a 223 semi-automatic rifle, all purchased on the US open market.

In Washington, about 200 people held a candlelight vigil for the victims outside the White House, whilst others protested there to call for tougher gun controls. This is not the first time such an incident has happened in the USA; these events show that western society is losing its value system. Most recently, there was a shooting incident reported in

Colorado USA on the November 19, 2022, late Saturday night. At least five people were killed when a man stormed into a night club and opened fire, at least 25 other people were said to be injured in the chaos.

As a matter of fact, when children are brought up without an education in ethical values, they can harbour hatred until adulthood and take revenge on innocent victims.

It is the responsibility of governments to control gun law and introduce strict regulations, however law itself cannot prevent anyone unlawfully using weapons.

There is a Buddhist proverb that says "Those who take up weapons get destroyed by weapons"; this discourages the use or ownership of any kind of weapon. Similarly, in the West it is said, 'If you live by the sword, you die by the sword'.

A similar tragedy happened in July 2011 in northwest Oslo, Norway, when a ferocious attack on youth summer camp took place by a far right racist named Anders Breivik, who massacred about 91 and injured at least another 110 innocent youths. It was the deadliest attack in Norway since World War II. The U.S. Secretary of State at that time, Mrs Hillary Clinton, among many world leaders, publicly condemned the attack in Norway, "this tragedy strikes right at the heart of the soul of a peaceful people", she said. The tragedy of the destruction caused in wars by modern weapons needs no further comment.

A mass shooting occurred near and in the Nakhon Ratchasima province of Thailand, colloquially known as Korat. The incident happened on the 8 February 2020 and continued to the next day. A soldier of the Royal Thai Army killed 29 people and wounded 58 others before he was eventually shot and killed by military marksmen. The attack began when the perpetrator shot and killed his commanding officer and two others at a military camp where he was stationed. The perpetrator then stole military weapons and a military vehicle to drive to the Terminal 21 Korat shopping mall, which had a large number of shoppers due to the public holiday, where he opened fire on shoppers.

The gun is, of course, a major accessory of serious pre-meditated crime. There have been many studies in public health literature about the illegal use of guns, many crimes reports and incidents of gun violence such as homicides, suicides, armed robberies, or gun accidents; however, only a few studies have examined the legal use of guns and the cultural elements associated with gun ownership.

The term "gun culture" was coined in 1970 by Hofstadter, he viewed it as monolithic and described it as the Americans' unique belief in the "notion that the people's right to bear arms is the greatest protection of their individual rights and a firm safeguard of democracy" (Hofstadter, 1970).

Douglas Richard Hofstadter is an American scholar of cognitive science, physics, and comparative literature whose research includes concepts such as the sense of self in relation to the external world, consciousness, analogy-making, artistic creation, and literary translation. He was the award-winning author of *The Age of Reform* 1956. The term "Gun culture" in the United States encompasses the behaviours, attitudes, and beliefs about firearms and their usage by civilians.

Legal ownership of guns in the United States is the highest in the world and politics tends to be polarized between conservatives who are advocates of gun rights, while liberals support stricter gun control. In accordance with Hofstadter's theory, some people believe that the people's right to bear arms is the greatest protection of their individual rights and a firm safeguard of democracy.

The orderly population think that gun culture brings serious damage to the economy and that there is no simple way of estimating the direct human or social cost, much less the indirect political costs, of having lax gun laws.

Hofstadter argued that American politics has always been an arena in which conflicts of interests have been fought out, compromised, and adjusted. Once, these interests were sectional, they now tend to follow class lines more clearly. From the beginning of American political parties, instead of representing single sections or classes clearly and forcefully, there have been intersectional and interclass parties, embracing a jumble of interests which often have reasons of contest among themselves.

During the November 2020 US election, some people were heavily armed when they came to the polling stations to vote, portraying a self-defence subculture. The temperament of those carrying arms was defensive, ready to standoff, and closer to retaliate if provoked. Today, the urban population of the nation is probably more heavily armed than at any other time in history, largely because of the conservatism, whereby guns and ammunition are easily available to purchase.

There can exist measurable variations in attitudes to gun culture across states. The core of the US gun culture is a complex psychological disposition that can be traced to a time of indigenous communities of Red Indians, there was a continued armed struggle between the natives and the white settlers' encroachments of their land. The history of this includes massacres of both sides, and this led to newly arrived settlers to always being armed. During colonial times, white settlers were encouraged to hunt because it gave them paramilitary training, it mostly compromised on subsistence hunting to feed their families.

The historical background and culture of native Americans are well depicted in the award winning epic historical drama film *The Last of the Mohicans (1992 film)*. It is a narrative of 1757 French and Indian war. It is a historical romance written by James Fenimore Cooper in 1826, a story of rescue operation in the crossfire of gruesome military conflict.

In the 19th century, new meanings were attributed to hunting. Because it had historically been reserved for aristocrats, it became a symbol of democracy in the newly formed United States. However, hunting, as with possession of guns was then mostly available to the wealthy elites and became a sport for white upper-class men similar to banned fox hunting in the UK.

Before we seek a solution for the criminal behaviour of people, it is worth understanding what underpins these emotional reactions and their relation to the function of society. The person who turns into a criminal and takes revenge does so as a response to unresolved grievances. It could be for a real reason or due to delusions of psychotic perception which are engraved in the perpetrator's mind over a period of time. According to Buddhist psychology, anger is a consciousness rooted in hatred. It manifests as an emotion relating to the perception of having been offended by the denial of experiencing satisfaction. This rejection provokes a person to react through retaliation. These acts are not necessarily spontaneous responses to stop an immediate threat but a premeditated crime. Those gunmen satisfy their ego and retribution by taking the lives of most vulnerable people.

There are many views of revenge. During the Middle Ages, revenge was an acceptable social norm. Anglo Saxon societies had a payment system that placed a monetary value on acts of violence to stop the spiral effect of revenge.

Many ancient arts and contemporary stories project revenge in different forms of justice. For example, in the modern film 'Star Wars Episode III Revenge of the Sith' (2005), the Emperor says, "Revenge is the foundation of justice. Justice began with revenge, and revenge is the only justice some beings can ever hope for".

Filmmakers and storytellers take these ideas from incidents that actually happened during those times, from history or from legends. Gun culture and gang cultures are still common in this world. For example, in February 2007 a fifteen-year-old boy was shot dead at point blank range inside his house, while he was sleeping, a victim of a South London gang war. Within eleven days three other teenagers were shot and killed.

During the journalistic investigation, it was said by a 16-year-old from the estate that, "Getting hold of a gun around here is as easy as going into a McDonald's and getting a McChicken sandwich. If I had the money, I could make a phone call and get a gun now... It wouldn't cost (as much as £150), you could ask anyone to borrow a gun... they would let you." A former member of the residents' association told the Guardian newspaper how a seemingly small slight could trigger a devastating response.

"It could easily have been that he had done something little, and that sparked this", said another youngster from Brixton. "These gangs operate on respect; if someone feels that they have been dissed, they have to act or it's them that looks bad, and they are seen as weak." (The Guardian 16.2.2007).

This sort of gang culture gives youths a sense of identity, a sense of belonging and being valued, often lacking in their family backgrounds. Young children from broken families are likely to join these gangs and there are many reasons and triggers for revenge. This sort of gang culture gives youths a sense of identity, a sense of belonging and being valued in an environment lacking in their family backgrounds.

A perceived injustice is often the basis of revenge, this can brew over many years. Untreated frustration will continue to build up until it erupts into violent behaviour. When capable of using weapons, such people make a direct aggressive response by taking revenge. It could be argued that such young men suffer from internal frustration born out of their own deficiencies and family environment, such deficiencies as the lack of effective parental control, lack of confidence to discuss personal issues and society's failure to offer them help.

They may not have developed mental faculties to reason out their problems and therefore act irrationally by attacking the perceived barriers. More research is needed to find out the actual contributory factors. Revenge has a psychological, moral, and cultural cause. From primitive times to modern-day advanced institutionalized societies, we can see evidence of revenge, often out of all proportion to the original encroachment.

These acts cause severe damage to the economy and, at present, are only dealt with by law and law enforcement agencies. Modern Western legal systems attempt to reform or re-educate convicted criminals. In some cases, a person is too internally weak to face the consequences of their actions which can result in suicide. An extreme example of revenge is terrorism. Anger becomes the predominant feeling behaviourally, cognitively, and physically leading to the conscious choice to act immediately and stop the threatening behaviour of another outside force.

There are always two sides to a story. Before deciding what course of action to take one has to weigh both sides. A person who experiences long term provocation or frustration may find it difficult to establish the original cause of his frustration and becomes angrier until it becomes a complex mental problem. A person with an angry disposition may seek violent and unpredictable methods to take revenge. The best solution to this situation is in its prevention rather than its cure. Of course, there may also be genetic reasons which push a person into being violent as well as dietary causes.

Gun violence is an urgent, complex, and multifaceted problem, thus requiring evidence-based, multifaceted solutions. An ill-defined problem poses challenges that are not easily solvable with no obvious answer. There may be many layers to the tasks that need to be completed in order to solve the problem.

Antecedent to gun violence is the gun culture that has existed from the beginning of white settlers and colonial times in America, now widely accepted by its society. Psychology can make important contributions to explain any account of gun violence in the United States. Policymakers must understand the history of the legal ownership of guns and the psychology of perpetrators in order to design a policy that prevents gun violence. Towards this end, more research-based conclusions and recommendations are needed on how to reduce the incidence of gun violence whether by homicide, suicide, or mass shootings at innocent victims. A complex and variable constellation of psychological factors makes a person more or less likely to use a firearm against themselves or others.

For this reason, there is no single profile that can reliably predict who will use a gun in a violent act. Instead, gun violence is associated with a confluence of individuals, families, schools, peers, communities, and sociocultural risk factors that interact over time during childhood and adolescence. Although many youths desist in aggressive and antisocial behaviour during late adolescence, others are disproportionately at risk of becoming involved in or otherwise affected by gun violence.

The most consistent and powerful predictor of future violence is the history of an individual's violent behaviour. The most obvious reasons for gun crimes are a lack of moral base, availability to purchase these weapons like any other commodity, exposure to violent movies and the like, that contribute to the formation of a mindset that characterises criminality as normal.

Economic theories that reject ethics and moral values are more likely to create societies that disregard human rights and moral responsibility for their actions. Economic development is not complete unless it creates an environment for peaceful living.

According to Buddhism, economic doctrine must be realistic and practical with an aim of improving human capital and intrinsic long-term sustainable development. It is valuable only if it serves a real purpose and the needs of people. Buddha addressed the reality of life and provided a practical solution to the truth of suffering.

Buddhism is not in conflict with other religions. Buddha did not advocate following and supporting him-self alone, he recognised the diversity in people's beliefs and advised people to follow their own religious leaders and social activities. For example, he addressed "samana and brahmana" meaning his contemporaries and other nonviolent religious followers. He advised them to follow their masters and come to his teaching only when they were ready to understand the advanced, absolute truth of life. Buddhist social philosophy recognises and supports good activities that improve the social welfare for many.

Modern economists are turning to Buddhist ideas of the middle path and are taking into consideration the human factor that these involve. Economic and political activities are the result of people's behaviour as performed by their actions. The Buddha identified that lifestyle is a series of actions which are performed by an individual during their employment. A right lifestyle would ensure that right actions are carried out so as not to acquire bad kamma (volitional action). The Buddha's discovery of the principles of kamma is pivotal to his teaching. The middle path encompasses all the important factors required to live our lives peacefully.

Choosing the right balance between what we need and what we want makes a big difference in our economic choices. One of the main theories of economics is supply and demand; in a free market economy, consumers demand what they need, and producers supply the goods and services. The price consumers are willing to pay is determined at the point where supply meets the demand. Price is controlled by the fluctuating market mechanism of supply and demand. Consumers can expect a reasonable price by moderation of consumption.

The employment market is also subject to the same principle of supply and demand for labour. An individual in the free-market economy can improve his or her standard of living by right livelihood.

To choose the right livelihood one must acquire the right knowledge and skills demanded by a given industry.

In modern society, this requires a broad commercial awareness. The concepts of 'specialization,' 'exchange' and the 'free market economy' were first introduced by British economist Adam Smith (Wealth of Nations 1776). Smith was a moral philosopher and pioneer in the Scottish Enlightenment. He was greatly influenced by his senior philosopher, David Hume. Smith proposed that by skilful means one can be a specialist and exchange one's skills to meet one's needs. In this way, a nation's wealth can be increased by advanced labour skills. Smith lectured that the cause of any increase in national wealth is labour, rather than the nation's quantity of gold or silver, which is the basis for mercantilism. Smith had a more moderate view of wealth and how wealth is created than Karl Marx.

Modern economists further developed Smith's ideas and gave more recognition to human input. In America, they introduced a new concept of 'knowledge workers', a different view of labour from that of the traditionalists.

According to Professor Michael Todaro, economic development is an improvement in living conditions and of people's self-esteem, it needs a free and just society. He suggested that the most accurate method of measuring economic development is the Human Development Index which considers literacy rates, mortality, and life expectancy.

An educated workforce is more productive which can make a strong impact on Economic Growth.

There are not only quantitative but also qualitative economic measurements. This can be achieved by investing in human capital. Increasing the literacy ratio, improving the infrastructure of the education system, improvement in health and safety and other areas such as healthcare can increase the welfare of people. These improvements are decided by governments through policies and spending plans.

Planning and its implementations need political stability, usually a term of five years in the UK and four years in USA. Every government has economic development plans. These plans would be more successful if only the whole nation would collectively support and contribute to the achievement of the plan's targets. Any political division jeopardises a country's progress. There are many factors which influence an economy including new discoveries in science and technology.

This can improve the use of scarce resources which creates the need for modernisation in every major economic activity such as transport, healthcare, sustainable renewable energy, digital products, food production and the construction industry. Before 2020, Covid-19, many organizations were beginning, or even well underway to some level of digital transformation. And once the pandemic hit, organizations had to accelerate their digital transformations like never before.

These changes require new skills and knowledge; to create new jobs the way people work has to adapt. Investing in human capital and human development is important to help people adapt and meet the challenges of new and emerging industries. For example, invention of vaccines in particular Covid-19 vaccine made the world safe from corona virus that made havoc in 2020/21.

An individual has to accept the responsibility and ownership of his or her self-development. Only the best can survive in a competitive market and employers only want the best workers who can contribute to their commercial and organisational goals. A person without developed skills is like an invalid coin that is not accepted for exchange.

Economic growth can improve household income and the temporal needs of a family. It is the responsibility of the leader of the household to ensure his or her family's welfare and encourage children in their education, skills, social ethics, and spiritual development. Good parenting is also essential for a family's emotional welfare and investing in spiritual development is equally important because it helps personal discipline, an area badly neglected in today society. Most family problems can be resolved by simple means, all religions address family values and individual responsibility within the family. In Buddhism, discipline is the foundation of family harmony, basic skills and understanding higher spiritual values.

A person who is disciplined gains respect and is an asset to society, a law-abiding citizen also makes a greater contribution to the economy. In the same way, a happy worker is more productive and contributes to economic success, therefore employers should also look after their workforce. Antisocial behaviour causes damage to economic progress and discourages hard-working people.

Economic development will be successful only if the whole nation is willing to give their best towards achieving it. It also requires right policies, good leadership, realistic targets, and transparency of government information on which these decisions are made. The government has to prioritise its improvements plans according to the industry sectors and needs of the people.

There are many qualitative indicators that measure the economic health of a nation. Today's children are the generation who will be responsible for the country in the future, but to build a strong economy in the future the government has to identify what the current problems are and take immediate corrective measures. These can be measured by indicators such as the child poverty rate, child literacy rates, infant morbidity, and juvenile crime rate. Economic prosperity should not be an illusion for them. Currently, many sectors are underfunded, redistribution may help balance this deficit.

There is an opportunity cost that need to take into consideration when allocating resources. Money spent on developing weapons and wars could have been spent on education, research, development, the health sector, environmental protection, renewable energy sources, eco-friendly technology, and human capital. Another area is the need to improve international relations between nations to improve trade between countries taking comparative advantage. Comparative advantage is an economy's ability to produce a particular good or service at a lower opportunity cost than its trading partners. Comparative advantage is used to explain why companies, countries, or individuals can benefit from trade.

The United Nation Organisation which was set up after World War II (originally established as the League of Nations established after World War I) could be more active in its position and function as a true catalyst to improve cooperation between nations, tackling child poverty and to ensure the welfare of all.

## Investing in Economic Development

Economic development is an essential part of meeting the basic needs of people and the long-term sustainable growth of economic activity. This growth depends on various factors i.e. the geographical location of a country. For example, if a country is geographically isolated with big distances to markets, it could be difficult to sell any products at competitive prices. Other factors are poor infrastructure, corruption, political instability, and ethnic division, all of which can make a country unattractive to foreign direct investment (FDI) in a global economic environment.

Among other things, a country's natural resources and its culture are the most important factors that influence decisions about which are the best areas for development. A country's economic model should be built by taking into consideration the welfare of the many in order to distribute wealth to the benefit of all, reducing inequality and poverty.

The workforce of a country is equally important for any investment decision; if the workforce is not flexible and adaptable to new technological changes no one will want to invest. In Buddhist countries, workforces can be trained in intermediate to high technology industries very easily because they have flexible attitudes to work and the ability to learn advanced skills quickly.

Buddhism has a culture of patience and teaches people to learn new knowledge and practice new skills, they have an aptitude of developing art and crafts. More importantly, people accept responsibility for their families and want to be self-reliant, this is one of the main principles of Buddhism for families to take responsibility. These personal attributes cannot be imprinted on people's minds without a suitable cultural upbringing.

Social culture, values, and industry are inseparable aspects in a highly developed industrial country like Japan for example. Some of the Japanese corporations apply Zen Buddhist principles to train corporate executives to improve productivity, competitiveness, inventions, and innovations.

The Japanese Motor Company Toyota introduced its world-class business philosophy by process reengineering and empowering its workforce through teamwork. Delivery cycle time was reduced to a 'just in time' philosophy, goods are purchased only when needed thereby reducing the cost of stocks. These ideas were later applied to service industries such as banking, insurance, and transport. It was not long before many Western and emerging industrial countries adopted these concepts to improve their production outputs.

Many countries overlook the link between economic growth to the rate of growth in population. This can lead to a high level of educated youths in unemployment. Many civil revolutions and much social unrest have been instigated by educated university students.

Since the Russian revolution, started by the Marxist movement and led by Lenin, many underdeveloped countries have followed these ideas causing long term damage to their economies. For example, in Sri Lanka, the far leftist youth movement twice attempted to overthrow elected governments by armed struggle, copying the Argentine Marxist Revolutionary leader Che Guevara.

He was a young medical student who was moved by poverty, hunger and disease in Latin America and turned into an insurgent against capitalist American exploitation of his people. He played a key role in the Cuban Revolution and extended his active participation until the Cuban missile crisis that fuelled the Cold War. There are active youth movements in universities in developed countries also.

Knowledge can be dangerous unless it is used with wisdom. Wisdom in this sense is to understand how everything is interdependent and interconnected whilst assessing the consequence of actions by concentrating on collectivist thinking to improving the welfare of all.

There are many mathematical, statistical, and computerised tools to predict the behaviour of consumer markets. In the modern world, the global economy is controlled not only by market mechanisms but also by banking systems that allows the flow of capital between countries.

There are two main contributors in an economy, providers of capital and providers of labour. Financial instruments such as shares, bonds and debentures are used as forms of capital. International corporations have taken over the main supplies of essential goods and services, and they control large parts of world resources that inevitably control the employment market.

The Free-Market model has shifted to oligopoly and monopoly markets which leaves small businesses unable to compete directly with them. These corporations are more efficient because they can take advantage of the economies of scale thus reducing costs associated with production and distribution. However, pure profit motivation could lead to market failures causing government intervention.

Governments in developed countries rely on small to medium-size enterprises for job creation. They prefer mix of both private and public partnership in business activities. Profit-making businesses in modern technologically driven production and service industries recruit people with the right aptitude and attitude to flourish in a competitive environment. It requires potential employees to have the right level of education, skills, and ability to train. At present there is a disparity. There are not enough organised institutions to train young people even in areas of skill shortage. For example, nurse-training schemes in the UK, which constitute one of the most important jobs in the healthcare industry are underfunded. Many small nations are struggling to compete with developed nations without adequate support by monetary funding. Their trained young people are leaving native country to take up jobs abroad and those remaining have to work under difficult conditions.

In this sense, the principles of the Young Men's Christian Association (YMCA) constitute noble ideas of George Williams on which the organisation was founded in the West. In 1844, he organised facilities to support young men in response to unhealthy social conditions arising from the Industrial Revolution (roughly 1750 - 1850). The centralisation of commercial activities and improvement of the rail transport system in the UK brought many young men to big cities like London. However, the social and living conditions were not at all good at that time. There wasn't a proper sewage system and there was the risk of contagious diseases. Streets were full of pickpockets, thugs, beggars, drunks, and abundant children. Young men were exposed to various dangers and life was largely miserable.

George William was a shop worker who wanted to help his other fellow young men and started the Christian organisation. This crossed the rigid line that separated all other churches and social classes that divided England in those days. His philosophy was to help all young men, women, and children without discrimination of race, religion, or nationality with honest compassion towards improving the social needs in the community.

His idea soon spread to America, and it was endorsed by President Abraham Lincoln. All YMCA members were volunteers, during the war they even assisted troops and prisoners of war. George Williams was knighted by Queen Victoria in 1894. During the Great Depression YMCAs became aware of the social problems which faced them. They extended their programme and mission in partnership with other social welfare agencies in order to meet the challenges of the time, identifying the need for group work, sports, and character building exercises.

The YMCA later became a training centre for office skills, commercial studies, vocational training and is a major influence on the welfare of young people. In America, the YMCA works in collaboration with most prestigious institutions of higher education. Williams set an unforgettable and remarkable example of care for vulnerable young people. He died in 1905 and was buried under the floor of St. Paul's Cathedral among the great British nation's heroes and statesmen. This noble act proves that "if you have a will there is a way" to develop yourselves even in on a time of economic difficulties.

Everything around us may not be very pleasant and pleasing, especially in an economic depression, our situations can be hard and harsh. Ernst Barlach was one of the few among the Western writers who had a closer understanding of this reality. Barlach was a German expressionist sculptor and a writer, projecting his ideas of reality through art and sculpture. From 1888 to 1985, he studied at the Gewerbeschule Hamburg and the Royal Art School Dresden. He was moved by poverty and street beggars, which led him to question what might lighten up their lives. During this time, the western world was desperate for new ideas of economic change. Ernst Barlach perceived war might change the lives of people. His arts portrayed dramatic attitudes expressing powerful emotions of men yearning for spiritual ecstasy, hope and enlightenment.

In the years before World War I, Barlach was a patriotic and enthusiastic supporter of the war and in 1915 he volunteered to join the German Army as an infantry soldier. However, the experience of war changed his views, and he soon became an anti-war pacifist. The horror of the war, human suffering, loss of loved ones, its effects on families and the cruelty of war influenced all his subsequent artworks. Instead of heroic German soldiers fighting for their glorious country, Barlach projected a controversial hallmark of horror, pain, desperation, and despair of the war. During the rise of the Nazi movement, he was the target of criticism, and his artwork was removed from city centres. In 1936, his works were branded "degenerate art", he was prohibited from working as a sculptor and was seen as pessimistic about the achievements of war.

Seeing the truth of war, as it was, Barlach stood up to what he honestly believed. The facts of life can often be stubborn influences and may not be very pleasant to discuss. A realistic solution may only be found if we understand the facts and the truth behind the problem.

Many economists believe war is not totally evil but can change the world to be a better place. There is an English saying, 'Water is the mother of civilisation and war is the daughter of civilisation'. Many economists ignore human feelings and decisions to go to war are often made without much concern for emotions. Art can be a powerful vehicle and conveys the truth of life which many people fail to see. Barlach was brave to tell the truth and the new generations of Germans appreciate his work.

Suffering is common to everyone; it does not discriminate and can be a very powerful emotion for awakening to reality.

## Drivers of Economic Development

Sustainable economic development depends on the moderation of consumption and the use of natural resources within regenerative limits. Planning for economic development begins with identifying the growth factors that drive economic activities of a particular field. The economist has to evaluate the industry structure of a given economy and invest in areas that have optimal growth, measuring cost and benefits. For example, a well-managed Agriculture has the benefit of food security. On the other hand, cutting down rain-forest for farming may be damaging to the ecological balance of the environment that can erode the fertile land and cause drought.

In Brazil, controlled deforestation and conversion to agriculture has been successful. The target industry must generate maximum sustainable returns from promising opportunities thereby improving trading activities, strengthening relations with investors at home and abroad which in turn expands exports to foreign markets. Compared with government programmes the private sector is more efficient and effective in terms of market exploitation because it reduces bureaucratic decision-making and enables quick business decisions.

Trade between countries can be also improved by international agreements giving fair market price to the producers and facilitating supply chain development, i.e. Fair-Trade coffee.

There is a need for the world leaders to come together to address challenges and barriers that prevent international trade and instead to foster a climate of economic cooperation. Major infrastructure developments such as shipping, civil aviation, rail, and transport should be carried out with planning and be coordinated with other countries, taking into consideration the effects on those countries, taking best geographical advantage for the best international business environment.

Government fiscal policies and tax systems can be made attractive for international trade to enable a better business environment. Most facilitation of international business is carried out by investment banks and centralised organisations such as the International Monetary Fund. Easy access to finance is an important factor for improving trade between countries recognising their production possibility frontier and comparative advantage.

## Fine Material Consciousness Era

Material things have great usefulness in improving living standards. Our knowledge and understanding of the properties of materials and our skills to shape their form for specific purposes has gone through many stages of development. For example, the building industry and automotive industry have achieved greater efficiency of use of materials and have contributed to improving the living standards of the general population.

The use of materials has gone through a detailed refining process along with the development of science and technology. In the area of chemistry and physics, scientists have discovered principles and methods to refine earth materials to an ultrafine specification. For example, the pharmaceutical and textile industry has reached such a high level of refinement that we find it hard to believe the raw materials for their production have come from the earth. This period in Buddhism is known as the *Fine Materials Consciousness Era*, whereby man is using his consciousness to seek the best material forms. Significant amounts of money are spent on pure research and developmental research. For example, the Imperial College of London has dedicated a vast amount of resources for the development of knowledge in science and engineering. The development of fibre optic network communications in the 5G computer technology has created fast and efficient communication channels that were unthinkable a century ago. Data storage, social media platforms has changed the way we work and live. To keep up with the growing demand for content, enterprises must prioritize digital transformation, use new technology and become digital factories that continuously deliver innovation across their digital landscape.

Buddhism views these human capabilities as valuable and helpful in improving the quality of life. On the other hand, these achievements should not be taken as ends in themselves, nor is consumerism the only purpose of life, this is only the materialistic view of life. Beyond the simple application of materials for everyday use, the Buddha discovered that the human consciousness can be further refined. There are meditation methods that refine consciousness beyond the material sphere to the immaterial sphere. In this realm, the mind reaches its ultimate conditional state of neither perception nor non-perception.

Reaching this level of higher concentration and consciousness is difficult to achieve for laypeople who are busily engaged in economic activities. Anyone wishing to refine the mind to a higher spiritual level through concentration meditation is expected to leave the attachment of worldly gains and enter the path of purification.

Our attachment to wealth can cause suffering. Our understanding of wealth, how we define and perceive it makes a big difference to our happiness. In the modern economy, wealth is defined in terms of asset value and disposable cash. What we can buy with money for our enjoyment and our general spending power makes a significant difference to our standard of living. Rich and famous people are currently enjoying a high life. However, it also brings them worry and anxiety due to the need to earn and maintain that level of wealth. For example, famous people are very sensitive about public criticism, especially with the use of social media. Their popularity can be affected by the slightest mistake or improper behaviour. Many famous people suffer from personality disorders and depression. Much pressure is exerted on them with regard to their public image and how they present themselves. This kind of constant pressure can lead to breakdowns in relationships, especially with family and children. They also have high levels of anxiety surrounding issues of divorce and money matters showing the impermance nature of worldly happiness that depend on something else.

# CHAPTER 18

# PHILOSOPHY OF ETHICS

## Introduction - In search of Excellence

THE PURPOSE OF THIS CHAPTER (Part II) is to discuss and explain a framework for ethics as it was understood by earlier contributors and its development throughout history. The framework for teaching ethics has now been employed in mainstream education from GCE/GCSE to A Levels and also several universities and schools of higher education around the world, including the University of Oxford as one of the most prestigious universities teaching philosophy.

The study of moral philosophy or ethics can deepen our reflections on and critical examination of some important questions in life. From a young age, it is valuable to learn, understand and be prepared in an ethical sense, to be able to look at our own lives, to evaluate our own actions, choices and take wise decisions especially when faced with difficult and complex situations.

Even in this 21$^{st}$ century, with the advancement of technology and scientific knowledge continually expanding, we are unable to resolve complex social and political moral dilemmas. Philosophical questions on ethics and moral values which have been asked since the time of the Ancient Greek philosophers still continue to perplex us.

Buddhism is one such answer to moral philosophy based on nonviolence; it can influence and enrich Western ethics with natural laws, to make them of a more practical value, to know ourselves better, to reach our personal inner peace, happiness, and make ourselves free.

Moral philosophy and ethical principles have been developed through centuries by the careful evaluation of cultural values, social governance, and norms. Moral philosophy can help us strengthen our personal traits and clarify our moral positions when making judgements, improving our perspective by reflecting on wider social relationships. Our actions affect ourselves and, in some ways, affect others.

A person with integrity and honesty is able to set guiding principles that can help others to decide what actions are to be taken in a difficult situation. To be in control of your emotions and to be resilient are the defining character attributes of a stable personality.

Philosophy of ethics is the study of the fundamental nature of knowledge, human behaviour, reality, and existence. It is an activity people undertake when they seek to understand themselves, the world they live in, and their relations to the world and each other. People in their daily life make both explicit and implicit choices that extend beyond the objective and practical way of life, this can cause a conflict of interests with others or could contest existing customs and norms of the society.

The major cultural traditions that influenced Europe are Greek and Roman cultures. These can be traced back as early as 700 BCE to the Greek poet Hesiod who contributed to bringing order to a rather chaotic Greek culture at that time. Yet, it was the Socratic period to give the primary impulse that prompts many to study ethics.

The Romans adopted most of the Greek myths to suit their imperial interests as characterised by a pagan culture and military might. There were no developed ethical values to be found during their dominant power culture until Emperor Constantine's period, who rejected paganism and replaced it with Christianity.

Ethics is an ambitious and multifaceted subject which can be traced back to the time of Socrates, however the proper direction of its development was soon lost after his execution, thought to be an unjust act by many of his followers. The work begun by Socrates laid the foundation for the discussions of ethics and soon his followers applied this theme to seek social justice.

Aristotle became the head of the Academy of Athens, being influential to the government he engaged in teaching and formulating a public policy by taking most of the aspects of Socrates's doctrine to formulate a political philosophy that defined citizens' position and their freedom within a social system. Rather than intellectual study, his vision was the application of practical values and the efficacy of ethics in daily life and public affairs.

Crucially, Aristotle did not challenge or question the authority, instead, he simply set out a description of what he honestly believed to be the common good and moral values for human development, this was presented in a persuasive manner to reform social justice. Since then, ethics has been very much entangled in politics.

## Ethics and Public Policy

In many ways, the central, deeply complex task of government policy perspectives is in balancing and coming to conclusions about the rights and duties of individuals, communities, and populations and with regard to protecting and maintaining individual rights.

People's conduct is hence regulated by law and order which has been derived from public policy.

Governments then delegate authority to law enforcement agencies who carry out this task. Yet, evidence strongly suggests that agents representing the government often receive little training or guidance on how to reach decisions informed by careful ethical thinking to become confident in a moral sense about the 'trade-offs' they are frequently required to enact in practice. For example, in recent years, the number of deaths in police custody has increased in US cities causing resentment in people to repudiate against the authority.

Climate change is another hot topic in the years 2019 – 2020, causing demonstrations in big European cities that demanded governments to take corrective action. Then, the Covid-19 outbreak in March 2020 lead to school closures, social distancing rules, national lockdown measures and a subsequent vaccine rollout in the UK and US which further highlighted various ethical questions.

These incidents call into question the fundamentals of public policy, forcing politicians to critically evaluate key values, examining the concepts of moral and ethical values that should inform public policy. Public policy in practice must promote the careful and critical evaluation of ethical thinking that underpins good policy decisions, reviewing underlining assumptions and reflecting on the moral complexities.

Policymakers must engage with and address class-based inequalities, especially in a multi-ethnic society so that everyone is treated equally. It should explore practical dilemmas when the government's purpose may conflict with fundamental values such as basic human rights and treating people with dignity. Public policy is to promote common good and common standard that are fundamentally moral which brings value and integrity to society.

Those who work in government agencies rarely act without having taken up normative positions on the purpose of the agency by which they are employed, this corresponds to the nature of its particular interventions and activities. They appear to operate with certain beliefs about, for example, the kind of society that people should be aiming to reproduce or about the sorts of ways in which individuals, communities or populations should lead their lives, this allows for segregation within the society. So, an important outcome of reinvestigating ethics is the capacity to make reasoned evaluations on a range of normative beliefs and values at work in society by applying a broader concept of ethics where possible. On the other hand, individuals must understand their role in the society they choose to live in, by respecting public property, the common good, the impact of their action on the economy, considering the unification of social relations, embracing the culture, and strengthening the social fabric. Not complying with the customs and norms of society would result in a conflict of interests.

## Normative Ethics

Ethics is a branch of philosophy, but nonetheless, it stands on its own right when it comes to understanding human behaviour. It can be considered as a guiding star when people doubt epistemological justification, moral values, and moral philosophical conceptions of what is valuable. Its validity has been recognised in all ancient religions, modern professions, and disciplines, for example it is currently vigorously applied in medical professions in the UK. Aspects of moral philosophy discuss value theory, normative ethics and metaethics.

Value theory investigates into: What is the good life? What is worth pursuing for its own sake? How do we improve our lives in terms of standard of living and quality of life?

These questions have been discussed since early Greek civilisation. It is argued in utilitarian theory that pleasure and enjoyment of life are valued over pain or suffering, happiness is thus a combination of pleasure and the absence of pain, pleasure is the only thing that is intrinsically good for people. Normative ethics was established over a period of time to determine norms or standards, discussing: What are our fundamental moral duties? Which character traits are virtues, and which are vices? Do the ends always justify means? How should we select our leaders?

Self-interest vs. the Common Good has been the central issue in Economic Ethics. The supposed conflict between individual self-interest and the common good is one of the hottest debated issues in economic ethics, environmental ethics as well as at the intersection between ecology and economics. Examples concerning earth ecology include air, water and seawater pollution, overfishing, the clearing of rain forest for agriculture, animal habitat destruction, the overexploitation of natural resources especially in the so-called *Third World countries*, carbon emissions and the burning of fossil fuels/non-renewable energy resources, and consequentially global warming and climate change.

The 2008 Economic and Banking collapse led to new discussions on the role of banking. From an economics perspective, both politicians and academics have debated the role of privilege through rent, special interest groups, investors, the phenomena of lobbyism and corruption, moral hazards, corporate scandals, overseas tax havens, the role of investment banking, gambling/speculation on the stock exchange, insider-dealings, market rigging, and market manipulation. This is fundamentally based on the alleged greed, avarice, and other forms of unethical behaviour as well as the near-sightedness of *some* managers, false accounting, tax fraud, the short-term oriented incentive systems in a range of practices by shareholder-value capitalism (e.g. bonus payments, short-term economic gain), etc. This all seems at odds with the broader long-term interests of other legitimate stakeholder groups like customers, suppliers, employees, and the general public.

All these phenomena may be summarized under the heading 'tragedy of the commons', given their lack of economic, social, and environmental sustainability.

These malpractices led to rethinking the role of governments and forced them to adjust potential trade-offs and compatibilities between self-interest and common welfare by remodelling economic policy and introducing new political concepts and regulations.

The value of ethics, public compliance and the need for an ethical framework has never been as necessary as at the end of the last decade with the additional burden of the Covid-19 outbreak.

To recap, today, both self-interest and competition are very important economic forces. In a capitalist model, self-interest is the primary motivator of economic activity while competition is seen as the regulator of economic activity. Together, they form what Adam Smith called the invisible hand, which guides resources to their most valued use.

Self-interest is defined as being focused on yourself or putting yourself at an advantage. An example of self-interest is thinking about your needs above the needs of others around you, thereby selfish individuals may act in a manner that's detrimental to others. Having a healthy self-interest doesn't preclude caring about others. As a result, a person with conscience may feel guilty about acting in their own self-interest. The reasoning is that taking care of your own needs will invariably have a negative impact on someone else especially if one controls economic resources out of proportion. In other words to make you better off without making someone else worse off.

Humans are clearly driven by selfishness, every action they make is intended to somehow benefit themselves. Such actions may often be perceived as kind or altruistic but the underlying motivation behind this behaviour is always driven by some form of self-interest.

The Principle of Proportionality states that responses should be proportional to the good that can be achieved and the harm that may be caused.

Relating this to medical ethics means that medical interventions and risks should be proportionate to the possible lives saved. This principle is also extended to military operations whereby civil casualties disproportionately increase with heavy artillery fire and arial bombing. The principle of proportionality prohibits attacks against military objectives which are "expected to cause incidental loss of civilian life, injury to civilians, damage to civilian objects, or a combination thereof, which would be excessive in relation to the concrete and direct military advantage anticipated".

Some evidence points to humans being innately cooperative. Studies show that in the first year of life, infants exhibit empathy toward others in distress. For example, there are always some people who come forward with humanitarian aid whether in times of war, civil unrest, or natural disasters.

It seems that human nature supports both prosocial and selfish traits. Genetic studies have made some progress toward identifying their biological roots.

Humans are certainly born with a capacity to be kind, even leaning toward kindness in many situations. Neuroscience tells us that we have certain neurons in our brains called mirror neurons, they respond when we see someone else experiencing pain in the same way as when we experience the same thing. Kindness improves our quality of life in the workplace as well as in the community, it brings people together.

Doing good for others also feels good, showing kindness to others is just as rewarding as receiving it from someone else. Similarly, compassion is a human instinct. Economic policies can improve by including these direct human qualities to benefit people in a global context.

# NOVEMBER 2020 US PRESIDENTIAL ELECTION

THE DANGER OF NOT ADDRESSING ethical values in political theory was very well demonstrated during the November 2020 US presidential election. One party claimed, 'election fraud', trying to overturn close election results and disrupt the subsequent announcement of power transition to the newly elected president.

This resulted in an angry violent mob at the Capitol Building of the US Congress where the announcement took place on 6th of January 2021. The Republicans' party-political ideology appeared to have shifted to the extreme right and the outgoing president was accused of *incitement of insurrection*, consequently he was charged with impeachment as a constitutional remedy, thus questioning his integrity to run a public office.

Capitol Building is considered as the symbol of democracy and shining light of self-rule since 1800; democracy is highly esteemed by a majority of American voters and the Capitol Building is equated to the Temple of their political system. Invading this building and the forceful attempt to overturn election results indicated the narrow self-interest of a few which shows the limitation of utility theory in its political application.

When people are deluded by political power, they over-look what is commonly valued, what they stand for and what makes life harmonious. Something is instrumentally valuable if it is valuable because of the good it brings about. In this line of argument 'Law and Order' is a good thing and something that people should value.

The political landscape of the USA has changed to a radical right-wing political preference that leans towards extreme nationalistic conservatism. This is marked by various ethnic supremacy ideologies and other right-wing beliefs in a hierarchical structure that divides society, making minority groups more vulnerable to injustice.

It characteristically shows their belief that a certain group of people is superior to all others as defined by their specific ethnic identity. This political ideology embraces the view that supremacy is a natural right for privileges in the social order and hierarchies based on socio-economic factors like wealth, income, education, occupations, social status, or derived power. As such, they seek a social position above minority groups and typically support this position based on natural law, economics, or tradition and view inequalities as inevitable.

The reactionary section of this political party holds the view that favours a return to a previous state of society which they believe possessed characteristics that are now absent in contemporary society or taken away from them, willing to take it back by excessive force and using a harsher tone of politics. These extreme groups and their leaders disregard core values; truth, accountability, civility in public discourse, opposition to racism, common ground solutions to the nation's problems, and steadfast support for the first amendment rights in the constitution.

Leaders would say "we will make this country great again", "We will take back what was stolen from us" seeking popularity and loyalty within the group. They would avoid the above ethical principles, instead, making falser or misleading statements, ducking responsibility for their actions, spewing streams of invective at their critics, inducing racial fear, and dividing people to preserve a perceived threat to national identity.

This is portrayed as a symptom of rapid social change, often due to mass immigration from corrupt countries, claiming equal rights, engaging in illegal activities, fraud, drug cartels, economic decline, and the emergence of undesirable subcultures filter that through from the influx of foreign cultures that change the character of a city or country at large.

Unmanaged cultural change and national identity can provoke extremists and those who resist social change. It is like giving ammunition and other component parts to weapons that engage a direct effect on the target they seek.

Racial differences, institutional racism and inequalities in America has it its roots going back to 1860s. Since the abolition of slavery, African Americans and their like-minded supporters always have been calling to end racial discrimination and racial segregation.

President Abraham Lincoln (1861 - 1865) led the nation through the American Civil War, the country's greatest moral, constitutional, and political crisis. American society has been divided by systemic, capitalist privatisation of economy and other philanthropic ideas keeping the privilege of distance, increasing the racial gap, making minority groups unable to reach white people's standard of living and quality of life.

The 1954 Civil Right Movement gained considerable protection in federal law for human rights against white supremacy through nonviolent resistance and civil disobedience campaigns that highlighted inequalities faced by African Americans across the country. Any kind of violence and civil unrest would petrify people.

Martin Luther King Jr., 1964 Nobel Peace Prize winner, was one of the major activists of the Civil Right Movement born to combat racial inequalities through nonviolent resistance. Minority students were able to get proper higher education and enter legal professions. A legal strategy was developed to fight within the constitution for more inclusiveness, equal rights, and most importantly ethical value of justice for all. This is the current theme of this divided nation; it requires a valued nation to build a philosophy of social governance for lasting peace and happiness.

Under the 2021 new administration, there was a visible attempt to reverse the past practices of discrimination. Societies can be greatly rewarded by dismantling politics from ethics and many other non-political themes such as art, music, and charitable activities that contain humanity. The new administration can greatly benefit from achieving higher goals such as social change, social reform, transformation of attitudes, equality, tolerance, and world peace. Especially in this period of the post Covid-19 health crisis, there is much more scope and opportunity to promote goodwill and defusing political tension by taking a leading role not only in America, but also providing leadership, special intervention, and support to rebuilding all affected countries in the world, thus improving international relations and regaining confidence.

Ethics of political speech is much debatable, whether there is any within it when comes to leading politicians speaking either directly to their supporters or in the national interest when they are under the efficacy of oaths to the office. Recent calls for ethical reforms have included questions about how or whether these declarations are honoured.

In the fraught politics of today's secularized, pluralistic society, scepticism about oaths may be tempting, but it is insufficient as the topic deserves critical reflection.

In a legal argument, prosecutors have an ethical consideration to not charge anyone for criminal offence without any firm ground on which to do so.

Political prominence is driven by emergency of the need, so the political message must be clear and effective. For example, issues concerning national security need swift action in the interest of the nation they represent.

In January 1775, Benjamin Franklin (1796-1790) was part of an American delegation sent to Britain in the attempt to resolve the outstanding disagreements between the Crown and the colonies. Seventeen points were up for discussion of which several were rejected outright by the Crown as "inadmissible" while others were rejected by the colonies.

Franklin's comments regarding the last two points produced one of his most famous sayings from the period: "Those who would give up essential liberty to purchase a little temporary safety, deserve neither liberty nor safety."

Franklin was foundational in defining the American ethos as a marriage of the practical values of thrift, hard work, education, community spirit, self-governing institutions, and opposition to authoritarianism both political and religious, with the scientific and tolerant values of the Age of Enlightenment. Franklin's remarks about the trade-offs between "essential liberty" and "a little temporary safety" seem to have been directed at those in the colonies who could see that further compromise was no longer possible by the Crown and that it was up to the colonies to cave-in to maintain the peace. Franklin warned them that to do this would be equivalent to give up the entire game and thereby scuttle any chance for real liberty and independence in the colonies. Nearly 250 years ago, he was speaking for the best interest and unity of America and all other British colonies at that time.

Over a period of time many things have changed with many wars, crisis, fluctuating economies, the influx of immigrants, and the shifting demographics of societies are complex.

Free speech is not necessarily desirable if it causes disunity and fruitless if it cannot resolve matters of national importance without causing political chaos. There is a difference between free speech and right speech. If one speaks the truth and it leads to, unity, peace, and happiness of many then one should speak. If one speaks the truth that leads to disunity, insurrection, and violence then one should not speak.

The usefulness of free speech was tested in the trial of the former president facing charges of "incitement of insurrection". This was in connection with the mob that invaded the U.S. Capitol on January 6, 2021, his theory of election fraud and trying to overturn election results.

It is interesting to see where the main lines of disagreement lay between the Democrats and Republican senators under their oaths to defend the American Constitution. One would think they could reach some kind of reconciliation to bring unity, heal the old wounds, maintain the integrity of a free election, respect the will of the people, bring peace not only in the U.S. but for protecting democracy in the world. Without this democracy, neither ethical nor moral values could be upheld in a public office, let alone facts to speak the truth.

The sequence of events that led to the violent incident was vigorously tested to identify whether the former president deliberately and intentionally orchestrated or incited this violence. Impeachment managers presented a series of social media postings and graphic content and violent images of video clips as evidence.

Changing ideological dogmas and the mindset of a populace needs more than legal proceedings. Resolving both current domestic and international challenges toward lasting peace requires a political philosophy that builds trust and confidence in all people and a strategic approach to fulfil the core interests and win the international agreements achieving global stability.

A balanced approach to military competition is to avoid conflict, this needs wisdom in what ingredients to add to the foreign policy globally and to specific regions in order to regain confidence. Hatred and violence cannot be resolved by hatred and violence, it requires an ethical, moral, and humanitarian approach to win back support, to hold hands with other nations for lasting domestic and international peace agreements.

The theory of utilitarianism is linked to the early Greek concept of Happiness rooted in Hedonism which comes from the Greek hédoné, meaning "pleasure". They argue that happiness is a combination of pleasure and the absence of pain. Pleasure is the only thing that is intrinsically good for people, which is also known as Ethical Egoism, self-centred pleasure. In the same way, not only physical pleasure but also mental pleasure is a value of goodness.

Russ Shafer-Landau makes a distinction that people who are inclined towards pleasure and have a positive attitude of enjoyment are generally welcomed by everyone.

(The Fundamentals of Ethics, Oxford University Press 2021)

However, enjoying the victory of the political party make those who voted for it happy whereas those losing the election may feel unhappy, this is no different from watching your favourite baseball team loose. Therefore, attitudinal pleasure has no intrinsic value but rather is conditional.

Thus, what makes you happy might not make others happy and seeking pleasure by violent means such as resolving a dispute against a public institution, is a crime that compromises the peace, security, and stability of all concerned and cannot be reasoned out by normative ethics alone.

Attitudes of people and subjective judgements on what is right and wrong cannot evaluate the objectivity of ethics by normative conventions.

Plato was the first to discuss moral distinctions. Callicles in Plato's Gorgias (482c-486d) advances the thesis that Nature does not recognize moral distinctions, and that such distinctions are solely constructions of human convention. Thrasymachus (336b-354c), in *Plato's Republic* advocates a type of metaethical nihilism by defending the view that justice is nothing above and beyond whatever the strong say that it is.

When there is a difficulty in accommodating or accounting for the existing moral agreements, metaethics has been thought to provide some insight concerning how we should respond to such differences at the normative or political level. (Kevin M Delapp Converse College USA. Internet Encyclopaedia of Philosophy)

Social motivation is the idea that people in general have a motivation to engage and interact with other people. This has been very important to human survival: people tend not to survive very well on their own. It's a psychological requirement for people to feel belongingness. Traditionally, people live together as families, tribes, clans, groups, teams, and it has now developed into broader social and political groups.

The concept of belongingness entails a leader-follower relationship which is the social interaction that occurs between leaders and followers as they fulfil (and occasionally alternate in) these roles. It is a complex and continuously changing relationship subject which leads to numerous demands, choices, and constraints.

Leaders and followers are unified in an interdependent relationship. Ethical concerns are among the evaluating elements essential to developing loyalty and trust in this relationship. However, because of their need to maintain power, distance, and self-serving leaders may become detached from how their actions are perceived and reacted to by followers.

This pattern can be especially damaging to political identity such as when leaders continue to receive criticism and consequently lose their election, especially when coupled with the complex political issues of today.

Implications are drawn regarding the ethics of equity, responsibility, and accountability in the exercise of authority and power. A major component for a leader is their perception of themselves and how followers perceive him or her. This perception implicates important ethical issues concerning how followers are involved, used, or abused, especially in a relationship that favours the leader's power. Within this dominance motif, followers are essentially seen to be compliant and can easily be manipulated and in the extreme, they can be signalled to act, even violently.

The leader's role is still often seen as preeminent by their power over others, rather than as stewardship or even as a service to others. Misleading followers is a tactic of an unscrupulous leader and was apparent in the recent Capitol Building incident. Misleading people for violence is dysfunctional to the entire democratic system especially when world attention is focused on the US political stage. This dysfunctional system contracts with one that shows the discipline and unity of purpose represented in "teamwork" aimed at clear performance goals.

Successful teamwork demands concern for maintaining responsibility, accountability, authenticity, and integrity in the leader-follower relationship recognised in developed ethics. Indeed, the often mentioned "crisis of leadership" usually reveals the absence of these elements.

This normative position has a distinctly functional value as a universal perspective applicable to the political and organisational spheres. Though this position comes out of a democratic ethos, its generality is evident in the organisational psychology literature on leadership.

When a President of a country also becomes a celebrity in the eyes of the world or has elevated to that level of acceptance by virtue of his position this becomes more complex, especially if the individual has interest in private enterprising, is egotistical and hungers for power, thereby one is unable to distinguish between, person, personality, and purpose of the office. They may cling to their position and abuse their fame to the detriment of the responsibilities of their office.

Systematic use of online activities and popular social media platforms have hugely contributed to the dynamics of power and position, to the point of inducing riots and violence in the US capital as these platforms are not regulated by ethics and law. Twitter immediately banned the outgoing president of the US, Mr Donald Trump from using their facilities soon after he was accused of giving tacit approval for insurrection.

The politicians have much to learn about celebrity ethics from global superstars.

*"The real measure of celebrity success is not how he became famous but what he does with that fame is more important. Especially with today's technological and media advanced society, the attention focused on an individual celebrity is often immensely disproportionate to his or her achievements. Today, a person can literally become a global celebrity overnight and that kind of attention can be difficult for an individual to handle.*

*But I have also learnt that such fame also be an enormous effective medium to focus attention and mobilise resources for worthy causes. I have been blessed with so much and had the opportunity to do what others cannot, but I believe it is not just an opportunity but a duty. I feel to reap and enjoy the fruit of my talents for myself but that would be selfish, irresponsible, and unconscionable. And these days with such abundance and advancement in what we can do, it pains me to think that we do very little for our children (to future generations).*

*In some ways, I feel undeserving to receive an award for something that is my duty. I accept this award as a gesture of encouragement from the people of India and as a commission to do more for mankind. Mahatma Gandhi knew how important it was for him to bring the world's attention to gain independence to India without using any weapons (by nonviolence).*

*In some ways, he was the first person to truly understand the importance and power of the public. He has always been an inspiration to me."*

(Michael Jackson at the Bollywood Awards New York 2009).

*November 2020 US Presidential Election*

What was displayed on January 6th, 2021, at the Capitol Building in Washington DC need no further interpretation. The world witnessed the most dramatic political power transition of our living memory in front of the media's cameras. Powerful actors in the political arena are encouraging the dehumanization of certain segments of society by their political rhetoric.

This is nothing short of a moral crisis, one for which we need a rich moral language to comprehend the integral morality and ethics involved. The moral vocabulary used by the media and party spokesmen has been tenuous, the moral repertoire they provide is inadequate. Some of these ideas have themselves become corrupted and entail commercial elements.

These assessments lack the moral gravity to grasp this deep-rooted division of society which goes back to the times of forming the Union. It requires evidence-based psychological analysis of behaviour, beliefs, sound political paradigms, root causes and motives of what kind of society people want to create. To make sound moral judgments one needs robust moral language and open discussions. To rebuild the moral foundation of a country begins with individuals concluding that there is a real truth about questions that matter. Society is comprised of people who hold certain assumptions about good and evil, and right and wrong.

*"Most people would not want to live in a society in which morality was unimportant, in which conceptions of right and wrong carried little weight. In fact, it is unlikely that any sort of civilized society could continue unless it had concern for important moral values such as fairness, justice, truthfulness, and compassion. Ethics are important because they give direction to people and societies, who have some sense that they cannot flourish without being moral."*

These words are by Scott Rae, who is an American Old Testament scholar, theologian, and professor of Christian ethics. He serves as dean of the faculty and chair of the department of philosophy at Biola University's Talbot School of Theology.

One of the main struggles many people face when they immigrate to a new country is how to integrate, to develop an authentic community in unfamiliar urban cities. One of the most challenging things some face is simply getting to know others, the coexistence of life together.

Why is that important?

To some, this question is misplaced, as the answer may seem obvious. To others, the question of the value of community is a legitimate one. After all, it is your choice to adopt and settle in a new society. Nothing is permanent and things are going to change over time. In this modern economic world, changes are inevitable. Studies have shown that a meaningful sense of belonging to the community is crucial to personal success.

All traditional religions believe and teach that a deep fellowship in a community is essential for spiritual as well as intellectual growth. Rejecting these values is a mistake which is hard to correct. After all, what one soon rejects might turn out to be the truth.

The hope of forming a democratic government in Myanmar was ceased by the coup d'état on the morning of 1st of February 2021 when, democratically elected members of the National League for the Democracy Party were deposed by Myanmar's military.

Myanmar, also known as Burma, is largely a Buddhist country in Southeast Asia and neighbours Thailand, Laos, Bangladesh, China, and India. The country gained independence from Britain in 1948. It was ruled by the armed forces from 1962, until 2011 when a new government began ushering in a return to civilian rule. This was achieved by scarifying civil liberties from the party leader Ms Suu Kyi who spent nearly 15 years in detention between 1989 and 2010 after organising rallies calling for democratic reform and free elections. She was awarded the Nobel Peace Prize while under house arrest in 1991 and she received the popular support of large numbers of people working for basic social, economic, and political change.

The military rulership rarely altered the nation's fundamental social and economic policies, nor did it significantly redistribute power among competing political groups, but all lucrative businesses were controlled by conglomerates of the military.

The revenue from these businesses directly benefited the coup leaders and their connected families.

Despite trade sanctions from the Western governments, business continued because of the weaknesses of the business model and the supply chain.

Similar incidents have happened in other countries, notably in Haiti. The impoverished country of Haiti - already an economic disaster zone with organised crime and kidnapping for ransom out of control - now finds itself facing a constitutional crisis with violent confrontations between anti-government protesters and the police as a daily occurrence. The dispute is caused by the country's leading opposition parties. The judiciary and activist groups say the current presidency ended on Sunday the 7th of February 2021 after a five-year term, the president says he has one year left in office, as an interim government ran the country for a year after his election.

(Source; Sky News 09 February 2021)

These political dilemmas show that democracy today is under serious threat. The underpinning causes of these political unrests can be related to declining economic conditions and mismanaged wealth distribution by power-hungry leaders who disregard the will of their people. Tyrants appear to take advantage of weakening economies and social structures. Most of these crisis happened in the middle of the Covid-19 pandemic and it calls into question whether this is ethical social governance systems, or could we improve this political behaviour?

# CHAPTER 20

# NEED FOR ETHICAL PRINCIPLES

THERE ARE FIVE MAIN PRINCIPLES of ethics that put together form the contextual grounds for many professional organisations and educational institutions. These are truthfulness and confidentiality, autonomy, and informed consent, beneficence, nonmaleficence, and justice. These principles can be motivation as a frame-work for moral issues, for commercial enterprises, for their economic motivation, and to build into business policy. They carry positive values that influence the wellbeing of others or society as an end in itself, this can be expected to contribute to its financial performance in the long run. The goal is to propel people towards behaving in a way that will benefit the organisation.

In Western philosophy, there are a lot of theories regarding moral philosophy, each can be traced back to several other theories that have been developed across different countries in the western hemisphere and at different times.

As a discipline, ethics is itself (at least in part) normative; it is about identifying and attempting to agree on the importance of particular values (or kinds of values), how and why separate values might influence decisions and choices of action.

This is very different to Buddhist ethics which stems solely from the enlightened Buddha and is directed toward an individual mind for its liberation.

The western theories of ethics were developed for policies and politics concerning the collective behaviour of society at large hence it has a character of hierarchical systems. It's formed of overarching theories which are often coupled with theology to attempt an explanation and justification of some peculiar normative positions, this filters down to a range of particular rules expressed in terms of a code of practice or conduct to regulate behaviour thus making one guilty if they break such code (at least in public).

With the dawn of democracy, free speech and freedom of journalism, ethics is a topic widely open for public debate. In fact, the task of evaluating normative beliefs within the public domain rests on the one hand, while normative judgments made by philosophers holds on the other, and yet these are complementary and are indeed intertwined.

It is sometimes needed to disentangle politics from ethics, this can be more effective in highlighting the pre-eminent duty of moral consideration, focusing on the consequential importance of ethical deliberation through critical appraisals and evaluation of principles.

For example, the March 2020 Covid-19 outbreak drew attention to the role of the World Health Organisation (WHO) as a specialised agency in the UN system. Questions were raised as to whether WHO acted within their capacity to protect member states according to their ethical principles; there were heated comments from leading politicians in the world without an effective solution offered or constructive suggestions as the severity of the pandemic unfolded.

Did WHO act soon enough to stop the spread of the virus, or did politicians ignore their advice?

With the advantage of hindsight, we can see where we made the big mistakes. This can be compared to the Spanish flu which was a global calamity to grip the world during 1918 – 1920.

Much can be learned from each of these pandemics. With the advancement of science and communications technology we would have been able to tackle the spread of the contagious virus more effectively than in 1918.

Unfortunately, we were counting the toll of this invisible enemy because we ignored the warnings from history. It is important from an epidemiology and virology point of view to understand the origin of the virus, the roots from which this pandemic grew, how it arrived in the country, how it mutated and evolved. This knowledge can be used to control the virus, allocate world resources better and would have reduced the number of deaths.

Regardless, this can only be achieved in a global pandemic if we have sound, credible ethics, robust systems of knowledge share, and cooperation between nations. It is the right thing to do to bring this unity, especially in a critical global situation such as in the middle of a pandemic to reduce the virus' transmission rather than follow misguided beliefs of political division.

## Benedict de Spinoza (1632 AD – 1677AD)

Benedict de Spinoza also known as Baruch Spinoza is a 17$^{th}$ century philosopher, who lived during the Age of Enlightenment. *Ethics* is the most famous work of Benedict de Spinoza, who is considered one of the great rationalists of his time. Spinoza was born of Jewish and Portuguese ancestry in 1632 and lived a simple life in Amsterdam as an optical lens grinder. His controversial ideas made him excommunicated by his own Jewish circles.

His greatest fame came about when *Ethics*, a collection of several of his philosophical works, was published anonymously by his close friends in 1677, shortly after Spinoza's untimely death at the age of 44. He rightfully deserves to be recognised alongside the likes of Descartes and Leibniz.

Spinoza was one of the first to recognise the perfection, accuracy, precision, and symmetrical order in nature as represented by mathematics. *Ethics Demonstrated in Geometrical Order* (in Latin: *Ethica, ordine geometrico demonstrata*) is perhaps the most ambitious attempt to apply the Euclidean method in philosophy (Euclid was a Greek mathematician). Spinoza lays out his ethical philosophy in precise geometrical order. He argues expressly against the dualism of Descartes and contends instead that everything in the world flows from the essential nature of reality, or God, echoing the Ariyan concept of the universe.

According to Spinoza, human perception of this ultimate truth is imperfect and thus much of human knowledge is incomplete and faulty. It follows that individuals must strive toward a more perfect and virtuous knowledge of truth and reality by controlling their emotions and employing a more scientific and objective approach.

This masterpiece of reason and rationality remains one of the most important philosophical treatises on the subject of ethics. Along the lines of Plato's allegory of the cave, Spinoza's approach confirms that reality is hidden, and that truth is not available to those who accept only 'shadows' as reality without investigating the object behind it.

Among western philosophers, Spinoza is best known for challenging traditional the normative beliefs that guide our behaviour. His work presents an ethical vision that unfolds out of a monistic metaphysics in which God and Nature are identified, whereby God is no longer the transcendent creator of the universe who rules it via providence, but Nature itself, understood as an infinite, necessary, and fully deterministic system of which humans are a part. Humans only find happiness through a rational understanding of this system and their place within it.

On account of his critical evaluations of existing beliefs and the many other provocative positions he advocates, Spinoza has remained an enormously controversial figure.

Spinoza wrote in the style of geometrical treatise, mapping a technically engineered blueprint of ethics. Through a long philosophical highway via metaphysics and manifestations of nature he gave clear signposts by way of definitions, axioms, propositions, and scholia.

In this noble task Spinoza used both analytical and synthesis methods for his critical investigation based on a set of ethical premises, he formed his argument by critical appraisal and evaluation of these principles. These resulting positions were driven by challenging the contemporary normative beliefs on political theology, that 'this is the way that things ought to be in the world' an attitude he saw extended well beyond the existing traditions and customs.

Follower of his map who is willing to give sufficient attention to every point, junction methodically, and take the right turning will surely arrive at the correct destination even he wishes to explore different subways, or lost in tunnels, passageways of ideas because Spinoza has shown clearly what contained in speculative views.

Spinoza equates nature to God, concerning the understanding of nature, he provides us with three types of epistemological knowledges. The knowledge one may gain from random experience is imperfect because it is obscured by distorted sensory perceptions and emotions. This type of knowledge is learnt from sight sounds and signs associated with experience corresponding to traditional learning customary to the language or social ethnic group, this lacks rational order between the words and objects.

For example, an infant responding to their environment according to early learning methods have an absence of rational structure. The second type of knowledge is gained by reason; when a child grows up, his or her reasoning ascends from an inadequate to an adequate perception of things. This type of knowledge is gained "from the fact that we have common notions and adequate ideas of the properties of things". For example, scientific knowledge gained from detailed study and by experiment, ascertaining the arrangement of nature and make use of it for our benefit; the properties of materials, its behaviour and its use for mankind is learnt through the subjects of chemistry, physics, biology, and botany etc.

Unlike the first kind of knowledge, this is a rational order of ideas. We might think that in attaining this second kind of knowledge we have attained all that is available to us, however Spinoza adds a third type, which he regards as superior. He calls this intuitive knowledge *(scientia intuitiva)* and tells us that it "proceeds from an adequate idea of the formal essence of certain attributes of God to the adequate knowledge of the [formal] essence of things".

There are many ways people interpret this third type of knowledge. According to ancient Indian Vedic science intuitive knowledge is interpreted as divine and accessible only to a certain religious clan in the social hierarchy.

Ancient Egyptians interpreted it as the mystical power of God. Similarly, different religions interpret it according to their religious beliefs. As an exception, Buddhism gives a clear method of acquiring such knowledge and purpose for intuitive wisdom in attainment of full liberation and supreme happiness.

Spinoza meets with Buddhism at this cross junction as its title of Ethics indicates. Its ultimate aim is to aid us in the attainment of happiness, which he believed to be found in the intellectual love of God. This love, according to Spinoza, arises out of the knowledge that we gain of the divine essence insofar as we see how the essences of singular things necessarily follow from it.

At this point Spinoza makes a distinct proposition concerning God to show how all other things can be derived from God. In grasping the order of propositions as they are demonstrated in his Ethics, we can thus attain the kind of knowledge that underwrites human happiness.

We are, as it were, put on the road towards happiness; of the two methods it is only the synthetic method that is suitable for this purpose, knowledge derived from the analysis of nature.

Spinoza viewed God and Nature as two names for the same reality, namely a single, fundamental substance, "that which stands beneath" rather than "matter" itself, this is the basis of the universe and of which all lesser "entities" are modes or modifications, that all things are determined to exist by Nature.

Early in his Ethics, Spinoza argues that there is only one substance, which is absolutely infinite, self-caused, and eternal. He calls this substance "God" or "Nature", the rest are variations of the properties of materials as different modes. A mode is any other property of a substance, Descartes defined a substance as a thing that does not depend on anything else for its existence. However, Spinoza argued that there is no such thing as a substance without its principal attribute.

Body cannot exist without extension, and mind cannot exist without thought. Arriving at these conclusions, Spinoza has investigated mind, cognition, sense perceptions, imagination, the psychology behind these patterns of mental constructions, and the eternity of the mind rejecting free will. In working out this new perspective, the first thing on Spinoza's agenda is to clear away what he sees as the most pervasive confusion that we as humans have about ourselves, the belief in free-will. Spinoza has nothing but scorn for this belief and treats it as a delusion that arises from the fact that the ideas, we have of our actions are inadequate.

"Men believe themselves to be free," he writes, "because they are conscious of their own actions and are ignorant of the causes by which they are determined".

Adequate ideas of our actions would carry with them knowledge of their causes, with this knowledge we would immediately see this belief as the delusion that it is. He rejects any concern of passion as well. Spinoza tells us that "the model human life – the life lived by the 'free-man' is one that is lived by the guidance of reason rather than under the sway of the passions." If passion is to be recognised as a necessary condition for motivation, then it should be directed towards a purpose that would benefit many rather than self-centred interest and emotionally driven actions.

Being a rationalist along with his contemporary philosophers in the Age of Enlightenment, Spinoza, advocated that since reason demands nothing contrary to Nature, it follows that everyone love himself, seek his own advantage, what is really useful to him, wish for what will really lead him/her to greater perfection, and that everyone should strive to preserve his own being as far as he can. This, indeed, is as necessarily true as it is that the whole is greater than its part.

Ethical prescription derived from reasoning along is egoistic in the sense that we act in accordance with our nature, whereby our nature is identical to our striving to persevere in being. Thus, reason prescribes that we do whatever is to our advantage and seek whatever aids us in our striving. To act this way, Spinoza insists, is to act virtuously, giving us important advice to decouple politics from ethics. He goes so far as to say that in a society in which everyone lives by the guidance of reason there would be no need for political authority to restrict action.

It is only insofar as individuals live under the sway of the passions that they come into conflict with one another and need political authority. Those who live by the guidance of reason understand this and recognize its authority as legitimate, he respects rule of law established by learned men of ethics.

Spinoza also introduces an axiom of cause and effect.

"The knowledge of an effect depends on, and involves, the knowledge of its cause".

He argues that knowledge of an attribute is combined knowledge of other attributes as identified and proved in scientific empirical methods. Both Issacs Newton in classical physics and Albert Einstein in his relativity theory state that matter and energy are relative manifestations of the same thing, that beneath the structure of matter there is a vast pool of energy beyond what man can handle. For example, the volcano irruption is due to the heat produced by matter itself and the explosion of built-up heated gas over a small period of time. Melted lava burst through the mountain walls flow like a reiver absorbing heat back to earth. In this example, heat is a property of matter produced by vibrating molecules.

In conclusion Spinoza admits that the road to happiness through an ethical life is not easy, to attain intuitive knowledge requires lot of hard work, but it can be attained to those who make the effort.

He closes the Ethics with these words: "If the way I have shown to lead to these things now seems very hard, still, it can be found. And of course, what is found so rarely must be hard. For if salvation were at hand, and could be found without great effort, how could nearly everyone neglect it? But all things excellent are as difficult as they are rare."

Spinoza's journey through ethics runs parallel to Buddhism which categorically says that ultimate happiness lies within one's ability and it is a state of mind without any admixture of theological or philosophical speculation. Both teachings meet at this junction whereby *"freedom from passion is the mark of wisdom"*.

In Buddhism the ethical path towards this final goal is inbuilt into the Noble Eightfold Path.

(History of Metaethics by Kevin M. DeLapp, Internet Encyclopaedia of Philosophy, Converse College, U. S. A.)

## Metaethics

Russ Shafer-Landau (born 1963) is an American philosopher and Professor of Philosophy at the University of Wisconsin Madison USA, he is a leading defender of a non-naturalistic moral realism.

Ethical non-naturalism is the meta-ethical view which claims that: Ethical sentences express propositions. Some such propositions are true. Those propositions are made true by objective features of the world, independent of human opinion.

Moral realism (also ethical realism) holds the same position, that a proposition may be true to the extent that it reports those features accurately. In the Fundamentals of Ethics, author Russ Shafer-Landau introduces the essential ideas of moral philosophy (Oxford University Press 2021).

It offers a comprehensive coverage of the good life and normative ethics. He establishes his views in the major work *Moral Realism*, stating that the term 'good' cannot be described in terms of what is pleasurable and painful, nor conclusions within science. This is a remarkable challenge to the early utilitarian theory, searching for a more altruistic set of values beyond the dualism of right and wrong. The meta-ethical understanding of the meaning of good life, questions first what morality actually is.

Metaethics is a subject area seeking answers to various puzzling questions digging deeper than normative ethics, it will greatly help in questioning the status of moral claims and the validity of a policy built upon moral values. Metaethics is the branch of knowledge that considers the foundational issues of morality and deals especially with the nature of ethical statements.

Philosophers doing metaethics ask vital and fundamental questions such as these: Is morality merely conventional, or are there objective standards of right and wrong? How can we gain moral knowledge? Why should we be moral? Can there be a science of morality?

Discussion of metaethics was first found in Immanuel Kant's publications. It was an attempt to identify an absolute value in ethics to evaluate the moral theory that articulates and defends general moral principles made to serve, explaining when and why various types of action, institutions, or characters count as right or wrong, just, or unjust, virtuous, or vicious. The assumption on which these presumptions were made never identified who is accountable for actions that stem from a policy formulated using those theories. For example, responsibility of corporate man-slaughter, corporate fraud, institutional racism, and war crimes are complex issues to resolve, and answers are sought somewhat outside the domain of ethics through lengthy legal proceedings based on conventions.

How can we justify one case of cruelty might be wrong and another not wrong without there being any ground that would justify treating them as different? Why is it so natural to suppose that there must be some other difference - say a difference in their consequences, or a difference in what has led up to the act of cruelty - that underwrites and justifies the thought that one is wrong, but not the other? Why not grant that one of the two just happened to be wrong and the other happened not to be? Could not moral properties just happen to have been distributed randomly so that, in the end, there is no justification for one action having a certain moral standing while another, otherwise the same, has a different standing?

Following various wars, human tragedies in the past and recent history, and economic failures over the past thirty years, there has been a great surge of interest in metaethics. Examples and severity of those incidents were discussed in Part II highlighting the error of human thought, whereby freedom sought through reasoning shifted the political ideology to both far right and left, resulting in man-made politically, economically, and socially calamities that are forcefully changing the world order by aggressive military means.

The result of this intervention temporarily suppressed the perceived immediate threat to the West; however, it caused a vacuum with economic and banking collapse increasing the gap between rich and poor.

Metaethics can be considered and valued as an attempt to understand metaphysical, epistemological, semantic, and psychological presuppositions and commitments of moral thought, speech, and practice. As such, it accounts within its domain a broad range of questions and puzzles, including: Is morality more a matter of taste than truth? Are moral standards culturally relative? Are there moral facts? If there are moral facts, what is their origin? How is it that they set an appropriate standard for our behaviour? How might moral facts be related to other facts about psychology, happiness, human conventions...? And how do we learn about the moral facts if there are any?

These questions lead naturally to puzzles about the meaning of moral claims as well as about moral truth and the justification of our moral commitments.

Metaethics also explores the connection between values, reasons for action, and human motivation, asking how it is that moral standards might provide us with reasons to do or refrain from doing as it demands. It addresses many of the issues commonly bound up with the nature of freedom and its significance (or not) for moral responsibility.

(Stanford Encyclopaedia of Philosophy *author unknown*)

https://plato.stanford.edu/entries/metaethics/

Establishment of metaethics would allow for an improvement to the general principles of existing moral theories and subsequent reformations of policies when introduced through the vehicle of politics. It would allow us to assess the plausibility and central aims of a moral philosophy using other competing interests with rational argument. For example, is it morally right to oppose an agreement for one's own political advantage that would have otherwise been beneficial to all?

Philosophers and policy makers could try taking a neutral stance by stepping back from particular substantive political debates within morality and address the views, assumptions, and commitments that are otherwise shared by those who engage in the debate, to unentangle politics from ethics and reach out for an absolute value beneficial for many.

In this modern world the political and social issues are complex and are compounded by various overlapping beliefs and theories, hence the need for a coherent and consistent set of principles, successfully articulating a common policy that is fully adequate and practical to address the universal issues in human life.

Answers to all metaethical questions cannot be found by reasoning alone as is clearly shown by Benedict de Spinoza in proposing his third type of knowledge. There are other operating laws in the universe that govern the moral order of our lives. These natural laws are found in a transcendental reality identified by ancient religious sages and modern psychologists with their different interpretations.

Philosophy is yet to be enriched with these new psychological and neurological discoveries that explains our behaviour and motivations to act. Buddhism shows that it would be more productive if we set a clear objective and goal in life that is moral. It advocates a middle way of living by not getting carried away by passion, this was also clearly shown by Benedict de Spinoza. The common goal here is happiness and the questions to ask is how one pursue happiness?

Buddhism identifies man's mind as being defiled by birth and it requires work hard to acquire virtues in the pursuit of happiness with clearly defined moral values and ethics. These ethical guidelines are discussed and established in Theravada Buddhist texts. When one advances in this middle path towards happiness, they can surpass the duality of nature and embrace the oneness of the universe, a crucial junction in life that one cannot arrive at by reasoning alone.

Buddhism describes this knowledge as direct knowledge, to see things as they are, this is only accessible by insight meditation. If moral truth is understood in the traditional sense, as corresponding to reality, what sort of features of reality could suffice to accommodate this correspondence? What sort of entity is "wrongness" or "goodness" in the first place?

Buddhist higher philosophical psychology provides a detailed ontological view of life that explains the absolute truth of who we really are rather than who we think we are. This distinction of reality is not a culturally invented belief system but can be discovered by an individual earnestly seeking to understand the truth of life, moved out of necessity to discover a solution to suffering.

One of the most pressing questions within analytic metaethics concerns how morality engages with our embodied human psychologies. Specifically, how (if at all) do moral judgments move us to act in accordance with them? Is there any reason to be moral for its own sake? Can we give any psychologically persuasive reasons to others to act morally if they do not already acknowledge such reasons?

Before becoming the Buddha, the unenlightened prince Siddhartha had many puzzling questions of contemporary religious beliefs, unsatisfactory answers pertaining to suffering, its cause, and its cessation.

There were many speculative views of life that were interpreted by an Eternalism and Nihilistic theory of the law of action. By seeing the suffering of his people, prince Siddhartha had the moral conviction to find a solution and moved to embark on a difficult decision on leaving the royal palace to search for what is right and wrong. He realised that by living in the realm of comfort one cannot see the reality outside of it and encountered difficult life experiences to discover the solution which he presented to the world in the form of the Four Noble Truths, a practical method of ethics to end suffering.

In recent years metaethics has been of interest to psychologists. This branch of study is known as Experimental Philosophy which seeks to supplement theoretical philosophical claims with empirical attention to how people think and act. It has yielded numerous suggestive findings about a variety of metaethical positions. For example, by drawing on empirical research in social psychology, several philosophers have suggested that moral judgments, motivations, and evaluations are highly sensitive to situational variables and in a way that might challenge the universality or autonomy of morality. (Flanagan 1991; Doris 2002).

## Analysis of Spinoza's Contribution to Ethics

Among all the thinkers in history, Benedict Spinoza's treatise on ethics is the most relevant today.

His theme of ethics is well grounded on a critical evaluation of contemporary political theology which lays a foundation for independent, democratic political thought.

He combines his thoughts by extremely naturalistic views on God, explaining the knowledge required to understand the manifestation of nature and tells us that men have to control their passions and cultivate virtues to access true happiness, thus challenging their traditional roles in spiritual texts. Spinoza's monumental work consists in showing that our happiness and wellbeing lie not in a life enslaved to the passions and to the transitory goods (pleasure) we ordinarily pursue, nor in the unreflective attachment to superstitions that pass as religion, but rather in the life of reason.

To clarify and support these broadly ethical conclusions Spinoza articulated his philosophical arguments in a structured way, using mathematical method to reject dualism, this both destroys world-weary views and heralds the arrival of a new world in its place. Spinoza engages in a detailed analysis of the composition of human beings because it was essential to his goal of showing how the human being is a part of Nature, existing within the same deterministic causal nexus as other extended mental beings. He argues that the nature of the mind and men's way of living can be explained like any other substance with the aid of common laws of nature such as physics.

This has serious ethical implications. He rejects the idea of free will and explains the nature of the mind and events in our minds are simply ideas that exist; imagination is a distorted mental construction, similarly, our actions and volitions are as necessarily determined as any other natural events. He introduced an important psychological phenomenon of cause and effect that has no beginning or an end (eternal). Spinoza believed that this is something that has not been sufficiently understood by previous thinkers, who seem to have wanted to place the human being on a pedestal outside of (or above) nature.

His radical approach is distanced from contemporary beliefs, explaining that human nature provides an insight into wider implications of man's behaviour and organic unity within the world, examining the true nature of a political society and attempting to give intellectual and religious freedom.

Spinoza distinguished human nature as body, mind, passion, and action, and in so doing he gave a range of psychological factors that affect human beings including love, anger hate, envy, pride, jealousy, etc. Indeed, he explains that these emotions follow from the same necessity and force of nature and that they can be determined in their occurrence by applied mathematics or physics just like any other phenomenon in nature, he attributes the cause for the impact of change as the power of the mind. All beings are naturally endowed with such a power of striving to achieve joy and happiness and to avoid or destroy what would lead to their sadness.

Our hopes and fears are fluctuating depending on the uncertainties we face in relation to the end goal, not knowing that the external objects of our passion are completely beyond our control, thus the more we allow ourselves to be controlled by external objects the more we are subject to passion. This is egoistic view supports self-interest as egoistic people believe we all put our own needs before those of others.

To be egotistic is to have too inflated an opinion of yourself - in other words, it's a form of self-delusion rather than a particular way of looking at the world. Spinoza gives two set of expiations to the contrary, first he must show that such freedom is not only compatible with political wellbeing but essential to it and then justify his argument by asking people to control their passion.

The individual egoism of Spinoza's Ethics is expressed in a pre-political context under the heading "state of nature". This is a universal condition where there is no law or religion, justice or injustice, every individual has the right to do whatever he can to preserve himself.

*"Whatever every person, whenever he is considered as solely under the dominion of Nature, believes to be to his advantage, whether under the guidance of sound reason or under passion's sway, he may by sovereign natural right seek and get for himself by any means, by force, deceit, entreaty, or in any other way he best can, and he may consequently regard as his enemy anyone who tries to hinder him from getting what he wants".*

Needless to say, this is a rather insecure and dangerous condition under which to live, similar to the prehistorical era, where the end justifies the means and only the fittest can survive, as is the case of the animal kingdom.

The difficultly of accepting natural law was shown long before Spinoza by British thinker Thomas Hobbes who wrote that life in the state of nature is "solitary, poor, nasty, brutish and short".

As rational creatures we soon realize that we would be better off, still from a thoroughly egoistic perspective, by coming to an agreement among ourselves to restrain our opposing desires and the unbounded pursuit of self-interest - in sum, that it would be in our greater self-interest to live under the law of reason rather than the law of nature. We thus agree to hand over to a sovereign our natural right and power to do whatever we can to satisfy our interests. Therefore, Spinoza agrees with Plato's idea of the Social Contract, that we agree to handover our natural rights and power to do whatever we can to satisfy our interest by state authority, this suggests a social democrat political system that recognises freedom of thought.

Obedience to the sovereign does not infringe upon our autonomy, since in following the commands of the sovereign we are following an authority whom we have freely authorized and whose commands have no other object than our own rational self-interest.

The type of government most likely to respect and preserve that autonomy would issue laws based on sound reason to serve the ends for which government is instituted, democracy. The "most natural" form of governance arises out of a social contract - since in a democracy the people obey only laws that issue from the general will of the body politic - and the least are subject to various abuses of power.

As a matter of fact, in a democracy, the rationality of the sovereign's command is practically secured, since it is unlikely that a majority of a large number of people will agree to an irrational design. Monarchy, on the other hand, is the least stable form of government and the one most likely to degenerate into tyranny.

While Spinoza ascribes the passing of responsibilities of our socioeconomic needs to the democratic government, he underlines how personal happiness and virtues depend on the individual.

Since we cannot control the objects that we tend to value and that we allow to influence our wellbeing, we ought instead to try to control our evaluations themselves and thereby minimize the sway that external objects and the passions have over us. We can never eliminate the passive affects entirely. We are essentially a part of nature and can never fully remove ourselves from the causal series that link us to external things. But we can, ultimately, counteract the passions, control them, and achieve a certain degree of relief from their turmoil. What Spinoza has in mind is the impact of our emotions on happiness and not allowing us to take reactive decisions.

The path to restraining and moderating the affects is through virtue. In this aspect of ethical behaviour, Spinoza is a psychological and ethical egoist. All beings naturally seek their own advantage - to preserve their own being and increase their power - and it is right for them do so as this is what virtue consists of.

Since we are thinking beings, endowed with intelligence and reason what is to our greatest advantage is knowledge. Our virtue, therefore, consists in the pursuit of knowledge and understanding, of adequate ideas. The best kind of knowledge is a purely intellectual intuition of the essences of things.

This "third kind of knowledge" - beyond both random experience and ratiocination - sees things not in their temporal dimension, not in their durational existence and in relation to other particular things, but under the lens of eternity (*sub specie aeternitatis*), that is, abstracted from all considerations of time and place, situated in their relationship to God and its attributes. That is to say identify common characteristics of natural phenomena would change our perception of the world.

They are apprehended, that is, in their conceptual and causal relationship to the universal essences (thought and extension) and the eternal laws of nature. Spinoza however does not give a method to obtain this third kind of knowledge or an explanation as to what prevents men reaching that level of understanding. Neither has he explained explicitly what made people believe in God in the first place, only to provide an insight that we should look beyond our sensory perceptions. Like any other philosopher of the Age of Enlightenment, Spinoza relied on plausible reason, knowledge, and logic to free himself from political theology and reveal important psychological concepts.

Fear and hope are fleeting phenomena subject to fluctuation whereby religious ceremonies, festivals and rituals could only be a remedy for anxiety born of uncertainty.

Through metaphysical hypothesis, Spinoza demonstrates what is useful for society and how to live a good moral life by crucial ethical principles that are needed for true happiness. He encourages people to re-examine traditional philosophical and theological conceptions in religious texts in order to find the doctrines of the "true religion". Spinoza's work is a major critique of passion with the view that life could be better only if people controlled their emotions and in particular passion, which is a very intense, compelling, and powerful emotion, capable of creating a strong liking or desire towards a person or an object.

It could also be the opposite, as disliking, aversion, and anger. This suggests that passion can be positive or negative and unpleasant at times. It could involve pain and obsessive forms that can destroy the self and even others. Passion can be useful as a means of motivation if combined with purpose; purpose is the reason behind your emotions that drive you to achieve something.

Ethical guidelines can direct our passions towards a purposive goal to benefit the individual and society alike. Similarly, knowledge also has the nature of duality. It can be useful and can be dangerous. The knowledge you seek could cause harm to yourself and others, it can also be a barrier that prevents us from coming to know more profound knowledge.

Knowledge is a powerful weapon, and it would indeed become dangerous if people do not know how to wield it properly. The general inference derived by people who have a competence in interpreting this is that a little knowledge makes people believe they are more of an expert than they really are. This can lead to errors in judgment and wrong decisions. To surpass the duality of nature one has to cultivate insight wisdom while supported by an ethical conduct to determine what is truly beneficial for mankind. Spinoza proposed to replace faith with intellectual love. What he equates to the third kind of knowledge generates a love for its object, in this love consists not a passionate joy but an active one, even blessedness itself.

He argues that we can understand the universal laws, acquire virtue, happiness, wellbeing and finally our freedom and autonomy by developing higher knowledge. In this way, everyone becomes equal and supports the welfare of one another in a way that is typically regarded as "ethical, even altruistic".

Spinoza's "free person" is one who bears the gifts and losses of fortune with equanimity and does only those things that he believes to be "the most important in life". He takes care for the wellbeing and virtuous flourishing of other human beings. He does what he can through rational benevolence (as opposed to pity or some other form of passion) to ensure that they too achieve relief from the disturbances of their passions through understanding.

Access to higher knowledge and the path of liberation has been discovered by the fully enlightened Buddha about 2.6 thousand years ago. The Buddhist higher philosophical psychology is a system that simultaneously articulates all three aspects of philosophy, psychology, and ethics. This is known as the Abhidhamma, an integrated framework presented as a programme for liberation. The justification of ethical injunctions derived from the cornerstone of the Buddha's teaching is summarised into the Four Noble Truths.

To appreciate this teaching one has to understand the noble truth of suffering, the world of conditioned phenomena has an inherent character to its nature, impermanence. Analysis of the mind is not motivated by metaphysical hypothesis but by the overriding practical aim of the Buddha's teaching which is to end suffering. The Buddha traces suffering to our tainted attitudes as a mental orientation rooted in greed, hatred, and delusion.

The Abhidhamma's phenomenological psychology takes on the character of psychological ethics, understanding the term not as *ethics per se* but as a complete guide to noble living and mental purification. The system analyses the nature of the based on ethical criteria: the wholesome, unwholesome states of consciousness, the beautiful mental factors, and the defilements. Its schematisation of consciousness and functions of the mind follows a hierarchical path of progress that corresponds to the successive stages of purity one can attain through meditative absorption by tranquillity and insight meditation.

The prominence of mental defilements and requisites of enlightenment in its schemes of categories is indicative of its psychological and ethical concerns, thus connecting the Abhidhamma to the second and fourth noble truths, the origin of suffering and the way leading to end of suffering.

The set of teachings provides the method to reach its consummation in understanding the knowledge of the "unconditioned element", Nibbana, this is the third noble truth, the cessation of suffering.

Buddhism is not in conflict with other religions. Its atheistic position neutralises the power of supernatural or divine beings to pass both the responsibility of man's liberation and his attaining of supreme happiness to the man himself.

# CHAPTER 21

# FRAMEWORK OF ETHICS AND THE BELMONT REPORT

Reading through the historical literature on philosophy, I realised I could not easily identify a developed and structured framework for ethics as the philosophy of ethics is narrated at overtly intellectual level through many logical arguments. Ethical principles have to be deciphered through a narration of philosophical positions established by various philosophers at various intervals of time.

During the period of Western Enlightenment ethics had a renewed interest as reignited by Immanuel Kant but this faded away by the strong winds of the World War II. The need for ethical principles arose following the reported atrocities inflicted on human subjects during World War II. As it happens, among other obscured objectives, Hitler wanted to create a superhuman race and notably at war time Hitler's army forcefully conducted various biological and gynaecological experiments which were later revealed after the war had ended.

Other than the Geneva conventions on treating prisoners of war there was nothing to identify the crimes against humanity on innocent civilians. On 20 November 1945 the first of multiple trials began in Nuremberg, Germany where the surviving leaders of Nazi Germany were tried for crimes committed during World War Two, which included the Holocaust.

During the Nuremberg War Crime Trials, the Nuremberg Code was drafted, and this set forth standards to judge physicians and scientists who conducted biomedical experiments on concentration camp prisoners. The Nuremberg Code set the example for subsequent codes that established rules to help protect human subjects involved in research. These rules however were found to be inadequate to cover complex situations at times of conflict and were frequently difficult to interpret or apply.

In 1974, following the Tuskegee Experiment scandal, an unethical natural history study on African ethnic groups for disease control and prevention, the National Commission for the Protection of Human Subjects of Biomedical and Behavioural Research was commissioned to develop a policy for Biomedical research in USA by the US Department of Human Services (Health & Education). The report took its name from the Belmont Conference Centre where the document was drafted in part. The Belmont Report: *Ethical Principles and Guidelines for the Protection of Human Research* (Bethesda, Md.)

The Commission, 1978. To avoid the limitations of these past codes, the Belmont Report was deliberately broader and established three basic ethical principles:

1) respect for persons, 2) beneficence, and 3) justice.

Since then, these principles became the central content of medical ethics and further developed to meet the need of various other research areas in innovative bioscience technologies and commercialisation to help enable deliver healthcare solutions that can truly make a difference to people's lives. These principles represent normative thinking that might stem from more than one moral philosophical theory and thus can be connected back to several theories.

Metaethics serves as a guideline to evaluate ethical theories and principles concerning their suitability, political correctness, ultimate value, and purpose. The Belmont Report set the standard for ethical principles, taking of its content from the academic community and professional bodies that have agreed to five main principles of ethics.

These are: Truthfulness and confidentiality; Autonomy and informed consent; Beneficence; Nonmaleficence; Justice. These principles are now articulated and fully integrated into the law and are enacted through various legislations as rules, for example the Data protection Act which is upheld by the General Data Protection Regulation (GDPR) of the European Parliament Council.

Governments and organisations are now required to maintain confidentially of information and at the same time be transparent with their policies and activities other than information which might not concern public interest.

Broader ethical principles are discussed in relation to professional relationships. The importance of ethics in medical and healthcare professions is very clear because it has almost excluded any political interference. This branch of philosophy therefore established ethical principles in the context of medical ethics; nonetheless, they are easily transferable to other areas, including the one regarding individual life for personal development towards happiness.

## Truthfulness and confidentiality

The concept of truthfulness corresponds to the quality of being honest. Its basic ethical value involves the moral duty to be honest. In a professional relationship it is generally necessary to build such trust. Modern medical ethics insists that a physician's attitude be honest and warrants and openness with patients about their conditions, medications, procedures, and risks. This can often be difficult, but it is generally necessary to foster a good relationship and for a better treatment outcome.

This is not as easy as it sounds; telling the patient the whole truth could interfere with the doctor's primary moral duty, which is to do no harm. Honesty is still preferred, but there are two situations where it is considered acceptable to not be completely truthful.

Firstly, the oldest moral codes in Western history deal with the rights and obligations of medical professionals whereby a physician may withhold some information if they truly believe that complete honesty will lead to greater harm, an ethical right called the therapeutic privilege.

A fear of suicide in patients suffering from depression is an example of this. The concept of truthfulness urges the professional not to lie, but on the other hand, the concept of confidentiality urges you to keep a secret – by which we mean knowledge or information that a person has the right or obligation to conceal.

"Principle 1, Rule: Individuals shall protect the confidentiality of any professional or personal information about persons served professionally or participants involved in research and scholarly activities and may disclose confidential information only when doing so is necessary to protect the welfare of the person."

In sum, the keeping of patient confidentiality is considered important because it is basic to a relationship built on trust and respect. It is important also because the consequences of keeping confidentiality are generally beneficial to patients in that it ensures better outcomes for them.

In his book *Social Work Ethics: Politics, Principles and Practice* (Red Globe Press 1999) Chris L. Clark offers a critical introduction to professional ethics for social workers. Clark argues that social workers and others in the social care field hold positions of responsibility and trust for the welfare of vulnerable and disempowered people, they also apply support and control to individuals who act in self-damaging or socially unacceptable ways. Whether in the state or independent sectors professionals carry responsibilities on behalf of society as a whole. Professional ethics therefore have a political as well as a moral basis. Clark recognises that social work is largely a state sponsored activity which therefore poses issues in political theory.

Typically, this is more indirect and less clearly expressed than the expectation of confidentiality. In social work, Clark identifies 'honesty and truthfulness' as one of eight rules of code of practice. Service and care should be offered and given in a manner that is honest, open, truthful, and transparent. Officers in the duty of social care and mental health professionals are required to document all the work they do with their clients.

The principle of confidentiality is not absolute. There are in fact, some exceptional circumstances where health professionals may ethically and legally qualify the principle of confidentiality centre on concerns about protecting the wellbeing of the patient themselves and protecting others from harm. Confidentiality is the duty owed by health care providers to protect the privacy of patient information. This duty stems largely from the right to privacy, but courts have imposed liability based on statutes defining expected conduct, ethical duties owed to the patient, breach of the fiduciary duty to maintain confidentiality, and breach of contract or implied contract between the patient and physician or healthcare facility.

Confidential information is private information that a person shares with another on the understanding that it will not be disclosed to third parties. It includes identifiable patient information – written, computerized, visually or audio recorded – that health professionals have access to. Keeping patient confidentiality is important because it builds trust, respects patient autonomy and privacy and contributes to good patient outcomes. Health professionals should ask competent patients for permission to share information with third parties.

In exceptional circumstances such as abuse or threatened suicide, it may not be appropriate to seek permission on medical grounds. These circumstances have not been considered by the courts of law, but they are likely to look for very strong evidence regarding the medical grounds as to why it was not considered desirable to seek the patient's consent.

So, there is an exception to the rule, if patients lack the capacity to consent to sharing information that health professionals may need to distribute.

## Autonomy and informed consent

The word autonomy comes from the Greek autos-nomos meaning "self-rule" or "self-determination".

The quality or state of being self-governing especially the right of self-government of the territory was granted autonomy. Autonomy is not an all-or-nothing matter. This is because principled autonomy is also neutral between good and evil. Indeed, a person is neither morally better nor worse than another person merely on account of being more rather than less autonomous.

It goes without saying that the most sophisticated defence of autonomy is Kant's. According to Kantian ethics, autonomy is based on the human capacity to direct one's life according to rational principles. He states, "Everything in nature works in accordance with laws." Kant does not provide explicit explanation as to whether those laws are defined or natural laws.

Spinoza has pointed out that reason demands nothing contrary to Nature hence we can argue autonomy is the natural right to be independent.

People can be informed or educated to make their own decision to be autonomous and work in unification and implication for cooperation with others.

The first ethical principle in the Belmont Report, respect for persons, is made up of two important, but distinct, requirements. The first is the recognition that people are autonomous and entitled to their own opinions and choices, unless detrimental to others. The second is the recognition that due to various reasons, not all people are capable of self-determination and instead require protection. The amount of protection provided to an individual should depend on the risk of harm and the likelihood of benefit offered by the research.

The Report promotes the idea that in most cases, respect for persons demands that people enter research voluntarily and with adequate information. However, these two requirements are assumptions and not deterministic by any form of evaluation, hence, the policy needs reviewing if the expected outcome is different to the actual.

There are four components of informed consent including decision capacity, documentation of consent, disclosure, and competency. Doctors will give you information about a particular treatment or test in order for you to decide whether or not you wish to undergo a treatment or test.

A minor, someone who is 17 years and younger, is generally considered not competent to make informed consent decisions. As a result, it is the minor's parents who provide the informed consent for treatment.

## Beneficence

Beneficence is defined as an act of charity, mercy, and kindness with a strong connotation of doing good to others which also include moral obligation. In healthcare, beneficence is one of the fundamental ethics. Beneficence is a concept in research ethics which states that researchers should have the welfare of the research participant as a goal of any clinical trial or other research study. The antonym of this term, maleficence, describes a practice which opposes the welfare of any research participant.

Beneficence is defined as kindness and charity; this requires action on the part of the nurse to benefit others. An example of a nurse demonstrating this ethical principle is by holding a dying patient's hand. It is the obligation to produce benefit for individual patients or clients, as implied in medical ethics narrations.

The medical profession is dedicated to wellbeing and not intended to harm, physicians should heal and help their patients according to the physician's abilities and judgment. In modern practice they conduct various scientific tests to determine the course of treatment, procedure or type of surgery needed. Patient treatments are prioritised according to their clinical needs. For example, accidents and emergency wards are to treat patients for emergencies, here they are faced with a trade-off between saving lives and following procedure in a medical emergency.

Beneficence, the second ethical principle in the Belmont Report, underlines how people need to be treated in an ethical manner not only by respecting their decisions and protecting them from harm, but also by making efforts, or, more specifically, making it an obligation to secure their wellbeing.

The Belmont Report identifies two general and complementary rules regarding beneficence:

1) do not harm, and 2) maximize possible benefits and minimize possible harms.

While the obligation to "do no harm" is often the focus of discussions, the obligation to maximize possible benefits while minimizing possible harms is an obligation that warrants equal consideration. The Report notes that it is the obligation of scientific investigators and members of their institutions to think about both maximizing benefits and reducing risks in their research.

Another object of discussion is the obligation of society at large, to recognize longer term benefits and the risks that may result from the improvement of knowledge and the development of novel medical, psychotherapeutic, and social procedures.

These obligations closely align with the Cancer Support Community's belief that in order to maximize the benefits and minimize the risks of clinical trials, both physical data and patient experience data should be collected as part of the research.

There are lessons to be learnt from history. Dr Mary Dobson, Historian of Medicine at St John's College, has been working in a University of

Cambridge documentary to mark the centenary of the 1918 pandemic named *Spanish flue* after it was first reported in a Spanish newspaper to highlight vital scientific research.

Dr Dobson said: "Spanish flu" has been what some people called a 'forgotten pandemic' but it was a huge global calamity that killed between 50 million and 100 million people - far greater than the casualties of the First World War."

Around May 1918, simultaneously the carnage of the First World War this unknown enemy started to sweep through the US, Europe, and the trenches. Its early origins and initial geographical starting point remain a mystery but, in the summer of 1918, there was a second wave of a far more virulent form of the influenza virus which no one could have anticipated. Soon dubbed 'Spanish Flu' after its effects were reported in the country's newspapers, the virus rapidly spread across much of the globe to become one of the worst natural disasters in human history.

Reporting these major incidents and educating medical students and public is also beneficial to find preventive medicine and measures to control a global pandemic. It is important that intellectual community highlight the vital ethical components of medical science so that decision makers are well-informed to benefit many.

## Non-maleficence

The principle of non-maleficence holds that there is an obligation not to inflict harm on others.

It is closely associated with the maxim primum non no-cere (first do no harm). Although not identical with medical ethics, it was an antecedent to historical development as the first constitutional principle on how we could treat people using an instrument of policy.

The principle of *non-Maleficence* requires an intention to avoid needless harm or injury that can arise through acts of commission or omission. In common language, it can be considered "negligence" if you impose a careless or unreasonable risk of harm upon another, this is a vigorously tested concept in medical care. Treatment is medically futile or non-beneficial because if it offers no reasonable hope of recovery or improvement, or because the patient is permanently unable to experience any benefit.

"Treatments that offer no physiological benefits to the patient are futile".

The principle of non-maleficence is also a consideration when treatment is futile. This treatment option in some cases minimizes harm to the infant and prevents prolongation of futile treatment.

However, it is also important to respect and support the wishes of the family who requests continuation of interventions. This principle is further tested in the administration of euthanasia, treatment withdrawal and palliative care.

Psychological and spiritual support is recognised as valuable to make patients comfortable on reaching such decisions.

## Justice

The notion of justice as a virtue first appeared in Homer's epic poetry. Homer's most important contribution to Greek culture was to provide a common set of values that enshrined the Greeks' own ideas about themselves. His poems, notably *the Iliad* and *the Odyssey* made a huge influence, providing a fixed model of heroism, nobility, and the good life to which all Greeks, especially aristocrats, subscribed. Early Greeks considered justice as a virtue of individual character, a personal trait which manifests in a person's character in relation to interpersonal behaviours and social interactions.

Plato attempted to conceptualise 'justice' in his treatise, *The Republic*. He treated the topic in relation to happiness through a variety of dialogues of political tone, giving it a much broader social political scope. Moving away from traditionalists, he made his views explicit by saying that justice is simply the "advantage of the stronger." This method of treatment involves the provocative idea that justice in the city (polis) is the same thing as justice in the individual, assuming that rules are set by an elite ruling class supported by the force behind the ruling.

Plato was the first to point out that justice is the primary virtue of government institutions, where public good and public concern should be the priority of a government. This introduces the principle of Social Justice, making it a political theme. Further, Plato argues that justice is a master virtue in a sense because both the city and the individuals are reciprocally interdependent.

Along with wisdom and courage he assumes that each and every individual has the same moral capacity to evaluate and make an ethical judgement. Plato eventually seeks to show that someone with a healthy, harmonious soul wouldn't lie, kill, or steal, however this does not make clear the difference between an individual mind and the collective mind set. The concept of public goods in economics is developed from this idea that more can benefit if government provide what private owners might exclude others using their property or goods that leads to market failure. In this way nonrivalry and non-discrimination is maintained in society.

Plato gives a somewhat different treatment of justice in Crito, a critical dialogue that depicts a conversation between Socrates and his wealthy friend Crito regarding justice, injustice, and the appropriate response to injustice. Socrates tries to use reason (rather than the values embedded in his culture) to determine whether an action is right or wrong. In Crito, Socrates believes injustice should not be answered with injustice. This is personified in the Laws of Athens, to prove this he refuses Crito's offer to bribe his escape from prison. The only question at hand is whether or not it would be just for Socrates to attempt an escape. If it is just, he will go with Crito, if it is unjust, he must remain in prison and face his death.

A philosopher has a conviction, rather than simply breaking the Laws and escaping, Socrates chose to try and persuade the Law to let him go. When the ballots were counted, 280 jurors had voted to find Socrates guilty, 220 jurors for acquittal. After the conviction of Socrates, the trial entered its penalty phase. Each side, the accusers, and the defendant, were given an opportunity to propose a punishment. Socrates was a very well-known philosopher in Athens during his lifetime and his execution in 399 BC catapulted him into even greater and more lasting fame.

The dialogue contains an ancient example of the social contract theory of government. In contemporary discussions, the meaning of Crito is debated to determine whether it is a plea for unconditional obedience to the laws of a society. It is not clear in the sequence of events whether justice is a property of how a society treats one another or if it has an absolute value.

Justice is a concept of moral rightness based on ethics, rationality, law, natural law, religion, or equity. It is also the act of simply being just and, or fair. Justice means to make sure things are seen equally. It means everyone should have the same responsibilities and rights as everyone else. The most fundamental principle of justice - one that has been widely accepted since it was first defined by Aristotle more than two thousand years ago, is the principle that states: "equals should be treated equally and unequals unequally."

In its contemporary form, this principle is sometimes expressed as follows: "Individuals should be treated the same, unless they differ in ways that are relevant to the situation in which they are involved."

For example, two people with the same illness should be treated equally by physicians irrespective of their social ethnic backgrounds. The right of all people and individuals to equal protection by the law. These sentencing principles reflect all three key principles of fairness, equality, and access.

The scales of justice are a symbol for the justice system in the United States. The Constitution protects justice for all citizens in the United States, although throughout history people have been treated unequally by their rulers.

The definition of justice is the use of power as appointed by law, honour, or standards to support fair treatment and due reward though there are incidents of miscarriages of justice. An example of justice in law is someone being set free from prison after strong evidence shows that they are innocent. State leaders have the privilege of pardoning convicted criminals at certain occasions of their career, usually having an element of politics attached to it.

There was a time in which there were attempts to separate the political entanglement of ethics, particularly to identify the principle of justice as a quality in itself. Political interference into justice system has dented the authenticity of ethics. Violation of human rights of opponents is common in some developing countries. Nevertheless, medical ethics has successfully managed to disconnect the element of politics from their medical ethics. However, it has been unable to resolve risk against benefit, balancing the risk of clinical trials against the anticipated likelihood of future benefits for many.

The last of the Belmont Report's three basic ethical principles, justice, raises questions about who ought to receive the benefits of research and who ought to bear its burdens. Following a provocative discussion of equality and differential treatment, the Belmont Report considers the need to scrutinize whether some classes of people - economically disadvantaged, racial, and ethnic minorities, or persons confined to institutions are systematically selected as research subjects due to their position or vulnerability rather than their connection to the problem being researched.

Today, the principle of justice may demand scrutiny of whether classes of people considered compromised or vulnerable are excluded from participation in clinical trials due to financial and other barriers even though they have a connection to the problem being considered.

The Report states that justice demands therapeutic devices and procedures developed from public funds must not only provide advantages to those who can afford them. The hope is that clinical research can bring benefits and the outcome is prioritised according to their clinical needs.

The importance of a speedy and effective clinical research and subsequent vaccine rollout was the central focus of the scientific community during the Mach 2020 Covid-19 pandemic. Medical ethics, knowledge sharing, and government policy enormously contributed to those efforts.

CHAPTER 22

# BUDDHIST ETHICS

### Philosophy of Buddhist Precepts

To test whether an ethical principle is valid and makes sense we need to examine it carefully.

If we want to develop traits for personal growth and welfare for many, we need to know what benefits it brings to us and the wider community. A consensus is needed to build trust and confidence within communities.

Once we've developed this, we need to understand how it will help, whether these benefits make sense, and if they accord with the basic nature of things. If the principle passes all these criteria, we can be confident about putting it into practice.

The Buddha outlined five precepts (no killing, stealing, sexual misconduct, lying, drinking alcohol, or taking intoxicants) which were to be followed by his disciples, laypeople, and monastics. The Buddha gave various reasons to explain why someone should be ethical. He showed its relation to the law of action, that it is in conformity with cause and effect; the first axiom of Buddhism states that certain things depend on other things as their base or condition. Every action has consequences, the outcome could be beneficial or not.

The second is the axiom of functionality. Every phenomenon that is affected by causes and conditions performs its specific function. For example, consciousness is a function of the mind, it relates to an experience that needs to be investigated, to have confidence in the truth sought before accepting its validity. Besides, to carry this out effectively one must separate emotions, normative beliefs, and perceptions from analysis.

The third is the axiom of establishment by reason. This means to establish facts proven by valid means; it corresponds to factual evidence that is not in contradiction, by this arises the need to investigate anything before determining it as true.

The last is the axiom of the nature of things. This is the axiom that certain facts are just the nature of things. This includes the intrinsic nature of phenomena, insight of interconnectedness and the underlying natural laws of the four great elements of the wider universe from which human beings are made of. For example, properties of earth, water fire and wind. Life forms and the physical universe are governed according to a fixed moral order. Breaking this order increases suffering, therefore ethical injunctions are introduced in the form of a practical ethical code of conduct, this allows us to have a realistic attitude to life.

One of the central aims of Buddhist moral philosophy is to assess the plausibility of the middle path by rejecting extreme practices, such as those that prevailed in contemporary India during the Buddha's time. Buddhism shows clearly that man's happiness and ultimate liberation depends on his own effort. Swaying towards extremes only prolongs suffering, hence suffering is the gauge with which to measure whether a principle is appropriate or not.

In the middle path all factors are prefixed, 'right' is a value attribution that exclusively presupposes a wrong way of practice, this increases suffering and is not conducive to happiness. The basic doctrines of the Buddha, from which his entire teachings stem from, are common to all Buddhists traditions. This includes the four noble truths: existence is suffering (dukhka); suffering has a cause, namely craving and attachment; there is a cessation of suffering, nirvana; and there is a path to the cessation of suffering. The path to end suffering was discovered by deep investigation into the connection between psychological factors and the function of the mind as the forerunner of behaviour.

Human beings are born with a temperament of selfish craving that sees us seeking pleasure throughout life. Uninformed people seek to satisfy their senses in variety of ways, endlessly craving for more which is the cause of suffering. Not knowing this fact adds more to suffering.

Ethical guidelines are set out to reduce suffering and for the protection of the individual and society alike. Precepts are ethical guidelines to regulate choice, these aim at developing the qualities of the person who practices them. Non-maleficence is the first principle proposed in Buddhism. The principle of non-maleficence - to do no harm - asserts that people should act in such a way that he or she does no harm to another intentionally.

In a border social context, do no harm and nonviolence is taught by showing the importance of accepting responsibility for one's physical, verbal, and mental actions. People are encouraged to practice benevolence, generosity, love, kindness and compassion towards fellow citizens and all other beings to achieve inner peace and social harmony thus promoting goodwill to all without discrimination.

Stealing is defined as taking what is not given, with this we must recognise the property rights of others. The obligation to produce benefits to an individual and to the larger society is implied as doing good, this is intimately connected to non-maleficence. Its importance is self-evident, it marks the outline of the other core principles within the Buddhist tradition of honesty and truthfulness. Last but not least, are mindfulness and awareness. These are the key factors to investigate the cause of suffering, intoxication makes the mind careless.

If one breaks the last precept, he or she is likely to break all other four ethical codes and violate social norms, that person contributes no benefit to society. It might not be simple to conceive that the principle of social justice is the same in a broader social or political scope as in an organised society where the individual accepts responsibility to reduce suffering for himself and others. The distinctive difference between the principle of non-maleficence on the one hand and that of beneficence on the other lies in the fact that the former frequently - but not always involves the omission of harmful action whereas the latter actively contributes towards the welfare of others.

The path of peace and happiness was found after strenuous effort. The Buddha renounced pleasure and the responsibilities of a household and political office, therefore Buddhist ethics are free from mental distortions and political interference.

Practising Buddha training factors is known as 'Parmi dhamma', this is a Buddhist term often translated as "perfection", also considered as higher virtues. It is described in Buddhist commentaries as the noble character and the qualities generally associated with enlightened beings.

The Pali canon gives ten substantive perfect qualities of an individual through which the path of enlightenment is sought.

The ten perfections in the Theravada tradition are:

1. generosity (dāna)
2. morality (sīla)
3. renunciation (nekhamma)
4. insight (paññā)
5. energy (viriya)
6. patience (khanti)
7. truthfulness (sacca)
8. resolution (adhiṭṭhāna)
9. loving-kindness (metta)
10. equanimity (upekkhā)

These ten factors of intrinsic value have been discovered and identified according to the natural law of cause and effect, moral order, and insight wisdom of connectivity. It is a natural process of the mind's evolution by taking ethical and moral life as its foundation. These factors are arranged in an order such a way that one support the cultivation of quality of the other until equanimity and stability of the mind is achieved starting from giving to develop detachment.

The historical Buddha possessed all ten qualities of perfection. He then formulated a set of ethical principles compatible with metaethics; these question the status of normative ethics by disagreeing with outdated practices which had no rational basis towards one's wellbeing and enlightenment. For example, the Buddha advised a group of fire worshipers to look at the fire inside their minds instead.

That's why, his transcendental wisdom of the world, the universal truths about being, and man's philosophical position in represents the world, there is crucial difference between Buddhism and all other contemporary philosophies.

Buddhism's sole focus is to reach the end goal which is the end of suffering and to achieve supreme happiness. The Buddhist higher philosophical psychology provides an ontological view of life that describes ultimate truth. The theory of enlightenment is formulated into the Four Noble Truths. Its ethical values and principles are practical, stemming from the three main doctrines of impermanence, suffering and insubstantiality of all phenomena.

This was then consolidated into eight concise factors according to the natural order of ethical importance. (The Eightfold Path consists of eight practices: right view, right resolve, right speech, right conduct, right livelihood, right effort, right mindfulness, and right concentration, insight, and tranquillity).

## Summary of Buddhist teachings

Summary of all the legendary Buddha's teachings have nothing to do with evil; instead it's all about cultivating a good and clear mind. To do good really means the generation and development of skilful acts, from ordination to the realization of the path of enlightenment.

Purification of the mind implies elimination of hindrances and defilements, namely greed, hatred and delusion and the attachments which are obstacles. By choosing the right path we can cultivate good moral conduct that ultimately leads to happiness.

Buddhist ethics are unique, they are based on the many outstanding qualities of the enlightened Buddha who taught without expecting anything in return. These qualities are compared to the divine adobes of heavenly gods that do not depend on worldly conditions; they are hence classed as supramundane. Buddha's compassion is unlimited and extends to all beings without exception. He understood the principle of cause, condition and mental phenomena that dependently arise from one another.

The reverse application of this truth is the dependent cessation of phenomena. These are without permanent substance and cease when the supporting conditions cease. For example, one thought arises dependent on another, similar to lotus flowers that appear on the water, wither when the water dries up and reappear when conditions are again suitable.

Ethics follows doctrinal principles; they are to help to maintain a suitable ethical environment to understand the deeper meaning of

Dhamma, intricately connected, not further reducible constituents that make up a being. They can be broadly divided into mind and mater or mentality and materiality. Teachings are timeless because they are addressed to the present moment, all-embracing, adaptable, and flexible to accommodate the needs of the modern world.

Buddhism covers all aspects of life without being impractical or impossible to understand. It is free from restrictions and open to everyone, serving as guidelines to people of all walks of life.

The universal principles of life equally apply to rich and poor as well as powerful and powerless.

To conform to Buddhist ethics, one need not have to be a Buddhist, yet it can serve as a norm to measure the ethical standard of other teachings. The search for moral excellence runs parallel in both East and Western thought. Buddha succeeded in presenting his doctrinal findings because he did not forcefully try to correct the world but gave freedom to think.

Buddhism is adaptable to cultural differences, if correctly understood in the context of ethics, it could serve as a basis to reform any society. True happiness comes from changing your heart, it lies deep inside you where others cannot see. The beauty of purity manifests in the form of words, actions and what you can offer to the world to make it a better place for all.

# CHAPTER 23

# CRITICAL REFLECTION ON ETHICS

T HOUGH MANY CENTURIES HAVE PASSED since Socrates' execution the foundation he set out for ethics remains sound and valid for today. Debates on values and political power have shifted from side to side, sometimes to the extreme right as is still visible in US politics today *(2021)*, but humanity always prevailed because human beings would hardly survive without an ethical foundation to life.

Punitive measures are painful. Society cannot successfully mitigate suffering by adding more of it to improve the living standards and quality of life. Ethics is based on well-founded standards of right and wrong prescribing what humans ought to do, usually in terms of rights, obligations, benefits to society, fairness, or specific virtues where most of these are integrated into jurisdiction legislative powers to exercise authority although there are many social standards are customary.

"Being ethical is doing what the law requires."

Ethics consists of the standards of behaviour that society accepts. Much philosophical thinking has shaped our societies to value democracy as a method of social governance, taking justice as its kernel point of ethics to protect people, this is the standard by which we can test the integrity of leaders, even at times of uncertainty.

There is a difference between seeking justice and revenge. The fine line between these two ends is decided by ethical values. Instigating insurrection, violence, deflecting blame for their actions is the mismanagement of justice, this has severe consequences on the social order and the system it aims to protect.

The narrow view of Hedonists promotes pleasure and self-interest, often entangled with economics and politics.

If people are not self-disciplined, their behaviour could contradict public interest. Understanding the psychology of behaviour, reducing the factors that contribute to unfair treatment such as greed, hatred and delusion might improve a Hedonist's view of ethics. Broader discussions of ethics would facilitate the evaluation of the purpose of public policy, government, and understand the role of the individual within an organised social system.

People can be educated in ethics and can improve their quality of life, eventually reaching a higher standard of living. In truth, understanding the moral values on a metaethical level can influence the distinctions between what decisions to make and how to make them for the welfare of people, in the global context as well as at an individual level.

Published in 1979, the Belmont Report identified three basic ethical principles and set forth guidelines for the conduct of biomedical and behavioural research involving human subjects.

These principles and guidelines are the results of an ethical enquiry into errors of thought, assumptions, and sub-sequent judgments that has helped thinkers and professionals to develop standards of measure against deliberate or accidental mistakes without which no progress could be made in any discipline.

Respect for persons, beneficence, and justice remain particularly relevant and necessary, not only for biomedical science but all areas of activity.

Buddhist ethics are compatible with the cosmic laws. Applying the four Buddhist axioms to investigate principles such as respect for person, beneficence, and justice, would help you to develop a realistic attitude about how to approach ethics. Buddhist axioms allow us to vigorously test normative beliefs before accepting their validity, it encourages us to investigate deeply, as a goldsmith testing gold, into whether it is real or fake.

Buddhist ethical principles were developed completely independent of political interference and theological belief for the benefit of an individual's liberation of mind.

Its general principle is that everything we do originates in the mind, where a set of other principles tells us what is morally right as well as how individuals should interact and integrate within society. These guidelines are still relevant for today's modern society. Buddhist morality is codified into five precepts and extended further as the trainee progresses on the path of happiness. Though they appear to be a religious code of practice, the Buddha formulated these principles from deep philosophical roots to connect behaviour to the psychological tenants of an individual.

When an individual accepts responsibility for his or her actions and self-regulates behaviour, no harm is done individually or collectively. Buddhist ethics are for one specific goal, to end suffering. Social, economic, and political policies can benefit from these Buddhist values because suffering is common to all.

The theories in ethics and the related abstract literature, represent philosophers' views to understand behavioural processes that cause people to act in a certain way in the context of their relationships with one another, for the benefit of society and what they believe is best for social harmony.

This book attempted to investigate several components of literature from the standpoint of ethical views, historical development, and their effects expressed by the same lineage of philosophers since Ancient Greece. Socrates was the first to question ethical values in Western philosophy.

Since his unjust execution, the development of ethics has been entangled with politics. There was an attempt to rediscover an absolute value of ethics by the philosophers of the Age of Enlightenment, notably Immanuel Kant, who contributed towards taking the subject to new heights. Kant believed that there was a supreme principle of morality that laid the foundation for metaethics which in turn, tests the status of ethical principles to guide behaviour.

People need some sort of a moral guide through life. Historically religion was the moral guidance that codified ethics into a set of rules that were followed by their converts. Religious leaders, on the other hand, are generally abetted in their purposes by the civil authority which threatens to punish all deviations from theological orthodoxy as "sedition" and exerts obedience.

These days many may think that they can get by without one, but chances are that they are egoists and do still have a principle that is guiding them.

During Ancient Greek civilisation, ethical egoism seemed attractive to people who sought their own selfish pleasure by promoting self-interest. As a general guide for all people that principle would lead and does lead to many conflicts since we live in a world of scarce resources.

The great thinkers of history started to contemplate their decisions on the theory of pleasure also known as hedonism, they soon rejected these selfish ideologies and thought of what would be good for many.

Utilitarianism says to profess the greatest amount of pleasure for the greatest number of people.

During the Age of Enlightenment, people valued "reason" above aristocratic power and religious authority and sought for greater values to benefit society. The political freedom they gained through reason resulted in three major civil wars to overthrow aristocratic power in America, France, and Russia.

The United States of America was the first country in the world to fully implement Plato's moral-political theory of *The Republic* into practice, becoming the world's first country to claim democratic freedom as characterised by "Liberty", a quality or state of being free. After that, Russia adopted Karl Marx's communist ideology.

Immanuel Kant was a German philosopher and one of the central Enlightenment thinkers.

Immanuel Kant's comprehensive and systematic works in epistemology, metaphysics, ethics, and aesthetics have made him one of the most influential figures in modern Western philosophy. He argued that the supreme principle of morality is a standard of rationality that he dubbed the "Categorical Imperative" which says to "Act according to the maxim that you would wish all other rational people to follow as if it were a universal law".

Inspired by a mathematical presentation of ethics, Benedict Spinoza was a Dutch philosopher of Portuguese Sephardi origin and one of the early thinkers of the Enlightenment and modern biblical criticism. His ideas included modern conceptions of the self and the universe; he came to be considered as one of the greatest rationalists of 17th-century philosophy.

He advocated Natural Law, stating that what follows the natural law is morally right and what does not follow the natural law is morally wrong.

He was one of the great naturalists and a rationalist who valued reason above all else. He proposed that people control their passions to worldly pleasure, to restrain and seek higher virtues and higher knowledge. He went even to the extent of challenging the contemporary political theology and uncoupled the western thought of ethics from politics and religion, showing the true freedom of thought by rejecting world-weary views and the way to true happiness, showing a man in his rightful place in society.

During the great economic depression, good ethical values founded by philosophers of the Age of Enlightenment were doomed. Far right extremists took militarised political power into their own hands in Germany and Italy. They promoted their Nazi ideology resulting in World War II and this brought a catastrophic effect to the rest of the world with unaccounted human tragedies and numerous atrocities.

At the same time, Japan expanded its military activities with a view to creating a controlled Asian economic region. The war ended with the testing of nuclear bombs on two cities in Japan.

After the war, world political opinion divided the West and East, both gaining considerable military strengths and nuclear know-how.

Political divisions were exacerbated to gain nuclear supremacy and capitalise world oil and energy supply resulting in what was known as the Cold War. Both the American and Soviet superpowers openly contended their interests in the Asia Pacific causing the Capitalist and Communist division resulting in the Vietnam War.

In the years 1991 and 2003, America led the western alliance forces, twice, to invade Iraq and change the world order, causing much unrest in many middle eastern countries including Syria.

Former USSR was devolved by the reconfiguration of the former eastern bloc with violent eruptions of ethnic conflict in Balkans states. War crimes, human tragedies, and atrocities were similar to World War II.

During this era, people's lifestyles were changed by increasing money circulation conforming to one of the elusive theories of monetary economics substantive by quantitative easing (QE).

Material possessions, consumerisation, and self-interest appeared to be the dominant values of all societies and military spending was at its highest for political agendas.

This unsustainable artificial economy and lifestyle collapsed in the 2008's banking and economic crisis, that involved all superpower countries unable to balance their books. This unconventional form of monetary policy QE, in which central banks purchases longer-term securities from the open market in order to increase the money supply and encourage lending and investment, has now become a standard practice of monetary policy stimulation.

The gap between rich and poor has widened, and the recent Covid-19 pandemic has added more to human misery. It highlighted the value of ethics.

The most recent January 2021 power transition of the US presidential election caused much controversy, violence, and dented the people's freedom of choice, rule of law and challenged democracy.

It also stressed the need to rethink ethics and test leadership styles defined by strength of character and his or her ethical foundation. These are the consequences of unethical conduct and lessons to learn from history, to reflect upon the errors of thought and unethical political philosophies, use of social media, technology and bad economic policies based on pure greed and self-interest. Hence, there is a need to improve relationships between communities, countries, and reinvestigate ethical and moral values so that they are sustainable and common to all human beings in the world, to have peace and justice.

The world is unimpressed with Russia's recent military activities in Ukraine. From 24 February 2022 to November 2022, the world has witnessed graphic content emanating from the warzone rejecting President Putin's narratives to justify his military actions.

Ukraine has never taken seriously Russia's demand for demilitarisation, and Moscow's insistence on "de-Nazification" is merely Russian propaganda.

The claims of Nazis and genocide in Ukraine were completely unfounded. Whatever its justification, soon or later Russian leader has to admit his mistakes as Russia's future and its future place in the world are at stake. This was unexpected to the Russian leader who wants to fundamentally redefine the status quo within Europe in line with his own vision to build a new Russian empire but was unable to propose an alternative ethical philosophical theory for better world order. Instead, President Putin began to use tough political rhetoric of using all his power. Russia has as many as 2,000 tactical nuclear weapons (TNW), lower-yield devices designed to defeat conventional forces on the battlefield (Reuters October 17,2022). Considering the setbacks Russia suffered, western leaders were concerned that they might use TNW to get Ukraine to negotiations. Moscow says that the west is misinterpreting their statements.

The world leaders were concern of Russia's unpredictability. The international community should "oppose the use of or the threat to use nuclear weapons, advocate that nuclear weapons cannot be used and that nuclear wars must not be fought and prevent a nuclear crisis in Eurasia," Chinese leader Xi Jinping said Nov. 4, 2022, according to Xinhua news agency. The comment is the first rebuke of its kind attributed to the Chinese leader since Russia invaded Ukraine in February, while President Xi Jinping met with German Chancellor Olaf Scholz on his official visit to China at the Great Hall of the People in Beijing to renew China-Germany relations. Noting the complex and fluid international landscape, President Xi underscored the need for China and Germany, two major countries with great influence, great civilizations from the west and east, to work together in times of change and instability and contribute more to world peace and development proving that ethics is the common ground for prosperity and success.

If the war continues it will certainly undermine the peace and stability not only in the West, but its global effects would be severe. Both Chinese and the Western leaders have now well realized the severe economic consequence of the unnecessary war Russia has started and want to build new constructive trade relations. In short, the worst is yet to come, and for many people 2023 will feel like a recession. Russia's invasion of Ukraine continues to powerfully destabilize the global economy. Beyond the escalating and senseless destruction of lives and livelihoods, it has led to a severe energy crisis in Europe that is sharply increasing costs of living and hampering economic activity and also caused humanitarian crisis in Ukraine. Many world leaders see this war as a turning point in the history of Europe.

One strategy aims to strengthen certain areas of people-oriented by ethical and ecologically friendly economic policies and practices by promoting friendliness and human values which underpin a sound ethical philosophical theory. These desires also imply the importance of establishing a sound ethical approach to achieving proper and lasting relationships between countries and wealth redistribution to reduce the wealth gap. Many societies are underserved, in need of public compliance and humanitarian aid; and this need has never been higher in our living memory given the added burden of the Covid-19 pandemic.

The differences and gaps in society correspond to the differences of moral values and gaps in ethical principles. Buddhism is a nonviolent, philosophical, and ethical set of teachings which were propounded by the enlightened Buddha. These teachings have contributed to achieving peace, economic prosperity, and personal happiness for those who accepted to follow them.

We thus assert that human experiences could be enriched further between Western and Buddhist philosophies by evaluating existing theories in an enlightened perspective and taking into consideration the profound psychology of broader human behaviour.

The 1976 Belmont Report set out Ethical Principles and Guidelines for the Protection of Human Subjects of Research. Thus, we believe that medical ethics are free from the admixture of politics, theological views, and other agendas. The Belmont Report serves as a framework and a benchmark for medical ethics and many other professional ethics in the US and UK. Therefore, a standard guideline of eight ethical principles derived from this report and other moral theories are discussed for practical application rather than intellectual study.

An ethical code is a listing of principles, values and aspirations based on a desired conduct and born in the traditions of the medical professions. It is more than a set of rules or a reason for promoting self-interest. Codes serve as a parameter by which all members of a profession can judge the acceptable level of behaviour and is the basis for self-regulation which helps to build good therapeutic relations.

Hopefully, by considering the various theories and examining how they could be applied to various situations involving medical practices and institutions each person will become more aware of their fundamental values and which of the theories is most in keeping with what they think of as the good. Such a theory would then serve as a source of moral guidance for the institutions and the individuals that act as an agent of an institution.

We believe that people should have some principles by which they make their decisions as to what is the morally correct thing to do, a sort of unified approach to ethical coexistence. This discussion of the Western philosophy of ethics, enriched with Eastern Buddhist values, would help for personal growth and personal development to enhance the value system for one who pursues happiness through peace. Buddhism is pragmatic; because it is based on empirical evidence, its validity can be tested here and now, and personal development, success, and happiness are its final good. If a person is tempted to think that several of the theories could be employed in a single life the result would be a person who would choose which theory is best employed to support the decision.

In Buddhist culture, doing the right thing is seen as more important than material wealth and duty is considered more important than personal pride. Happiness comes from being generous and benevolent.

It is up to you as to which principles will guide your decisions. There is advice that others can and do give you, but it is your decision. Choose wisely. For Plato, this was the whole point of Philosophy: to assist someone in choosing wisely, in choosing what truly is the Good.

The Buddha showed us the path for personal liberation. Other than philosophy there are other sources of ethics; this book has explored the ethical values of literature, biblical stories, Shakespeare, and epic stories that have inspired many generations for their practical value.

Ethical Egoist and self-centred ideas coupled with religious fanaticism only led to violence and terror. The world community clearly appears to be unwilling to accept blind principle that has no rationality as the basis for moral conflict resolution. History suggests that ethical values do not flourish under autocratic regimes but work well in a socialist democracy, political systems which recognise human rights and that operate with the principle of Utility in an effort to resolve conflicts and avoid violence.

The Path of Peace and Happiness shows you the way out of the woods to a clear vision of life. What is needed in a moral code is something that will enable humans to live with one another in order rather than a chaos of self-interested action. The law of action dictates that every action has its consequences, whether you like it or not, all consequences are yours.

CHAPTER 24

# ETHICAL DILEMMAS

Historically religious leaders advocated the ethical and moral conduct of individuals. People's behaviour was regulated by religious codes of practice; the principal factors of ethics in religion are faith and obedience, its main psychological factor is hope. The oldest code of practice is the Ten Commandments which could be found in Judeo-Christian societies. The moral laws are solidified into ten great mandates. These commands form the basis of covenants, a voluntary acceptance of a supreme authority of the creator God that needed to maintain discipline, social harmony among people, at the historical time, it was under tough conditions.

Civic leaders needed to bring unity among their people, hence needed a common set of rules to keep them together. They perceived that transgression to Creator as the main reason for personal and collective social failure and persuaded men to behave. The way of restoration, of salvation, redemption was possible and promised that all may come to the knowledge of the Creator, and to have fellowship with him again, from whom all the children of men are separated in the state of enmity, and are ignorant of him, and drove from his presence.

Followers were motivated by freedom, from slavery in Egypt, and a promise of a Freeland or the kingdom of heaven where they could live in peace and happiness. According to this doctrine, only through obedience to moral laws could one be delivered from the bondage of slavery to those powerful Pharaohs of ancient Egypt (c.3150 BCE).

During the time AD 30-36, Christians were brutally punished and crushed by Roman rulers.

Christians suffered from systemic, sporadic, and localised persecution under Roman Imperialism that perceived rising religions as a threat. This hostility against religions lasted for nearly two and half centuries until the 4th century CE, it was then that Emperor Constantine the Great began to transition Christianity into becoming the dominant religion of the Roman Empire.

All religions in the world have their own methods and motives to guide converts including maintaining discipline and unity. Moral traditions and most of the codes are common to many religions, it was the way that people lived in peace. This was characterised by many churches and cathedrals indicating that these traditions were highly valued by society until today.

With the development of political freedom, people began to question religious authority and demanded better explanations concerning their freedom of thought, whilst certain hypocritical behaviour and scandals of the clergy made people distance themselves from religions. These human weaknesses towards temptation are interpreted as a demon's spell in order to destroy life. This was felt strongly enough to excommunicate the perpetrator from society or subjugate them to capital punishment by the ruling authority, incidents of which are described in biblical stories founded on contemporary ethical values and moral standards.

The structure and the law of politically and economically organised societies became increasingly complex, social, and religious institutions needed to adapt to the changes of the day and people became more and more distanced from these religious institutions. For example, education, healthcare, and marriage are no longer the responsibilities of religious institutions but have been taken over by central and local government councils replacing church councils. There were increased philosophical inquiries into political theology and people began to reject religious authority and aristocratic power, accepting instead democratic rules of social governance.

However, many people in the world have a religion and still keep their passive traditions alive.

Religion is a comfort zone, established by institutions of developed ethics to guide moral values for a peaceful, friendly, and contented life.

Ethical dilemmas are situations in which there is a difficult choice to be made between two or more options, neither of which seems to resolve the situation in a manner that is consistent with accepted ethical guidelines. When faced with an ethical dilemma, a person has to select an option that does not align with an established code of ethics or societal norms, such as a code of law, religious teachings, or their internal moral perceptions of right and wrong.

People are faced with ethical dilemmas all too frequently in their everyday lives, either in domestic situations or in public. For example, queuing theory is a situation where people have to wait until their turn comes for service in line at a bank, food store, a bus, traffic, medical treatment, and vaccinations, yet some people jump the queue before their turn. The theory covers a wide range of applications to provide faster service to customers and move traffic, avoid congestion or conflicts.

There is rarely a clear answer regarding right and wrong. Instead of being able to rely on external standards, people have to rely on their moral values to resolve such situations. In a homogeneous society, there is much understanding and appreciation of help among people as exhibited in cultural practices. Breaking a code is mitigated with a simple apology.

In cosmopolitan cities, particularly in a political and economic situation, this is a more formal procedure sometimes needing litigation to resolve a dispute. In multi-ethnic and multicultural cities, ethics and morals are much more complicated as people can begin to lose their identity and moral social standards, replaced with rules, contractual obligations, policies, procedures, and legal proceedings.

One could easily get into trouble; therefore, people avoid each other rather than wanting to help one another. Rather than a collectiveness, societies are segregated, and individualism is the norm in these crowded cities.

These separations are visible in a work environment, a deliberate segregation of duties discourage colluding with one another to avoid the misuse, abuse or misappropriation of employers' or public resources. For example, digital communication and digital data storage have created some ethical dilemmas involving information access and privacy, staff need for an authorisation of access and a reason for legitimate use of other people's personal data. You could find yourself in a situation of requiring written permission to get information needed for your work. Policies aim at justice for all people and can reduce conflicts by changing past mindsets to facilitate people's friendly relations.

Good parenting entails bringing up children in an ethical background and encouraging them to learn moral standards at a young age. A storytelling approach is a conventional tradition for early learning stages to learn good habits. Introduced by Lawrence Kohlberg in the 1930s, he proposed that we use these to encourage children to think through possible outcomes and consequences of ethical dilemmas. Lawrence Kohlberg was an American psychologist best known for his theory of stages of moral development. He served as a professor in the Psychology Department at the University of Chicago and at the Graduate School of Education at Harvard University. Kohlberg's theory proposes that there are three levels of moral development, with each level split into two stages. Kohlberg introduces child psychology into ethics and suggests that children move through these stages in a fixed order because moral understanding is linked to cognitive development. The three levels of moral reasoning include preconventional, conventional, and post-conventional.

By using children's responses to a series of moral dilemmas, Kohlberg established that the reasoning behind the decision was a greater indication of moral development than the actual answer. A more detailed study of the behaviour of children aged between 18 months to 12 years has been carried out by Jean Piaget. Jean Piaget was a Swiss psychologist known for his work on child development. Piaget's 1936 theory of cognitive development and his epistemological views are called *genetic epistemology*.

Piaget placed great importance on the education of children. The key concepts of Piaget's theory of cognitive development suggest that intelligence changes as children grow. He conducted a kind of IQ test for children and observed that a child's cognitive development is not just about acquiring knowledge, the child has to develop or construct a mental model of the world. Cognitive development occurs through the interaction of innate capacities and environmental events, with which children pass through four stages of development.

The theory explains that a child responds to the perceived world around them, and responses change as they grow. As we know children learn moral habits from parents' teachers and adults. It is important that parents take responsibility for the upbringing of their children in a positive ethical environment setting which is exampled by their own conduct.

Piaget was employed at the Binet Institute in the 1920s, his job was to develop French translations of questions on English intelligence tests. He became intrigued with the reasons children gave for their wrong answers to the questions that required logical thinking. He believed that these incorrect answers revealed important differences between the thinking of adults and children.

Piaget branched out on his own a new set of assumptions about children's intelligence. His theory focuses not only on understanding how children acquire knowledge but also on understanding the nature of intelligence from an infant stage to a formal operational stage, where children learn more abstract knowledge of their environment. He then concluded that the sequence of these stages is universal across cultures and follow the same unvarying order. All children go through the same stages in the same order, but some children have the ability to learn faster or are gifted by birth. These talents in children need to be identified at their primacy age so that they can be developed further and become useful to society at large. This would be to the benefit of many in conformity with utility theory thus multiplying the positive effects to benefit the wider world when these talented children accept civic responsibilities at later stage of their lives.

Examples of teaching moral values through storytelling can be found in ancient Greek times.

The most prolific source of moral lessons in literature is Aesop's Fables. Aesop was a Greek storyteller. The main characters in his stories are animals, through which each story demonstrates a moral lesson.

For example, 'there is no believing a liar, even when he speaks the truth' – "*The Shepherd's Boy and the Wolf*".

These examples of morals and moral lessons demonstrate that although there are certain morals followed by society as a whole, they are also highly personal. Morals are based on a personal belief system, as such religions, biblical stories, epics can have a great influence on moral values. Children learn certain moral values from these stories at a young age which become their guidance in adult life. Some stories project role models.

In literature, often the moral of the story stems from a central character's set of morals or evolved personality traits, it is interesting to see how someone's morals move the story along.

In real life situations, these stories help to resolve ethical dilemmas in personal relationships or when the impact of our decision needs serious consideration, even to the extent of risking your own life to save others.

For example, consider a hypothetical situation in which a group of friends are going for a swim in the ocean together and one of them is drowning. The group has to make an extremely difficult decision. Only someone with strong moral conviction, character, strength, and skill would come forward to save the one in distress. This is one of the most extreme examples of a moral and ethical dilemma. The choice is between actively causing one person's death or allowing other people, including oneself to die.

Someone following a utilitarian approach to ethics would likely choose to save the friend who is drowning, this philosophy is based on choosing actions that result in the greatest good for the greatest number of people. It would be a very rare individual who is brave enough to save others and risk his own life but there are true stories like this. There are very striking and dramatic stories and parables in literature and the Bible that highlight the high standards of moral and ethical values in many advanced cultures which have inspired generations.

The latter of this book demonstrates both morals and morale within conceptions of universal art, wherein the story is relevant to everyone by conveying ethical characters, leadership, and economic models more effectively than political and philosophical narratives.

There are many ethical perspectives. People learn ethics from childhood, both from a religious and a philosophical point of view.

There are five branches of ethics, each of which offers a different perspective:

- Normative Ethics

  The normative approach is the largest branch of ethics, it deals with how individuals can figure out the correct moral action that they should take. This branch of ethics has largely been developed by philosophers since the Socratic time.

- Meta Ethics

  The metaethics branch seeks to understand the nature of ethical properties and judgments, such as whether truth values can be found and the theory behind moral principles. It questions what morality in its absolute sense is.

- Applied Ethics

  Applied ethics is the study of applying ethical theories from philosophers to everyday life.

  For example, this area of ethics asks questions such as - "Is it acceptable to allow euthanasia?" and "Should you turn in your colleague at your workplace for fiddling with petty cash?" A framework of ethics was developed to benefit professional services in line with this type of ethical inquiry.

- Moral Ethics

  The branch of moral ethics questions how individuals develop their morality, why certain aspects of morality differ between cultures, and why certain aspects of morality are generally universal. For example, religious moral values such as universal loving-kindness are taught in Buddhism.

- Descriptive Ethics

  Descriptive ethics is more scientific in its approach. It focuses on how human beings actually operate in the real world, rather than attempting to theorize about how they should operate. The study of genetic patterns is one such example of descriptive ethics.

Deciding how best to resolve difficult moral and ethical dilemmas is never easy, especially when our options violate the societal and ethical standards by which we have been taught to govern our lives. The most pressing issues in modern societies is economics and politics. It is not economically viable and impossible to live alone, and we often must choose to interact with larger more politically motivated organised societies.

Man's most important question in economics is whether the end justifies the means. Various dilemmas and conflicts, including wars, are the result of man's inability to dissolve tensions through dialogue and resolve an issue by means of ethical principles and conduct.

In international dilemmas, countries have to find a way to abandon ideological prejudice and political agendas and instead, jointly follow a path of peaceful coexistence and mutual benefit, in a system where all win by their participation and cooperation thus avoiding violence and resolving conflict in a peaceful way.

Ethics clearly define the boundaries of freedom, assuming that freedom is conditional, affected by external rules concerning a subjective understanding of "right" and "wrong". On the other hand, moral values can be broader, unbounded, and can be universally shared values of right and wrong.

Disputes arise due to misunderstandings and ignorance concerning the boundaries of freedom.

Disputes can be resolved amicably but, if not, by deferring to the organisational hierarchy of society; historically, an ultimate power decreed absolutely on what is right and wrong such as was bestowed on kings, however over time and because of successive social change, this power has been successfully transferred to the legal system to resolve many of these issues.

The term *dispute resolution* is sometimes used interchangeably with *conflict resolution* although conflicts are generally more deep-rooted and lengthier than disputes.

Dispute resolution techniques assist the resolution of antagonisms between parties that can include citizens, corporations even between governments, political leaders internally or externally. In developed countries, unicameralism is the practice of having a single legislative house or parliamentary chamber. This can be extended to governments to consider the role of bicameral conflict resolution in a legislative agenda-setting. This can also be useful in the event of unicameral conflict when promoting policy change, especially when facing uncertainty over the policy preference on matters of critical importance.

Bicameral conflict resolution committees play a more sophisticated role in government policy than making unilateral decisions characterised by autocratic dictatorial leaders. In democratic party politics, the enactment of primary legislation often requires a concurrent majority of the house, the approval of a majority of members in each of the chambers of legislature.

When this is the case, the legislature may be called an example of perfect bicameralism. However, in many parliamentary and semi-presidential systems, the house to which the executive is responsible can overrule the other house which may be regarded as an example of imperfect bicameralism.

Some legislatures lie in between these two positions, with one house able to overrule the other only under certain circumstances. In the UK, this bicameralism is represented by the Westminster Parliament of the House of Commons and the House of Lords while in the United States of America, Congress and Senate share the legislative power with the popular assemblies of elected members by the public representatives and elected president with executive powers. These are both form of government that embody the basic ethical premise of the principle of accountability. The integrity of the elected member is formalised by taking oaths administered by the representative of the law. A person undertakes the oath to support, defend, and uphold the Constitution, bearing true faith and allegiance to the country and constitution. The process is very conventional and established by long tradition, the validity of oaths solely depends on the person's moral standards and public acceptance of what people perceive as morality. Violation of oaths such as deception is an impeachable offence to be followed by legal proceedings.

This conventional juridical system by design assumes the premise that no one is above the law and all legal requirements are embedded in the constitution, which is open to amendments if required, subject to the approval of the house.

Oaths, affirmations, pledges, declarations, and political manifestos constitute a shared core of moral values in public service. These are undertaken by politicians representing the citizens, civil servants, or uniformed services such as police officers and medical nurses. The powers and responsibilities granted by oaths to a public office or profession is a technical legal matter, however, in simple terms it is a promise to do their job well.

At the highest level of public office, such as Executive President, many powers and privileges are given by the Constitution so the responsibility to serve the nation is also very great. He or she can give executive orders. The oath of office, and most cases of law, do not grant any protection when deciding that an order is a bad idea, bad policy, or morally wrong. In fact, the oath does not grant any protection from anything, it is solely an oath of allegiance and a promise to do good work. For this reason, having an opposition is a good idea to test the ethical and moral value of a policy.

Freedom of speech and freedom of journalism are very important elements in evaluating the moral standards and efficacy of policy decisions, they affect public questioning as to the integrity of political leaders.

Ethical dilemmas arise when an employee believes that they are being ordered to act in a manner inconsistent with his or her oaths of office. Disobeying direct orders is generally not an available option but they may pursue other avenues provided by law or regulations, perhaps trade unions can help to mitigate critical issues.

Government employees are accountable to the people, not to politicians. Professional employees understand their oaths of office and take it seriously, knowing their moral duty is to do the job right. The public judges their duty, not by the oaths they took but typically by the role they play. For example, the value of the nursing role in the UK was well recognised by the public during the Covid-19 pandemic, which led to a campaign of clapping to them visibly and openly expressing appreciation.

## January 2021 U.S. Presidential Impeachment Trial

A much controversial and unpresidential dilemma of ethics and moral duty concerns the outgoing President of United Sates Mr Donald J Trump. This was staged on the 6th January 2021, in the US electoral power transition. It was an incident of a violent nature by Trump supporters who believed that the election was stolen from them. This resulted in Mr Trump being accused of an impeachable offence by an incitement of insurrection.

The incident which came to debate, it is not yet resolved as to what is right and wrong in politics and whether it warrants constitutional reform to avoid such disputes in future. This is the result of political ideologies, agendas, personal pride, and prejudice becoming so much entangled with moral principles and ethics to make someone unable to assess the integrity of a public office bearer.

There are no guidelines or standards of measure to assess the integrity of a leader or candidate of a presidential election. Leaders are often created by their exceptional abilities in public speech, by situations and charisma and this is easily predictable.

Mr Trump's reaction to the election results and subsequent behaviour was predicted almost a year ago by Dr Jerrold M Post in his book, *Dangerous Charisma: The Political Psychology of Donald Trump and His Followers*, originally published by Pegasus Books, 05 November 2019.

Dr Post wrote "If Trump loses in 2020, and he chooses to call foul or tout conspiracy theories," he wrote, "it is unclear just how extreme the reaction of some of his supporters may be."

Dr Post was the long-time head of psychological profiling at the C.I.A., he put President Trump under the psychiatric microscope, examining the unique connection between Trump and his base. He came under criticism within the psychiatric community but a year later he had the consolation of being proved right.

The American Psychiatric Association, of which Dr Post was a lifetime fellow, accused him of violating the so-called Goldwater Rule, which bars a member from publicly offering a professional opinion about someone without interviewing the person or getting that person's consent. It was a dilemma of professional ethics vs moral conviction for the writer. To Dr Post, such criticism was ridiculous, if not irresponsible. He believed that it was his ethical obligation to offer his insights on political figures, especially if they presented a threat to the country.

Dr Post was a political psychologist who had analysed the characters of many dictators in the Cold War era. Besides, he would add, he wasn't offering Saddam Hussein medical advice. "We have satellite photography that can zero in on the dimples on a golf ball," he told The New Yorker newspaper, "but we can't peer into the minds of our adversaries."

In his last book, written with Stephanie R. Doucette, Dr Post used the tools of political psychology he had developed at the C.I.A., he also faced opposition within the C.I.A. from analysts who insisted that psychology offered limited insight - especially when, as was almost always the case, Dr Post was unable to interview the subjects in person. For that, Dr Post had to underline health conditions, however, his contribution to political psychology is insightful. Sadly, he died in November 2020 after testing positive for Covid-19 at the age of 86.

*US Impeachment Trial*

Then President Mr Donald Trump's controversial role in inciting the January 6 Capitol riot has led to a historic impeachment and to the first impeachment trial of a president after he's left office. The purpose of the trial is to invoke the constitutionally created sanction of "disqualification to hold and enjoy any Office of honour, Trust or Profit under the United States" – meaning he would have no future come-back attempt to contest for a presidential election.

This was an internal political process held by the Senators to trial the conduct of an office-bearer whilst holding an official position under oath. The sequence of events that led to the violent incident was vigorously investigated to identify whether the former President deliberately and intentionally orchestrated or incited violence. Impeachment managers presented a series of social media postings showing graphic contents and violent images of video clips as evidence.

The defence lawyers argued on the basis of the liberties granted for Free Speech, however, political free speech is not applicable as a defence against attempting to forcefully overturn election results. The defence relied on the fact that the Senate has no constitutional jurisdiction over an ex-president. This argument seemed to be the key theme of Trump's defence and the outcome was predetermined by the vast majority of the Senate GOP (The Republican Party, sometimes also referred to as the GOP - Grand Old Party) conference. 45 out of 50 had previously voted for a motion declaring that the Senate has no constitutional jurisdiction over an ex-president, both sides sparred over its merit.

During their presentations, rather than arguing on points of law, the House managers heavily relied on videos showing Trump's rhetoric leading up to Jan. 6, including his remarks the morning of the insurrection. Their political narratives were persuasive, facts people already knew but not in as much detail as to shift the pre-determined mindset of traditional orthodox conservatives.

Indeed, changing political paradigms implies more than social media postings evidence and the showing of video clips; it requires profound philosophical psychology and criminology knowledge to interpret violent events and criminal activities and to ultimately judge on the moral accountability and group behaviour of the far-right political ideology.

At the conclusion of the trial, the Senate voted 57 - 43 to convict, which was short of the required two - thirds majority ordered in the United States Constitution, thereby acquitting the former President Trump of the charge of inciting insurrection in the attack on the U.S. Capitol on January 6, 2021. Seven Republican senators voted on principle to convict Donald Trump, the largest bipartisan vote for an impeachment conviction of a U.S. president.

Despite voting to acquit on the grounds of a jurisdiction argument, the Republican Majority Leader Mr Mitch McConnel made a statement expressing his displeasure at the incident, he fully condemned former president Trump's actions preceding the riot as a disgraceful dereliction of duty to protect the constitution, saying that there is no question that President Trump is practically and morally responsible for provoking the events of the day. He stated that the impeachment trial was not an overarching tribunal to test the moral obligations, but a narrow purpose of Senators tasked against a current office bearer; the trial was only a political ramification, not implied by the criminal justice system.

However, with the foresight of the evidence provided there was nothing stopping him with his assertions to set a new precedent to impeach an ex-president on the grounds of gross misconduct. Mr McConnell also left open this moral dilemma with the possibility for civil and criminal charges against the former President saying, "He didn't get away with anything yet."

In his closing remarks the defending lawyer also stated that the impeachment trial was not a political theatre, a place for an emotional appeal, but an opportunity to professionally test the legal merits of arguments according to the existing constitution and rule of law. It was a carefully measured display of American party politics to patch their own embarrassment.

The evidence is strong to suggest that social media networks are disseminating disinformation, fake news, and obfuscation, to confuse users of these networks. In this modern era of technology, some people are obsessed with these methods of communication and take them seriously, adding a kind of new form of identity.

Disinformation can be a strong weapon, offensive in an information war, especially when deployed against political opponents at the time of a critical event such as the presidential transition of power. It is difficult to verify the authenticity of information and videos posted online.

Professional journalists and broadband network providers have a moral and ethical obligation to intercept any alleged wave of *fake news* and methodically investigate the transcripts of text and audio files on the subject. To avoid unpleasant situations, they then warn the public that such news should be regarded with scepticism.

Currently, there is no such control by any regulatory body in individual countries affected by global networks that are accessible by anyone, anywhere in the world. Countries can be vulnerable to disinformation known as misinformation by cyber-attacks spread deliberately to deceive, while fake news might create mass public hysteria or damage international relations on sensitive matters. Disinformation is a weapon that could be intentionally used on a targeted audience as there are no ethical standards on these type of communication channels and users should regard the subject with scepticism. Perhaps by hindsight, other independent media networks might be able to intervene. Cyber space should be treated with respect with rule based order as much as space is controlled.

Misinformation amongst political rivalry can cause severe damage and can almost tear apart the social fabric unless retracted by those who are responsible for such devious actions. Lessons need to be learnt from social media speculations, whereby people are provoked, leading to a loss of lives and that fundamentally threaten our democracy.

U.S. House Speaker Nancy Pelosi said that lawmakers will establish an outside, independent commission to review the "facts and causes" related to the deadly Jan. 6 attack on the U.S. Capitol by supporters of then-President Donald Trump (Reuters 15 February 2021).

The new administration has a hopeful tone, indicating the right direction for tackling difficulties of greater political, economic, and health issues with some key provisions in economic relief. If not acted upon sooner, this would end federal economies in high unemployment and cut back on aid to small businesses, leaving any recovery painfully prolonged.

Among other goals, the Covid-19 vaccine rollout and reopening of schools were the highest priories on the list, bringing ethical values to political decisions. Restoring ethics means protecting democracy and allowing for timely action on the most pressing issues of the people whom they represent. In this way, ethics is made to be of a more practical value through every step of the journey as envisaged by Aristotle.

The U.S. political media landscape has changed since Rush Limbaugh took over the Conservative talk radio show. Limbaugh wasn't the first to start this genre, radio hosts have talked politics before him, but Rush Limbaugh was more than just a radio host, he was the master-mind behind dividing the American nation and infusing racial hatred. He was a sensation among people who liked to tweak liberals, outraging with political incorrectness by attacking Barack Obama's presidency with harsh tones and racial comments.

Politics seemed second to entertainment in Limbaugh's early years without any underlying set of ethical principles. He set the rules and his comments became the topic of entertainment, reaching an estimated 15.5 million people each week. This dominated the media world attracting the largest audience to his political talks, he charged advertisers confiscatory advertising rates, working in concert with other routine cable news networks like Fox, CNN, and MSNBC.

Soon his purpose became evident; "He refused to accept the attacks that came against this country from within," Levin said on Fox News. "He refused to accept the ideological changes in this country. He defended the traditions of this country. And he spoke for tens of millions of us."

"It wasn't just that he transformed the media landscape, but he transformed the Republican Party," said Nicole Hemmer, author of *Messengers of the Right: Conservative Media and the Transformation of American Politics*. "He became a power player and someone who could move voters."

Limbaugh suggested in a media interview in December 2020 that he believed the country was "trending towards secession," the act in which states could attempt to leave the Union, these were the conditions that resulted in the American Civil War. Later, he made clear with carefully measured words that he wasn't advocating that. These sensitive comments were noted by Media Matters for America (MMfA) who act as a watchdog for securitizing politically right-leaning media outlets. To the end, however, he remained loyal to Trump, who awarded Limbaugh a Presidential Medal of Freedom at the State of the Union address in the year 2020. They all subscribed to this false confidence and the security of political rivalry but got neither liberty nor security. The legal justice system will hunt them until they find the truth.

Rush Limbaugh died on the 17 February 2021. He left a legacy. To his fans, Limbaugh's death of lung cancer at the age of 70 was an occasion for deep mourning. For his foes, it was good riddance. Somewhere, Rush could surely appreciate it.

"He was the most important individual media figure of the last four decades," said Ian Reifowitz, professor of historical studies at the State University of New York and author of "The Tribalization of Politics: How Rush Limbaugh's Race-Baiting Rhetoric on the Obama Presidency Paved the Way for Trump."

## Tribalization of Politics

The Tribalization of Politics explores how the conservative radio host "tribalized" U.S. politics through his racially divisive, falsehood-ridden portrayal of President Obama.

(Ian Reifowitz published by IG Publishing 1 June 2019).

By playing and preying on white anxiety, Limbaugh laid the groundwork for the election of a president who essentially adopted his views of the Obama presidency. Dr Reifowitz says that Limbaugh repeatedly used a technique called 'racial priming' against America's first black president - language designed to heighten racial or cultural resentment. Limbaugh's aim was to convince his audience that America is for white people and shift the voters back to conservatism.

The book describes how Limbaugh's divisive rhetoric against Obama was designed to cleave America into two, creating a conservative 'tribe' animated by a passionate racial and cultural hatred toward the opposing tribe.

Dr Reifowitz blames Limbaugh for setting a blueprint for white identity politics and the dividing of the nation into uneasy tribes. This racially motivated radio broadcasting process divided the nation, threatening the democratic principles upon which the US constitution was built. Limbaugh succeeded in his attempt to regain political power using racial tactics which has now internationally tarnished the image of America after the January 6th incident, when a crowd of Trump's supporters stormed the Capital.

The riot ended up doing damage, not only to the building itself but also to some of the monuments and artwork depicting the history of enslaved Black people. In the culture wars that spilt over during President Donald Trump's time in office, the most visible flashpoint was whether to preserve or destroy monuments depicting figures from America's racist history.

Reconciliation of racial differences is difficult unless all Senators of both sides are willing to recognise the contribution of those enslaved by early Americans and publicly recognise the reminiscence of their history. To restore the balance of power in the Senate needs a common goal, centrist political views, and common ground rather than grappling with party politics in a way that could cause irreversible damage to America.

Opportunists can change the narrative, put their own content towards a political movement and gain from someone else's suffering, without caring for the long-term effects on the next generation. Under these circumstances, criminal gangs could join political movements under disguised identity. This is contrary to the stream and ideas of the Age of Enlightenment; instead, they are going backward in time to tribal rivalry against each other, two sides competing for the same interest. There are better ways of winning voters in an election in the modern world, by progressive social-economic policies that are fair, timely, transparent, and aim to build unity and prosperity for all concerned in dignity and integrity by reshaping political ideology and subsequently governments.

The Conservative radio host Mark Levin called Limbaugh "a tremendous patriot." Once a universally accepted compliment, the term "patriot" has become more complicated through its use by some of the rioters at the U.S. Capitol on Jan. 6.

On 21st February 2021, the Scottish newspaper, The National, reported "Rush Limbaugh's death is a reminder that toxic views deserve no platform." Columnist, Stuart Cosgrove of The National wrote, "When will we see his like again? Hopefully, not very soon and preferably never again. Rush Limbaugh is dead, my eyes are bone dry, and the florist is closed due to Covid-19 lock-down."

The death of Limbaugh has drawn attention to the noisy cult of right-wing radio in America and marked the death of a pioneer and a thoroughly detestable personality. When it comes to modern media there is always a space for bigots, racists, and coded hate speech. Media platforms are powerful methods to reach out to people effectively, as such, even without listening you live in a world influenced by media.

Personality is created by the society you live in, not in the one in which you are born; it can become a strong influential political ideology that blinds followers to get entrapped in a vicious cycle for generations to come. This mystery has vexed us all hitherto; until light is shed to illuminate this dark political era, to help clarify by making intelligible the hidden messages, and cast off the toxins that pollute the minds and awaken us to decent political debate.

It would be interesting to see how any comeback of Conservatives materialise in the future of American politics. (Source: Independent 19 February 2021)

The Presidential power transition to the new administration took place on the 20th January 2021 in Washington DC and under heavy security; 25,000 heavily armed National Guards were deployed to protect the extended security zone of the US Congress Capitol Building where the presidential inauguration and oaths took place.

The incident demands much self-introspection and reflection, not only by American voters but all peace-loving people in the world who value democracy. It causes us to rethink ethics, moral values, the integrity of elections, and above all the integrity of political leaders to uphold the stability of a democratic social system.

The serious key questions to ask and contemplate are, "what is our protection?", "who can protect us?" and "how are we protected?"

A power-hungry dictator would use extremism and everything at his disposal to secure his power by getting rid of all his opponents and challenges. He has no moral values or conviction and deep inside he suffers from a superiority complex. He portrays himself in impeccably smart outfits, lives in pristine and extravagant luxury, surrounded by important people, seeking affirmation from the public, making people believe that he is the only one who can save the country, to provide stability and security whilst promoting chaos to intimidate his opponents. He would say "my people love me", viewing people as a flock of sheep to which he gives leadership. A person without ethics and moral values would use attorneys to represent him with caveat emptor attached, not to act as lawyers but as criminal co-conspirators.

An unindicted co-conspirator, or unindicted conspirator, is a person or entity that has an alleged indictment for having engaged in conspiracy but who is not charged by the same indictment. Prosecutors choose to name persons as unindicted co-conspirators for a variety of reasons including grants of immunity, pardon, pragmatic considerations, and evidentiary concerns.

Absolute power needs absolute legion. Such people think that they inherit the country as a kind of royalty, expanding their base and terrorising people causing displacement and refugees. These scenarios were evidently visible at the end of Cold War in Iraq, Libya, and Syria, it is the product of dictatorship that disregards ethics and morals and the loss of democracy.

At the time, millions of Americans struggle daily with the challenges of a pandemic, the aftermath of Trump's chaotic era, political uncertainty, a dire economic situation, and a sluggish recovery. The Incident at the U.S. Capitol building on the January 6th might be a wakeup call to rethink the underpinning political philosophy.

There was a lack of preparation from civic leaders in the state of national emergency, a downplay of the pandemic and mishandling of Covid-19 was related to a high number of deaths in the past year. For much of the past six years, former President Donald J. Trump has dominated the political conversation, prompting days of outrage, finger-pointing and general news cycle made havoc with nearly every tweet, the results of those messages were astonishingly damaging to the democratic ethos.

Social media platforms have a great responsibility to strengthen society rather than allowing one dominant figure to stir up, divide and rule a nation for their political advantage by delivering a constant stream of chaos that is very damaging for international image and relations. On the other hand, journalists and TV stations have a bigger role, to neutralise fake news and disinformation that are enmeshed in controversy themselves, magnifying and amplifying disinformation.

Most of these phenomena can be subsumed under two broad categories: Firstly, misuse of free speech and freedom of expression and secondly, lack of political insight to win voters and settle disputes of national importance. Fake news and media recognition are short lived, though it has already created a void in politics and media representation. The truth will emerge in due course and people will recognise it; nothing is hidden forever.

Some connected people or the privileged may in some ways feel protected from the widening chasm that divides society for the sake of short gain or media recognition. Independent journalism has a much more prominent role of responsibility to educate their audience, to unentangle the facts from political rhetoric, to promote norm abiding behaviour rather than reporting a deluge of biased, polarised, twisted news, and promoting unethical social trends.

The slowdown of the global economy due to the pandemic and the weakness of internal social structures have challenged the sustainability of the United States economic growth model.

Lessons learnt from the Capitol riots need critical analysis, to focus on its core values and a strategy that unites people with a common good of economic success. Emotional fallout and mental impacts take time to heal. There were substantial weaknesses in the premise and propositions on both sides of the arguments in the Impeachment Trial. It displayed their ideological divisions well.

Punishment is not necessarily curing the crime. Policies are most effective when they are built on ethical values and principles towards social reforms. Excessive political involvement in the health crisis has contributed to high mortality rates in the past year and an increased dependence on vaccinations inoculation campaign has been the main contributor to reassuring our return to any normality.

In the year 2022, the biggest challenge the US was facing, a sharp decline in economic activity and an increase in unemployment and poverty. The Covid-19 pandemic has further reinforced the urgent need for reforms, to reverse the declining growth capacity, and accelerate the scheme of vaccination rollouts to strengthen the health of working-population, challenges that the new administration have successfully met.

The nation's fiscal health is also an important matter, the Federal Reserve and Treasury officials assure to keep low interest rates and stable inflation rates for the foreseeable future to help improve the labour market that needs to see substantial progress towards full employment.

Inflation rates have been on the low side for decades, in line with other advanced economies, indicating a fall in global demand for goods and weak price gains due to high unemployment rates shifting consumer preferences.

It is hard to expect these low trends will change anytime soon, therefore the nation has to awaken to the truth, learn from its mistakes, adjust, give up narrow political interest to avoid gridlock for fast track economic and social progress. Additionally, there are a large number of undocumented immigrants awaiting legal entry to engage in active participation to contribute to the economy. These important social, economic, and political issues need a speedy response, ethical value systems, and a change of attitude towards fellow citizens.

In November 2022, U.S. midterm elections reflected how American voters have reacted to the Capitol riots. According to the Pew Research Centre, many Americans were filled with shock, horror, and anguish. Their responses to the Capitol riot were, in many cases, raw and emotional. "Saddened, hurt, disgusted," one woman in her 50s said. "Never thought I would see anything like this in my life."

When the results were expected, President Biden struck an optimistic tone at the White House. "It was a good day for democracy, and I think a good day for America," Biden said. (New York Times November 10, 2022). Many seats in United States elections always go to the same party. So control of the Senate and House of Representatives depends on a relatively small number of competitive seats, or "battlegrounds". This is an indication of fixed mindset of voters behaviour irrespective of how world outside see them. When the election results were released Democrats won the Senate and Republicans won the House or Congress. But the party in power normally loses in the midterms, and inflation and gas prices are high and Biden's not especially popular, and the red wave is still somewhere out at sea.

Identity has become very prominent in American culture in recent years and political identity is a hot theme. Since Americans don't have an identical ethnic, national, religious, or linguistic background, it's complicated to define the term American identity. What you look like; where you come from; how much you earn and how you talk, are the superficial indices that many use to peg you into one group or another. What is being lost is an appreciation of a deeper identity; one that manifests itself through a person's character.

The present American administration has bigger challenges ahead as the global economy continues to face steep challenges, shaped by the lingering effects of three powerful forces: the Russian invasion of Ukraine, a cost-of-living crisis caused by persistent and broadening inflation pressures, and the slowdown in China. According to the IMF most recent forecasts in October 2022, project global growth to remain unchanged in 2022 at 3.2 percent and to slow to 2.7 percent in 2023. More than a third of the global economy will contract this year or next, while the three largest economies, the United States, the European Union, and China will continue to stall. In short, the worst is yet to come, and for many people 2023 will feel like a recession.

Russia's invasion of Ukraine continues to powerfully destabilize the global economy. Beyond the escalating and senseless destruction of lives and livelihoods, it has led to a severe energy crisis in Europe that is sharply increasing costs of living and hampering economic activity. Gas prices in Europe have increased more than four-fold since 2021, with Russia cutting deliveries to less than 20 percent of their 2021 levels, raising the prospect of energy shortages over the next winter and beyond. More broadly, the conflict has also pushed up food prices on world markets, causing serious hardship for low-income households worldwide, and especially so in low-income countries. These are the real issues need to be addressed by the world leader meeting a two-day summit hosted by the Indonesian G20 summit November 2022 in Bali Indonesia. The summit was a testing ground for the US President Mr Biden's master diplomacy who met in good terms with his Chinese counterpart Mr Xi Jinping.

China has lot to offer to the world than heated geopolitical tensions, reducing uncertainty, once protected by a Great Wall China has increased integration with the world on many dimensions in terms of scale. For example, China has made huge strides in innovation in recent years. China is a global force in the world's digital economy and artificial intelligence (AI) technologies.

The G20, including Russia, has deplored the economic impact of the Ukraine conflict, according to a draft communique, with 'most' members also condemning the war. The Ukraine leader Volodymyr Zelensky has outlined a 'Ukrainian formula for peace' in an address to world leaders gathered in Bali for the draft discussion, a moment of hope that G20 leaders have come together to find resolution to the crisis applying diplomacy.

# CHAPTER 25

## MORAL NARCISSISM

Moral narcissism is a new concept used to describe a moral indignation to consequences of action or those caused by a policy or a policy's instruments. It is widely used in recent political rhetoric and narratives in US political critique. Writers have used the term when analysing both domestic and global US policies to show the momentous impact of the time period since the end of the Cold War.

Narcissism is defined as an excessive interest in or admiration of oneself or one's physical appearance. It has a psychological connotation, characterising a personality type that exhibits symptoms of selfishness, involving a sense of entitlement, a lack of empathy, and a need for admiration. The term is also used in psychoanalysis to describe self-centredness arising from failure to distinguish the self from external objects, either in very young babies or as a feature of mental disorder.

In 1979, the cultural historian Christopher Lasch published the epochal *The Culture of Narcissism: American Life in an Age of Diminishing Expectations* (W. W. Norton & Co 1979, New York), where he warned people about the normalisation of narcissism in American society.

In his award-winning book, the author explores the roots and the ramifications of the process of normalizing pathological narcissism in the 20th-century American culture by using psychological, cultural, artistic, and historical synthesis. Lasch analysed personality types since World War II, explaining that it was post-war America which produced new personalities consistent with clinical definitions of "pathological narcissism".

This pathology, he argues, is not akin to everyday narcissism, a hedonistic egoism described in the definition, but instead adopts a clinical diagnosis of narcissistic personality disorder.

For Lasch, "pathology represents a heightened version of normality." He locates symptoms of this personality disorder in the radical political movements of the 1960s, as well as in the cult movements of the 1970s. Narcissistic personality disorder (NPD) is described as a personality disorder characterized by a long-term pattern of exaggerated feelings of self-importance, an excessive craving for admiration, and struggles with empathy.

A person with these symptoms is akin to the dictators who caused much harm to the world; therefore, their influence could be damaging. The result of these intrusive ideas of personality was disruptive to the American traditional family values.

The book content was significant enough to warrant the highest political authority, Lasch notably visited Camp David to advise then President Jimmy Carter who was concerned about ideological changes that might have happened.

Thirty-five years later, the author Roger L Simon reintroduced the term *Moral Narcissism* in his book *I Know Best: How Moral Narcissism Is Destroying Our Republic, If It Hasn't Already*, (Published June 14th, 2016 by Encounter Books) in which Simon reveals the inside story of a widespread epidemic of schizophrenic social division causing mental fragmentation of present American political society.

In the Obama era, Simon writes that there was a parade of endless, often inexplicable, scandals.

*I Know Best* goes beyond Lasch to lay bare how this moral narcissism is behind all those scandals from Obamacare to various other chaotic incidents in the Middle East displacing civilians and more. Simon's critique is aimed at everything the Obama administration did only to make them feel good about them-selves, but the results be damned. Simon pointed out that ideological philosophies of both political parties have been infested with this toxic attitude that is dividing the nation, segregating by race, colour, or tribe, thus leading to culture wars.

In 2020 and 2021 increased right-wing activities indicated the destruction of the very foundation of democracy and dereliction of duty by failing to sustain the will of the people. In 2021, the National Intelligence Community assessed that domestic extremist violence (DEV) has posed an elevated threat to Homeland security.

Enduring DEV's motivations pertaining to biases against minority populations and perceived government overreach will almost certainly continue to drive DEV's radicalisation and mobilization to violence (MSNBC News March 2021).

According to Simon, it is a true epidemic that must be cured in order to save American democratic republic and their futures. America needs a serious moral discussion to address these ongoing issues. The topic has caught the attention of the academic community and the conversation has extended to overlapping ethical questions of moral narcissism and moral complicity in global health, bioethics, and humanitarian aid to war-torn countries.

Dr Mark Sheehan of Oxford Biomedical Research Centre (BRC), Ethics Fellow at the Ethox Centre and a Research Fellow at the Uehiro Centre for Practical Ethics in the Faculty of Philosophy, has submitted a research paper to discuss some of the best instances of bioethics.

These are scientific applications of ethical concept analysis of real-world cases; this is done in a way that prompts both reflections on the part of the practitioners involved in the real-world case and reflections by the bioethicist on the way in which the field of bioethics understands the concept in question.

As a fine example, referring to Buth *et al*'s paper on this issue, Dr Sheehan pointed out three important concepts that straddle the worlds of politics and ethics, to some extent these are undertheorized in applied settings. These three concepts - moral narcissism, moral complicity, and dirty hands are related, raising particular problems for the activities of researchers, aid workers, and others, as those from richer countries working in poorer or conflict-torn parts of the world.

Moral complicity has been shown by definition and by common usage to be the wrongdoing of another in which we have part. Buth *et al* set out a general account of these concepts and their relationship.

Their focus is substantially on complicity issues raised in particular complex regions.

According to these research, charitable organisations have been accused of wrongdoing in Myanmar, Libya, and on the border between Syria and Jordan. Charities have been accountable for driving back refugees to war zones. These regions are notably under coercive control due to political instability and civil wars. Charities or Non-Governmental Organisations (NGO) are accused of continuing to operate by providing medical interventions and other aid but not speaking out what they witness, that innocent people are being used as a coercive pawn providing aid. There are some important nuances embedded in the paper that are worth bringing out.

First, moral narcissism as they define it, comes about at the point at which "an appropriate concern for one's own moral integrity turns into moral self-indulgence" or a concern for the preservation of the agent's self-image, as Bernard Williams describes it.

Interestingly it's as though how I appear, how I seem, in performing an action comes to matter more than what I do and its rightness. I, the self-centred person, acting as the agent. The self-centred 'I' is the central axis of the concept of moral narcissism. It could be extended to a collective mindset such as a political party or group of people. One thing to notice here (as Buth *et al* do) is that there is a balance to be struck between being indulgent and being unreflective.

This is a slightly different way of understanding the idea of moral narcissism, as distinct from Williams' context, where he wants to contrast the consequentialist position with the integrity of the agent in acting - a contrast between the importance of what happens as a result of what the agent does and the importance of the nature of what the agent does.

Being reflective (in the sense that being overly reflective can be self-indulgent) is related to recognising and being aware of the place that an agent has in the context of action - being aware of how they are viewed, what is expected of them, what their values are in relation to those around them and how the proposed act or acts are expressive in the context. We can imagine at one extreme that an agent who is naive and unaware, blunders into a situation with the best of intentions but completely misses the context.

At the other extreme, and this is the moral narcissism, we can imagine an agent who is completely hamstrung by what others will think and how they will be judged seemingly if they do anything at all. At this extreme, the agent is too concerned with the politics of the situation and their role in it if they act: to be an agent here would be to become embroiled in the politics. Evidence shows in some sensitive regions political and corporate scandals of fraud, bribery, and breach of trust. It is a common allegation of businessmen working for political parties for favour. It is a novelty in deregulated, market independent newspapers that offer positive coverage called media bribery, basically getting flattering coverage on a news site in return for favourable regulations worth substantial monetary value.

Political influence and policies taken by those corrupt leaders directly affect the world of vulnerable populations in many ways by the directions they take and ultimately changing the international order in distressing ways. For example, in March 2021 there is a large number of internally displaced people in the Ethiopian city of Mekelle. Four months after Ethiopia's prime minister, Abiy Ahmed, began a sweeping military operation, the restive region of Tigray is being wracked by bitter civil conflict. Accounts of egregious rights violations - massacres, sexual violence, ethnic cleansing, and fears that starvation is being used as a war tactic - have set off alarms across the world but without any outside help.

In Mekelle, the region's biggest city, hospitals are filled with casualties from the fighting that rages in the countryside, many of them terrified civilians arriving with grievous wounds. Schools houses were full of some of the 71,000 people who have fled to the city, often bringing accounts of horrific abuses at the hands of pro-government forces. (Source: New York Times 19 Mar2021)

These extremes map neatly onto certain kinds of objectivism, ethics at one end, contrasted with a kind of relativism that is often tempting in the face of value and contextual difference at the other. The self-image focus of the moral narcissist is sometimes the product of the idea that there is nothing else for me to be concerned with but what I value.

At the other end of the spectrum, the kind of blind objectivist has things right and immediately sees the demand to act on the unambiguous demands of the context. The following example vividly illustrates moral complicity in a legal context when testing moral accountability.

In his 1968 article on collective responsibility Joel Feinberg presents the following example: Suppose C and D plan a bank robbery, present their plan to a respected friend A, receive his encouragement, borrow weapons from B for their purpose, hire E as a getaway driver, and then execute the plan. Pursued by the police, they are forced to leave their escape route and take refuge at the farm of E's kindly uncle F. F congratulates them, entertains them hospitably, and sends them on their way with his blessing.

F's neighbour G learns of all this, disapproves, but does nothing. Another neighbour, H, learns of it but is bribed into silence. Clearly, participants C and D are the perpetrators of the crime, and they can be regarded as the principal actors in this scenario. But six other individuals are involved as well in a variety of ways. What can be said about their status as participants in crime?

Those who are involved as contributors in a sequence of events like the one described but not as principal actors are commonly referred to as accomplices. As such, they can be said to be complicit in the events or complicit in the outcome to which these events lead. One of the central themes of this book is that complicity carries its own ethical consequences. A person who is complicit in what another does is morally accountable. This concept is not much different to hypocrisy where the practice of claiming to have higher standards or more noble beliefs than is the case. A person who puts on a false appearance of virtue or religion and then acts in contradiction to his or her stated beliefs or feelings.

Moral narcissism has its roots in Max Weber's social theory. Maximilian Karl Emil Weber was a German sociologist, historian, jurist, and political economist, who is regarded as being among the most important theorists on the development of modern Western society and whose ideas would profoundly influence social theory and social research. Arguably Weber is the most influential sociologist and architect of social modernisation in the 20th century.

Weber's wide-ranging contributions gave critical impetus to the birth of new academic disciplines such as sociology as well as significant reorientations in law, economics, political science, and religious studies. In his famous lecture on *Politics as a Vocation*, Max Weber coined and elaborated the antithesis between the ethics of conviction and the ethics of responsibility, which has had a far-reaching impact on the ethical discussions, particularly in German-speaking countries. His main point is that the politician needs to balance an *Ethic of Moral Conviction* with an Ethic of Responsibility.

The *Ethic of Moral Conviction* refers to the core unshakeable belief that a politician must hold, Weber finds this to be a common characteristic among politicians. On the other hand, responsibility is an ethical concept traditionally recognised by many developed cultures including Buddhist and Judeo-Christian societies that refers to the fact that individuals and groups have morally based obligations and duties to others and to larger ethical and moral codes, standards, and traditions.

Max Weber's distinction between the ethic of conviction and the ethic of responsibility is best understood as a contrast between mutually exclusive ethical worldviews. Interpretations that correlate the two ethics with Weber's distinction between value-rational social action and instrumental-rational social action are misleading. Weber assumes that both types of rational social action are present in both ethics.

The ethic of conviction recognizes a given hierarchy of values as the context for moral endeavour. The ethic of responsibility, on the other hand, acknowledges value obligations but assumes the absence of any given hierarchy of values and the inevitability of value conflict as the context for moral endeavour.

When interpreted in the context of his multi-layered understanding of value conflict, Weber's ethic of responsibility emerges as a coherent ethical perspective. For example, foreign policy of many western countries projects their own past experience and recollections of World War II and the history of Colonisation, this avoids the responsibility of consequence and direct effect of that policy, nor does it have a clear policy to end an ongoing conflict. This attitude was projected in foreign policy debates, for example about Kosovo, Iraq, and the ongoing conflict between Israel and Palestine. None of those policies addressed the human suffering involved as victims of war.

Moral Narcissism in its application is a concept that divides the conscience between intentions and results. For it to no longer matter how anything turns out, as long as your intentions were good, that you were "moral." And, just as importantly, the only determinant of those intentions, the only one who defines that morality, is you.

This trend of attitude to morality spreading through cultural values is the new method for feeling good about yourself. These new ideas are manifest in collective human intellect, customs, social behaviour, and achievements in art, popular cinema, academy, and media which have a great influence on people on a daily basis. They are ever willing to ratify those good intentions and ignore the results. For example, violence is projected in movies as heroic for its excitement and entertainment value, but it ignores the social impact of promoting violence as normal.

When contained in domestic and public policy, including only the moral conviction not responsibility, the effect of this one-sided element of moral justification would be damaging to the social cohesion dividing the society, holding diametrically opposite interpretations of values and can lead to militia groups within. In a political arena, this could cause fragmentation and damage the union, defeating its common object of unity while shifting views to both far left and right especially in an economic declining period.

In a racially motivated social ideology, it can divide people into regrouping themselves under different ethnic and nationalistic identities. A new policy cannot be applied in retrospect to correct such damage, but it might help to identify a range of underlining contradictory policies which led to such a division. An evaluation of ethics and metaethics can provide a new and different foundation for social justice to overcome the trade-off of the antithesis between the ethics of conviction and the ethics of responsibility.

New policy based on such profound foundations can significantly improve social cohesion, reduce the tensions between internal attitudes and external action results. In the Western model of ethic of responsibility there are no guiding principles of intention to test what is right and wrong.

According to Buddhist psychology, intention is the factor that forms "karma" and moral precepts are the guidelines for good intention that would produce good results. Insight of this law of action in practice is the guiding and contributing principle for the path of peace and happiness. The ethic of responsibility is the best answer to the meaning and meaningfulness of life.

Most of us are trapped in modern urban cities and are brought to believe that media postings and news coverage as the gospel truth. Technology by design is very smart, giving the user a false security and a novel identity. We work hard and daily to meet our ends, taking the economy and political trend as a given, unable to question its validity.

We have placed our trust in independence and freedom of journalism as replacement for questioning political decisions.

Most voters are unaware of the underpinning political doctrines and hidden agendas of party politics. Belonging to a political party and its uprising gives a sense of identity, belongingness, and euphoria.

We are liable to get caught up in overwhelming trends of false promises that cannot be delivered or under delivered by those who profess it but are unable to recognise the culpability of them too, instead to feel carefree and safe in the company of perceived powerful leadership.

Certain political activities, rallies, critiques of opponents and promise of rewards can induce a state of euphoria.

There are few selected speakers who have the psychological abilities to draw attention and polarise their audience with moral narcissism of the radical left. This segregation within a society may emerge from income inequality, economic displacement, insecurities, and result in such differentiation as would consist of various social groups believing themselves to have power. This tendency to think about morality in terms of how your actions make you feel about yourself rather than in terms of their consequences for others is frequently reflected in policy instruments, thinking that all which matters is being right, regardless of the effect.

For example, in the epic story of Robinhood, to rob the rich to give to the poor, entailing the principle that the "end justifies the means." Associated gun culture is a dangerous combination, it gives a further false confidence in security.

What transpired on January 6th, 2021, suggests that people had convened secretly for a specific purpose, organising the targeting of the then Vice President Mr Michael Pence who was believed to have special legal powers overpower transition. The chants of 'Hanging Mike Pence' were heard and gallows were erected outside as Trump's supporters laid siege to the Capitol building in Washington DC on January 6 following a rally held by the then president outside the White House. The situation was brought under control by wise thinking and quick action of internal security personnel. Mr Pence had to be evacuated through the tunnels in the building to escape.

Political assassinations are the result of strongly disagreements and a perceived threat of ideological differences, when in situations of extreme nationalism even nonviolent movements are seen as risky and bring danger to its members. For example, in India, Gandhi's dynasty ended through a series of political assassinations. It is an ever-important goal to have peace and stability in your own country with political wisdom to heal a divided nation.

Although the appearance and character of incidents appear to be different in time, historical analysis shows that the concepts and political motives are the same. It requires a deeper understanding of human behaviour, political psychology, and insight into political science, to help in gaining the necessary lessons that must be learnt from history.

When looking for pragmatic solutions, Lenin characterized the NEP in 1922 as an economic system that would include "a free market and capitalism, both subject to state control," while socialized state enterprises would operate on "a profit basis." Other policies included monetary reform (1922–1924) and the attraction of foreign capital. The NEP represented a more market-oriented economic policy deemed necessary to reverse the dire economic condition that was left after the Russian Civil War. Many extremists opposed to fostering this capitalist model though they themselves had no other alternative. This approach was proved to be a success.

Lenin adjusted the economic and social impact of his decision very wisely, quickly and accepted the responsibility of his policy with political wisdom. There was no evidence whatsoever that Lenin sought fame and popularity though it was bloody revolution he intended a social change for a better society.

Economics and psychology are closely related but their interdependency was not recognised by the Western Enlightenment movement until recent evidence showed that economies can greatly benefit from modernisation, specialisation, and exchange.

Developed economic concepts and taking multiple-step strategies are able to shift the old paradigm of extremist ideas, unite people and bring nations together. More than any previous generation in history, we have come to see the individual as the sole source of meaning. The gossamer filaments of connection between us and others, which once held together families, communities, and societies, have become attenuated. We have become lonely selves in search of purely personal fulfilment.

Today's generation has become more dependent on technology and media platforms to stay connected. This perception of belongingness must surely be an illusion not knowing what toxic views filter through those everyday media platforms. A life lived grappled to mobile devices is one of only partial satisfaction that tempts towards craving more and more information.

Time spent pursuing the satisfaction of desire is less than satisfying and never actually provides all we desire. It is a law of economics that states our induced consumption is directly proportional to a marginal propensity to consume to satisfy. When our disposable income diminishes, we crave for other things to satisfy ourselves by engaging in useless conversations and ideas that come free as a package. The things we spend most of our time pursuing turn out to be curiously irrelevant when it comes to seeing the value of a life as a whole.

So, it is worth reminding ourselves that there is such a thing as ethics, and it belongs to the life we live together and the goods we share - the goods that only exist in virtue of being shared.

People who own the most are only as happy as those who have the least, and half as happy as those who are content with what they have. The desire to give is stronger than the desire to have. This alone is enough to defeat cynicism and fatalism about the human condition.

# CHAPTER 26

# EASTERN RELIGIOUS PHILOSOPHY VEDANTA

### Philosophy of Vedanta

SIMILAR TO THE WAY GREEK philosophy spread from the Mediterranean to the West, a different set of philosophical traditions emerged within the Eastern Asian regions of India and China. Hinduism is one of the oldest religious traditions, it covers a diversity of views of the people of India dating as far back as 3,500 BCE.

Their sacred text is a large work called the Vedas, which literally means "bodies of knowledge," handed down by generations up until today. It is written in the ancient Indian language of Sanskrit. It describes features of various gods, emphasizing the pantheistic notion of the divine reality that permeates the cosmos.

Before the arrival of Buddhism, Islam, and Christianity, Hindu concepts influenced the philosophical thought of Asia, and many share a specific conception of God and the cosmos. Philosophers and theologians of all traditions try to understand how God, or some ultimate reality, relates to the world, and there are two general approaches to this: transcendence and immanence.

The *transcendence approach* maintains that God is entirely separate or distinct from the finite world in which we live. There are rituals, hymns, worship, and transcendental meditation practices to appease them, and to be in union with them. By contrast, *the immanence approach* views that God is not external to the cosmos, but dwells within it or is immanent to it.

The Hindu religious, philosophical, and theological interpretation is that one should look inwards upon oneself to a secluded divine realm beyond the cosmos, in this way it is possible to communicate and form a union with God by adopting a strict religious discipline such as yoga and meditation that prescribes ethical living.

Mystical experiences associated with these religious practices are further interpreted by coupling it with a permanent self that transmigrates from life to life perpetually and by taking a turn towards purification one can ultimately reunite with God. This view is often called pantheism, a term literally meaning all-God. On this view, God dwells within everyone since we all are part of the cosmos. On the other hand, one who rebels against God is cast from heaven to hell.

In classical mythology, this is often personified as the Devil or tempter, whose purpose is to destroy achieving this divinity or final liberation. Pantheism is the belief that reality is identical with divinity, or that all things compose an all-encompassing, immanent God.

Pantheism was popularized in Western culture as a theology and philosophy based on the work of the 17th-century philosopher Baruch Spinoza, particularly in his book *Ethics*. Pantheist belief does not recognize a distinct personal god, anthropomorphic or otherwise, but instead characterizes a broad range of doctrines differing in forms of relationships between reality and divinity. Spinoza developed highly controversial ideas regarding the authenticity of the Hebrew Bible and the nature of the Divine and was effectively excommunicated from Jewish society at age 23.

Pantheistic concepts date back thousands of years and pantheistic elements have been identified in various religious traditions including Hinduism. Furthermore, the term *pantheism* was coined by mathematician Joseph Raphson in 1697 and has since been used to describe the beliefs of a variety of people and organizations.

Influenced by Spinoza, the freedom gained from theological restriction helped philosophers and scientists to understand nature better while developing an ethical approach to further scientific knowledge due to nature's arrangement as a discrete ethical order.

Deviation of this order has been identified colloquially as bad Karma in Hindu religion, a law of cause and effect that would eventually take one to a bad destination, thus realms of hells and heaven were explained as destiny. Cosmology was developed on the basis of heavenly and hell realms of existence.

The Buddhist understanding of the "middle path" is the cross junction of both East and West, meeting to reflect on our own limitations in understanding the entire cosmos, it would be more beneficial to take ethics further to find true happiness and liberation. The Buddha did not reject or accepted existing culture and related concepts of cosmology but simply used those ideas as a vehicle to convey his teachings. Lately in the history, Buddhism mingled with Hindu ideas and mythological concepts and rituals were added to explain some teachings. For example, the Hindu concept of *Mara* is widely used to explain adversaries.

Buddhist philosophy has had a powerful influence on social governance in the countries which have adopted it. Buddhism views that our ultimate protection is dependent on our value system. According to Buddhism, moral shame and moral dread are the two guardians of the world. When these two psychological factors diminish from man's mind there lies before him the entire destruction of mankind.

The first cause, continual world cycles and final destruction of the world are the themes of the Vedic teaching to which the Buddha did not pay much attention. The concept of creator, protector and destroyer is symbolised in the Hindu religion. Hinduism is an Indian religion rooted in Vedic philosophy which developed long before the arrival of Buddhism, it is one of the most ancient religions in the world. Originally called "Sanatana Dharma" by Hindus, Hinduism is characterized by beliefs in "samsara" (reincarnation), cycles of "karma" (all actions have consequences),

"moksha" (freedom from the cycle of reincarnation), aspects including the "yogas" and "vedas" from literary works such as the Upanishads, Bhagavat Geeta, Vedas. It embraces the concept of multiplicity, or the ideology that there are multiple gods that represent one divine being. The teachings are fascinating, described through colourful stories of many gods and demigods who were the foundation of Hinduism when Aryans brought their beliefs and practices to India around 1500 BC.

There are some Hindus that don't necessarily believe in the concept of multiplicity, instead they simply pick one God to worship. However, many

Hindus believe in the Trinity: Brahma (the creator), the iconic symbol of Swastika that represents duality of power of Brahma and Good Luck on the other hand. Vishnu (the preserver) and Shiva (the destroyer).

Vishnu, in particular, was seen as a prominent figure in Hinduism for many generations because of his unique nature and reincarnations, and thus continues to be worshipped today. Vishnu symbolizes the preserver, the protector, the guardian, and the sustainer of the world, as created by Brahma and Vedic law. Compared to other deities he was believed to have a very collected and benevolent nature.

Vishnu is colourfully portrayed with many features, carrying many instruments that could be used as powerful military weapons, he was also accompanied by his consort Lakshmi, the goddess of good fortune and prosperity.

Lakshmi's presence "balances his male intellect and spiritual sophistication with female physicality and passion" (Cummins et al. 79), this balance is essential to Vishnu and his performance as the protector of the universe. Vishnu's vehicle is a loyal eagle named Garuda on which Vishnu travels in grace. These unique characteristics of Vishnu are essential to his duty as the preserver and protector of the created world, helping him with "full control of time and space and subjective realities".

Throughout Vishnu's continuing existence, he reincarnated himself in order to carry out his duty of preserving and protecting the world as well as the law of the Vedas. There are ten episodes corresponding to ten reincarnations of Vishnu in which his role is to protect the world from evil.

The moral as taught by these roles were to "outgrow the beast to discover the divine", once again symbolizing Vishnu's duty of preserving righteousness and faith in the supreme power. Hindus believe he has already reincarnated himself nine times and his tenth reincarnation is yet to come.

Before his next appearance there comes the dark age of the Kali Yuga, the last phase of the cycle of existence. Hindus have held the belief that this is the age when everything would gradually disappear and then the world would end in total destruction. Vishnu's eighth incarnation is one of Hinduism's most famous and prominent heroes, known as Krishna.

The classical story of Bhagavad Gita is part of the Prasthanatrayi, which also includes the Upanishads and Brahma sutras. These are the three starting points for the Vedanta school of Hindu philosophy. The story depicts the moral dilemma of war or peace.

The Bhagavad Gita is a conversation between Prince Arjuna and Krishna, a mortal incarnation of the god Vishnu. Arjuna is worried about an upcoming battle for succession since he will be fighting against his kinsmen or brothers and hesitant. In explaining why Arjuna should fight, Krishna goes over a wide variety of spiritual and religious topics relating to dharma, karma, spirituality, and the cycle of reincarnation.

The Gita is one of the most famous pieces of Hindu literature, a dramatic psychological warfare, and the lessons it teaches are central to that faith. As a cultural touchstone and a spiritual guide, it's one of the most important ancient texts in the world. The translation and commentary by Eknath Easwaran help even those who aren't learned in Hindu mythology to understand its teachings. (Shortform webpage)

The concept of psychological warfare is depicted in the epic stories of Mahabharata, a Sanskrit poem of India dealing mainly with the struggle between two rival families on the brink of destruction and the reverse psychology of neutralising the tension of war. Krishna is well-known for his role in this famous epic, specifically the conversation between Krishna and Arjuna in the *Bhagavad Gita* where he emphasizes the importance of "dharma", duty, action, and bhakti (devotion).

Vishnu is believed to have taken the form of Krishna in his role of advisor to the commander of the battlefield, where to preserve righteousness and faith in the supreme power, Arjuna would have to kill his uncle Kamsa who was filled with excessive pride and power. Through his major role and teachings in the Mahabharata and the Bhagavad Gita, as the narrator Devdutt Pattanaik indicates, Krishna's purpose was to teach the lesson, "Know the thought before the action" (157).

Classical Vedic philosophy paints an eloquent picture of the universe and forms the basis of both Hindu and Buddhist cosmology, a vast and complex phenomenon that is difficult to comprehend and decipher. It delivers stories from which we have to work out the moral values, what is right and wrong, yet the moral dilemma remains of whether to kill or not to kill.

In the *Bhagavad Gita*, Arjuna was asked to choose between killing his own brothers or losing the battle. It shows us that ordinary folks cannot decide for themselves, such divine knowledge is not easily available to them; a powerful dramatical psychological drama of war in the mind.

Looking through the lens of Buddhism, the Buddha has successfully resolved moral dilemmas, discovered the truth, explained the consciousness and mental construction of psychological warfare. He identified the symptoms, the causes of the degeneration of morality and wisdom that inevitably lead to our own destruction. He neither accepted nor denied the validity of a central creator or first cause but showed that by a sequence of cause and effect the mind gets defiled or purified by one's own action. According to Buddhism, the first cause is irrelevant for our salvation.

The misuse of power has severe consequences. The determining psychological factor of morality is wisdom, where two paths are open equally to everyone. Choosing the right path to peace and happiness and prosperity is a wise choice marked by "right view". Choosing the wrong path to self-destruction is a factor of ignorance marked by greed, hatred, and delusion.

One thought on Vishnu: The Saviour, the Preserver, and the Protector. (Dr David B Gowler)

When we look to the past, we find that history is filled with many graphic events that have changed the course of our lives. The memories of World War I and World War II are two major events that changed the world but also have brought us together to rebuild the shattered remains and heal the old wounds. Details on a tableau of war are an objective depiction of these events, whilst human sentiments of those destroyed by war's ravages are indeed the only evocative portrayal of the conditions of the human soul, we have to understand what it was like to live in such conditions.

There is a few poignant recounting of the actual experiences of soldiers and innocent civilians when caught up in the battlefields, tortured or having died in concentration camps. It invites thoughtful and cultured people to become involved with reasoning, to understand what went wrong and learn lessons from past mistakes.

The method of the theory which can define easily all things happening around us is the best we have to discover our own mistakes. Ethical enquiry is one such method that helps us to resolve dilemmas and come to terms and accept the given reality.

In 1938, a British war hero of the First World War, Henry Tandey, received a phone call from Prime Minister Neville Chamberlain. The Prime Minister had just returned from Germany after a fruitless meeting with Hitler to persuade him not to start another war. In Germany, Chamberlain was invited to Bavaria, Hitler's hilltop retreat, where he was shown a reproduction of the famous painting "The Menin Crossroads."

The painting depicted a soldier carrying his wounded comrade on his back at the Battle of Ypres in 1914. The man carrying the wounded soldier was Henry Tandey. During the phone conversation, Chamberlain told Tandey that Hitler has recognized him as the man who had spared his life on a battlefield twenty years ago. According to Hitler, on September 28, 1918, Private Henry Tandey was serving near a French village where he encountered a wounded German soldier. But instead of shooting him, Tandey let him go. The then 29-year-old soldier was Adolf Hitler.

English soldier Henry Tandey came face to face with young Adolf Hitler on a French battlefield during World War I but decided to spare the wounded soldier's life. Had Tandey shot Hitler that day, the world would have been saved from one of the most reviled dictators and mass murderer of all time. Was this a grave mistake, the noble character of Henry Tandey or was this our fate?

From retrospect and with the advantage of hindsight we may say that should Tandey have shot the wounded soldier, the world would have been saved from the horror of World War II. We cannot explain every event in the world with reasoning alone, there are other forces we do not know nor understand.

The natural law of action, Karma, is one of those mystical principles in ancient religions shared by both Hindus and Buddhists with different interpretations. How could this be possible two men think diametrically opposite ways of humanity. The philosophy of ethics and truth shared by all Buddhist schools, teaches us that all human beings have the same needs for safety, freedom, and wellbeing.

There are some people among us grossly deluded, who have no insight, blindly following political leaders and their ideology.

Buddhism offers a new perspective of how to cut through the net of delusion, to look at your opponents with a practical way of offering kindness to those who disagree with you whether politically, domestically, or globally.

To truly love and be kind to someone you do not even have to know them. The Buddhist loving-kindness is universal and allows you to explore deeper into who you are, rather than identify yourself with any kind of political-economic or social theory. Political ideologies formed based on such theories are not permanent, unless adopt and change with real needs and concerns of people they would not produce satisfactory results for the benefit of many. The Pali term *metta* is described in Buddhist psychology as absence of hatred, that you do not wish any harm to anyone anywhere, whether born or awaiting to be born seen or unseen. The expansion of your mind into broader dimensions is to show that there is an ever-present possibility for us to experience liberation from hatred, rivalry, and ignorance. By training our minds we can develop wisdom and understand the truth of suffering.

Buddhism provides a systematic and comprehensive training scheme, the way towards the end of suffering, this is the Path of peace and happiness, the noble eight-fold path. The universal ethical and moral principles are well articulated in this path of liberation.

CHAPTER 27

# GRASS ROOTS ETHICS

THIS CHAPTER ACKNOWLEDGES MULTIPLE FORMS of practical ethics and recognizes the role of parents, teachers, and leadership. These roles set examples at a grassroots level, affecting behavioural change, and achieving positive outcomes for personal development, social harmony, and economic prosperity.

The use of the term "grass roots" as a metaphor is to illustrate the basic ethical values, the very foundation, and principles one can learn at a young age. This approach is to cultivate the acceptance of responsibility, of decision making, of right and wrong. It is associated with a bottom-up hierarchy, rather than a top-down, a traditional power structure imposing lawful rules concerning behaviour, this is considered more natural and effective. When children are brought up in an ethical cultural background, they are encouraged to contribute towards the welfare of their community, accepting their responsibility in shaping a progressive society by assuming the code of conduct for their actions.

When children are brought up in an ethical environment, they naturally tend to be legally abiding citizens as they grow up, adopting responsible roles in society and becoming valid contributors to its progress, welfare, and advancement on a personal and national level. Grassroot ethics can encourage strong character traits which develop as they become adults, qualities suitable to future representatives and good leaders, conducting themselves in a manner befitting and appropriate to the organisation and chosen profession.

A sense of personal responsibility gifts one with the ability to grow by themselves whilst adhering to the highest levels of professional conduct. The fundamentals of such traits are honesty, bravery, work ethics, dutiful, reliability, compliant, and vetting procedures to ensure efficiency. These are a general set of principle behaviours and attitudes that form 'Good Conduct' in the workplace or as a leader exhibiting moral virtues.

There are always extra requirements for any role, in terms of good practice, safeguarding, and professional conduct that should be adhered to in relation to the nature and environment of the different professions. For example, an army officer in the armed forces is primarily a leader, he or she must command and manage a team of fighting specialists, developing their skills to a high level of competence and readiness, responsible for the welfare, morale, and motivation of a platoon in support of national security and defence.

They set the bar very high to establish an expected, required, or the desired standard of quality.

Some children demonstrate leadership qualities and can accept extra responsibilities at a young age, such as in the participation of sports, in extra curriculum activities or become school leaders capable of shaping the future generation of societies.

Teachers have a greater responsibility than most in guiding our children. Above all, they must demonstrate integrity and ethical behaviour in the classroom, and in their conduct with parents and staff. Teachers must model strong character traits, such as perseverance, honesty, respect, lawfulness, patience, fairness, responsibility, and unity.

Usually, it is the headteacher's responsibility to set the standards of the school which could have a unique philosophy as established by the founders. For example, Waldorf education, also known as Steiner education, is based on the educational philosophy of Rudolf Steiner, the founder of Anthroposophy. Its pedagogy strives to develop pupils' intellectual, artistic, and practical skills in an integrated ethical culture and holistic manner.

The cultivation of pupils' imagination and creativity is a central focus. The first Waldorf school opened in 1919 in Stuttgart, Germany. A century later, it has become the largest school movement in the world.

Nowadays, Educational Psychology is still an underinvested area of education. It is the application of psychological theory, research, and techniques to support children, young people, their families, and schools to promote the emotional and social wellbeing of young people. Its core approach is to give an insight into guiding principles, learning methods, social and behavioural issues that impede children's learning.

Educational psychologists study children of all ages aiming to understand how they learn. Results of these analytical studies are used to improve specialized training, provide advice, and interventions based on educational psychology and the orientation services at schools across its different stages (preschool, primary and secondary).

The application of educational psychology at schools can successfully address the guidance and advisement needs for student development from an approach of inclusivity. It concerns issues related to improving a schools' educational quality, training and innovation of faculties, tutoring, attention to diversity, learning difficulties, and vocational and professional guidance. It also allows for educational psychology advisement and intervention in other spheres such as adult educational settings that may need more awareness of social harmony by integrating ethical values into its curriculum and training. Investing in educational psychology can benefit both teachers and students with improved quality learning methods and successfully fill attainment gaps.

Organisations use a variety of strategies in selecting future leaders to take their businesses forward, including testing candidates' character traits. At an ethical level, everything we do at grassroots should be guided by a wish to live up to a developed ethical standard of our society. In particular, it is important to us that leadership and other roles can never be barred from someone because of their gender, race, health, or social status.

The issues that dictate whether someone can have these roles should be about their character, morals, experience, maturity, and gifts. Those who are strong in their character attributes have a purpose in life. Although they may rejoice with achievement, for having done something useful, they will always remember that the purpose of the service they render is not to feel good or to enhance their reputation.

Their duty is primarily for the greater purpose of serving their country and serving others for the glory of the values they uphold.

# Grassroots ethics 2

The challenge of strengthening social justice and the values of our modern atheistic society today is largely in the hands of politicians. An elevation of self-interest over the common good along with the loss of a strong, shared moral code has made people blindly follow leaders. The truth is that when a crowd runs out of control, there is no easy answer as to who is responsible to restore order.

If the political leadership misguides their followers, as was evident in the 2020/21 US election, and if there is no clause in the legal constitution stipulating how to deal with it, then it is quite an unfortunate situation. It is unfounded to believe that social order would adjust itself like any other commercial market mechanism, individuals must play their part in rebuilding a common moral foundation. Without such foundational values, a society is sure to be bound in anarchy, downward strides which are visible in many broken societies.

In moral crises, wise responses come from religious institutions and religious leaders, as evident today as it was in the past. There is a spectrum of competing views concerning how religion and ethics are related. In the past, religious discipline was the absolute bed-rock of ethics in Judeo Christian and Islamic societies.

Since the world has moved on in time, the influence of Aristotle's version of virtues to organisational reform and other political critiques, many religions have integrated his valuable ideas to reshape religious orthodox cultures within their own circles. Aristotle was one of the greatest intellectual figures in Western history. He was the author of philosophical and scientific systems that became the framework and vehicle for both Christian scholasticism and medieval Islamic philosophy.

Even after the intellectual revolutions of the Renaissance period, the Reformation, and the Age of Enlightenment, Aristotle's concepts of virtues, his vast range of intellectual contribution to science, arts, and development of philosophy remain embedded in Western thinking and continue to be studied by present scholars.

Aristotle's ideas have a profound influence on people's everyday life without even knowing it. There is evidence to suggest that his ideas have been spread as far as Asia Minor and beyond after his departure from the

Academy. While religious leaders hold on to the texts and their revelation, scholars argue that insight about life and its true meaning comes from the tenets of reason.

In the 17th century, Spinoza took this argument of reason further and added that insight wisdom is higher than the knowledge gained from reason alone; as a consequence, men should strive to reach happiness by controlling temptation and this idea is compatible with the Buddhist's direct knowledge, which comes from a moral life and introspective meditation. From this perspective, ethical principles direct societies towards a final goal of peace and happiness, irrespective of how and who advocated the moral virtues.

In a complex political world, equitability just seems an illusion to appear and disappear at different intervals of time. Thus, it would be much wiser for independent and responsible individuals to find their own path for liberation by living according to valuable moral guidelines and upholding ethical principles both for their own protection of happiness and for securing the welfare of others. (Ref: Anthony J.P. Kenny)

Sir Anthony Kenny has been Pro-Vice-Chancellor of the University of Oxford, Master of Balliol College, Oxford, Chairman of the Board of the British Library, and President of the British Academy.

Happiness is the ability to say: I lived for certain values and acted on them. I was part of a family, embracing it and being embraced by it. I was part of a community, honouring its traditions, sharing its griefs and joys, ready to help others, knowing that they were ready to help me. I did not only ask what I could take; I asked what I could contribute.

To know that you made a difference, that in this all-too-brief a span of years you lifted someone's spirits, relieved someone's poverty, pain or loneliness, or brought to the world a moment of grace or justice that would not have happened had it not been for you - these are as close as we get to the meaningfulness of life, and they are matters of everyday rather than heroic virtue movie characters that depict unrealistic heroism.

## Parenting

Children need to be taught right from wrong from a very young age. They should be guided by systematic instructions to follow appropriate codes of conduct. Many religious institutions have a standard code of conduct to help families and children to develop in conformity with religious teachings and to establish acceptable social habits. Parents and teachers are responsible for fostering good conduct in their children until the child can develop and maintain self-discipline.

A child's mind is like a seed that grows with age.

The socio-economic framework is like the field in which the seed grows. Social values, religious beliefs, customs, and the education system all transmit their culture, these are the conditions under which the child learns to act and to respond through various stages of his or her life. As one gets older, changes occur to one's physiology, anatomy, and psychology and different experiences of feelings and perception make a child begin to respond to the social environment according to his or her understanding and temperament. These conditions are many and vary in accordance with their context in time and are also influenced by economic and social trends.

In the modern world social trends are mainly political and in cosmopolitan cities they can be complex. For example, in a big city like London, many children are encouraged to appreciate more than one religion to promote religious tolerance. In Christianity, Jesus taught his disciples to "turn your left cheek to one who slaps your right". Buddha taught to give love and kindness to all, including your enemy.

Western society is now aware of the need for proper parenting and many child psychologists have contributed to new ideas in this field, such as "positive parenting", where good behaviour is encouraged and rewarded.

Over recent years, theories of childrearing and parenting have looked at various applications of reward and punishment. An important philosophical contribution to this area has been the ideas of John Locke, an English physician and philosopher, who argued that parents could reward good behaviour with their parental esteem.

Every society has young people experiencing and engaging in widespread drug abuse, bad behaviour, and civil disobedience.

Vandalism and violence are expressions of youth intolerance, frustration, and rejection of established social norms. Particularly in big cities, there is a high incidence of teenage pregnancies. In earlier centuries, especially during mediaeval times corporal punishment was a disciplinary action taken to shape behaviour.

As time moved on, modern psychologists rejected this idea and encouraged positive rewarding methods to correct children's behaviour. Indeed, a child cannot be wholly blamed for negative behaviour. Children need to be admonished, and parents have to spend quality time with them to understand, counsel, and advise them on important issues, to help them correct, resolve challenges, and improve their behaviour.

For example, Buddha had a son named Rahula. He was admitted to the order of monks and was assigned to be trained under the Buddha's chief disciple. Rahula was proud, resistant to instructions, lied and didn't listen to his mentor. When he complained, Buddha admonished him personally. Rahula was asked to bring a basin of clean water and - as was the custom of the day - the junior had to wash his teacher's feet. After Rahula had done this the Buddha asked, "Rahula would you drink this water?" Rahula answered, "No, sir. It is dirty and I wouldn't drink it". Then the Buddha asked, "Rahula, what would you do with it?" Without hesitation, Rahula replied, "I would throw it away". Buddha advised Rahula that he wouldn't hesitate to throw him away from the monastic order, as it would be like dirty water because there is no place in his order for those who are conceited and who tell lies. Rahula got the message and from then on corrected himself and became an exemplary monk.

This story shows how children can be stubborn but can be corrected. The Buddha had the wisdom to see through a problem and give the appropriate answer to correct anyone who is prepared to learn his teaching. Buddhist societies seek the Buddha's supreme wisdom at all times.

Raising a child with an ethical background is important so that they might understand what is right and wrong. A child learns these habits at an early stage from their parents. In this sense, parents are the child's first teachers. This responsibility of teaching ethical values can then be shared with schoolteachers when the child begins their formal education and onwards, Sunday schools can be very beneficial in this sense.

We can be certain that all religions have developed moral values. The parable of the sower taught by Jesus in Christianity is one of universal value; there is a moral to this story which helps the children discover how truly wonderful the world of ethical conduct is and how we must not let worry, selfishness, or greed steal it away.

Children can keep these lessons close to their hearts with truth and understanding. We must not let the evil one snatch it away. True happiness and the confidence to accept responsibility comes from sharing and caring for others. These moral lessons are the foundation stones for when one is grown up as an adult so that they can live in a community with respect and dignity. It protects the child from being delinquent.

Civilised societies are founded on religious ethical values. In these societies, children are encouraged to abide by these values whilst engaging in the community, to raise the bar for the future, to be higher achievers and contributors. Parents and teachers have a great responsibility, an emphasis should be placed on supporting the child's growth in a better ethical environment.

The first and foremost precept of Buddhism is:

"I undertake the training of not killing any living being".

This moral value is based on the karmic retribution of the action. The rest of the four precepts are to regulate our behaviour ensuring that no harm is done to anyone. The Buddhist education system teaches children at a young age the consequences of their actions. These moral values are embedded in the socio-economic framework in Buddhist countries and encourage 'right living', therefore promoting loving-kindness and compassion towards their fellow citizens. Buddha gave us a foundation and structure of values, Buddhists take the Buddha's wisdom, universal moral law, and perfect human qualities as their refuge.

This is the path of peace, happiness, and economic prosperity; without discipline no economic prosperity can be achieved.

# Marriage

## The Buddhist view of Marriage

Buddhism addresses the way to the path of liberation. The Buddha, when he was a young prince, married and had a son but eventually came to renounce the world. He left the palace to find a solution to universal suffering. Most of his disciples were married men who had left home in an act of emancipation to seek enlightenment. Buddhist monks are expected to live in complete celibacy and breaking that precept is self-defeating.

Marriage is a social arrangement in the pursuit of happiness through the earthly attachment to another person. According to Buddhist doctrinal teaching, the main cause of suffering is attachment; so, marriage would contradict the path to liberation if a monk were to have a partner. So, to avoid social disharmony, the Buddha made a rule that married men needed to obtain their wife's permission - and young men their parent's consent - to join the monastic order.

There is not much discussion on marriage itself in Buddhism as this has always been considered to be a secular affair. There are only a few essential guidelines written about marriage, which came about as a result of people asking the Buddha's advice in resolving certain marital difficulties.

The Buddha emphasized the importance of the compatibility of partners. He pointed out that the main reason for a man's downfall is his involvement with other women. In the discourse of Sigalovada, advice is given by the Buddha to a young man named Singala. He describes the values of marriage and of the need for a husband's and wife's respect for each other.

On another occasion, The Buddha described the duties and qualities of a good wife. A young wife should accept the culture of the new family, be friendly to her in-laws, her husband's friends, and thus be integrated into the new family. She must be capable of managing the household responsibilities and protecting the family wealth, not carelessly spending the husband's hard-earned money.

When the Buddha was teaching laypeople, he sometimes referred to issues concerning marriage. In Buddhism, laypeople's lives are regulated by the five precepts and principles of the middle path, this presupposes moderation. The third precept 'to refrain from sexual misconduct' could be directly applicable to marriage, although misconduct is not defined. From the Buddhist perspective misconduct has to be interpreted within a cultural context and thus can be very wide, depending on the local cultures. For example, polygamy is accepted in some cultures and rejected by others. Historically, many kings had more than one wife and consorts. Child abuse, rape, prostitution, grooming, and seduction of any engaged young woman are classed as misconduct in many cultures, including in Buddhism. Not only the third precept but all the other four are equally important for a stable and happy marriage.

If Buddhist principles are correctly understood, it is enough to maintain the harmony of family life no matter what trials and tribulations are to be faced. The underlining principles of those precepts are set according to the law of "karma". In simple terms, good actions produce good results and bad actions produce bad results. Marriage is sometimes known as wedlock; this commits a couple to a fixed life-style. Therefore, it is important to choose the right way of living without acquiring bad habits that would add more suffering to married life.

Positive communication along with loving intention can resolve problems by replacing the intention of hurt, control, fear, or rejection of one's partner. The Dalai Lama, the head priest of Tibetan Buddhism has written: "Too many people in the West have given up marriage. They do not understand that marriage is about developing a mutual admiration of someone, a deep respect and trust, and awareness of another human's needs."

The institution of marriage gives a wonderful opportunity to develop good actions and improve personal tenets. It is a delightful association of two people to nurture a good and loving culture, to grow and reach maturity in life through accepting individual responsibility for the upbringing of a family. Life is not a rose garden, but husband and wife can face challenges as they journey through life together.

With the right understanding, sharing responsibilities, with a tender and loving, caring attitude, married couples can overcome most issues. Buddhism agrees with Christianity that a husband and wife have a complementary role and that married life is incomplete without the other's contribution. Marriage provides companionship and fellowship that helps each person to live in harmony with the society they choose to live in.

There are three aspects to action, manifesting either physically, verbally, or mentally. One should be always mindful about one's actions. Verbal action can be very powerful therefore, words should be carefully chosen to suit the occasion and the mood of one's partner. The words can be sharper than a blade. Truthfulness and right speech are very important factors. One must not be harsh, humiliating or insulting to one's partner especially in the context of the social environment.

Guarding your mouth and protecting the boundaries of the family are equally important. The fourth precept, 'to refrain from false speech'

376

constitutes the only guideline needed to regulate verbal actions that may otherwise harm good relations.

Love and kindness, compassion, and generosity start at home. Husbands should take extra care of their wives when they are pregnant. This is a time of testing one's real character, of one's acceptance of responsibility and appreciation of life. One of the main damaging aspects of a marriage is the ignorance of birth control and abortion. Marriage should be planned. Ample medical advice is available through GP practices and health centres to facilitate a healthy marriage.

Buddhism does not approve of abortion because it constitutes killing. However, arranging the affairs of their life is up to a couple. Understanding the functional differences, disposition, sexuality, emotions, moods, feelings, and other complex functions of the mind requires more than common sense.

Buddhists seek knowledge and insight to enlighten their perception and can apply the Buddha's wisdom in many situations in daily life. Buddhist injunctions are to protect everyone. When addressing difficult situations, patience and gentleness are both important to see things more clearly. Anger, hatred, and anxiety can overcast the truth and lead to one taking a wrong course of action to resolve a problem. Anger dispels happiness and brings darkness.

To achieve peace in the household, we must minimize anger and cultivate kindness and compassion according to Buddhist guidelines. Developing a kind heart and loving attitude can transform your partner. Respect, honour, loyalty, and support to each other are the threads that strengthen the fabric of marriage, whilst appreciation and recognition enhance the joy of life.

Most importantly, emotional, and moral support to one's partner in challenging times is vital to a lasting happy marriage. One should be caring in thought and deed, especially at times of illness, it is an opportunity to show compassion. Meditation on loving-kindness is a very effective method of bringing happiness to another person and to a couple in a partnership.

This love, compassion and kindness can be extended to the children of the family, to friends and to the whole world, bringing complete tranquillity peace and happiness to all. These are factors of wisdom. They spring from right understanding and right thought. Depending on the occasion they manifest as sublime qualities and prompt appropriate action for the most positive outcome.

Separation is a consequence of marital union which inevitably entails suffering. While death is a natural phenomenon that can cause separation, in some unfortunate situations, marriage can end up in divorce. One of the main reasons for divorce is having diametrically opposite views of life from one's spouse.

Those who are unable to resolve marital differences need to undertake critical analysis of their overriding self-interests and contemplate deeply the meaning of life, purpose, and reasons for their marriage. An individual has to decide what he or she wants to achieve and what barriers cannot be overcome. Dhamma practise has great benefits for a peaceful life.

In Thai culture, young men become temporary monks before marriage, which gives them an edge over other eligible bachelors who do not have this opportunity. However, if there are persistent conditions which always result in disagreements that cannot be mitigated then divorce is an option, rather than acquiring bad karma to avoid a calamity.

There are many incidents of suicide, violent revenge, where men and women fall into complete mental blindness under the spell of greed, hatred, and delusion. On one hand, being with someone you dislike is suffering and on the other, separation from a loved one or not getting what you want is also suffering. Buddhism views marriage as undertaking a duty and responsibility for the welfare of the family. Even in the event of divorce, this principle is continued with respect to the children and the estranged wife. The law intervenes to redress the injustice to an injured party.

Human beings cannot live in isolation unless trained in altruistic wisdom, this is to live a completely detached life and to develop a higher level of consciousness for seeking enlightenment. Marriage is a good social arrangement that gives emotional stability and security to an individual, as well as at a social level. It also provides an economically more efficient way to live. It requires couples to have a deeper understanding of each other and to accept certain social norms i.e., it is a social arrangement as agreed by both parties to the marriage.

Religious teachings can help to increase the understanding of the purpose of marriage and make marriage more meaningful, by not allowing uncontrolled emotion and worldly views to make life more difficult than might otherwise be the case. Marriage is a personal choice, to enter into a legally binding contract that has evolved out of a social system.

The compatibility of partners, having common values, having a sharing and caring attitude are all essential for a purposeful and happy life. Buddhism provides a foundation, a framework and principles that encourage the exploration of its philosophical values and translates them into practical guidelines for the self-regulation of a marriage, for personal growth and to enable one to gain conventional wisdom in the attainment of happiness.

## Buddhist Psychology

How can we explain something which at one time has been passionately desired and yet another time most violently detested?

The fundamental difference between like and dislike is the mental attitude, the manifestation of inner mental factors that are associated with the given consciousness of an object. This object can be a person, a memory of a person, a time, place, incident, or a combination of all. The attitude is intricately connected to the active perception of that object. It is propelled by a predominant force of passion or aversion depending on the character of the subjective disposition of the mind which is in constant flux. The impermanent nature of the mind is aptly compared to a stream of water that is always in continuous flow.

Buddhism recognises that attitudes can be changed. The consciousness of an object arises together with a constellation of mental factors, these also vanish together according to the supporting causes and conditions. They are like ripples in a stream without permanent substance. There are fundamentally two types of mental factors, pleasant and unpleasant. It requires understanding and appreciation of the middle path propounded by the enlightened Buddha to investigate your own mind through this line of inquiry.

By letting go of attachment, passion, and aversion, one can arrive at a well-balanced middle point that is peaceful and tranquil. It is receptive to the sublime, higher teachings which are directed towards the liberation of suffering. Buddhism teaches us how suffering is related to our own actions. In Buddhist reasoning, karma is not an outside force, but an inherent property of every mental process that is activated by intentional and volitional actions. These produce results by way of feelings, thoughts, emotions, and mental constructions that further result in conditions of the mind, triggering mental factors to produce more results.

Buddha explained the chain of mental functions that dependently arise and their relation to our actions. Only with wisdom one can cut off the associated conditions and root causes of suffering. Buddhism encourages us to cultivate a mental attitude of skilful action, known in common Pali terminology as "kusala kamma". The word "kusala" denotes a sharp double-edged blade of grass called "kusa", found in tropical countries. It is a metaphor for a sharpened wisdom, capable of cutting off both the effect and the root causes of suffering with surgical precision.

On the other hand, unskilful actions are termed as "akusala kamma". These actions produce dull effects on the mind which make us unable to discern the thoughts and intentions of the heart, they are thus not conducive to liberation.

Over time, the mind gets conditioned by our own actions, and they become the attitude, habit, and character of a person. In times of difficulty, Buddhist people seek wisdom from monks in a confidential, safe environment whilst working through the effects of past traumatic experiences. This counselling can assist the seekers of truth to discover their own personal resources and capabilities which are sometimes hard to find during times of confusion, conflict, and anxiety.

Buddhist words of wisdom can help you see circumstances from a new perspective. They are supportive, encouraging and empower one to make positive changes in life. Buddhist advice of letting go and not harbouring anger or hatred can help one cope with current issues or a crisis of anxiety and despair.

Narrated through various sources of literature the *(chapter 28-30)* book explores classical examples of ethical behaviour of moral excellence.

CHAPTER 28

————— ⚬ —————

# ETHICS OF OLYMPIANS

## Olympians of Ancient Greece and Greek Mythology

GREEK MYTHOLOGY STEMS FROM THE naming of twelve Olympian gods. These twelve gods can be traced back to Athens in the 6th century BC. They represent various aspects of nature and society, having achieved perfection in those aspects. For example, Zeus is the ruler and God of the sky and thunder. Hera is the Queen of the gods and the Goddesses of marriage and family.

The gods were named Olympians because they were said to dwell on Mount Olympus, the highest mountain in Greece. Worshipping of these gods became the religion and cult practices in ancient Greece.

It was said to have evolved from Bronze Age Greece and can be related to a collection of similar beliefs and practices in ancient Egypt the preeminent civilization in the Mediterranean world. Egyptian religion was polytheistic. Most gods were generally benevolent, with characteristics of divine and human. These practices typically consisted of offerings and sacrifices at the altar of the temple dedicated to the gods.

The evidence of the existence of such practices can be found in ancient Greek epics. In Homer's epic *The Odyssey* (725 BC) he describes the use of an animal sacrifice ritual in times of danger or before some important personal or common endeavour to gain favours of the gods for success. In 776 BC, there was a change in the rituals. Instead of sacrifice, they introduced sporting events and games which were held in honour of

Zeus at a panoramic site named Olympia; later, these events became the Olympic Games. This change can be seen as deviating from rituals of blind faith towards practical achievements that encourage personal development to reach further human potential through competition.

Sports included athletics, wrestling, boxing, and chariot races; more games were later added. Sports and games are methods of harnessing energy that requires self-discipline, accepting responsibility for one's actions, confidence, and honesty. Winning attitudes need to meet the challenges of the game. These attitudes are essential in meeting the challenges of life intelligently and to giving leadership.

Ancient Greeks equated athletics to intelligence and used it as a means of achieving excellence. However, there were horrific events, unfair competition, cheating, bribery, and dishonesty in these games, which were punished with penalties. Hence, rules were brought in to maintain the spirit of the games. It was stated that Greece was often at war, and this made travel between cities dangerous for large crowds of spectators, entertainers, and traders. To make the travel safer to Olympia a 'sacred truce' was introduced, and peace messengers were sent out from Elis.

People regarded the Olympic Games as more important than wars, and this idea inspired the modern Olympic Games bringing the five continents together in peace. The Olympic Games are held every four years. The modern Olympic Games began in 1896, since then various countries have hosted the Games in their capital cities with an unbroken chain of passing the Olympic flame from one to another.

Olympic Games attract millions of visitors, and the Olympic flame is the emblem of goodwill, peace, and joy. Opening and closing ceremonies are spectacular cultural displays of the hosting nation, with a rationale of sharing goodwill across all the participating countries of the world with their varied cultures and religions.

## Olympic Rules

The ethics of the Olympics promotes *equality* and *fair play*. Some participants, who are aware of these ethics, use performance-enhancing drugs, the use of transparent information, and tests becomes an ethical and moral issue. Some of the arguments against allowing drugs are tied in with the arguments against cheating in general.

Allowing drugs would elaborate the focus on winning, rather than taking part and therefore it would not be in the spirit of the games. Allowing drugs also promotes unhealthy and dangerous behaviour, setting a bad example to children. Many performance-enhancing drugs pose severe health risks. If drugs are allowed, drug advertising and sponsorship would presumably follow. This resounds with similar ethical problems to the debate surrounding tobacco advertising in sports like Formula One. Since this dispute on drugs involves the established rules, the Olympic committee must draw the line between acceptable behaviour and cheating.

They have now added more rules to decide on allowable and disallowable drugs. Regardless of the outcome of the discussion about whether the rules should be changed, athletes must abide by them. Nobody is arguing that it's ethical to enter a competition and knowingly break the rules. A few people argue that if competitors choose to accept the risk of being caught then they are entitled to cheat, it's a personal choice in taking the risk of public humiliation.

The decisive universal ethical factor in such scenario is moral shame and moral dread, something to be taken seriously by an individual since in the Olympics they represent their country. There are occasions where the use of a special diet, medical treatment or therapy enhances athletic performance. Deciding on these issues and where to draw the line has become complicated because sports is now a profession.

Sport-related injuries affect their profession therefore it can be argued that sport ethics is already subservient to medical ethics. For example, a sports physician cannot and ought to not prescribe potentially performance-enhancing drugs, unless the athlete requires such drugs to alleviate any illness or pain. The moral questions concern the appropriateness of the use of drugs in sport. However, this matter is not straightforward, and it is no easy task for a physician to decide how best to treat their athlete-patient - more as an athlete or more as a patient.

Yet, if the individual gives a great deal of value to their sporting career and is prepared to make long-term health sacrifices in order to excel in their sport, then it might be in the patient's best interests to receive treatment that makes them well for sport, rather than well for life.

A comprehensive, well-informed study of the ethics of drug use in sport is certainly needed, hitherto, the Olympic Committee are the authority to decide what is in the best interest for the spirit of the Olympic Games. The Olympic Committee believes that performance-enhancing drugs should be banned because they can potentially damage the health of those taking them, whether they are elite athletes who stand the risk of being detected using them or the recreational sportsperson who is unlikely ever to be tested.

They should be banned also because anyone using them is trying to gain an unfair advantage over those athletes who wish to maintain normal health. They are 'cheating' because their use is against the rules of the sporting federations.

The Olympic Values Education Programme and The Olympic Committee have identified seven Olympic values which are: friendship, excellence, respect, courage, determination, inspiration, and equality. The objective of the Olympics is therefore to promote these values through the biographical narratives of Olympic athletes. The understanding of this group of seven Olympic values is to build constructive relationships with participating countries. The Olympic Movement strives to ensure that sport is practised without any form of discrimination.

The Olympic motto says that taking part is more important than winning. The concept of a level playing field in commerce was developed from this ethical principle of fair play, creating a situation that is fair because everyone has the same chance of succeeding.

At its core, the modern Olympics - first held in Athens in 1896 - symbolizes peace, harmony, and solidarity between nations, in accordance with the International Olympic Committee (IOC). But it would be hard to find an example of an Olympic Games free from political, economic, or cultural scandals. For example, in the 2018 Winter Olympics held in PyeongChang, Republic of Korea, the entire Russian team was banned from competing in Olympic games.

Still, it has been discovered that not only had Russian athletes been doping, but it was part of a large-scale state-sponsored scandal. To be fair, the IOC allowed those to compete who had not been part of the scandal by investigating on a case-by-case basis. The Russian anthem would be not played *(The McLaren Report 18 July 2016 by Professor Richard McLaren)*.

At the same time, Japanese Short Track Speed skater Kei Saito was caught using illegal doping and was also suspended from the Winter Olympics.

It is true sports can elevate the spirit for facing challenges in life and develops resilience.

Despite the Covid-19 pandemic, the Tokyo Olympic torch relay begins as a sign of hope in Japan on 25th March 2021. It is the first time in history that an Olympics and Paralympics will be held without overseas spectators, organizers have had to scale back their ambitions due to the pandemic. Seiko Hashimoto, the head of the Games' organizing committee, said that the start of the Olympic flame's journey was a sign of hope.

"For the past year, as the entire world went through a difficult period, the Olympic flame was kept alive quietly but powerfully," she said at the opening ceremony, which was attended by a small number of dignitaries.

"The small flame did not lose hope, and just like the cherry blossom buds that are ready to bloom, it was waiting for this day."

## London 2012 Olympic Games

One of the main aspects of the Olympic Games is team spirit and honesty. Winners of Gold medals bring pride, glory, and esteem to the nation they represent, the same as it was in ancient Greece.

Winners get a hero welcome back home with privileges and social status. The atmosphere during the London 2012 Olympic Games was electric. The achievements of Team GB made waves of euphoria across the British nation; the whole event was inspirational especially if compared to the London Street riots just a year before.

The 2012 Games transformed the community spirit into an enthusiastic sporting legacy. The Olympics improves the moral standards and morale of all nations, bringing forward ethical values. The Para Olympics (*Paralympic*) represents the compassion towards less able sportsmen and women to realize their full potential, it proves that disability is not a hindrance in achieving excellence of performance.

Paralympic started as a sports competition for injured Second World War soldiers in 1948, it has since become a major event which shows empathy for people who have gone through life-changing injuries. It gives them an opportunity to show courage, effort and to rebuild their lives. It can be hard to imagine for us what it would be like, for instance, to be blind or unable to walk.

The word 'Paralympics' has added a new dimension to social ethics, recognizing the importance of giving an equal opportunity for disabled sports, running parallel with the main Olympic Games and with the same spirit.

The Ancient Greek Olympic Games is the foundation for modern schoolhouse sport, regional and national sporting events. Apart from the Olympic Games, European Games, Commonwealth Games and Asian Games provide great opportunities to develop skills not only in sports but also in organisation, cultural display, and presentation.

These are also important for economic improvement by providing a wide range of job opportunities to many people. Super-talented iconic sportsmen and women become role models for the young generation. London 2012 games produced overnight legends in the history of sport. Jamaican Usain Bolt gained Gold in the men's 100- and 200-meters sprint. Sir Chris Hoy became the most successful British Olympian of all time. Mo Farah and Jessica Ennis added more to the glory. Paralympic athlete, above knee amputee Richard Whitehead, inspired the spectators by gaining Gold in 200m T42 category.

Self-development, honesty, acceptance of responsibility, compassion and community spirit are also valued in Buddhist societies. Ancient Buddhist masters recognized the fact that the mind can be trained, whereby human qualities and potential can be improved in various ways by identifying the temperament of a person. For example, Zen Buddhism uses archery, swordsmanship, and martial arts to train the mind in meditation. These techniques are used to remove the cruelty of warriors who use weapons. The underlining principle is to identify and remove mental defilements. These are mainly the greed, hatred and delusion that obscure vision.

## Roman Culture

Ancient Greek religion, culture, concepts, deities, and myths are used as a vehicle to convey philosophical ideas, to establish political power and also to strengthen the morale of its society.

Greek philosopher Xenophanes was the first to question such ideas. Both Plato and Aristotle disagreed with polytheistic mythical deities arguing that there is no empirical evidence to prove their existence. With the Renaissance and the contemporary Hellenic period, Greek religion has undergone a number of changes in the arts, humanities, and spirituality. In 146 BC Romans conquered Greece. Romans took much of the Greek religious ideas and other aspects of Greek culture and Romanised it. For example, Zeus was equated with Jupiter and Hera with Juno. Romans used Greek ideas of sports and games to strengthen the empire and the best performers were admitted to the Roman army's officer grades.

Yet jealousy, suspicion, and rivalry were common; when achievements are coupled with power and ego, they cause pride and conceit. The mind becomes blind with the pursuit of selfish motives and the act of betrayal is clearly projected in the story of Ben Hur, rewritten by Lew Wallace in 1880AD.

## Biblical Story of Ben Hur

Greek methods of human development reappear in the epic story of Ben Hur, a Biblical hero set during the time of Roman Empire in Jerusalem, Israel. The story unfolds with the Roman culture that prevailed during the time of Christ. It was considered "the most influential Christian book of the nineteenth century" written with an overtone of Biblical characters.

*Ben-Hur: A Tale of the Christ* is a novel by Lew Wallace, published by Harper and Brothers on November 12, 1880. The story recounts the adventures of Judah Ben-Hur, a Jewish prince from Jerusalem, who is enslaved by the Romans at the beginning of the first century and becomes a charioteer and a Christian. Running in parallel with Ben-Hur's narrative is the unfolding story of Jesus, from the same region and around the same age.

It gracefully and overtly presents the truly developed human qualities of Ben Hur, a Jewish prince and wealthy merchant. His childhood friend, Messala, turned out to be an ambitious and antagonized commanding officer of the Roman army. They both studied together in Rome and were good sportsmen, but they changed over time and came to hold very different views and aspirations.

Messala was blind with the glory of Rome and its imperial power while Ben Hur remained devoted to his traditional faith and became a generous supporter of Christianity. Messala later arrests Ben Hur, accusing him of an attempted assassination of the Roman governor of Judaea, without a trial he sent him to work until death as a Roman galley slave. Messala also imprisoned Ben Hur's mother and sister and had all the family's property confiscated. Messala betrayed his childhood friend the Jewish prince Judah Ben Hur, after Judah refused to help him with crushing the rebellious Zealots.

Ben Hur's fate magically turns around when the ship on which he was enslaved was struck by Greek pirates, as the ship was sinking, he saves his slave master's life, the commander of the ship. That act earns his freedom back and he gains Roman citizenship. After enjoying a privileged life of luxury as an adopted son of the Roman, Ben Hur returns to his city.

He finds out that his mother and sister contracted leprosy while in prison and were expelled from the city. He defeats his arch-rival Messala in an open competition of a chariot race, and before dying from fatal injuries caused in the competition, Messala reveals to Ben Hur the place where his mother and sister are.

During the race Messala races with a "Pict Chariot" - a chariot fitted with blades on the hubs. Messala is able to use these blades to destroy a couple of chariots and force their riders out of the race. When he tries to do the same with Ben Hur's chariot, the attempt backfires and it is Messala's chariot that is destroyed. Messala is thrown from the chariot, dragged along the ground, and then trampled by another team of horses.

Ben Hur seeks to heal his mother and sister through his faith in Jesus. They get a release order reviewed by the new governor of the city, Pontius Pilate, who saw a great injustice in the prison order. The story, a plot of revenge and redemption for his family through a high-risk chariot race becomes a story of compassion and forgiveness, highlighting the true character of Ben Hur.

Ben Hur fought against the injustices of imperial power with his own wisdom and strength for the cause he believed in. Buddhism shares the same value system of gratitude, taking care of sick parents, standing up for principles and the determination to achieve one's goal. For such a man, having given up his patrimony and privileges, heavenly rebirth is expected after their death.

Self-development through self-discipline, courageously meeting the challenges of life with patience and applying wisdom, is the character of a man seeking self-enlightenment. Buddhism is not a religion that binds a person to a faith; it helps that person release their full potential through ethical conduct. These mental faculties are identified and developed in Buddhist higher philosophy and psychology, shaping the character attributes of higher performers irrespective of their religious beliefs.

Mental faculties are universal. These can be further developed by virtuous acts. Sports psychologists use some of these techniques to improve confidence, concentration and to enhance the performance of star players. Ethics are guidelines applicable to every branch of knowledge and are also practically applied to reach the best outcome.

## Greco-Roman Culture

Greco-Roman culture is the term given to Roman culture greatly influenced by Greek culture. It was a fusion of Greek and Roman ideas which expanded across the Greco-Roman world. The influence of this culture spread to Greece, Cyprus, Italy, Asia Minor, Syria, Tunisia, and Libya. It also spread to some Alpine countries. There is evidence to suggest that in the 1st century CE Romans had closer contact with Germanic cultures which expanded across cultural relations. For example, Germanic people had a practice of worshipping Roman gods with Germanic names.

Greco-Roman culture fully developed with Imperial Roman power. Romans did not tolerate other religions. The execution of Jesus appears to have been a Roman plot to stop his teachings being popularized among their subjects. Christianity is the name given to his teachings.

Christianity was systematically destroyed; a law was introduced that banned Christianity and its followers were heavily persecuted. Refusal to participate in the 'Imperial cult practices' was treated as an act of treason. Roman soldiers arrested anyone in breach of the law and brutally tortured them to death. Cruel methods were employed to terrify religious prisoners by mutilating, burning, and starving them. Prisoners with a strong physique were condemned to fatal gladiatorial contests to amuse spectators.

This hostility continued for a period of two and half centuries. In 313 AD, Emperor Constantine the Great issued an edict of tolerance. This was after reviewing the religious practices during his time. It was called the Edict of Milan, it legalised Christian worship and superseded the previous edict issued by Emperor Galerius in April 311AD and granted Christians the right to practise their religion. Constantine favoured Christianity, he condemned the crucifixion of Jesus and introduced policies that enhanced and encouraged the ethical values of Christian teachings including religious tolerance and freedom of worship.

These policies emphasized the teachings and glorified the personality of Jesus and his apostles. Jesus' mother, Mary, was elevated to the status of a goddess. The Roman Catholic Church was founded on the ethical values of Christianity and brought the teachings of Jesus to its forefront. Constantine reformed the Roman culture by reinstating ethics and a regenerated sense of humanity.

Christianity is a monotheistic religion that reduced the esteem of polytheistic mythical gods and goddesses of Greco-Roman culture. The word 'Christianity' is rooted in the ancient Greek word 'christianos', meaning follower of Christ. The Catholic Church espoused the Christian saints. They replaced the Roman pantheon of gods and goddesses giving instead more realistic ideas and a purpose to worshippers. An important moral concept, the fear of committing sins, was introduced which brought paganism to an end.

With the collapse of the Roman Empire, mainly due to unsustainable imperialistic ideas and heavy military losses suffered, its satellite kingdoms adopted the Roman Catholic Church (RCC) with some changes to suit their local cultures. For example, the Church of England was established because the King of England disagreed with the divorce law advocated by RCC. However, the principal teachings and ethical values still remain intact.

The Church of England is more tolerant than the RCC towards freedom of thought and expression. Public services in England are grounded on Christian values. Education, patient care, hospital services, childcare, and elderly care are based on Christian ethical values, including respect for the dead. Greeks and Romans, on the other hand, were both literary societies. Satellite kingdoms inherited a vast wealth of literature infused during the Renaissance and Hellenic period. They were enriched with Aristotle's teaching and Christian ethical values. During the time of Alexander the Great, Greek culture mingled with Buddhist principles and ethics. There are historical links between ancient Greece and Northern India.

These Buddhist and Christian values are reproduced in English poet and playwright William Shakespeare's (1564AD) famous play *The Merchant of Venice.*

# CHAPTER 29

# ETHICS OF SHAKESPEARE

## The Merchant of Venice

THE STORY UNFOLDS THE CULTURE of wealthy merchants of Venice during the Late Middle Ages in Italy.

It is based on the prevailing law of contract settlements in trade agreements. Coming from the pen of William Shakespeare, the greatest dramatist of all times, this play mixes romance, ethical conduct, and conventional wisdom. Shakespeare deals with western ethics and values through the character of Bassanio. Then, these are specifically contextualised in the issues surrounding the law of contract and tortes of individual responsibilities and obligations. In common law, a tweak in law can cause a claimant to suffer loss, resulting in legal liability for the person who implies a tortious act to satisfy his personal grudge.

This delicately written story defines the business ethics. It blossoms into the incredible drama of a legal battle when the heiress, Portia, now the wife of Antonio's friend Bassanio, dresses as a lawyer and saves Antonio by establishing a legal doctrine.

Bassanio, a young gentleman of noble rank, wishes to win the beautiful and wealthy young lady Portia of Belmont. However, Bassanio has wasted his inheritance and is broke. He approaches his friend Antonio, a wealthy merchant of Venice, to help him out for three thousand ducats, needed for his expenditures as a suitor to visit the beautiful Portia. Antonio agrees to help but his ships and merchandise are busy at sea, therefore his cash flow is strained. As a trusted friend, Antonio does not want to disappoint Bassanio's romantic adventure. He, therefore, promises to cover a bond as a guarantor if Bassanio can find somewhere to borrow the money he needed.

Bassanio finds a Jewish moneylender, Shylock, who reluctantly agrees to lend the money without interest. Shylock takes this opportunity to take revenge on Antonio because of the abuse he had suffered at his anti-Semitic attitude.

The condition of the contract states that if Antonio fails to repay the money at a specific date, he may take a pound of Antonia's flesh. Although Bassanio does not want Antonio to accept such a risk, Antonio signs the contract for his friendship. With the money in hand, Bassanio leaves for Belmont with his friend Gratiano.

Gratiano is a good companion but warns him to have self-discipline for his talkative behaviour.

In the meantime, in Belmont, there are many suitors contesting to win Portia. Her father wants an intelligent man for his daughter so he left a will stipulating each contestant must choose correctly from one of three caskets. They are gold, silver, and lead. Inside the caskets there are three different verses of wisdom describing the nature of the choice. Whoever picks the right casket gets Portia.

Slogans are set to test the intelligence and character of each suitor as an equivalent to an IQ test.

The first suitor, the Prince of Morocco, who likes a luxurious life, chooses the gold casket with the slogan which says:

"who chooses me will get what many men desire".

The second suitor, the Prince of Arragon, who is full of conceit and imagination and who thinks that he is unique, chooses the silver casket with the slogan which says:

"who chooses me will get what he deserves", he imagines himself to be full of merit.

Both men leave empty-handed having rejected the lead casket because lead is considered as a poor material which does not suit their social status.

Bassanio is the favourite of Portia's household. He ponders upon his choice and chooses the Lead casket with the slogan which says:

"who chooses me must give and hazard all he hath".

It was the right choice and Bassanio wins Portia's hand.

The casket of gold (chosen by the Moroccan prince) contained a skull with a scroll in it that read:

"All that glistens is not gold; often have you heard that told. Many a man his life hath sold but my outside to behold, gilded tombs do worms enfold. Had you been as wise as bold, Young in limbs, in judgment old, your answer had not been inscrolled: Fare you well; your suit is cold."

This gold casket's skull and scroll simply represent the moral that "one should not judge a book by its cover".

In the casket of silver (chosen by the prince of Arragon), there was the smiling face of an idiot and it reads:

"The fire seven times tried this: Seven times tried that judgment is, that did never choose amiss. Some there be that shadow's kiss; Such have but a shadow's bliss: There be fools alive, I wish, Silver'd o'er; and so was this. Take what wife you will to bed, I will ever be your head: So be gone: you are sped."

This is the same moral lesson throughout. That "all that glitters is not gold", and thus Bassanio chose correctly.

In the casket of lead (chosen by Bassanio) there was a portrait of Portia with a scroll that read:

"You that choose not by the view, Chance as fair and choose as true! Since this fortune falls to you, be content and seek no new, if you be well pleased with this and hold your fortune for your bliss, turn you where your lady is and claim her with a loving kiss."

At Venice, Antonio's ships are lost at sea. The loss of expected income made Antonio unable to satisfy the contract terms by returning the money as promised. Shylock sees his opportunity and is more determined to take revenge on Antonio, a Christian.

At this time, Shylock's daughter, Jessica, had fled home with Antonio's friend Lorenzo, who is also a Christian. Without further notice, Shylock takes Antonio to court.

Bassanio realizes his responsibility and comes to rescue his friend Antonio. He offers Shylock double the amount, but he refuses and insists on the pound of flesh according to the terms and conditions of the contract.

The presiding judge of the court, the Duke of Venice, wishes to save Antonio but finds no precedent to nullify a contract. He refers to an advisor, a "doctor of law".

The lawyer representing Antonio repeatedly asks for mercy, "it is twice blest: it blessed him that gives and him that takes."

Shylock, who has a hidden motive to take revenge, adamantly refuses any compensation and insists on the pound of flesh which forces the case to continue. The court grants Shylock his bond, however the lawyer points out that although the contract allows Shylock to remove the flesh it does not allow for the blood of Antonio. Thus, if Shylock were to shed any drop of Antonio's blood it would constitute murder under Venetian law.

Such a criminal act would cause forfeiture of his "property and goods". Further, Shylock must cut precisely one pound of flesh, no more, no less. The lawyer advises him that "if the scale do turn, but in the estimation of a hair, thou deist and all thy goods are confiscate."

Seeing that this is an impossible case to win Shylock concedes, accepting Bassanio's offer of money for the defaulted bond. The lawyer points out that under the contract law, once the offer is rejected it cannot be reinstated, preventing Shylock to take the cash settlement. Further, a point of law outcasts Shylock as an 'alien' having attempted to take the life of a citizen. He had to forfeit all his property, half to the government and half to Antonio, leaving his life at the mercy of the Duke.

The Duke immediately pardons Shylock's life. Antonio generously gives back most of his share to Shylock's daughter, Jessica. At Antonio's request, the Duke grants remission of the state's half of the forfeiture but on the condition that Shylock converts to Christianity bequeathing his entire estate to Jessica and Lorenzo.

In this story it turns out that the supposed lawyer is Portia in disguise!

The story reveals human nature in contemporary Venetian society. Different characters represent various psychological aspects of the mind and the interplay of those aspects. Shylock, the protagonist, represents a self-centred and greedy man. He has hidden motives and is seeking revenge at the first opportunity. Antonio, instead, represents the generosity of a true friend and forgiveness.

Then, while Bassanio has gratitude, truthfulness and accepts responsibility to rescue a friend in need, who in turn has the character of a gentleman in returning the favour, Portia represents wisdom, mastery of ethics and justice in the legal profession. The Duke of Venice has compassion for both sides.

All these characters' attributes and traits are universal and not limited to a particular group of people or religion. They are valid in the modern business world although the form of its manifestation may differ from one place to another. The law is an evolving subject because the needs of people and their perceptions change with the environment and time period, but the principles remain the same. In the real world, law reflects the jurisdiction and politics of the society, nonetheless it serves as a valuable tool to measure ethical conduct.

It could be a better tool to measure ethical values more effectively if ancient principles of ethics are included in the reformation of criminal minds.

*Ethics of Shakespeare*

Shakespeare touches upon the connection between virtue and happiness with a pun intended on the poetic and humorous parenthetical comments precisely to tell the moral of the story. Ethics as portray by Shakespeare is that part of literature or kind of philosophy that deals with happiness and how it can be achieved, chiefly through virtue.

Metaphorically, happiness is called sweet, so the opposite of happiness could metaphorically be called sour or bitter. Shakespeare strikes right in the middle of human feelings, emotions, and intellect with his ethical philosophy, rightly comparing virtue to the health of the body which is between the two sick extremes of too much or too little. Shakespeare mentions at the beginning and the end so he can alliterate and reiterate.

In the dialogue between Bassanio, Lorenzo, and Gratiano he utilises logic with acquaintances by using practical rhetoric in common talk, and by depicting Aristotle's ethics, Shakespeare tells the moral codes of civilised society.

With Portia's reply to the words of Nerissa, Shakespeare touches upon the much greater difficulty of doing what is good rather than just knowing what is good:

*Portia:* Good sentences and well pronounced.
*Nerissa:* They would be better if well followed.

*Portia:* If to do were as easy as to know what were good to do, chapels had been churches, and poor men's cottages princes' palaces.

It is a good divine that follows his own instructions: I can easier teach twenty what were good to be done, than be one of the twenty to follow mine own teaching. The brain may devise laws for the blood, but a hot temper leaps o'er a cold decree: such a hare is the madness of youth, to skip o'er the meshes of good to counsel the cripple.

Since the end of ethics is to do what is good or what is better, it is important to see that knowledge is not enough and that ethics should be followed by the effort to do what one has learned is good or better and that herein lies the greatest difficulty.

"Action should speak louder than words".

Virtue, and especially moral virtue, abide in the middle or mean of greed and generosity. But the virtue of reason is also a mean for truth as being between two mistakes. Shakespeare clearly shows the master wisdom of nature, and he seems to put together logic and rhetoric to then formulate the legal argument for defeating greed by wisdom. He shows us how generous law could be by distributing the wealth of the 'fair and just' without hurting either party and reforming Shylock. These are the main or chief parts of his philosophy. And to hit the golden mean is to go a long way towards happiness.

The moral of the story highlights the doctrinal teachings of the enlightened Buddha. The impermanent nature of life is very well demonstrated in Shylock's character. His greed and hatred led him to lose not only the case but lose all his wealth and dignity.

The slogans of the caskets testing the intelligence of the suitors and the verses inside them contain words of wisdom as in Buddhism. There is nothing permanent in the world; everything is subjected to change, decay, and death.

"All that glitters is not gold" can be interpreted in the light of conventional wisdom; our choices are dependent on our perception. The true nature of things as they are can be concealed by luxury, conceit, and imaginings.

By mindfulness and investigation, we can discover the true nature of life that is often wrapped in elegance and vanity. According to Buddhism, there is nothing new in the world; therefore, we must be content with what we have got so that good things will come to us rather than chasing illusions.

As the story goes on, it conveys an important message of human's qualities to resolve life problems peacefully and intelligently without bloodshed.

This is a central teaching common to both Buddhism and Christianity. Compared to the Roman attitude of 14 centuries ago, *The Merchant of Venice* reveals a remarkable change in tolerance as when ethical values are properly understood. What finally remains is only the good we have done, whereby many generations can benefit from these good things.

In the Catholic Church, Constantine and his mother Helena are treated as saints. Their contribution changed the world and will benefit many generations to come.

CHAPTER 30

# KINGDOM OF THAILAND

Buddha's teaching had a profound influence on people's lives in countries which adopted Buddhist philosophy. Buddhist ethics, though always influential, gained renewed interest in modern Thailand's economic development programs initiated by His Majesty the Late King Bhumibol Adulyadej. If we want sustainable development for future generations, economic theories should incorporate the moral values of non-political systems and evolved social systems.

We have to learn lessons from the past. As Buddhists, we believe in peaceful dialogue and non-violent means as better ways of resolving issues. By these we can find solutions to the challenges of life, such as the sustainable use of resources so that many may find their peace and happiness.

A programme initiated by His Majesty the late king of Thailand introduced the application of Buddhist ethics into economic development, incorporating the Middle path, Right view, and Right livelihood. Having understood the need of his people and country in 1998, His Majesty the Late King Bhumibol introduced a rural economic development program through his philosophy of the "Sufficiency Economy".

*Sufficiency Economy* is a philosophy that stresses the middle path as the overriding principle for appropriate conduct and way of life by the populace at all levels, as the individual, family, and community. It is a balanced development strategy for the nation to develop in line with globalization and protect against inevitable shocks of market forces.

"Sufficiency" means moderation and due consideration in all modes of conduct, together with the need for sufficient protection from internal and external shocks. To achieve this, His Majesty realized that the most essential factors are strengthening the moral fibre of the nation and application of knowledge with prudence so that everyone adheres first and foremost to the principles of honesty and integrity. It requires a culture of a caring and sharing attitude.

Such an attitude was readily available in a Buddhist country like the Kingdom of Thailand. Thai culture is enriched with its traditional values and customs. In addition, a balanced approach combining patience, perseverance, diligence, wisdom, and prudence is indispensable to cope appropriately with critical challenges of rapid socio-economic and cultural changes that occur as a result of accelerated economic growth. Thailand successfully met those challenges.

Consequently, in May 2006 the United Nations Human Development Programme (UNDP) presented HM the Late King Bhumibol with the UNDP's inaugural Human Development Lifetime Achievement Award for HM's tireless efforts and dedication for the wellbeing of the Thai People and nation.

"Sufficiency is moderation. If one is moderate in one's desires, one will have less cravings. If one has less craving, one will take less advantage of others. If all nations hold this concept of moderation, without being extreme or insatiable in one's desires, the world will be happier." (HM the Late King Bhumibol)

The principles adopted by the philosophy of Sufficient Economy stem from the Buddhist 'middle path' to liberation, based on Buddhist ethics and moral values.

Historically, kings sought advice from Buddha with regard to social governance, how to rule a country and what qualities make a good king. There is evidence in the Pali Cannon that many kings supported Buddha and his disciples. Buddhist social philosophy recognizes that quality of life can be improved through education and training.

"Education is a major factor to create and develop a person's knowledge, ideas, behaviour and merit. Any society and country should provide good, complete, and well-balanced education, covering all aspects for the youth, so that the society and country will have qualified citizens. They will be able to sustain the country's prosperity and develop progressively…"

(His Majesty the Late King)

His Majesty the Late King's remarks echo Socrates' idea and concept of the "Philosopher King". His Majesty the Late King also realized that the development of education for the youth is an important foundation for the country. The Thai Encyclopaedia has been published for young people through His Majesty's initiative.

This specific encyclopaedia covers different branches of knowledge, including science, technology, social and humanity studies. Today, Thailand is not counted as a poor country. Thailand is a member of the G24 Nations which is one of the signature achievements of HM the Late King.

(Source: Department of Information, Ministry of Foreign Affairs, Kingdom of Thailand).

# CHAPTER 31

# MOTHER'S DAY

During the Middle Ages, the custom developed of allowing people who had moved away from where they grew up to come back to visit their home, their 'mother' churches, and their mothers and relatives.

This occurred on the fourth Sunday of the Christian festival of lent before Easter Sunday. At the time, it was not uncommon for children to leave home to work when they were just ten years old, so this was an opportunity for families to meet up again.

These young children both boys and girls worked as servants for rich families or farms. They were allowed to take home domestic farm products like eggs, milk, and grains. Some children painted eggs with colours and decorated them as presents to their mothers. Since then, the exchange of Easter Eggs became a custom in Europe. It is now a big commercial business; chocolate companies make chocolate eggs and millions of them are sold just before Easter Sunday.

This became Mothering Sunday in Britain. As the dates of Lent vary each year, so does the date of Mothering Sunday. Although it's often called Mother's Day in the UK, it has no connection with the American Mother's Day.

In the US, Mother's Day is celebrated on the second Sunday of May each year. The idea started in America when a woman called Anna Jarvis held a small memorial service for her own mother on 12 May 1907. Soon after, most places in America were observing the day and in 1914, the US president Mr Woodrow Wilson made it a national holiday, celebrated on the second Sunday of May. Lots of other countries celebrate Mother's Day at different times of the year as well.

The custom became a tradition, an evolution of a novel idea to keep family unity and visit mothers at least once a year. The idea spread to Asian Buddhist countries like Thailand as well.

*Mother's Day in Thailand*

August 12th is a very special day for the people of Thailand, it is the birthday of their beloved queen, Her Majesty Queen Sirikit. In commemoration of Her Majesty this day is also recognized as National Mother's Day.

Thailand is ruled by a King. Her husband was His Royal Highness the Late King Bhumibol Adulyadej. Queen Sirikit's story is not one exclusively of privilege. It is a story of romance, self-discipline, courage, motherhood, devotion, and above all support for her late husband and service to the people of Thailand.

The couple met when they were in Paris, the city of love and romance. At that time, young Princess Sirikit was living in France where her father was in diplomatic service. In the neighbouring country of Switzerland, there was a certain young gentleman, who often travelled to the Thai Embassy in Paris.

The young gentleman was none other than HRH the Late King Bhumibol of Thailand. The young couple met and perhaps due to the romance that hung in the air of Paris, fell in love. Later, the young king was injured during a Swiss motoring accident. Princess Sirikit, accompanied by her mother, visited Lausanne frequently to give support to the king. Their relationship grew up in this way.

Both of them were descending from the Royal Chakri dynasty known as Rama Dynasty. Princess Sirikit's father, Prince Nakkahatra, was also in the Thai diplomatic Corps to the UK and continental Europe.

The Royal couple married on 28th April 1950, one week prior to the ceremonial coronation of His Majesty the Late King Bhumibol. Since then, Queen Sirikit's love and devotion embraced not only her husband but encompassed her family and the entire nation of Thailand.

Here is a job that no one would envy as it demands great self-discipline in her public life, little privacy from the eye of the media, and long tiring hours of work and devotion to her county.

Contrary to the difficult nature of her responsibilities, HM Queen Sirikit has graciously and regally risen to her task. Because of her qualities of leadership to Thai women, she dedicated herself to promoting economic welfare and thanks to her contribution to the country, HM Queen Sirikit gained the status of Mother of the nation.

Motherhood is viewed in Buddhism as a position of high responsibility as well as respectability. If a woman goes through her household life honouring the responsibilities vested on her as a mother, she can lay claim to honour. By recognizing and highlighting this responsible and respectable position of motherhood, the Buddha raised the status of women in society. An authentic Buddhist ethical value was established in Buddhist culture.

A person has no one else as worthy of honour and respect as one's own mother, provided she has played the mother's role well and correct. It is such a mother, along with one's motherland, that is valued even higher than life in heaven. People are willing to give their lives to protect their motherland. So, this great and powerful concept of 'mother' is engraved so deeply into the mind to provoke emotions. In this respect, with Thailand being a Buddhist country, HM Queen Sirikit gained the respect of her people by fulfilling her royal duties.

Her Majesty accompanied the Late King on all of his overseas engagements and has been by his side when welcoming other Crowned Heads of State and Envoy to Thailand. In fact, when HM the Late King Bhumibol entered Buddhist monastic life in 1956, Queen Sirikit became Regent of the Kingdom of Thailand.

Her Majesty has been a constant source of support and inspiration to those less privileged, who may look up to the Royal family for guidance. She has started many projects to promote self-employment programs in rural Thailand such as helping village women start small enterprises for weaving, candle making, herbal medicine, fabric dying or any other means of income-generating business. Queen Sirikit is invariably directing funds to worthy projects including Arts and Crafts training centres to produce handicrafts using local materials. Some of them in the cities of Chiang Mai and Chiang Rai are jointly established with the Tourism Authority of Thailand such as Aquariums and Bird sanctuaries. These projects echo those of her late husband's rural development projects.

Thailand has a high level of rainfall, and it is largely an agricultural economy. The Late King of Thailand who was also deeply revered by his people, was involved in rural development through over 4000 projects mainly concerning irrigation and food production.

From the Buddhist point of view, a good mother must necessarily be a good wife as well. If the husband does not do his role, she may be helpless, but very often a good and efficient wife is able to get him on the right track. Because of the mother's position in the family to correct her children and direct them onto the right path, the mother possesses the authority to decide on important family affairs.

Singala Vada Sutta (discourse of Singala) stands as a charter for the lay man's code of practice, it explains the householder's duties. In this discourse, the Buddha explained the mother's role and mentioned that a husband must give his wife authority to run the family affairs. Here the main duty of the mother should be to dissuade the children from evil ways through precepts and practice, persuading them to do in like manner. She must give them a sound education, get them married to suitable partners, at the proper time, and hand over their inheritance when the time comes for it.

Successful motherhood ultimately depends on the proper discharge of reciprocal duties by all the members of the family. The duties of parents and children are very well explained in the Singala Discourse. (DN31 - Dīgha Nikāya - The Collection of Long Discourses)

However, when a mother fails in her duties, willingly or unwillingly, it spells hell and ruin for the unfortunate child, no one else in the world can replace their natural mother. This dark aspect of motherhood is not uncommon in modern society. Without the mother's protective cover, a child's life can become open to many serious dangers because no one else can provide that love of a mother to her children. Knowing this well, the Buddha used a simile in the Metta Sutta discourse of Loving Kindness, "Like a mother who protects her own only child even at the expense of her life, so in the same way towards all beings, one should cultivate a boundless heart".

The Buddha conceded this unique position to mother-hood because of the closely acquainted knowledge and understanding he had regarding human relations. A deity once came to him and asked, "who is the best friend one has at home?" unhesitatingly the Buddha replied, "mother is the best friend one has at home".

Upon this backdrop of the unique value of motherhood, a child unwanted by its mother is surely a victim of tragic circumstances. When a child becomes the victim of their mother's neglect and ill-treatment nothing can be more unfortunate for that poor soul.

A mother's position has never been ascribed to a father. In Eastern traditions, the mother is always mentioned first. We have a folk idiom that states: If the mother is lost, what can be expected from the father?

Buddhism recognizes the value and position of a mother. Being a Buddhist country, Thailand recognizes this value which is incorporated into their family value system. Mother's Day in Thailand is not only to celebrate their Queen's birthday but to recognize the value of every mother. This day is a public holiday to go and visit one's mother, grandmother, and family.

The Queen's birthday was selected to highlight the importance and significance of Mother's Day as well as respect for the Queen.

The mother's role is to look after the children when they are young. When they grow up it is their duty to look after her. In Buddhist traditions, we consider looking after one's mother and father as good merit or good kamma.

In one of the Jataka stories there was a Bodhisattva who was a music teacher. He taught music to students as a career so that he could look after his blind parents. By doing such merit the Bodhisattva perfected his wisdom until he attained supreme enlightenment.

Finally, I would like to conclude with a Dhammapada (43):

*"Neither mother, father nor any other relative can do one greater good than one's own well-directed mind".*

For a family man, the basic purpose of Buddhism is to discipline the mind to recognise the duty and ethical value of family. The best respect you can give to your mother and father is looking after them when they need it most. Hence, we have to learn the Buddhist principles and traditions that are of benefit to us and guide our lives in terms of knowledge and wisdom that improve the way of life.

In Thai culture, these principles are closely interwoven into the entire fabric of society. People of Thailand have accorded an almost divine reverence to Thai Monarchy and Buddhism for the directions and guidance they have given to them.

*Controversies*

There are controversies surrounding certain social practices about whether they are ethical or not. Questions are raised such as, what are the Buddhist view of such practices and why such practices are allowed in stronghold Buddhist countries? For example, abortion, death penalty, euthanasia, vegetarianism, homosexuality etc. I haven't done enough research or data to go into a detailed analysis of them, but I will briefly discuss the Buddhist way of looking into these critical issues. And although compelling studies on this topic are few and far between, based on my own observations–statistically insignificant though it may be these estimates seem to at least land in the ballpark of reality.

Firstly, Buddhism or Buddhist monks do not interfere with the law of the land but expect people to abide by them. Secondly, to examine the circumstances as they arise on a case-by-case basis and weigh all sides evaluate to make a rational decision. A decision has to be made in context of each individual scenario.

The Buddhist rationale is to look at the effect on consciousness based on the doctrine of cause and effect in such a way as to minimize suffering. Buddhist ethics are not for political debate, they are for progression in the path of enlightenment.

Evaluation of ethical systems relate to the motivation for adhering to the ethical rules of the system, whether religious or secular. In Buddhism the goal of ethical conduct is self-control, self-understanding, and self-knowledge emerging from self-development.

Ethics are the prerequisite for the training of the mind, the elimination of ignorance and the attainment of enlightenment. Some secular laws are more directly moral in nature, but these are often indirect social objectives.

The pursuit of Buddhist ethics leads to social harmony but in the Buddhist way of life this harmony is achieved through individual perfection. All Buddha's teachings are embedded on an ethical grounding.

That is to say, a self-knowledge that emerges towards enlightenment and the perfection of morality.

Buddhism addresses the real problem of life, that life is suffering and thus the path leading to the cessation of suffering. As a matter of fact, Buddha put suffering in the forefront of his doctrinal structure. He dedicated the rest of his life to teaching the path that leads to the cessation of suffering.

According to the Chinese school of thought, Buddha had identified 84,000 different personalities and engaged in discourses with them to correct their views towards the right understanding of moral conduct based on wisdom.

In the noble eightfold path, the elements corresponding to morality and ethics are right speech, right action, and right livelihood. These constitute sila (morality). Cultivation of sila normally proceeds alongside progress in the other two great constituents, namely mental training, and wisdom.

# NOTES AND REFERENCE PART I & II

## Reference: Part I

1. Dr Thomas Slakey; *Ethics According to Aristotle and Kant*, Thomas Aquinas College, California.
2. Dr Gunapala Dharmasiri; *Fundamentals of Buddhist Ethics*, University of Peradeniya Kandy, Sri Lanka, 1986.
3. J D Mabbott, President of St. John's College University of Oxford, *An Introduction to Ethics, 1966.*
4. Ernest Edward Kellett; *A Short History of Religions*, Wadham College, University of Oxford, 1962.
5. Publications by the Department of Information, Government of Thailand, 2002.
6. Author AGS Kariyawasam; *Buddhist Evaluation of Motherhood.*
7. Internet, Wikipedia.
8. New York Time, May 2021.
9. Al-Jazeera News, May 2021.
10. Prof. David Dale Holmes; *The Buddhist Ideals of Good Governance.* https://www.buddhistdoor.net/features/the-buddhist-ideals-of-good-governance/
11. New York Time 06 January 2022.
12. Blake Hounshell; Leah Askarinam; *On Politics: How many Americans support political violence?* New York Time 05 January 2022
13. Kenneth Roth; *How Democracy Can Defeat Autocracy*, January 2022. https://www.hrw.org/news/2022/01/14/how-democracy-can-defeat-autocracy
14. Russiapedia https://russiapedia.rt.com/of-russian-origin/siloviki/

15. Nina L Khrushcheva; *Putin's War Will Destroy Russia* 31 March 2022 Project Syndicate.

## Notes:

1. The **Allegory of the Cave** – also known as the **Analogy of the Cave**, **Plato's Cave**, or the **Parable of the Cave** – is an allegory used by the Greek philosopher Plato in his work *The Republic* to illustrate "our nature in its education and want of education" (514a). It is written as a fictional dialogue between Plato's teacher Socrates and Plato's brother Glaucon at the beginning of Book VII (chapter IX in Robin Waterfield's translation) (514a–520a).

   The Allegory of the Cave is presented after the metaphor of the sun (507b–509c) and the analogy of the divided line (509d–513e). Allegories are summarized in the viewpoint of dialectic at the end of Book VII and VIII (531d-534e).

   Plato describes a group of people who have lived chained to the wall of a cave all of their lives, facing a blank wall. The people watch shadows projected on the wall by things passing in front of a fire behind them and begin to ascribe forms to these shadows. According to Socrates, the shadows are as close as the prisoners get to viewing reality. He then explains how the philosopher is like a prisoner who is freed from the cave and comes to understand that the shadows on the wall do not constitute reality at all, as he can perceive the true form of reality rather than the mere shadows seen by the prisoners.

   The Allegory is related to Plato's Theory of Forms: according to which the "Forms" (or "Ideas"), and not the material world of change known to us through sensation, possess the highest and most fundamental kind of reality. Only knowledge of the Forms constitutes real knowledge. In addition, the Allegory of the Cave is an attempt to explain the philosopher's place in society: to attempt to enlighten the "prisoners" in the allegory of cave.

2. John Burgess Wilson (25 February 1917 - 22 November 1993) who published under the pen name Anthony Burgess was an

English author, poet, playwright, composer, linguist, translator, and critic. His remarks about ethics were directed towards Russian communist regime that introduced different set of ethics in human behaviour and a legal system.

3. Fyodor Mikhaylovich Dostoyevsky (11 November 1821 - 9 February 1881) was a Russian writer and essayist, best known for his novels *Crime and Punishment* and *The Brothers Karamazov*.

    Dostoyevsky's literary works explored human psychology in the troubled political, social and spiritual context of 19th-century Russian society. Considered by many as a founder or precursor of 20th-century existentialism, Dostoyevsky, wrote with the embittered voice of the anonymous *underground man Notes from Underground* (1864), which was called the "best overture for existentialism ever written" by Walter Kaufmann. Dostoyevsky is often acknowledged by critics as one of the greatest and most prominent psychologists in world literature.

4. Ajahn Khemadhammo was appointed an OBE

    (Officer of the Most Excellent Order of the British Empire) in the Queen's Birthday Honours, June 2003 for services to prisoners. In December 2004, on the birthday of the Late King of Thailand, he was made a *Chao Khun* with the ecclesiastical title of *Phra Bhavanavitayt*; he was only the second foreign-born monk to receive such an honour.

5. The Groundwork of the Metaphysic(s) of Morals

    (German: *Grundlegung zur Metaphysik der Sitten*, 1785), also known as *Foundations of the Metaphysics of Morals* or *Grounding of the Metaphysics of Morals*, is Immanuel Kant's first contribution to moral philosophy. It argues for an *a priori* basis for morality.

    Where the *Critique of Pure Reason* laid out Kant's metaphysical and epistemological ideas, this relatively short, primarily meta-ethical, work was intended to outline and define the concepts and arguments shaping his future work *The*

*Metaphysics of Morals.* However, the latter work is much less readable than the Groundwork.

The Groundwork is notable for its explanation of the categorical imperative, which is the central concept of Kant's moral philosophy.

Noble Eight-fold Path:

1. (Right view, Right thought)
2. (Right speech, Right action, Right livelihood)
3. (Right effort, Right mindfulness, and Right concentration).

6. Emergency Medical Services Response to Cardiac Arrest
   https://www.ncbi.nlm.nih.gov/books/NBK321505/

7. R. A. Berg et al., 2010). This conceptual model illustrates the sequence of events that can optimize care and outcomes for the approximately 395,000 individuals who experience an OHCA in the United States each year (Daya et al., 2015). Together, the first three steps com-prise the fundamental actions within basic life support (BLS) strategies for cardiac arrest
   (R. A. Berg et al., 2010), including early recognition of a cardiac arrest by bystanders and 911 call takers, as well as the delivery of initial treatments (i.e., CPR and defibrillation) by bystanders or trained first responders prior to the arrive of EMS providers (i.e., emergency medical technicians [EMTs] and paramedics).

8. Economics, Alain Anderton 6th edition 2015, Pearson Education

# Reference: Part II

1. The Stanford Encyclopaedia of Philosophy.
   https://plato.stanford.edu/entries/descartes/
2. Helene M Glaza; *Lenin's New Economic Policy: What it was and how it Changed the Soviet Union,* 2009, Vol.1 No 11 Pg.1/1
   http://www.inquiriesjournal.com/articles/1670/lenins-new-economic-policy-what-it-was-and-how-it-changed-the-soviet-union
3. Helene Glaza; M. 2009. *Lenin's New Economic Policy: What it was and how it Changed the Soviet Union.*
4. Inquiries Journal/Student Pulse 1 (11)
   http://www.inquiriesjournal.com/a?id=1670
5. World Bank publications July 2020.
   https://www.worldbank.org/en/country/kazakhstan/publication/economic-update-summer-2020
6. The Conversation. Adrian Brettle Lecturer in History, Arizona State University.
   https://theconversation.com/3-crisis-leadership-lessons-from-abraham-lincoln-136794
7. Jimmy Carter; Our Endangered Values: America's Moral Crisis.
8. Summary written by Brett Reeder, *Conflict Research Consortium.*
9. Jimmy Carter; *Our Endangered Values: America's Moral Crisis.* New York, NY: Simon & Schuster, 2005
10. National Archives, The Presidential Library and Museum
    https://www.beyondintractability.org/bksum/carter-our
    https://www.jimmycarterlibrary.gov/research/hos-tage_crisis_in_iran
    https://www.psychologytoday.com/us/blog/morality-ta-les/201812/america-s-moral-crisis
    https://theconversation.com/3-crisis-leadership-lessons-from-abraham-lincoln-136794
11. Pew Research Centre
    https://www.pewresearch.org/2017/01/10/how-america-changed-during-barack-obamas-presidency/

12. The Independent and BBC News May 2011
https://www.bbc.co.uk/news/uk-politics-13549927
https://www.independent.co.uk/news/uk/politics/obama-he-came-he-spoke-he-conquered-westminster-2289136.html
13. The Guardian, 17 March 2021.
https://www.theguardian.com/us-news/2021/mar/17/joe-biden-vladimir-putin-election-interference
14. New York Times March 26, 2021.
15. The White House March 25, 2021.
https://www.whitehouse.gov/briefing-room/speeches-remarks/2021/03/25/remarks-by-president-biden-in-press-conference/
16. What is gun culture? Cultural variations and trends across the United States, July 2020. Claire Boine et al, nature.com
17. American Psychological Association
https://www.apa.org/pubs/info/reports/gun-violence-prevention
18. Benjamin Franklin on the trade-off between essential liberty and temporary safety (1775).
https://oll.libertyfund.org/quotes/484
19. Business Ethics Quarterly Vol. 5, No. 1, Ethics and Leadership: The 1990s (Jan. 1995), pp. 55-65, Published by Cambridge University Press.
https://www.jstor.org/sta-ble/3857272?seq=2#metadata_info_tab_contents
20. Jonathan Morrow, Director of Cultural Engagement and Student Discipleship; *What Kind of Society Do You Want to Live in?*
21. Jonathan Morrow, Director of Cultural Engagement and Student Discipleship
https://www.impact360institute.org/articles/what-kind-of-society-do-you-want-to-live-in/
22. Blake D. Dutton Loyola University Chicago USA Internet Encyclopaedia of Philosophy)
https://iep.utm.edu/spinoza/

23. Stanford Encyclopaedia of Philosophy, (Author unknown).
https://plato.stanford.edu/entries/metaethics/
24. Internet Encyclopaedia of Philosophy.
Kevin M. DeLapp, Converse College USA.
https://iep.utm.edu/metaethi/
25. University of Cambridge; *The Forgotten Pandemic*
https://www.joh.cam.ac.uk/forgotten-pandemic-killed-more-50-million-people
26. Eric A Havelock; *The Greek Concept of Justice*, Harvard University 1978.
27. Russ Shafer-Landau; *The Fundamentals of Ethics,* Oxford University Press June 2020.
28. Mark LeBar; *Justice as a Virtue.*
https://plato.stanford.edu/entries/justice-virtue/
29. P. Schröder-Bäck, P. Duncan, W. Sherlaw, C. Brall, K. Czabanowska; *Teaching seven principles for public health ethics*; British Medical Council (BMC)
30. Kevin M. DeLapp; *Benedict Spinoza*; Converse College USA https://iep.utm.edu/metaethi/
31. Steven Nadler; *Baruch Spinoza*;
Stanford Encyclopaedia of Philosophy,
https://plato.stanford.edu/entries/spinoza/
32. Dr. Alexander Berzin; *The Four Axioms for Examining a Buddhist Teaching.*
33. Bhikkhu Bodhi; *A comprehensive Manual of Abhidhamma*; BPS Kandy, Sri Lanka, 1999.
34. Moral narcissism and moral complicity in global health and humanitarian aid.
BML Journals by Dr Mark Sheehan, Associate Editor
https://jme.bmj.com/content/44/5/287
Correspondence to Dr Mark Sheehan, 26/03/2021
http://dx.doi.org/10.1136/medethics-2018-104887
35. Author: Gregory Mellema; *Complicity and Moral Accountability*; April 2016; Notre Dame Press, University of Notre Dame.
36. Bradley E. S; *The structure of Max Weber's Ethic of Responsibility.*

37. Classical Eastern Philosophy, from: '*The History of Philosophy': A Short Survey* By James Fieser, Revised 6/1/2020.
https://www.utm.edu/staff/jfieser/class/110/4-east-ern.htm
https://en.wikipedia.org/wiki/Pantheism#:

38. Dr David B Gowler; *One thought on Vishnu: The Saviour, the Preserver, and the Protector.*

39. Kevin M. DeLapp; *History of Metaethics*, Internet Encyclopaedia of Philosophy, Converse College, U. S. A.
https://iep.utm.edu/metaethi/

**Sources:**

Cummins, Joan, Doris Srinivasan, Leslie C. Orr, Cynthia Packert, and Neeraja Poddar. *Vishnu: Hinduism's Blue-Skinned Savior.* Ocean Township, NJ: Grantha, 2011. Print.

Dimmitt, Cornelia, and J. A. B. Van Buitenen. *Classical Hindu Mythology: A Reader in the Sanskrit Purāṇas.* Philadelphia: Temple UP, 1978. Print.

Pattanaik, Devdutt. 7 Secrets of Vishnu. Chennai: Westland, 2011. Print.

(Devdutt Pattanaik is an Indian mythologist, speaker, illustrator, and author, known for his writing on sacred lore, legends, folklore, fables, and parables. His work focuses largely on the areas of myth, religion, mythology, and management.)

https://scholarblogs.emory.edu/rel100hindu-ism/2015/11/24/vishnu-the-savior-the-preserver-and-the-protector/

40. Jerrold M. Post, Stephanie Doucette, Dangerous *Charisma: The Political Psychology of Donald Trump and His Followers.* Publisher PEGASUS BOOKS, 2nd Edition Dec 2020.
https://www.nytimes.com/2020/12/12/us/

41. Absolute Power; Al Jazeera Media Network January 2021.

42. Henry Tandey.
https://unbelievable-facts.com/2017/09/biggest-mis-takes-in-history.html
https://en.wikipedia.org/wiki/Henry_Tandey

43. Ethics, Anthony J.P. Kenny et al
    Sir Anthony Kenny has been Pro-Vice-Chancellor of the University of Oxford, Master of Balliol College, Oxford, Chairman of the Board of the British Library, and President of the British Academy.

44. Jonathan Sacks; *Everyday virtue and the meaning of life*, March 2006.

45. Ethics guide; BBC, The Guardian.
    http://www.bbc.co.uk/ethics/sport/debate/drawing-line_1.shtml
    http://www.bbc.co.uk/ethics/sport/debate/against.shtml
    https://www.theguardian.com/sport/2021/mar/25/tokyo-olympic-torch-relay-begins-as-sign-of-hope-in-japan-amid-covid-curbs

46. Duane H. Berquist; *Shakespeare's Ethics*.
    https://www.atstudies.com/files/8714/2678/4903/Shake-speares_Ethics.pdf

47. Department of Information, Ministry of Foreign Affairs, Kingdom of Thailand.

48. Publications; Royal Thai Consulate General Vancouver, Vancouver BC Canada, BBC World Service
    *Early Buddhist theory of knowledge*, Book by K. N. Jayatilleke, George Allen & Unwin Ltd London, 1963, (Routledge Library Editions: Buddhism)

49. Stanford Encyclopaedia of Philosophy; Kolodny, Niko and John Brunero, *Instrumental Rationality*, The Stanford Encyclopaedia of Philosophy (Spring 2020 Edition), Edward N. Zalta (ed.)
    https://plato.stanford.edu/archives/spr2020/entries/ra-tionality-instrumental/

50. Emergency Medical Services Response to Cardiac Arrest.
    https://www.ncbi.nlm.nih.gov/books/NBK321505/

51. (R. A. Berg et al., 2010). This conceptual model illustrates the sequence of events that can optimize care and outcomes for the approximately 395,000 individuals who experience an OHCA in the United States each year (Daya et al., 2015). Together, the first three steps comprise the fundamental actions within basic life support (BLS) strategies for cardiac arrest.

52. (R. A. Berg et al., 2010), including early recognition of a cardiac arrest by bystanders1 and 911 call takers, as well as the delivery of initial treatments (i.e., CPR and defibrillation) by bystanders or trained first responders prior to the arrive of EMS providers (i.e., emergency medical technicians [EMTs] and paramedics).

53. New York Time May 2021, 06 January 2022, Al-Jazeera News May 2021.
Prof. David Dale Holmes; *The Buddhist Ideals of Good Governance*. https://www.buddhistdoor.net/features/the-buddhist-ideals-of-good-governance/
Blake Hounshell and Leah Askarinam; *On Politics: How many Americans support political violence?*

54. Chandra Lekha Sriram; *Responding to mass atrocities and human rights abuses*, Applied Knowledge Ser-vices November 2015. https://gsdrc.org/professional-dev/responding-to-mass-atrocities-and-human-rights-abuses/

55. The Canadian Jewish News June 20, 2016; https://thecjn.ca/perspectives/opinions/sun-stood-still/
Anna Ahronheim; *The Jerusalem Post*, Published: June 20, 2021 22:19.

56. Reference (Chapter 1)
Reference: New York Time May 2021, 06, 27 January 2022, Al-Jazeera News May 2021, *On Politics: How many Americans support political violence?*
David Dale Holmes; *The Buddhist Ideals of Good Governance*. https://www.buddhistdoor.net/features/the-buddhist-ideals-of-good-governance/

57. A Short History of NATO https://www.nato.int/cps/en/natohq/declassi-fied_139339.htm

58. https://twitter.com/globaltimesnews/sta-tus/1475531946998603777
Australian Strategic Policy Institute, The Strategist 31 January 2022. https://www.aspistrategist.org.au/how-china-views-the-ukraine-crisis/

59. Investopedia, https://www.investopedia.com/terms/
60. Vladimir Putin interviewed by the Financial Times | FT - https://www.youtube.com/watch?v=FbY0VpyjtuI
61. NATO Press office.
    https://www.nato.int/nato_static_fl2014/as-sets/pdf/pdf_2016_07/20160627_1607-russia-top5-myths_en.pdf
62. BBC News.
    https://www.bbc.co.uk/news/world-europe-56720589
63. Nina L Khrushcheva; *Putin's War Will Destroy Russia*, 31 March 2022, Project Syndicate
64. History of Kyiv.
    https://en.wikipedia.org/wiki/History_of_Kyiv
65. Of Russian origin: Siloviki.
    https://russiapedia.rt.com/of-russian-origin/siloviki